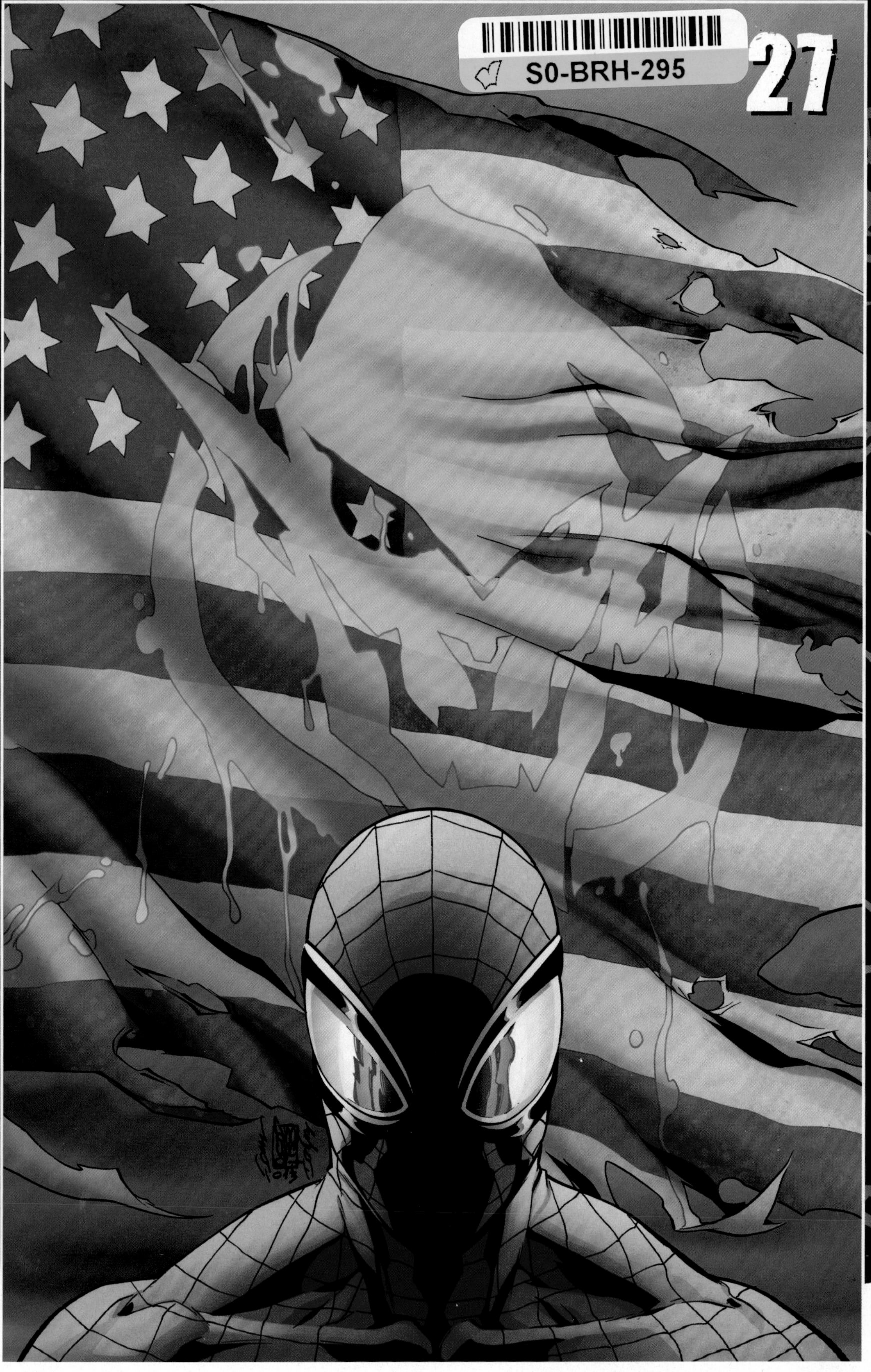
27

CARDS ON THE TABLE

31 DAYS LATER...

THE SUPERIOR SPIDER-MAN
GOBLIN NATION

SUPERIOR SPIDER-MAN #27-31

WRITERS
DAN SLOTT & CHRISTOS GAGE

PENCILER
GIUSEPPE CAMUNCOLI

INKERS
JOHN DELL WITH TERRY PALLOT (#30-31)

COLORIST
ANTONIO FABELA

LETTERER
CHRIS ELIOPOULOS

COVER ART
GIUSEPPE CAMUNCOLI & JOHN DELL WITH LAURA MARTIN (#27-28) **& EDGAR DELGADO** (#29-31)

"ACTIONS WITH CONSEQUENCES"

WRITER
CHRISTOS GAGE

ARTIST
WILL SLINEY

COLORIST
EDGAR DELGADO

LETTERER
CHRIS ELIOPOULOS

SUPERIOR SPIDER-MAN ANNUAL #2

WRITER
CHRISTOS GAGE

PENCILERS
JAVIER RODRIGUEZ & PHILIPPE BRIONES

INKERS
ALVARO LOPEZ & PHILIPPE BRIONES

COLORISTS
JAVIER RODRIGUEZ & VERONICA GANDINI

LETTERER
VC'S CLAYTON COWLES

COVER ART
MICHAEL DEL MUNDO

ASSISTANT EDITOR
ELLIE PYLE

EDITORS
STEPHEN WACKER & NICK LOWE

Collection Editor: **Jennifer Grünwald** • Assistant Editor: **Sarah Brunstad** • Associate Managing Editor: **Alex Starbuck**
Editor, Special Projects: **Mark D. Beazley** • Senior Editor, Special Projects: **Jeff Youngquist** • SVP Print, Sales & Marketing: **David Gabriel**

Editor in Chief: **Axel Alonso** • Chief Creative Officer: **Joe Quesada** • Publisher: **Dan Buckley** • Executive Producer: **Alan Fine**

SUPERIOR SPIDER-MAN VOL. 6: GOBLIN NATION. Contains material originally published in magazine form as SUPERIOR SPIDER-MAN #27-31 and ANNUAL #2. First printing 2014. ISBN# 978-0-7851-8797-4. Published by MARVEL WORLDWIDE, INC., a subsidiary of MARVEL ENTERTAINMENT, LLC. OFFICE OF PUBLICATION: 135 West 50th Street, New York, NY 10020. **Printed in Canada.** ALAN FINE, EVP - Office of the President, Marvel Worldwide, Inc. and EVP & CMO Marvel Characters B.V.; DAN BUCKLEY, Publisher & President - Print, Animation & Digital Divisions; JOE QUESADA, Chief Creative Officer; TOM BREVOORT, SVP of Publishing; DAVID BOGART, SVP of Operations & Procurement, Publishing; C.B. CEBULSKI, SVP of Creator & Content Development; DAVID GABRIEL, SVP Print, Sales & Marketing; JIM O'KEEFE, VP of Operations & Logistics; DAN CARR, Executive Director of Publishing Technology; SUSAN CRESPI, Editorial Operations Manager; ALEX MORALES, Publishing Operations Manager; STAN LEE, Chairman Emeritus. For information regarding advertising in Marvel Comics or on Marvel.com, please contact Niza Disla, Director of Marvel Partnerships, at ndisla@marvel.com. For Marvel subscription inquiries, please call 800-217-9158. **Manufactured between 4/25/2014 and 6/2/2014 by SOLISCO PRINTERS, SCOTT, QC, CANADA.**

0 9 8 7 6 5 4 3 2 1

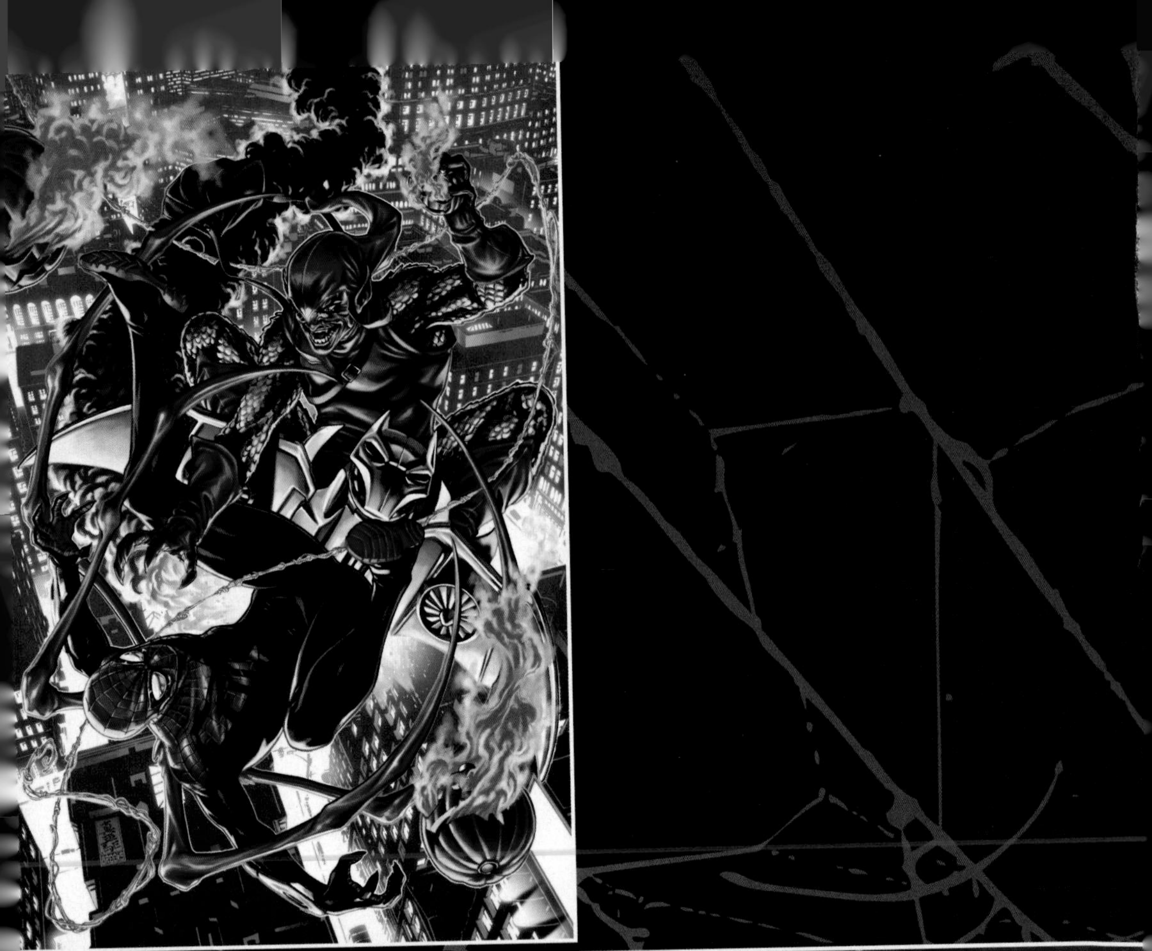

#27 VARIANT
BY MARK BROOKS

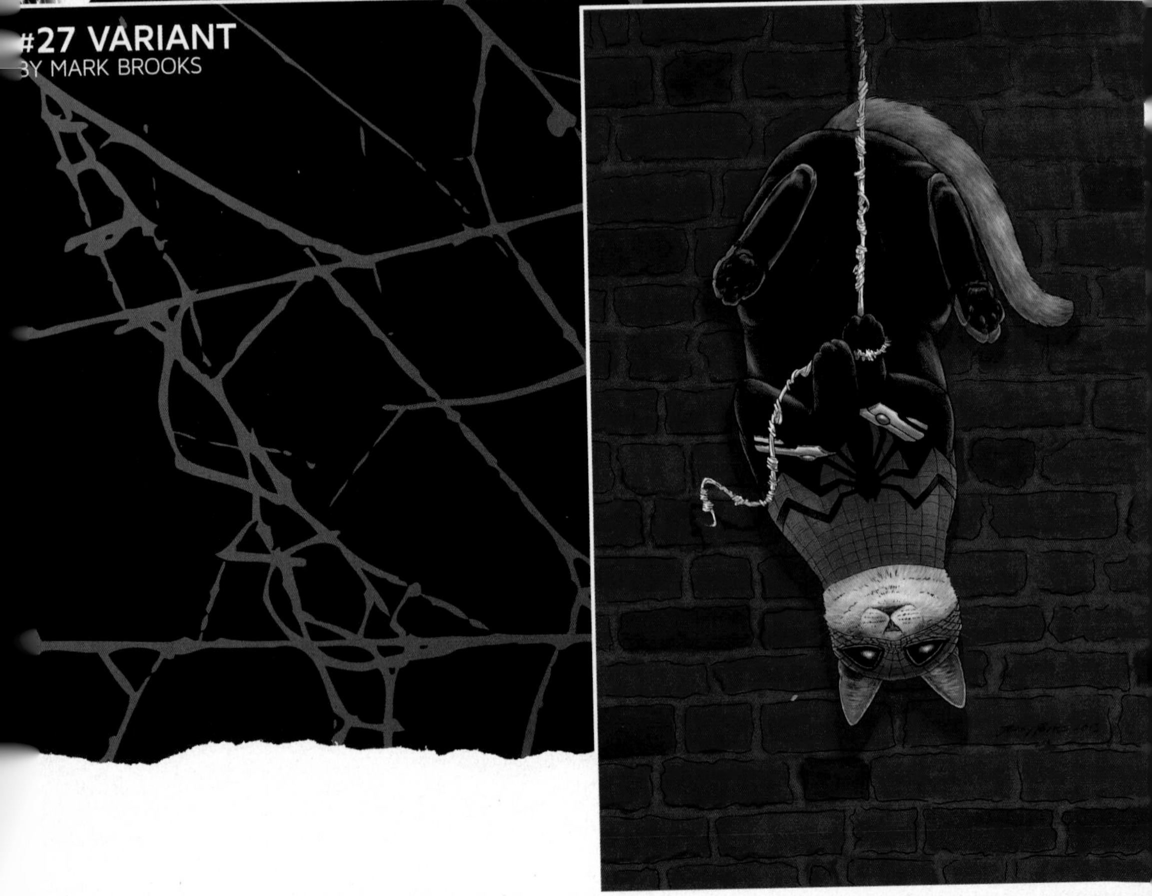

#27 ANIMAL VARIANT

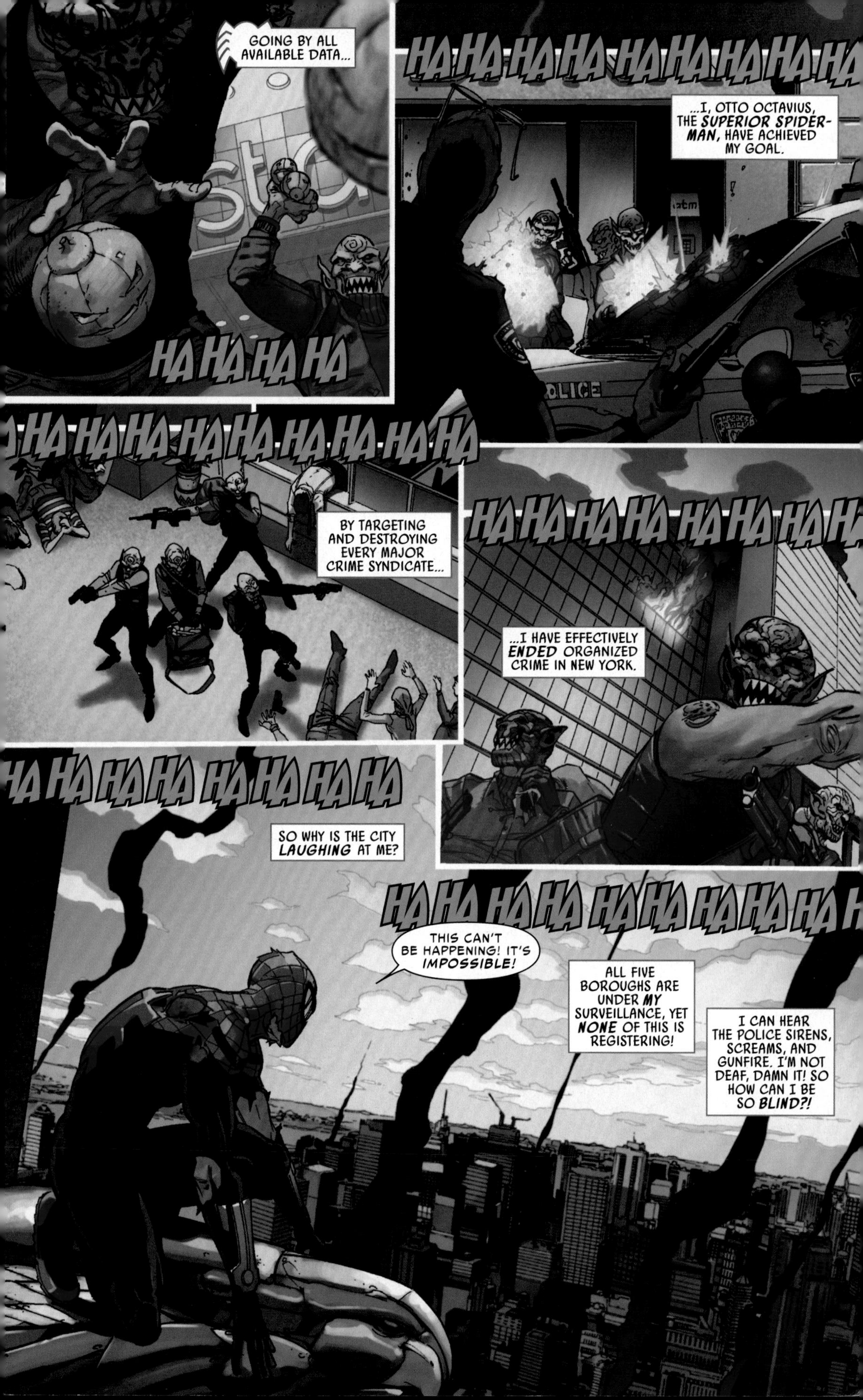
GOING BY ALL AVAILABLE DATA...
HA HA HA HA
HA HA HA HA HA HA HA HA HA
...I, OTTO OCTAVIUS, THE SUPERIOR SPIDER-MAN, HAVE ACHIEVED MY GOAL.
POLICE
HA HA HA HA HA HA HA HA HA HA
BY TARGETING AND DESTROYING EVERY MAJOR CRIME SYNDICATE...
HA HA HA HA HA HA HA HA
...I HAVE EFFECTIVELY ENDED ORGANIZED CRIME IN NEW YORK.
HA HA HA HA HA HA HA HA HA
SO WHY IS THE CITY LAUGHING AT ME?
HA HA HA HA HA HA HA HA HA HA
THIS CAN'T BE HAPPENING! IT'S IMPOSSIBLE!
ALL FIVE BOROUGHS ARE UNDER MY SURVEILLANCE, YET NONE OF THIS IS REGISTERING!
I CAN HEAR THE POLICE SIRENS, SCREAMS, AND GUNFIRE. I'M NOT DEAF, DAMN IT! SO HOW CAN I BE SO BLIND?!

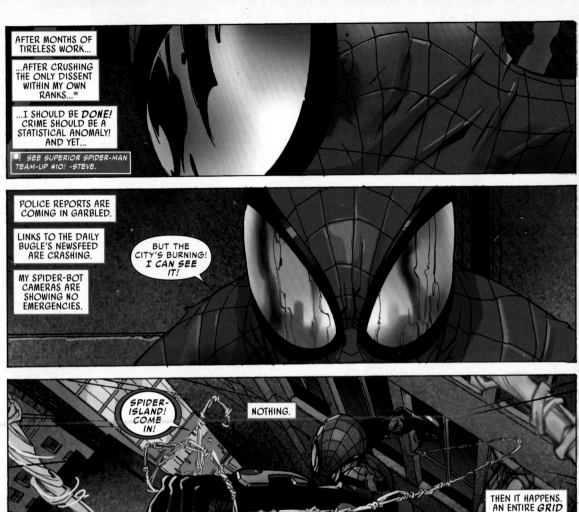

AFTER MONTHS OF TIRELESS WORK...

...AFTER CRUSHING THE ONLY DISSENT WITHIN MY OWN RANKS...*

...I SHOULD BE *DONE!* CRIME SHOULD BE A STATISTICAL ANOMALY! AND YET...

* SEE SUPERIOR SPIDER-MAN TEAM-UP #10! -STEVE.

POLICE REPORTS ARE COMING IN GARBLED.

LINKS TO THE DAILY BUGLE'S NEWSFEED ARE CRASHING.

BUT THE CITY'S BURNING! I CAN *SEE* IT!

MY SPIDER-BOT CAMERAS ARE SHOWING NO EMERGENCIES.

SPIDER-ISLAND! COME IN!

NOTHING.

THEN IT HAPPENS. AN ENTIRE *GRID* IN MY CITYWIDE SWEEP SHUTS DOWN.

THE AREA AROUND THE BROOKLYN BRIDGE. I HAVE TO GO.

HAVE TO SEE THIS WITH MY *OWN* EYES.

NO.

UNTIL NOW I'D THOUGHT ONLY *TWO* CRIMINALS HAD ESCAPED MY DETECTION.

THE TWO *HOBGOBLINS.* URICH AND KINGSLEY.

THE IDIOT AND THE COWARD.

I COULD NEVER ACCOUNT FOR THAT GLITCH IN THE SYSTEM. UNTIL NOW.

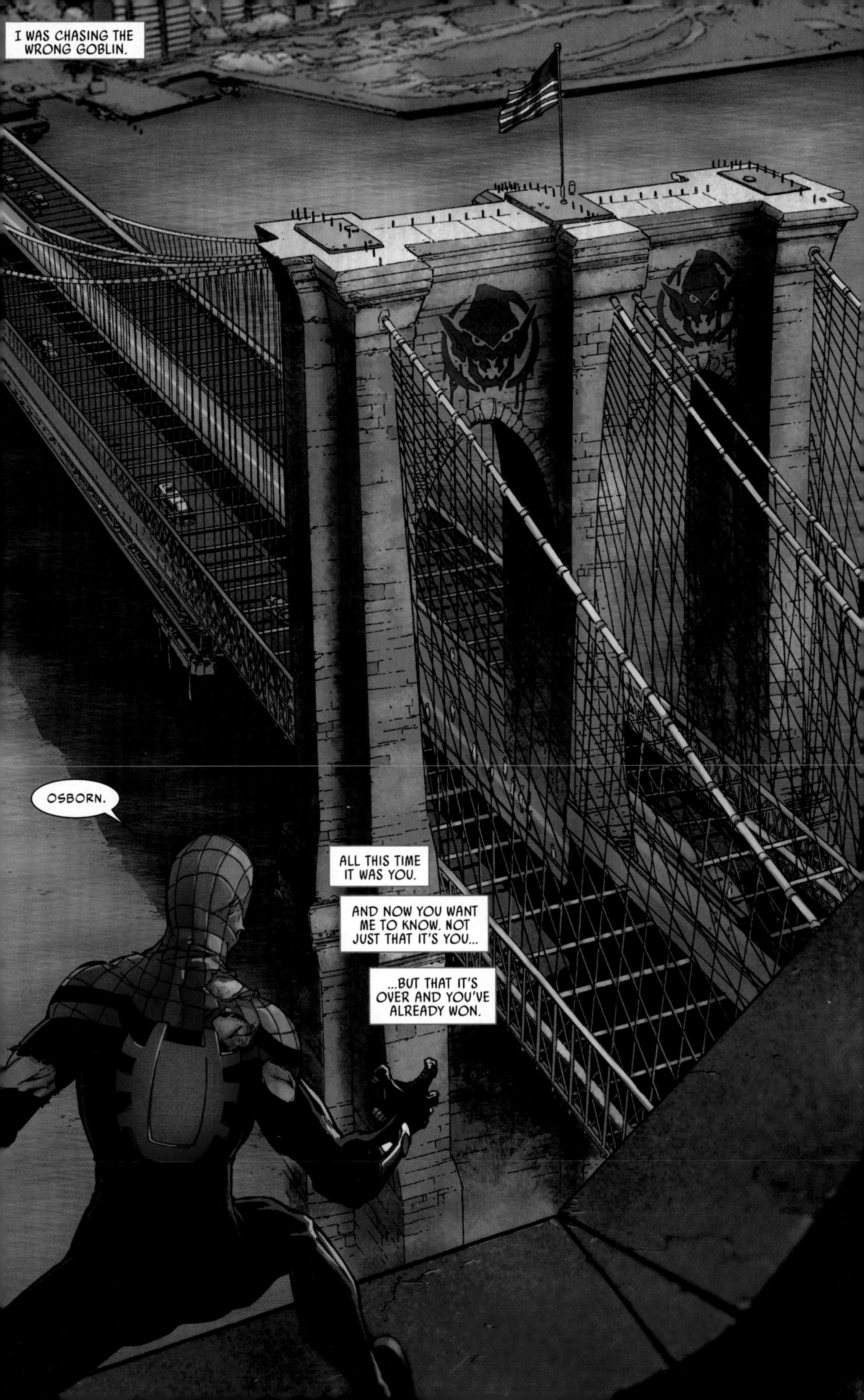
I WAS CHASING THE WRONG GOBLIN.
OSBORN.
ALL THIS TIME IT WAS YOU.
AND NOW YOU WANT ME TO KNOW. NOT JUST THAT IT'S YOU...
...BUT THAT IT'S OVER AND YOU'VE ALREADY WON.

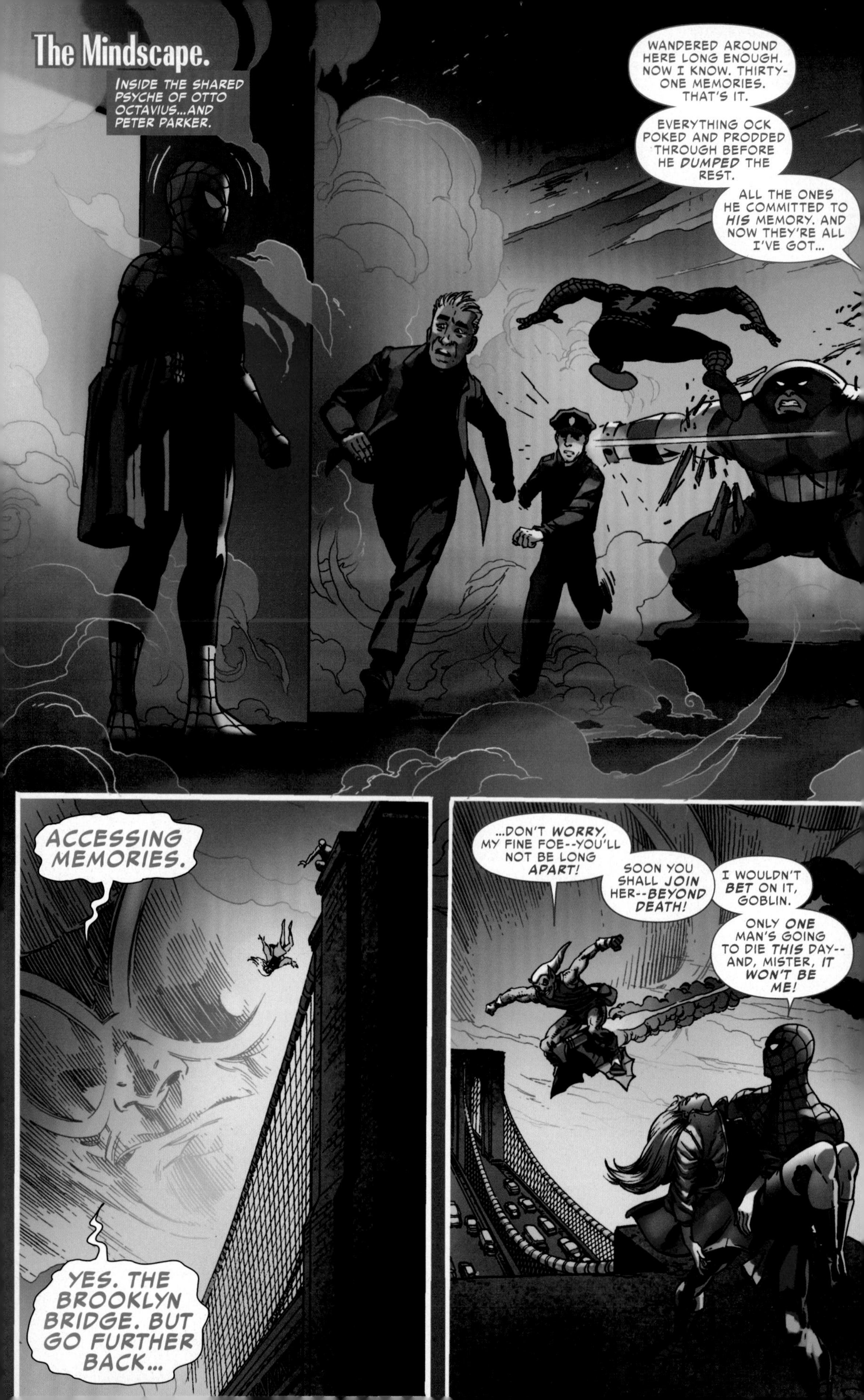
The Mindscape.
INSIDE THE SHARED PSYCHE OF OTTO OCTAVIUS...AND PETER PARKER.
WANDERED AROUND HERE LONG ENOUGH. NOW I KNOW. THIRTY-ONE MEMORIES. THAT'S IT.
EVERYTHING OCK POKED AND PRODDED THROUGH BEFORE HE DUMPED THE REST.
ALL THE ONES HE COMMITTED TO HIS MEMORY. AND NOW THEY'RE ALL I'VE GOT...
ACCESSING MEMORIES.
YES. THE BROOKLYN BRIDGE. BUT GO FURTHER BACK...
...DON'T WORRY, MY FINE FOE--YOU'LL NOT BE LONG APART!
SOON YOU SHALL JOIN HER--BEYOND DEATH!
I WOULDN'T BET ON IT, GOBLIN.
ONLY ONE MAN'S GOING TO DIE THIS DAY--AND, MISTER, IT WON'T BE ME!

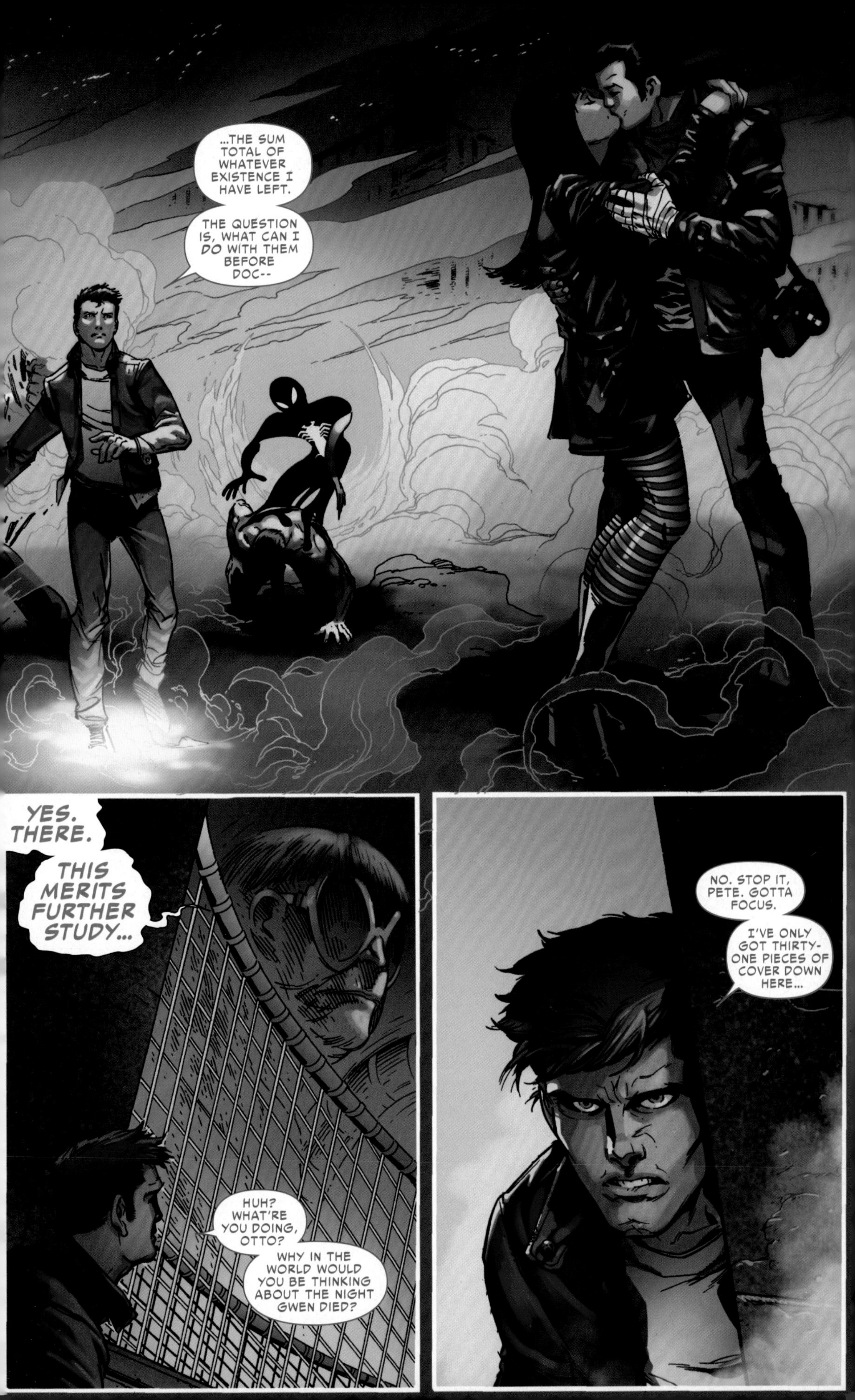
...THE SUM TOTAL OF WHATEVER EXISTENCE I HAVE LEFT.
THE QUESTION IS, WHAT CAN I DO WITH THEM BEFORE DOC--
YES. THERE.
THIS MERITS FURTHER STUDY...
HUH? WHAT'RE YOU DOING, OTTO?
WHY IN THE WORLD WOULD YOU BE THINKING ABOUT THE NIGHT GWEN DIED?
NO. STOP IT, PETE. GOTTA FOCUS.
I'VE ONLY GOT THIRTY-ONE PIECES OF COVER DOWN HERE...

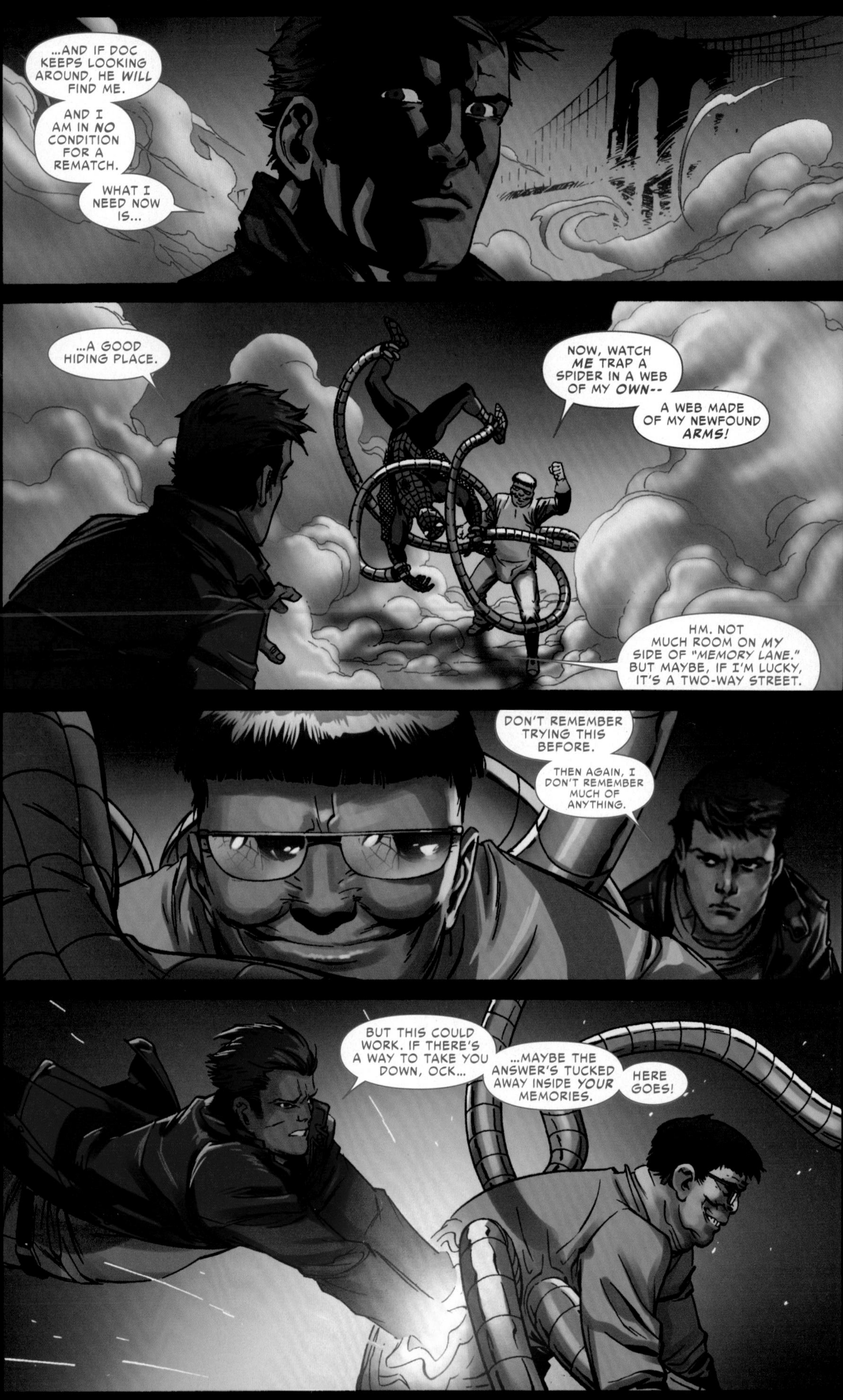

...AND IF DOC KEEPS LOOKING AROUND, HE WILL FIND ME.
AND I AM IN NO CONDITION FOR A REMATCH.
WHAT I NEED NOW IS...
...A GOOD HIDING PLACE.
NOW, WATCH ME TRAP A SPIDER IN A WEB OF MY OWN--
A WEB MADE OF MY NEWFOUND ARMS!
HM. NOT MUCH ROOM ON MY SIDE OF "MEMORY LANE." BUT MAYBE, IF I'M LUCKY, IT'S A TWO-WAY STREET.
DON'T REMEMBER TRYING THIS BEFORE.
THEN AGAIN, I DON'T REMEMBER MUCH OF ANYTHING.
BUT THIS COULD WORK. IF THERE'S A WAY TO TAKE YOU DOWN, OCK...
...MAYBE THE ANSWER'S TUCKED AWAY INSIDE YOUR MEMORIES.
HERE GOES!

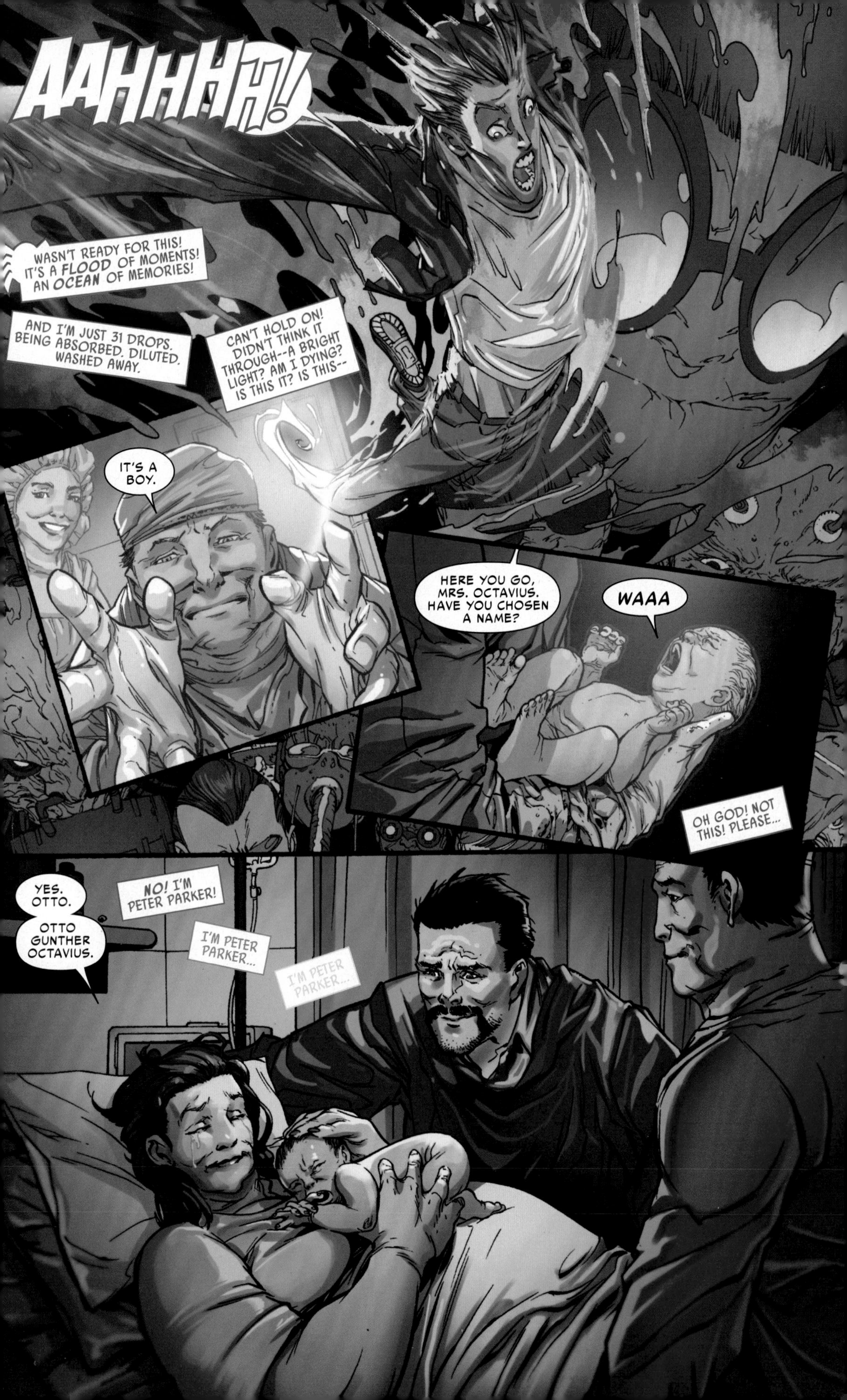
AAHHHH!
WASN'T READY FOR THIS! IT'S A FLOOD OF MOMENTS! AN OCEAN OF MEMORIES!
AND I'M JUST 31 DROPS. BEING ABSORBED. DILUTED. WASHED AWAY.
CAN'T HOLD ON! DIDN'T THINK IT THROUGH--A BRIGHT LIGHT? AM I DYING? IS THIS IT? IS THIS--
IT'S A BOY.
HERE YOU GO, MRS. OCTAVIUS. HAVE YOU CHOSEN A NAME?
WAAA
OH GOD! NOT THIS! PLEASE...
YES. OTTO.
OTTO GUNTHER OCTAVIUS.
NO! I'M PETER PARKER!
I'M PETER PARKER...
I'M PETER PARKER...

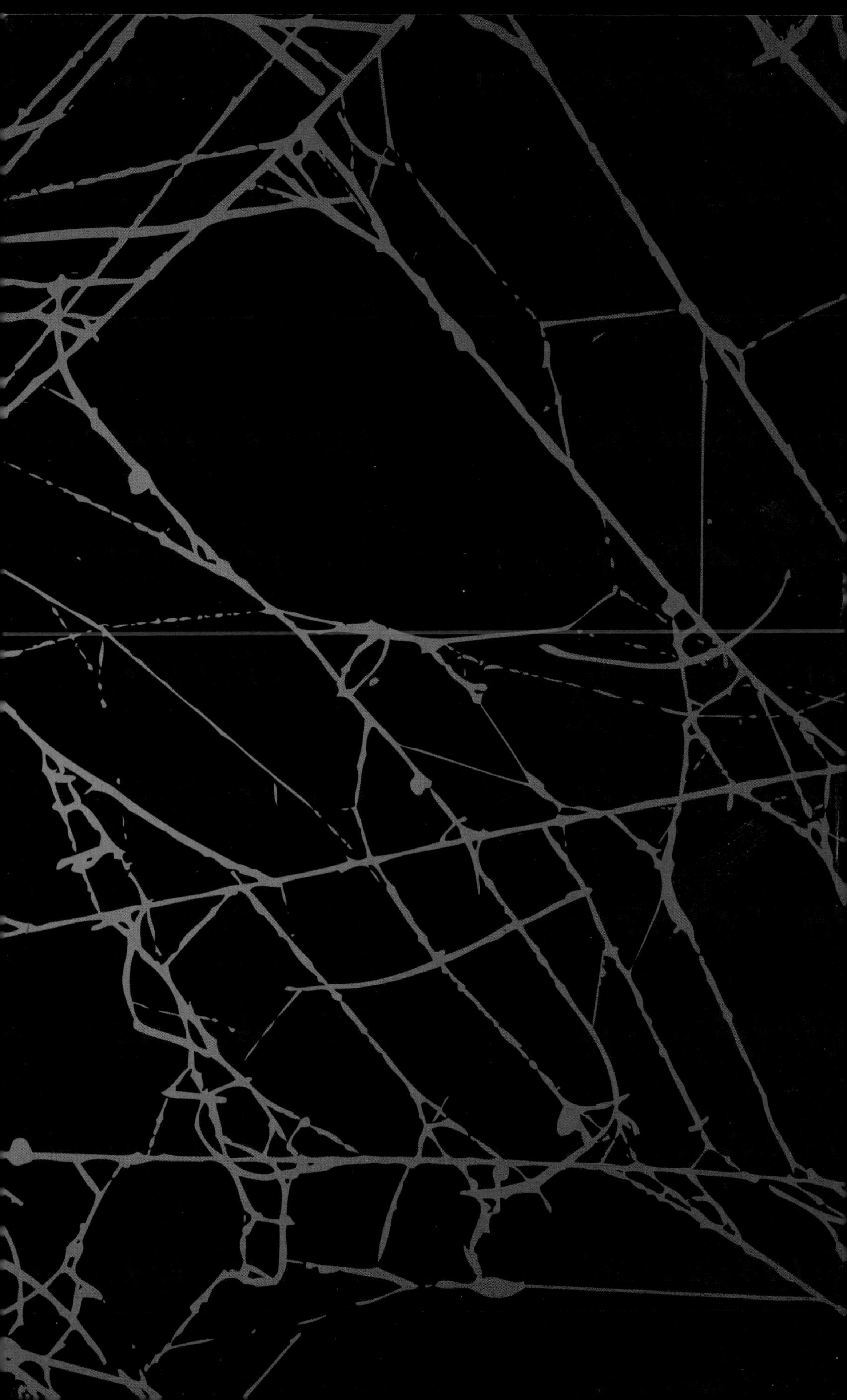

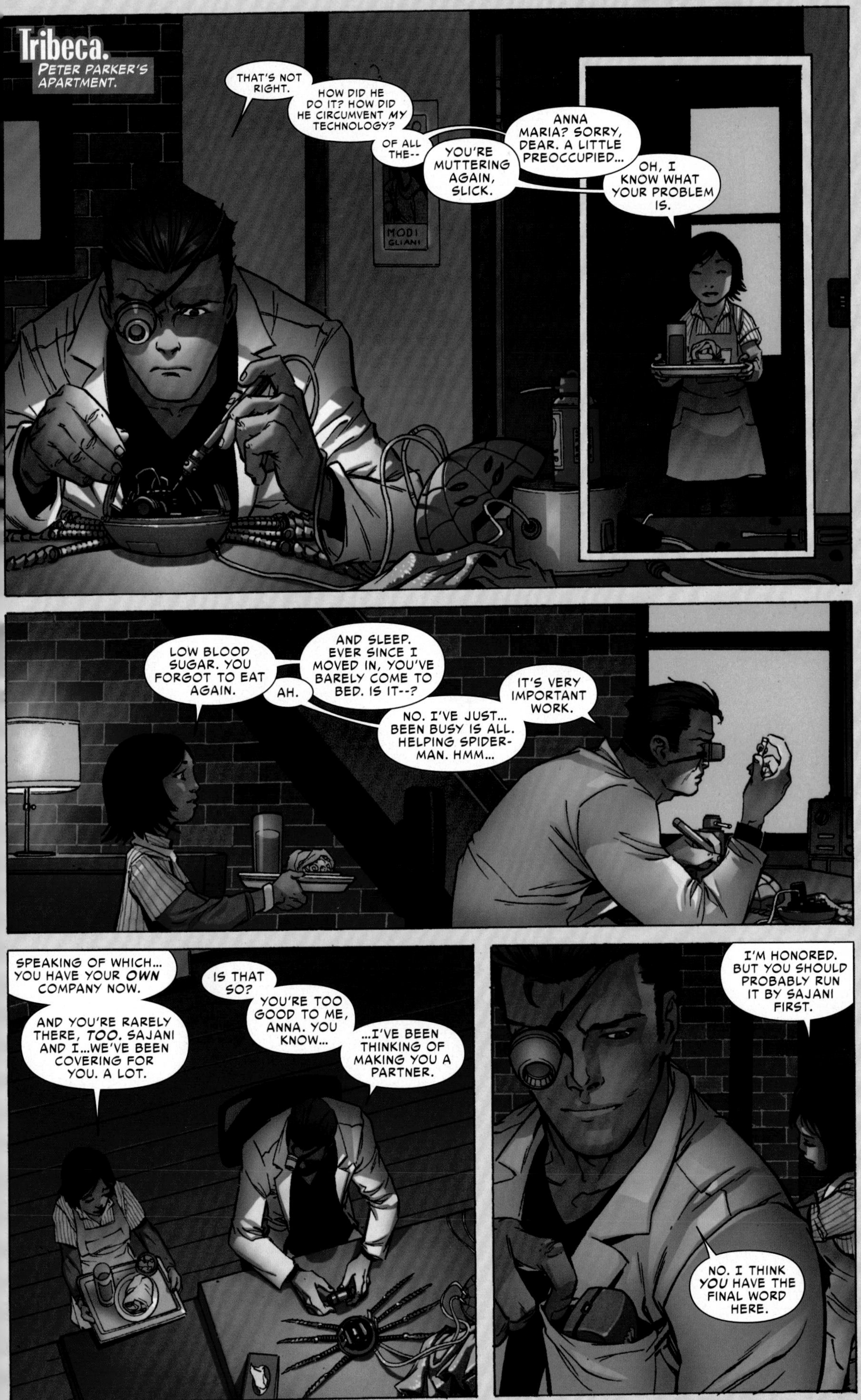
Tribeca.
PETER PARKER'S APARTMENT.
THAT'S NOT RIGHT.
HOW DID HE DO IT? HOW DID HE CIRCUMVENT MY TECHNOLOGY?
OF ALL THE--
YOU'RE MUTTERING AGAIN, SLICK.
ANNA MARIA? SORRY, DEAR. A LITTLE PREOCCUPIED...
OH, I KNOW WHAT YOUR PROBLEM IS.
MODI GLIANI
LOW BLOOD SUGAR. YOU FORGOT TO EAT AGAIN.
AH.
AND SLEEP. EVER SINCE I MOVED IN, YOU'VE BARELY COME TO BED. IS IT--?
NO. I'VE JUST... BEEN BUSY IS ALL. HELPING SPIDER-MAN. HMM...
IT'S VERY IMPORTANT WORK.
SPEAKING OF WHICH... YOU HAVE YOUR OWN COMPANY NOW.
AND YOU'RE RARELY THERE, TOO. SAJANI AND I...WE'VE BEEN COVERING FOR YOU. A LOT.
IS THAT SO?
YOU'RE TOO GOOD TO ME, ANNA. YOU KNOW...
...I'VE BEEN THINKING OF MAKING YOU A PARTNER.
I'M HONORED. BUT YOU SHOULD PROBABLY RUN IT BY SAJANI FIRST.
NO. I THINK YOU HAVE THE FINAL WORD HERE.

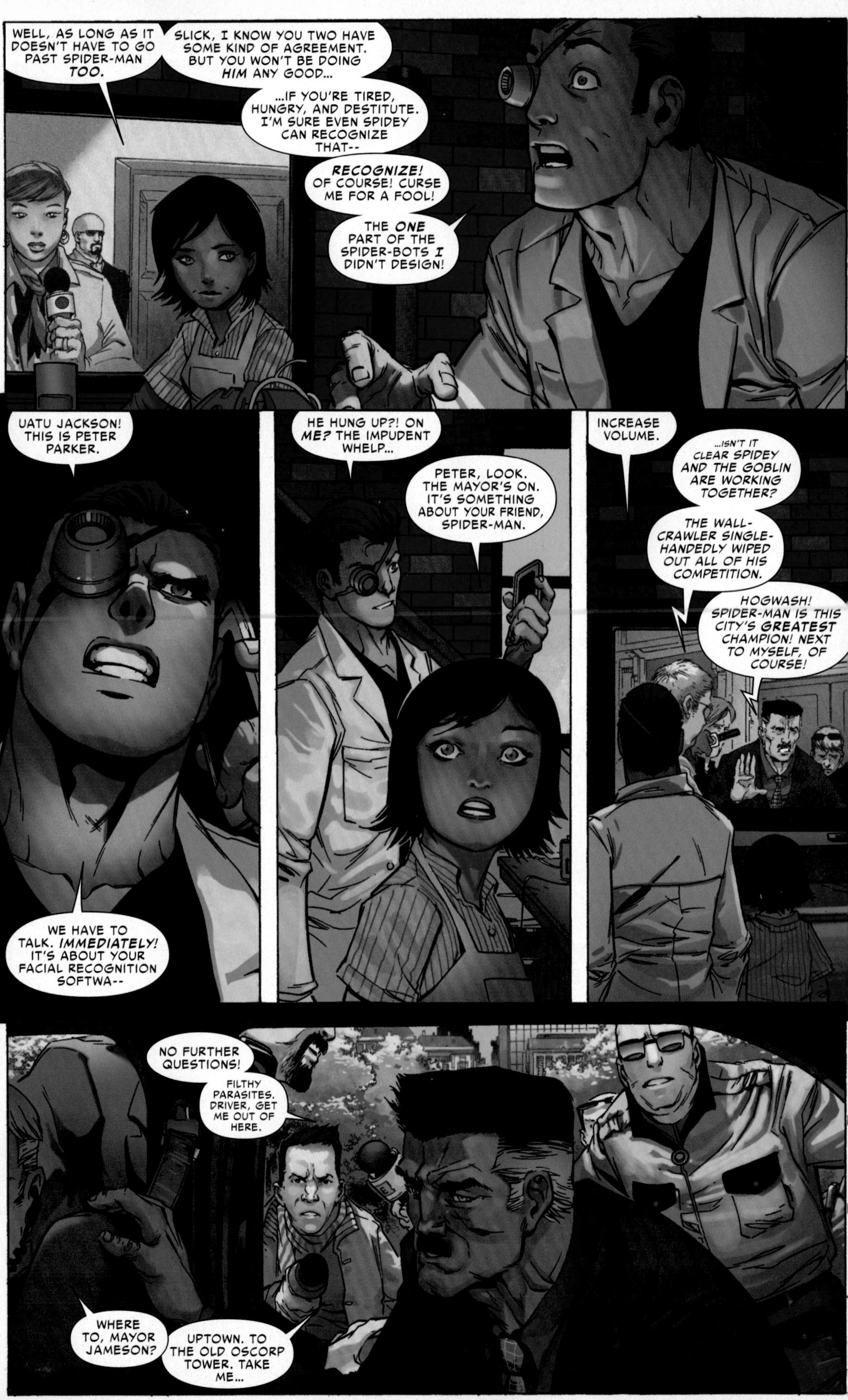
WELL, AS LONG AS IT DOESN'T HAVE TO GO PAST SPIDER-MAN *TOO.*
SLICK, I KNOW YOU TWO HAVE SOME KIND OF AGREEMENT. BUT YOU WON'T BE DOING *HIM* ANY GOOD...
...IF YOU'RE TIRED, HUNGRY, AND DESTITUTE. I'M SURE EVEN SPIDEY CAN RECOGNIZE THAT--
RECOGNIZE! OF COURSE! CURSE ME FOR A FOOL!
THE *ONE* PART OF THE SPIDER-BOTS *I* DIDN'T DESIGN!
UATU JACKSON! THIS IS PETER PARKER.
WE HAVE TO TALK. *IMMEDIATELY!* IT'S ABOUT YOUR FACIAL RECOGNITION SOFTWA--
HE HUNG UP?! ON *ME?* THE IMPUDENT WHELP...
PETER, LOOK. THE MAYOR'S ON. IT'S SOMETHING ABOUT YOUR FRIEND, SPIDER-MAN.
INCREASE VOLUME.
...ISN'T IT CLEAR SPIDEY AND THE GOBLIN ARE WORKING TOGETHER?
THE WALL-CRAWLER SINGLE-HANDEDLY WIPED OUT ALL OF HIS COMPETITION.
HOGWASH! SPIDER-MAN IS THIS CITY'S **GREATEST** CHAMPION! NEXT TO MYSELF, OF COURSE!
NO FURTHER QUESTIONS!
FILTHY PARASITES. DRIVER, GET ME OUT OF HERE.
WHERE TO, MAYOR JAMESON?
UPTOWN. TO THE OLD OSCORP TOWER. TAKE ME...

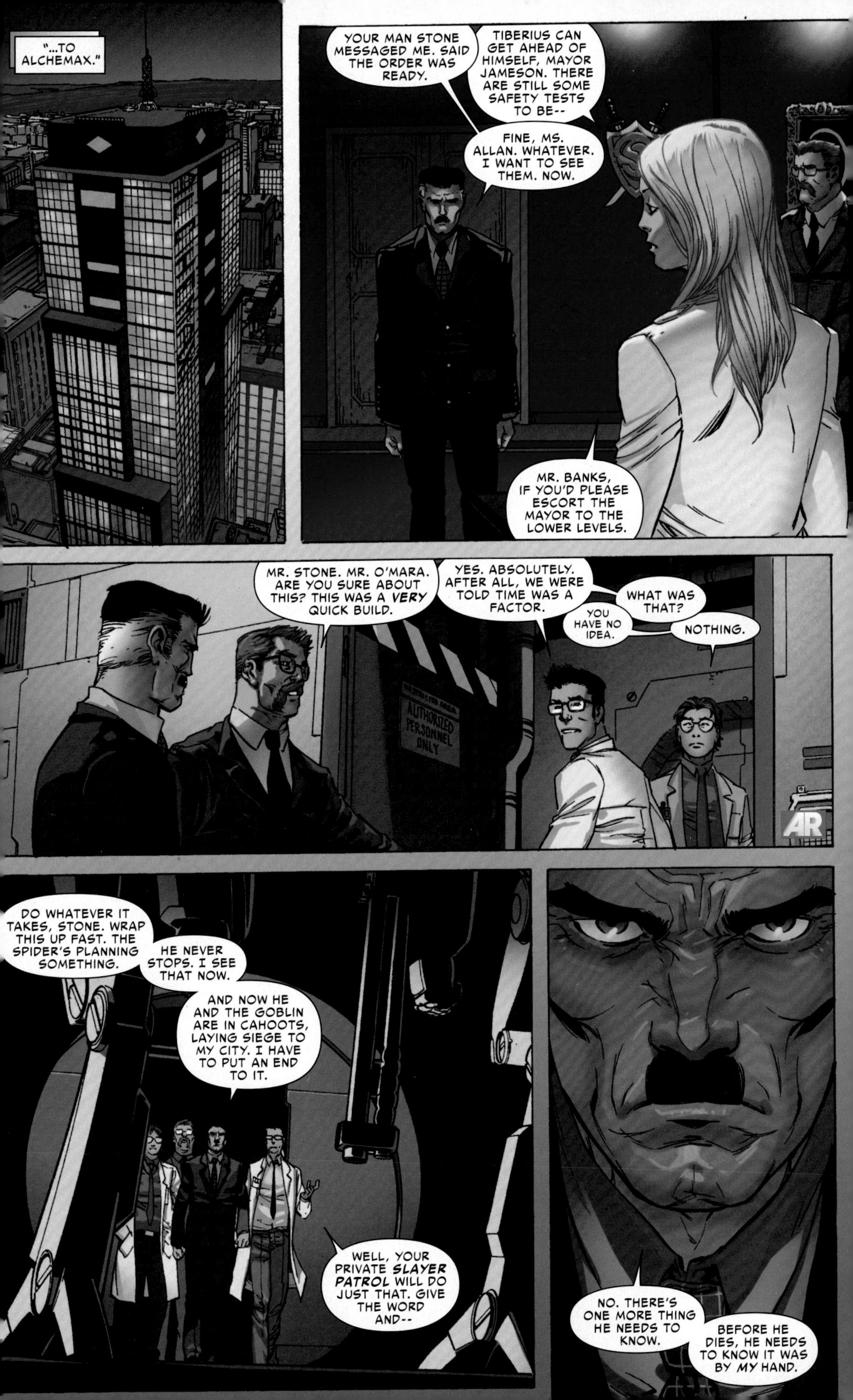
"...TO ALCHEMAX."
YOUR MAN STONE MESSAGED ME. SAID THE ORDER WAS READY.
TIBERIUS CAN GET AHEAD OF HIMSELF, MAYOR JAMESON. THERE ARE STILL SOME SAFETY TESTS TO BE--
FINE, MS. ALLAN. WHATEVER. I WANT TO SEE THEM. NOW.
MR. BANKS, IF YOU'D PLEASE ESCORT THE MAYOR TO THE LOWER LEVELS.
MR. STONE. MR. O'MARA. ARE YOU SURE ABOUT THIS? THIS WAS A *VERY* QUICK BUILD.
YES. ABSOLUTELY. AFTER ALL, WE WERE TOLD TIME WAS A FACTOR.
YOU HAVE NO IDEA.
WHAT WAS THAT?
NOTHING.
RESTRICTED AREA
AUTHORIZED PERSONNEL ONLY
DO WHATEVER IT TAKES, STONE. WRAP THIS UP FAST. THE SPIDER'S PLANNING SOMETHING.
HE NEVER STOPS. I SEE THAT NOW.
AND NOW HE AND THE GOBLIN ARE IN CAHOOTS, LAYING SIEGE TO MY CITY. I HAVE TO PUT AN END TO IT.
WELL, YOUR PRIVATE *SLAYER PATROL* WILL DO JUST THAT. GIVE THE WORD AND--
NO. THERE'S ONE MORE THING HE NEEDS TO KNOW.
BEFORE HE DIES, HE NEEDS TO KNOW IT WAS BY *MY* HAND.

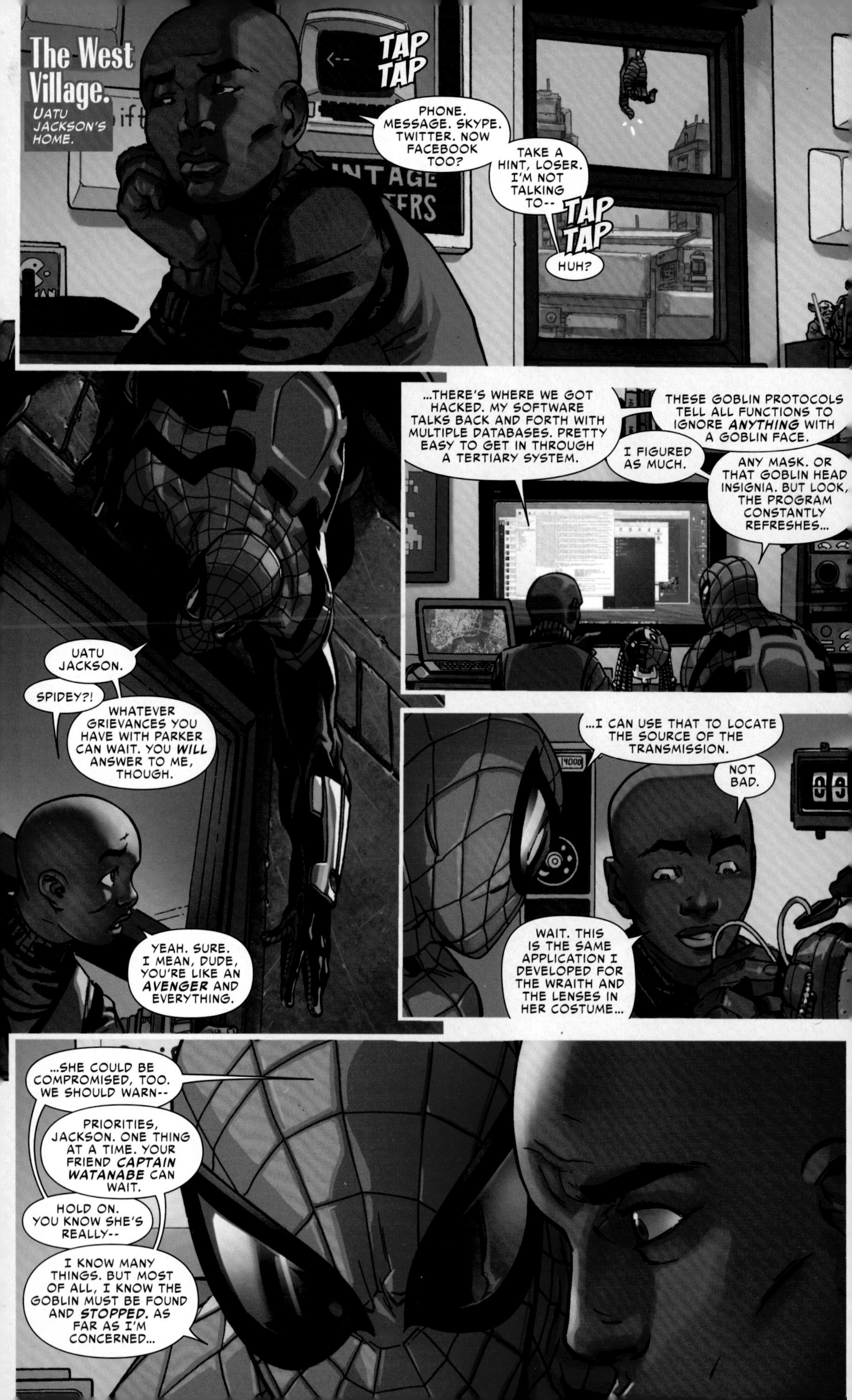

The West Village.
UATU JACKSON'S HOME.
TAP TAP
PHONE. MESSAGE. SKYPE. TWITTER. NOW FACEBOOK TOO?
TAKE A HINT, LOSER. I'M NOT TALKING TO--
TAP TAP
HUH?
UATU JACKSON.
SPIDEY?!
WHATEVER GRIEVANCES YOU HAVE WITH PARKER CAN WAIT. YOU WILL ANSWER TO ME, THOUGH.
YEAH. SURE. I MEAN, DUDE, YOU'RE LIKE AN AVENGER AND EVERYTHING.
...THERE'S WHERE WE GOT HACKED. MY SOFTWARE TALKS BACK AND FORTH WITH MULTIPLE DATABASES. PRETTY EASY TO GET IN THROUGH A TERTIARY SYSTEM.
THESE GOBLIN PROTOCOLS TELL ALL FUNCTIONS TO IGNORE ANYTHING WITH A GOBLIN FACE.
I FIGURED AS MUCH.
ANY MASK. OR THAT GOBLIN HEAD INSIGNIA. BUT LOOK, THE PROGRAM CONSTANTLY REFRESHES...
...I CAN USE THAT TO LOCATE THE SOURCE OF THE TRANSMISSION.
NOT BAD.
WAIT. THIS IS THE SAME APPLICATION I DEVELOPED FOR THE WRAITH AND THE LENSES IN HER COSTUME...
...SHE COULD BE COMPROMISED, TOO. WE SHOULD WARN--
PRIORITIES, JACKSON. ONE THING AT A TIME. YOUR FRIEND CAPTAIN WATANABE CAN WAIT.
HOLD ON. YOU KNOW SHE'S REALLY--
I KNOW MANY THINGS. BUT MOST OF ALL, I KNOW THE GOBLIN MUST BE FOUND AND STOPPED. AS FAR AS I'M CONCERNED...

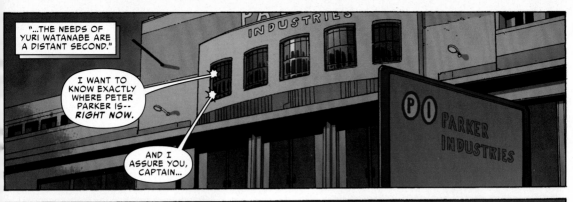

"...THE NEEDS OF YURI WATANABE ARE A DISTANT SECOND."

I WANT TO KNOW EXACTLY WHERE PETER PARKER IS-- RIGHT NOW.

AND I ASSURE YOU, CAPTAIN...

PI PARKER INDUSTRIES

...AS HIS BUSINESS PARTNER, I COULDN'T AGREE MORE.

THIS ISN'T A JOKE, MS. JAFFREY. PETER PARKER IS MY NUMBER ONE PERSON OF INTEREST...

...IN THE CASE OF A MISSING POLICE OFFICER.

I FIND IT HARD TO BELIEVE THAT THE OWNER OF A NEW START-UP COMPANY COULD GO DAYS WITHOUT CONTACTING ANY OF YOU.

TELL ME ABOUT IT.

BELIEVE ME, CAPTAIN, WHATEVER BACKROOM INTERROGATION GAMES YOU'VE GOT PLANNED FOR PARKER...

...ARE NOTHING COMPARED TO WHAT I'M GOING TO DO WHEN I GET MY HANDS ON HIM.

NICE TRY, MS. JAFFREY. BUT I'M NOT BUYING ANY OF IT.

YOU CAN EXPECT TO SEE OFFICERS CAMPED OUT HERE UNTIL THAT MAN DECIDES TO SHOW HIS FACE. THIS ISN'T OVER...

"...I WILL FIND HIM. NO MATTER WHAT ROCK HE'S HIDING UNDER."

SIGNAL'S HOLDING. AND STRONG. NO MATTER HOW FAR UNDER THE CITY IT'S LEADING ME.

ACCORDING TO MY FILES...

...THESE TUNNELS WERE FOR A SCRAPPED AND ABANDONED SUBWAY LINE THAT--

CORRECTION. A FULLY FUNCTIONING LINE.

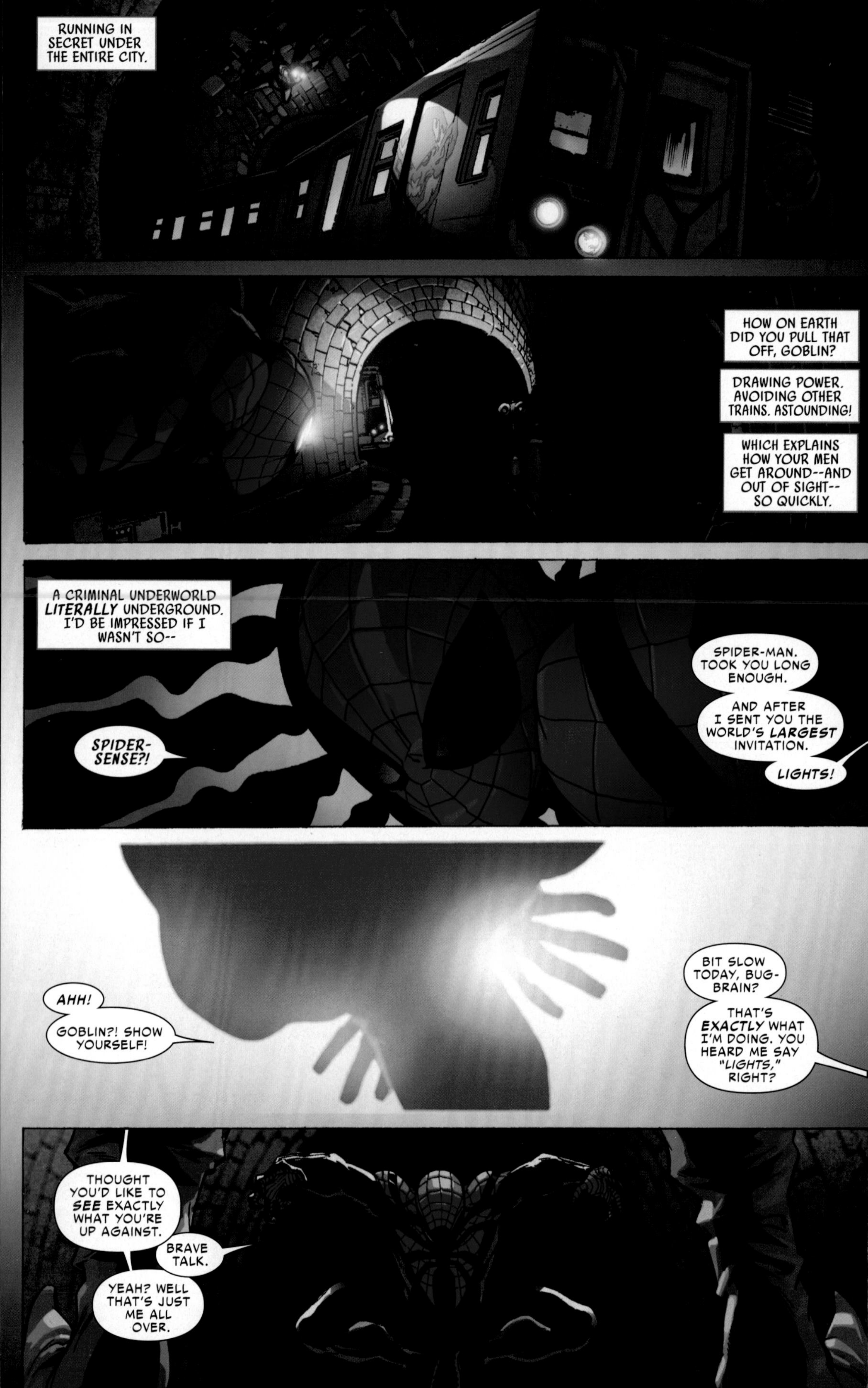
RUNNING IN SECRET UNDER THE ENTIRE CITY.
HOW ON EARTH DID YOU PULL THAT OFF, GOBLIN?
DRAWING POWER. AVOIDING OTHER TRAINS. ASTOUNDING!
WHICH EXPLAINS HOW YOUR MEN GET AROUND--AND OUT OF SIGHT--SO QUICKLY.
A CRIMINAL UNDERWORLD LITERALLY UNDERGROUND. I'D BE IMPRESSED IF I WASN'T SO--
SPIDER-SENSE?!
SPIDER-MAN. TOOK YOU LONG ENOUGH.
AND AFTER I SENT YOU THE WORLD'S LARGEST INVITATION.
LIGHTS!
AHH!
GOBLIN?! SHOW YOURSELF!
BIT SLOW TODAY, BUG-BRAIN?
THAT'S EXACTLY WHAT I'M DOING. YOU HEARD ME SAY "LIGHTS," RIGHT?
THOUGHT YOU'D LIKE TO SEE EXACTLY WHAT YOU'RE UP AGAINST.
BRAVE TALK.
YEAH? WELL THAT'S JUST ME ALL OVER.

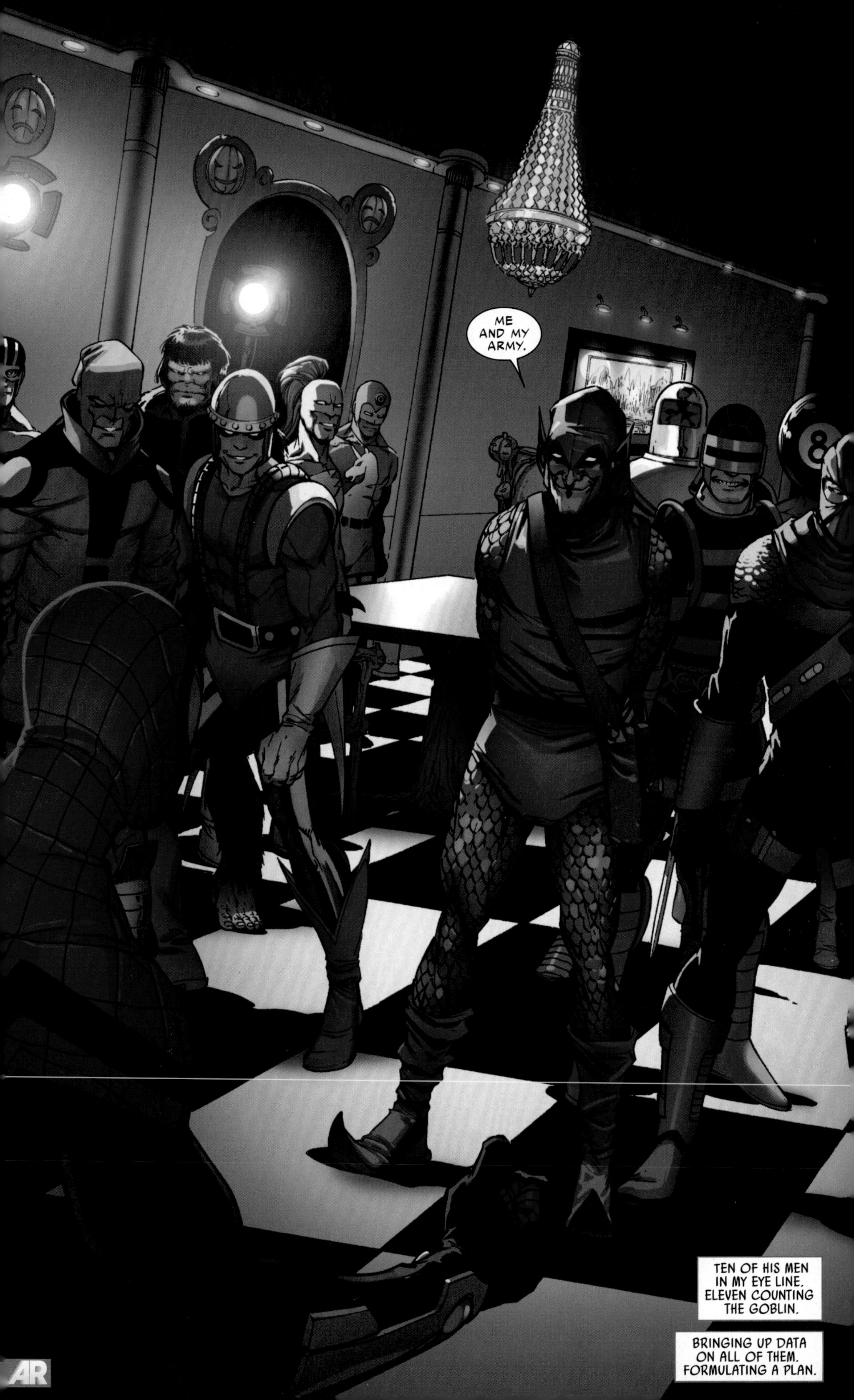

ME AND MY ARMY.
TEN OF HIS MEN IN MY EYE LINE. ELEVEN COUNTING THE GOBLIN.
BRINGING UP DATA ON ALL OF THEM. FORMULATING A PLAN.

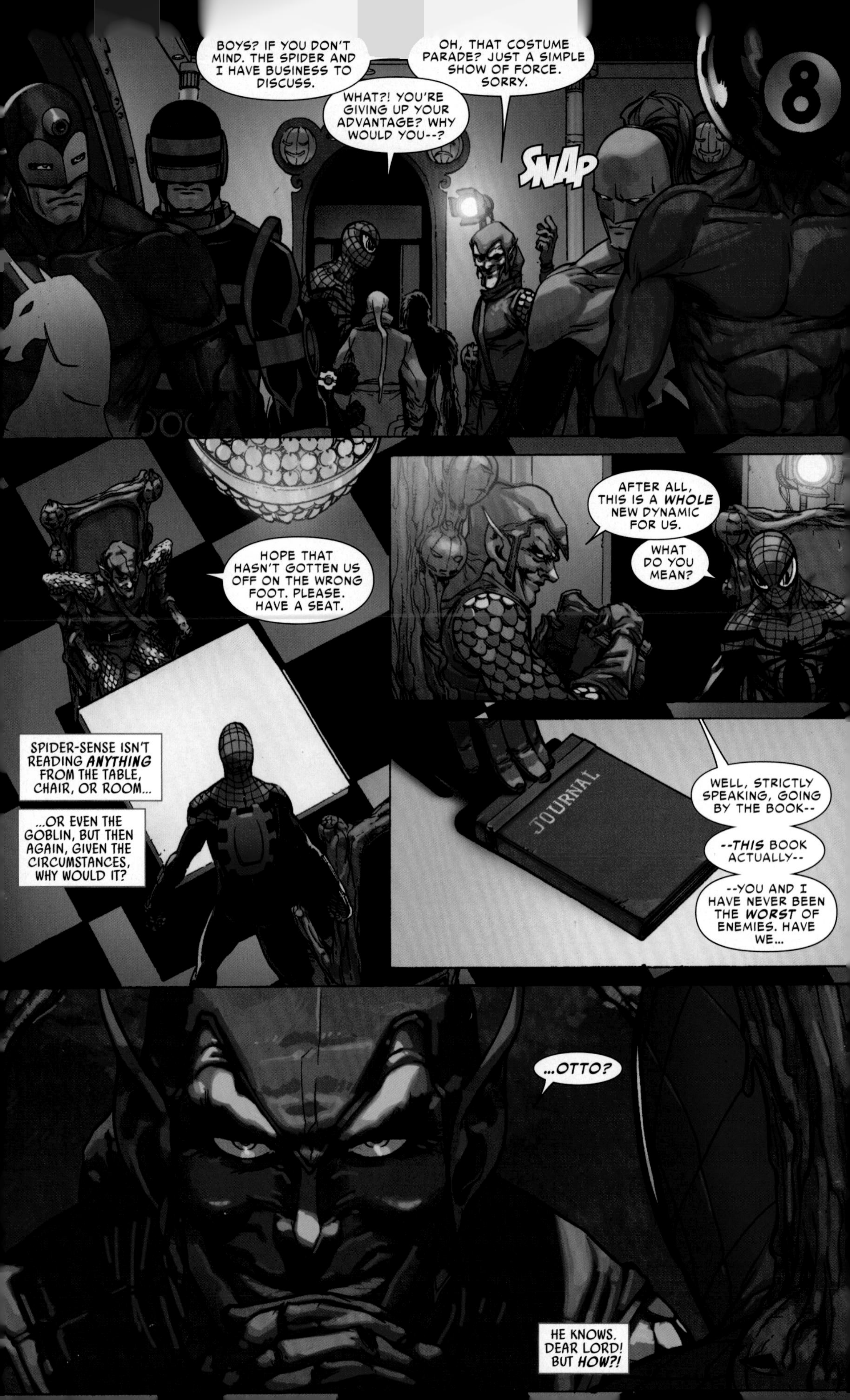
BOYS? IF YOU DON'T MIND. THE SPIDER AND I HAVE BUSINESS TO DISCUSS.
WHAT?! YOU'RE GIVING UP YOUR ADVANTAGE? WHY WOULD YOU--?
OH, THAT COSTUME PARADE? JUST A SIMPLE SHOW OF FORCE. SORRY.
SNAP
HOPE THAT HASN'T GOTTEN US OFF ON THE WRONG FOOT. PLEASE. HAVE A SEAT.
AFTER ALL, THIS IS A WHOLE NEW DYNAMIC FOR US.
WHAT DO YOU MEAN?
SPIDER-SENSE ISN'T READING ANYTHING FROM THE TABLE, CHAIR, OR ROOM...
...OR EVEN THE GOBLIN, BUT THEN AGAIN, GIVEN THE CIRCUMSTANCES, WHY WOULD IT?
JOURNAL
WELL, STRICTLY SPEAKING, GOING BY THE BOOK--
--THIS BOOK ACTUALLY--
--YOU AND I HAVE NEVER BEEN THE WORST OF ENEMIES. HAVE WE...
...OTTO?
HE KNOWS. DEAR LORD! BUT HOW?!

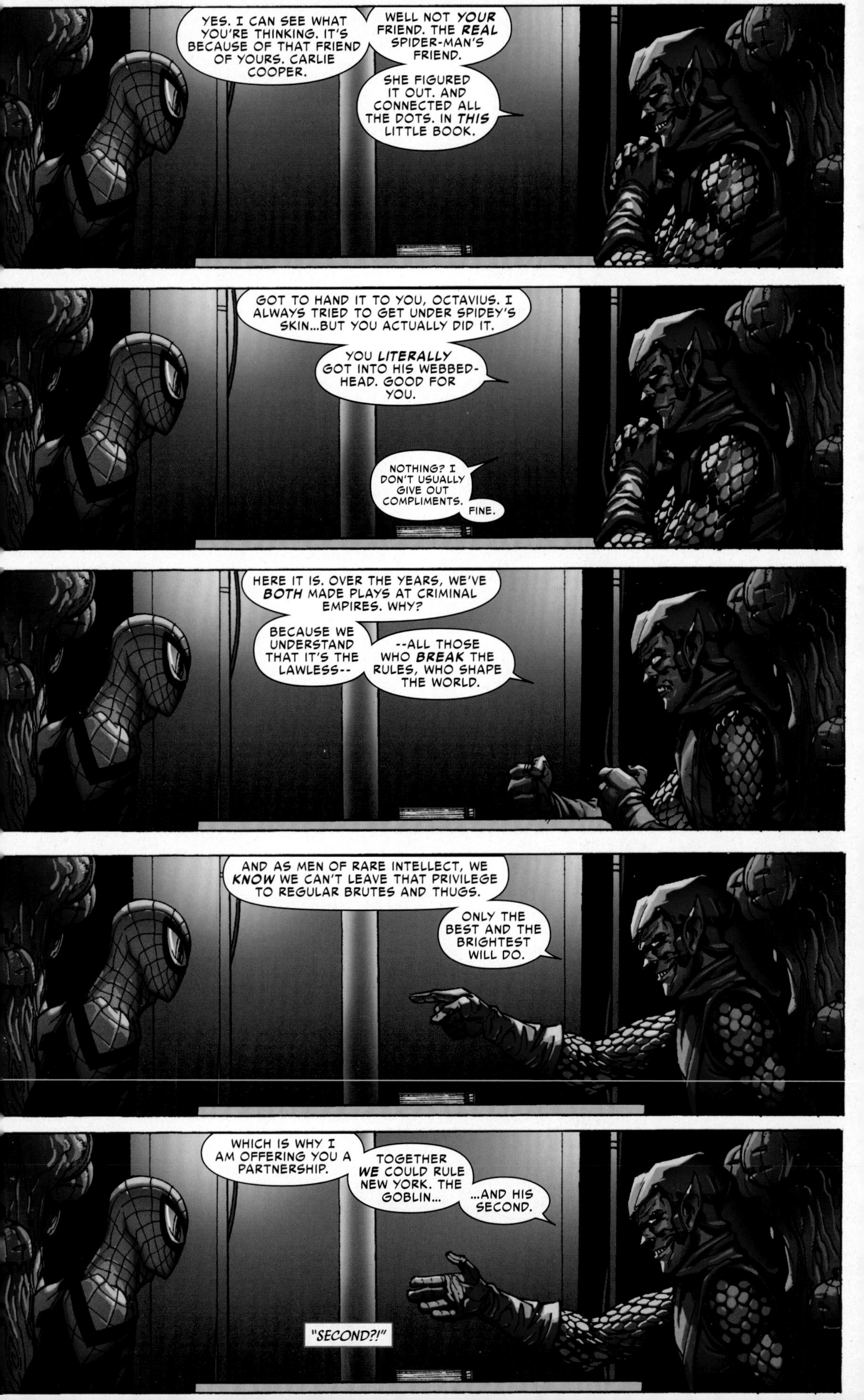
YES. I CAN SEE WHAT YOU'RE THINKING. IT'S BECAUSE OF THAT FRIEND OF YOURS. CARLIE COOPER.
WELL NOT *YOUR* FRIEND. THE *REAL* SPIDER-MAN'S FRIEND.
SHE FIGURED IT OUT. AND CONNECTED ALL THE DOTS. IN *THIS* LITTLE BOOK.
GOT TO HAND IT TO YOU, OCTAVIUS. I ALWAYS TRIED TO GET UNDER SPIDEY'S SKIN...BUT YOU ACTUALLY DID IT.
YOU *LITERALLY* GOT INTO HIS WEBBED-HEAD. GOOD FOR YOU.
NOTHING? I DON'T USUALLY GIVE OUT COMPLIMENTS.
FINE.
HERE IT IS. OVER THE YEARS, WE'VE *BOTH* MADE PLAYS AT CRIMINAL EMPIRES. WHY?
BECAUSE WE UNDERSTAND THAT IT'S THE LAWLESS--
--ALL THOSE WHO *BREAK* THE RULES, WHO SHAPE THE WORLD.
AND AS MEN OF RARE INTELLECT, WE *KNOW* WE CAN'T LEAVE THAT PRIVILEGE TO REGULAR BRUTES AND THUGS.
ONLY THE BEST AND THE BRIGHTEST WILL DO.
WHICH IS WHY I AM OFFERING YOU A PARTNERSHIP.
TOGETHER *WE* COULD RULE NEW YORK. THE GOBLIN...
...AND HIS SECOND.
"SECOND?!"

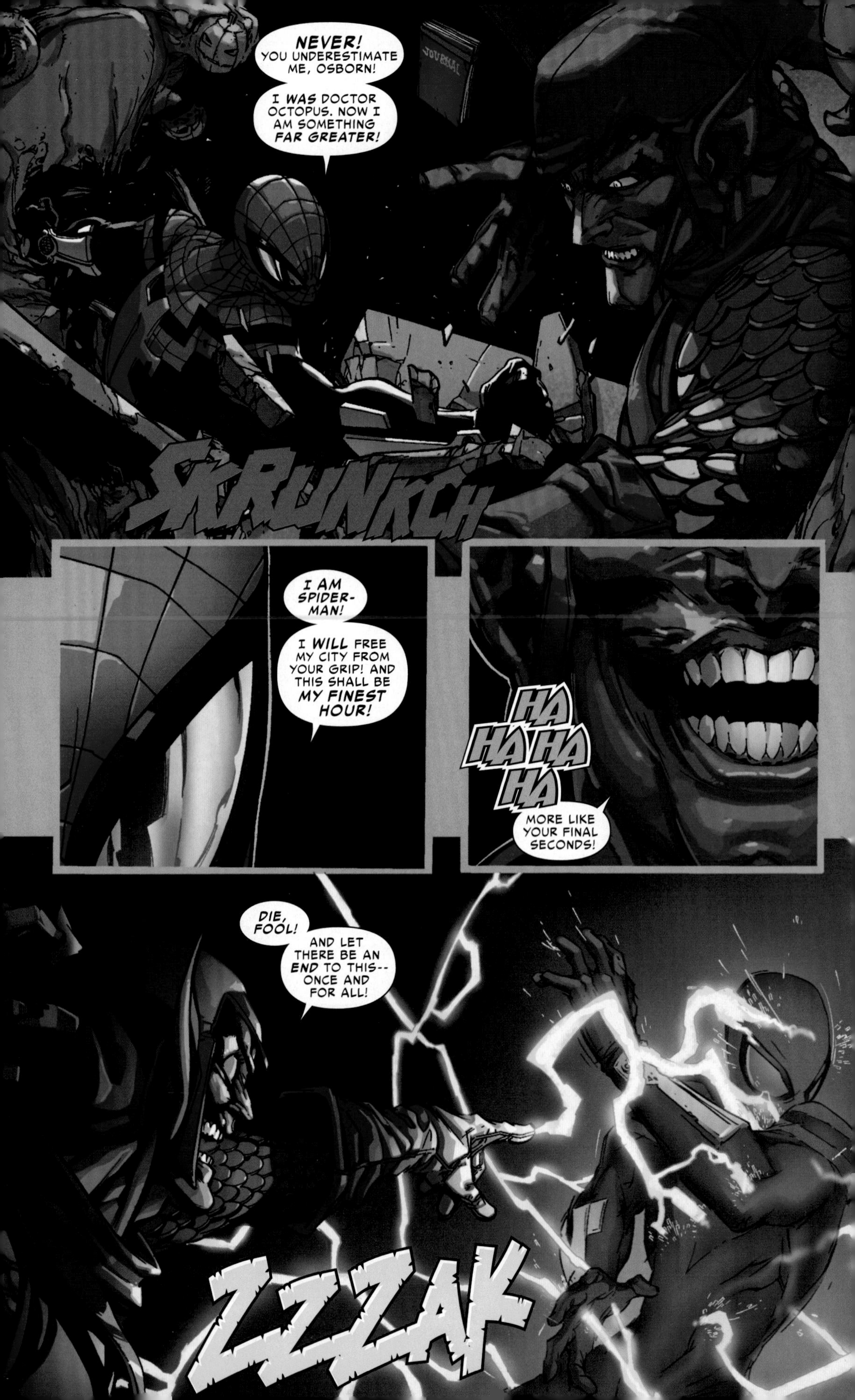
NEVER! YOU UNDERESTIMATE ME, OSBORN!
I WAS DOCTOR OCTOPUS. NOW I AM SOMETHING FAR GREATER!
SKRUNKCH
I AM SPIDER-MAN!
I WILL FREE MY CITY FROM YOUR GRIP! AND THIS SHALL BE MY FINEST HOUR!
HA HA HA HA
MORE LIKE YOUR FINAL SECONDS!
DIE, FOOL!
AND LET THERE BE AN END TO THIS-- ONCE AND FOR ALL!
ZZZAK

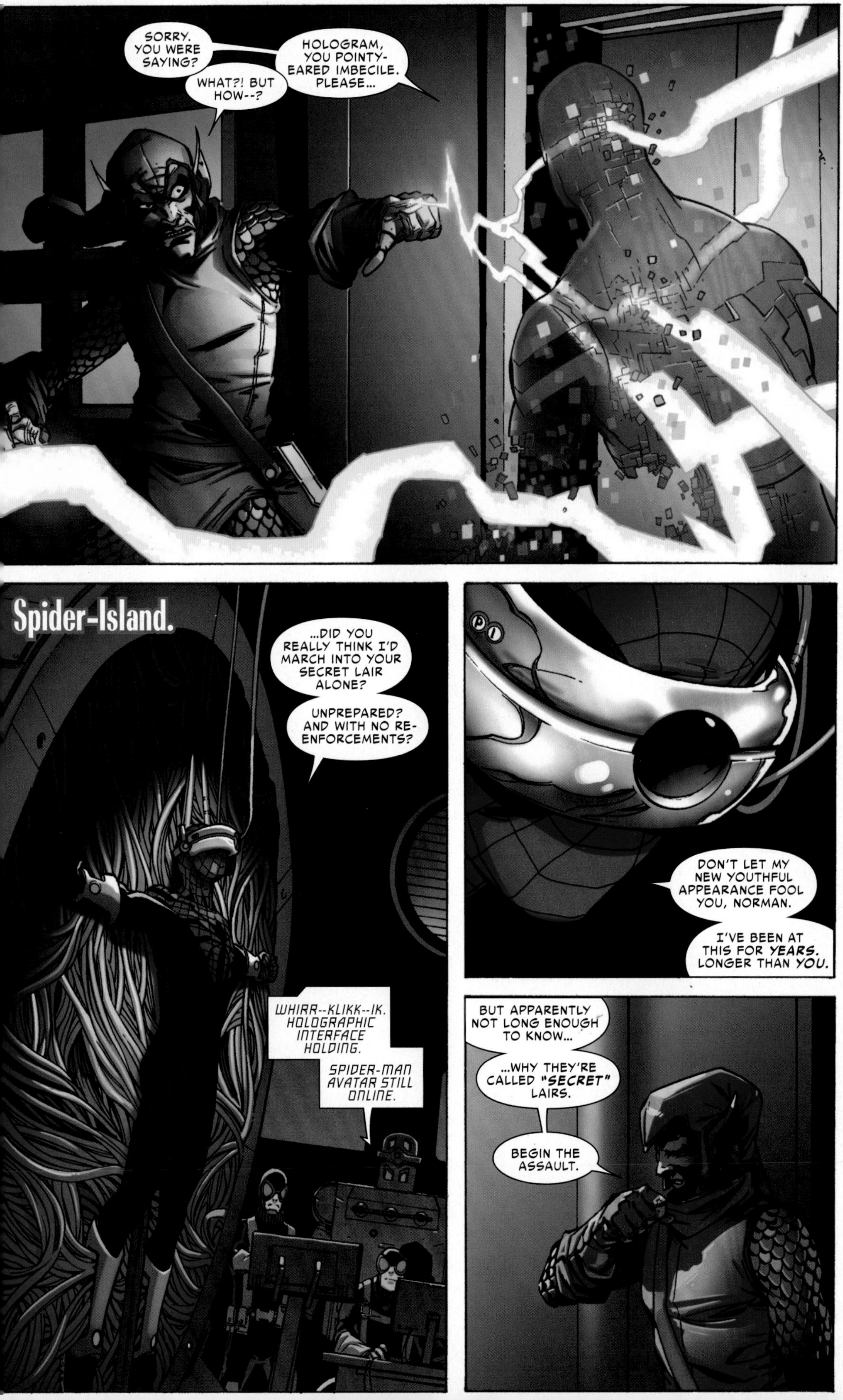
SORRY. YOU WERE SAYING?
HOLOGRAM, YOU POINTY-EARED IMBECILE. PLEASE...
WHAT?! BUT HOW--?
Spider-Island.
...DID YOU REALLY THINK I'D MARCH INTO YOUR SECRET LAIR ALONE?
UNPREPARED? AND WITH NO RE-ENFORCEMENTS?
WHIRR--KLIKK--IK. HOLOGRAPHIC INTERFACE HOLDING.
SPIDER-MAN AVATAR STILL ONLINE.
DON'T LET MY NEW YOUTHFUL APPEARANCE FOOL YOU, NORMAN.
I'VE BEEN AT THIS FOR YEARS. LONGER THAN YOU.
BUT APPARENTLY NOT LONG ENOUGH TO KNOW...
...WHY THEY'RE CALLED "SECRET" LAIRS.
BEGIN THE ASSAULT.

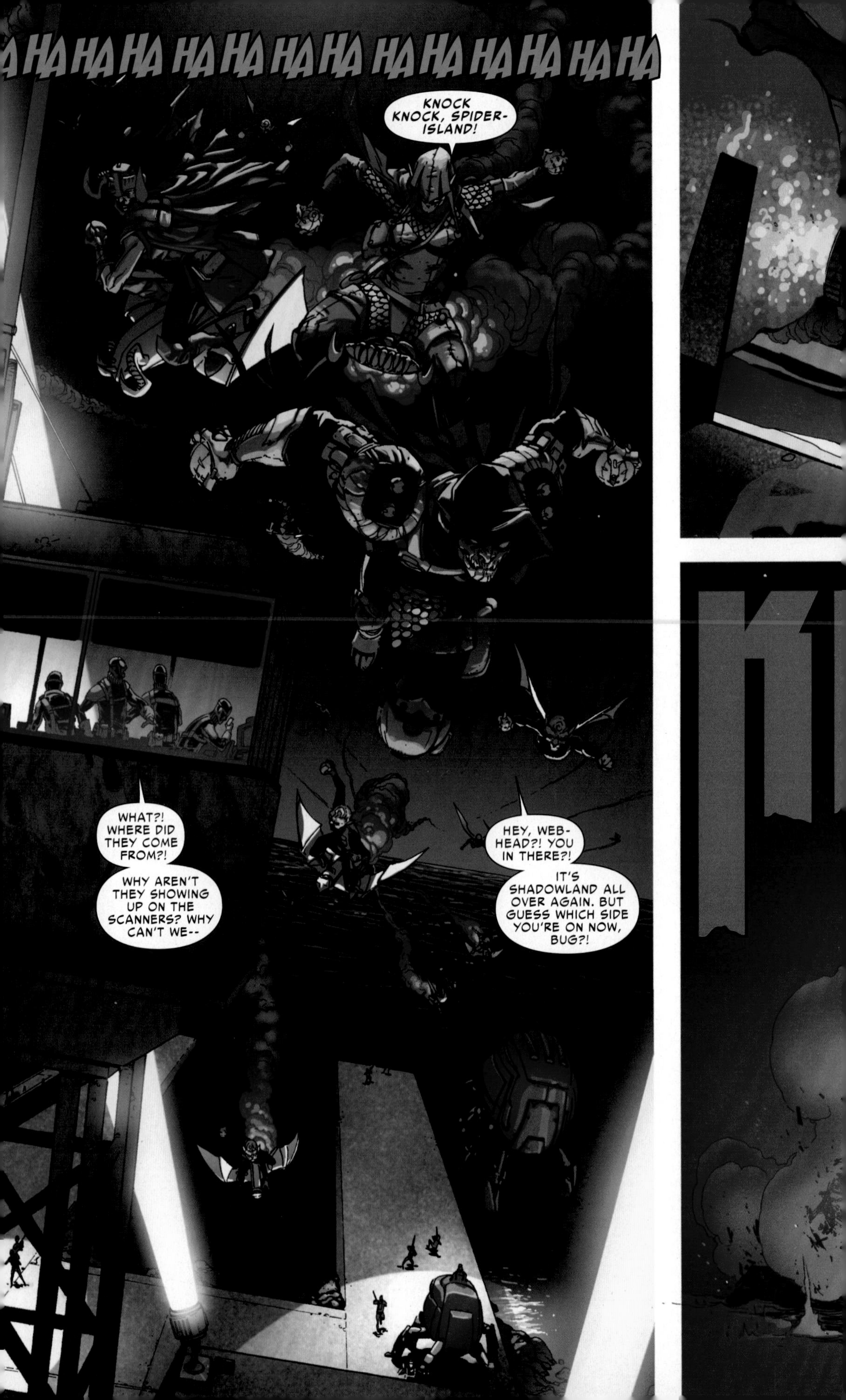
HA HA HA HA HA HA HA HA HA HA HA HA HA HA HA
KNOCK KNOCK, SPIDER-ISLAND!
WHAT?! WHERE DID THEY COME FROM?!
WHY AREN'T THEY SHOWING UP ON THE SCANNERS? WHY CAN'T WE--
HEY, WEB-HEAD?! YOU IN THERE?!
IT'S SHADOWLAND ALL OVER AGAIN. BUT GUESS WHICH SIDE YOU'RE ON NOW, BUG?!

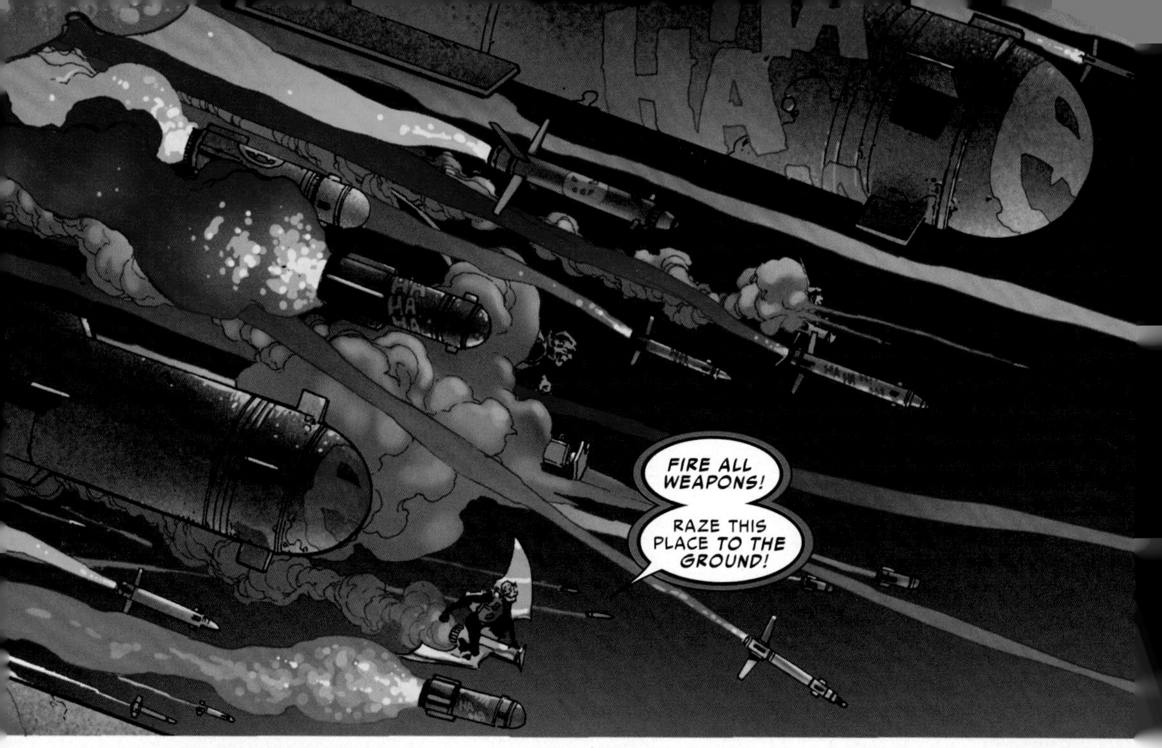
FIRE ALL WEAPONS!
RAZE THIS PLACE TO THE GROUND!

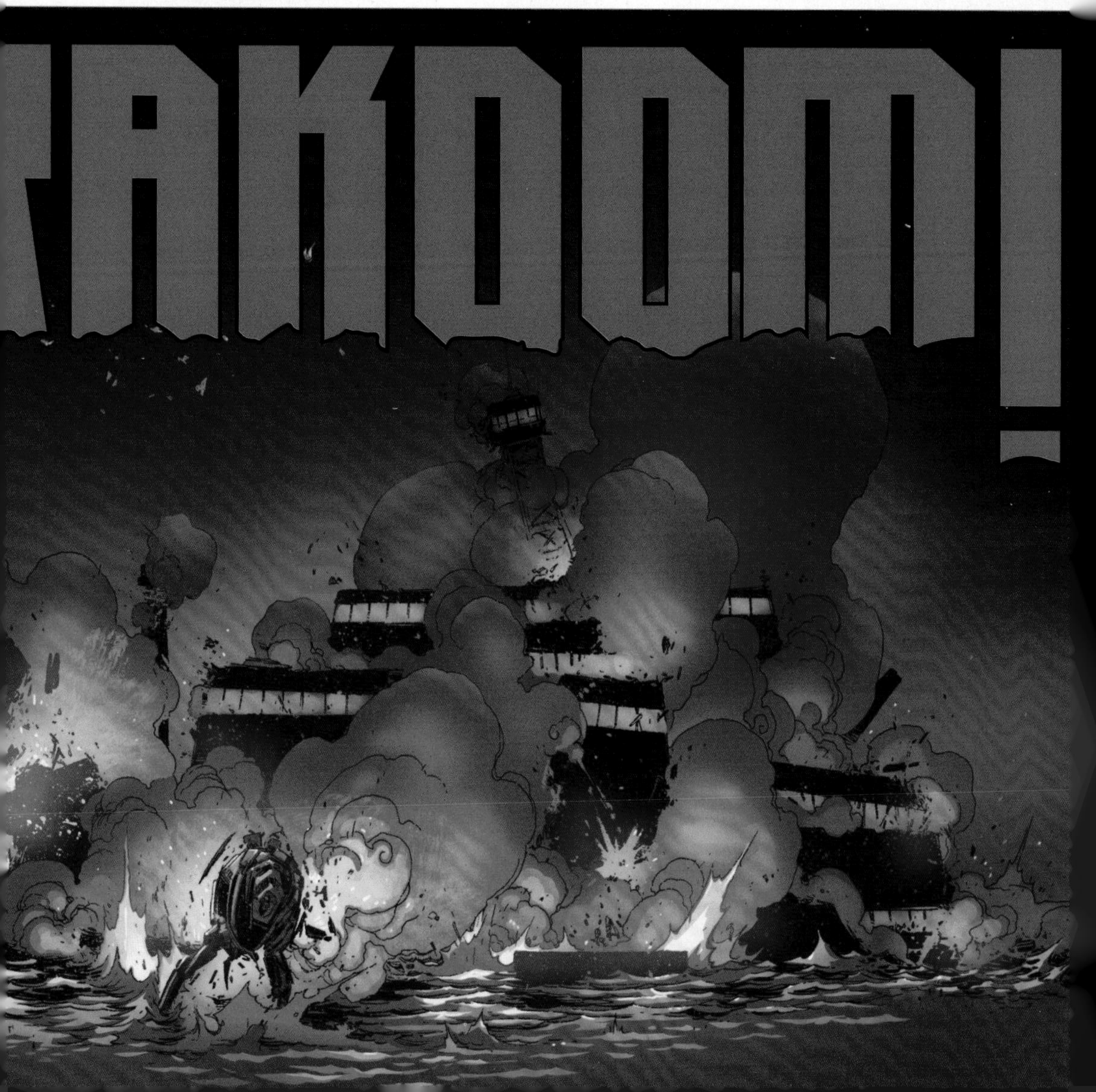
RAKOOM!

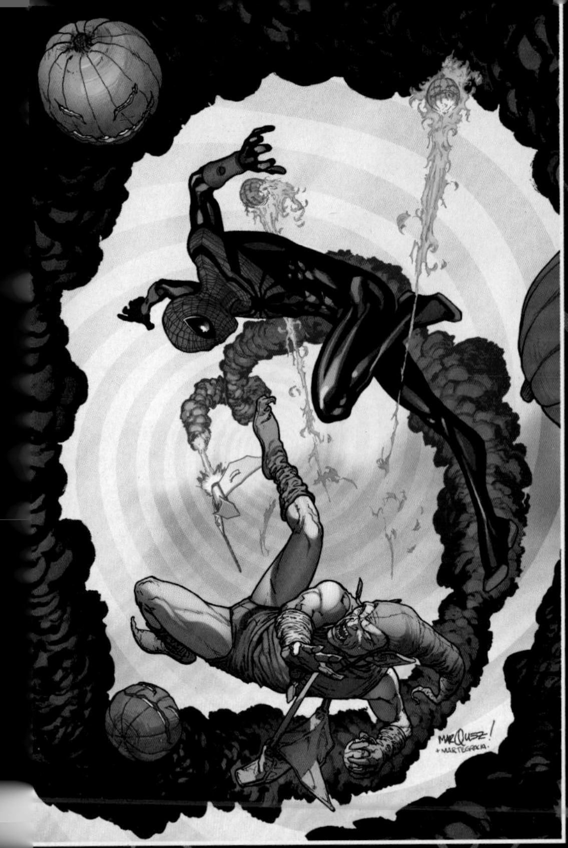

#28 VARIANT
BY DAVID MARQUEZ & MARTE GRACIA

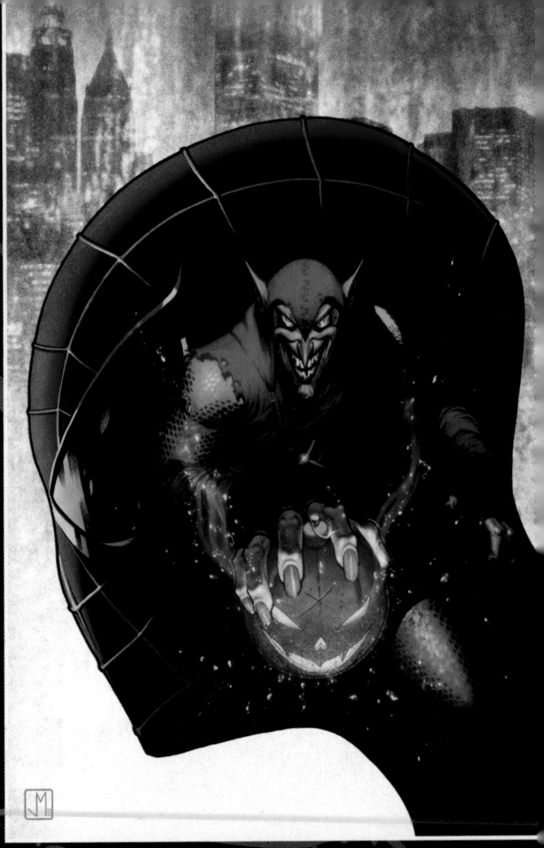

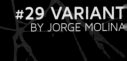

#29 VARIANT
BY JORGE MOLINA

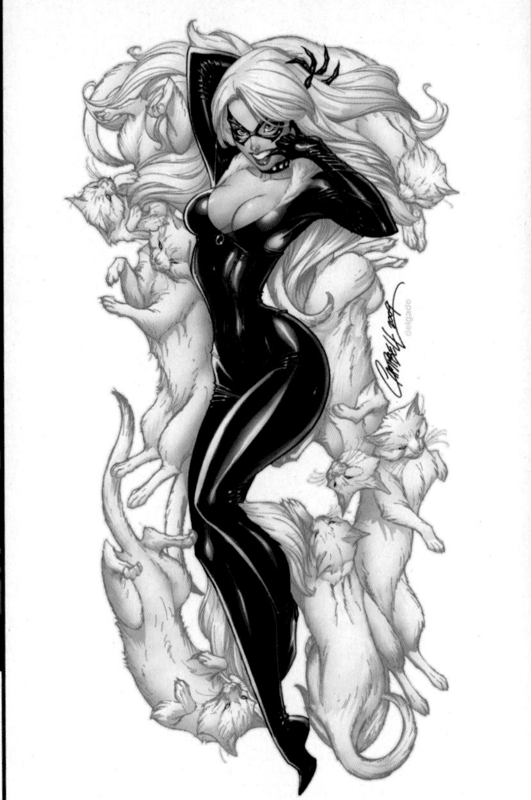

#29 VARIANT
BY J. SCOTT CAMPBELL & EDGAR DELGADO

28

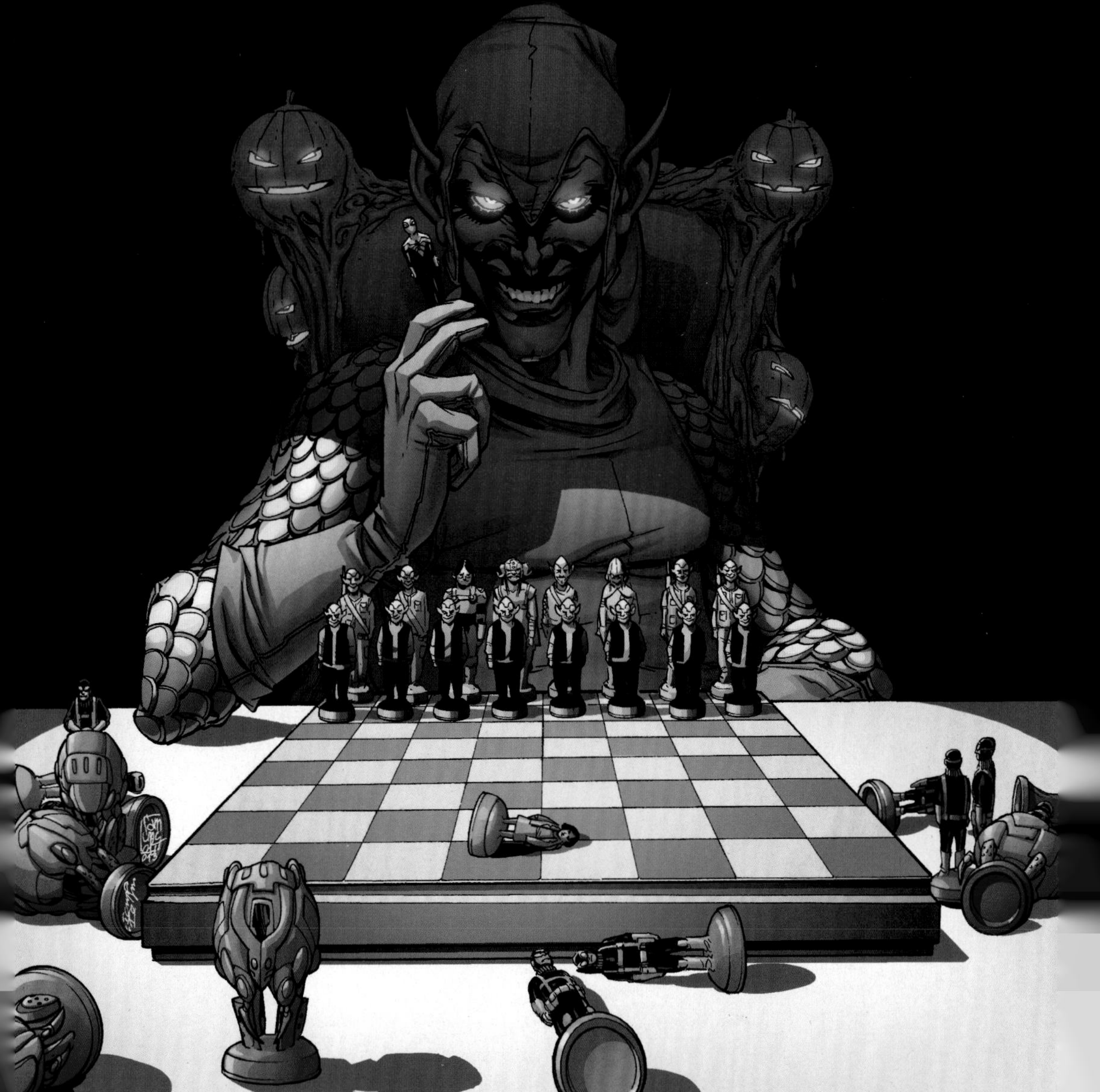

THE FALL OF SPIDER-ISLAND

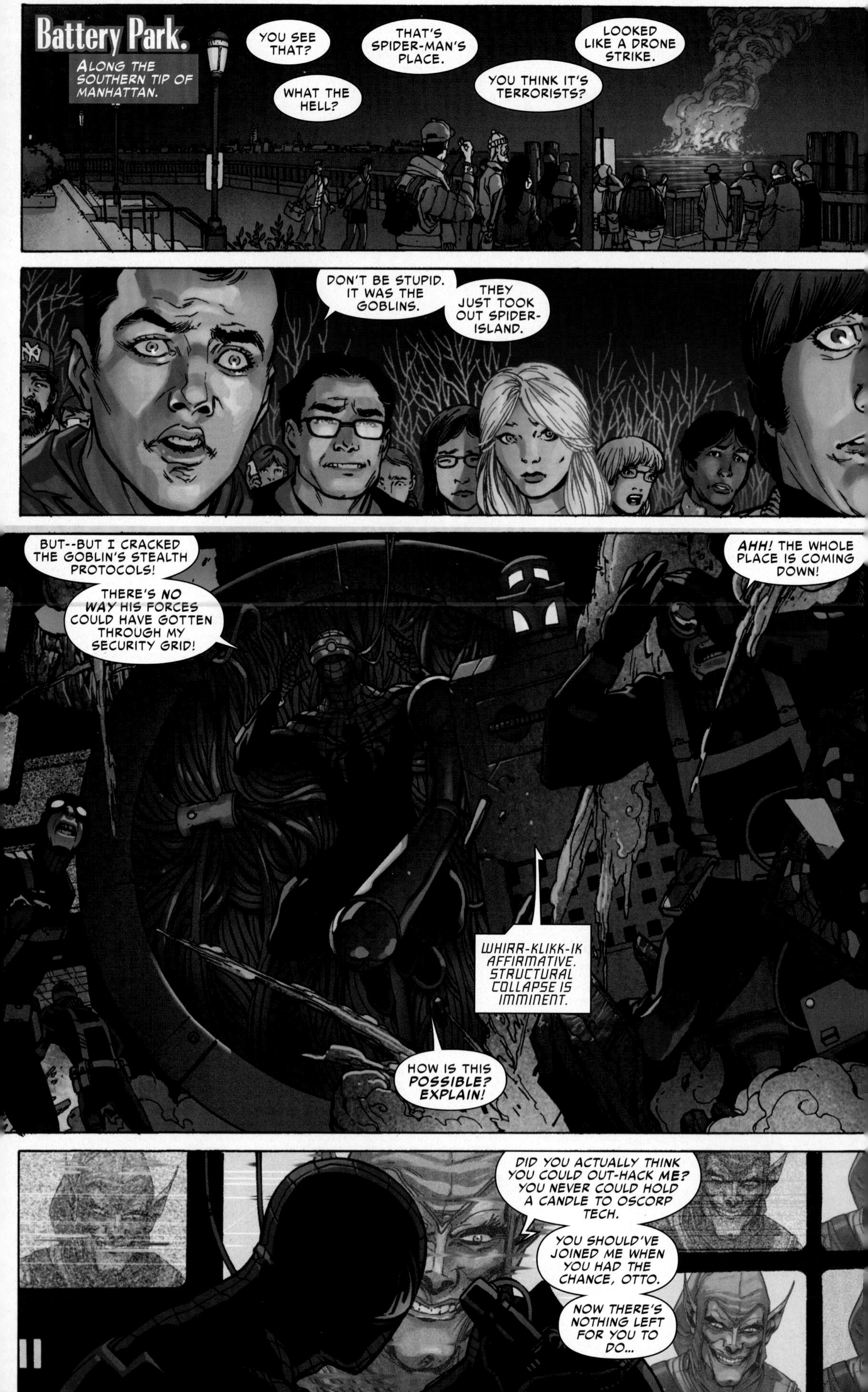

Battery Park.
Along the southern tip of Manhattan.
YOU SEE THAT?
WHAT THE HELL?
THAT'S SPIDER-MAN'S PLACE.
YOU THINK IT'S TERRORISTS?
LOOKED LIKE A DRONE STRIKE.
DON'T BE STUPID. IT WAS THE GOBLINS.
THEY JUST TOOK OUT SPIDER-ISLAND.
BUT--BUT I CRACKED THE GOBLIN'S STEALTH PROTOCOLS!
THERE'S NO WAY HIS FORCES COULD HAVE GOTTEN THROUGH MY SECURITY GRID!
AHH! THE WHOLE PLACE IS COMING DOWN!
WHIRR-KLIKK-IK AFFIRMATIVE. STRUCTURAL COLLAPSE IS IMMINENT.
HOW IS THIS POSSIBLE? EXPLAIN!
DID YOU ACTUALLY THINK YOU COULD OUT-HACK ME? YOU NEVER COULD HOLD A CANDLE TO OSCORP TECH.
YOU SHOULD'VE JOINED ME WHEN YOU HAD THE CHANCE, OTTO.
NOW THERE'S NOTHING LEFT FOR YOU TO DO...

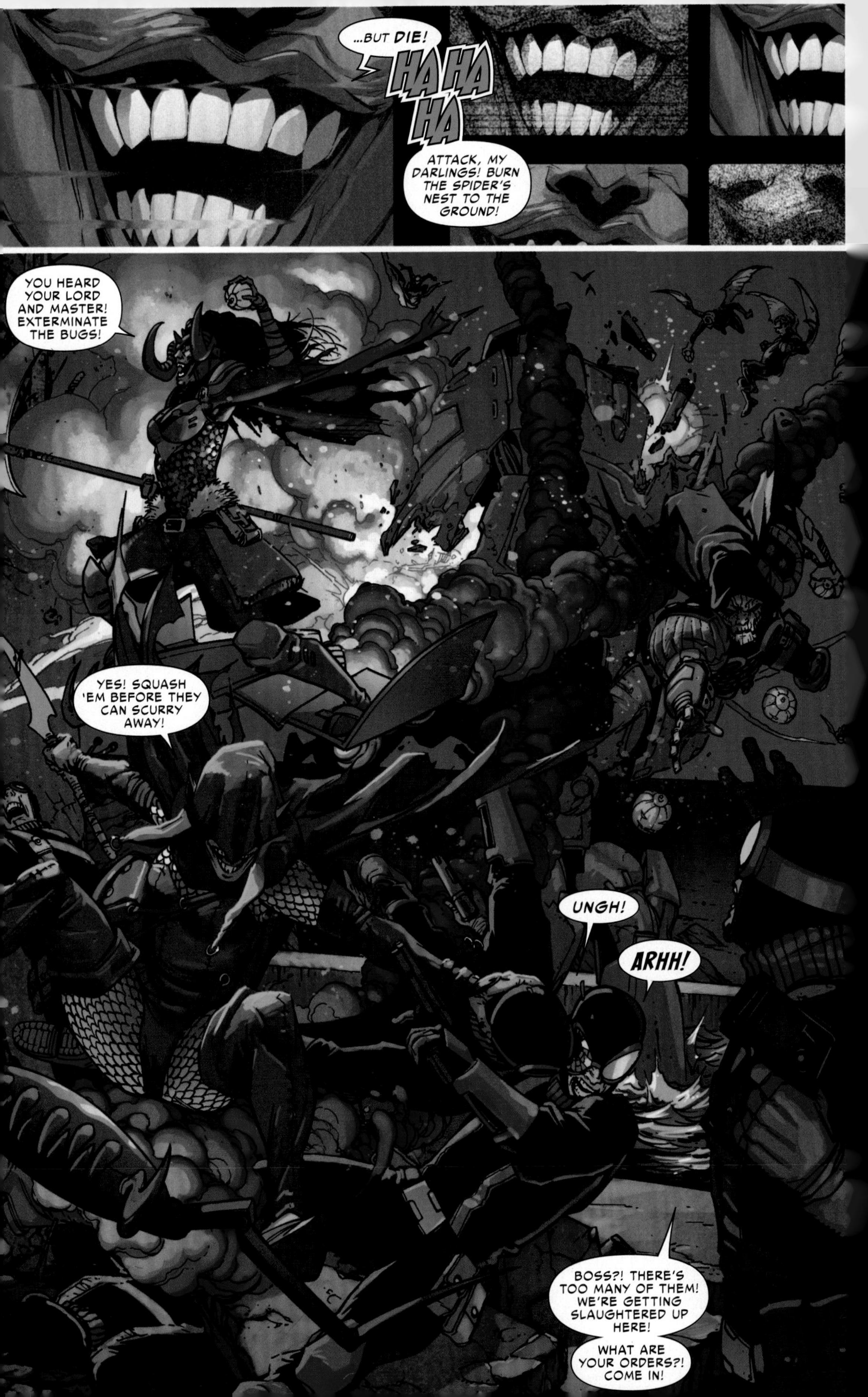
...BUT DIE!
HA HA HA
ATTACK, MY DARLINGS! BURN THE SPIDER'S NEST TO THE GROUND!
YOU HEARD YOUR LORD AND MASTER! EXTERMINATE THE BUGS!
YES! SQUASH 'EM BEFORE THEY CAN SCURRY AWAY!
UNGH!
ARHH!
BOSS?! THERE'S TOO MANY OF THEM! WE'RE GETTING SLAUGHTERED UP HERE!
WHAT ARE YOUR ORDERS?! COME IN!

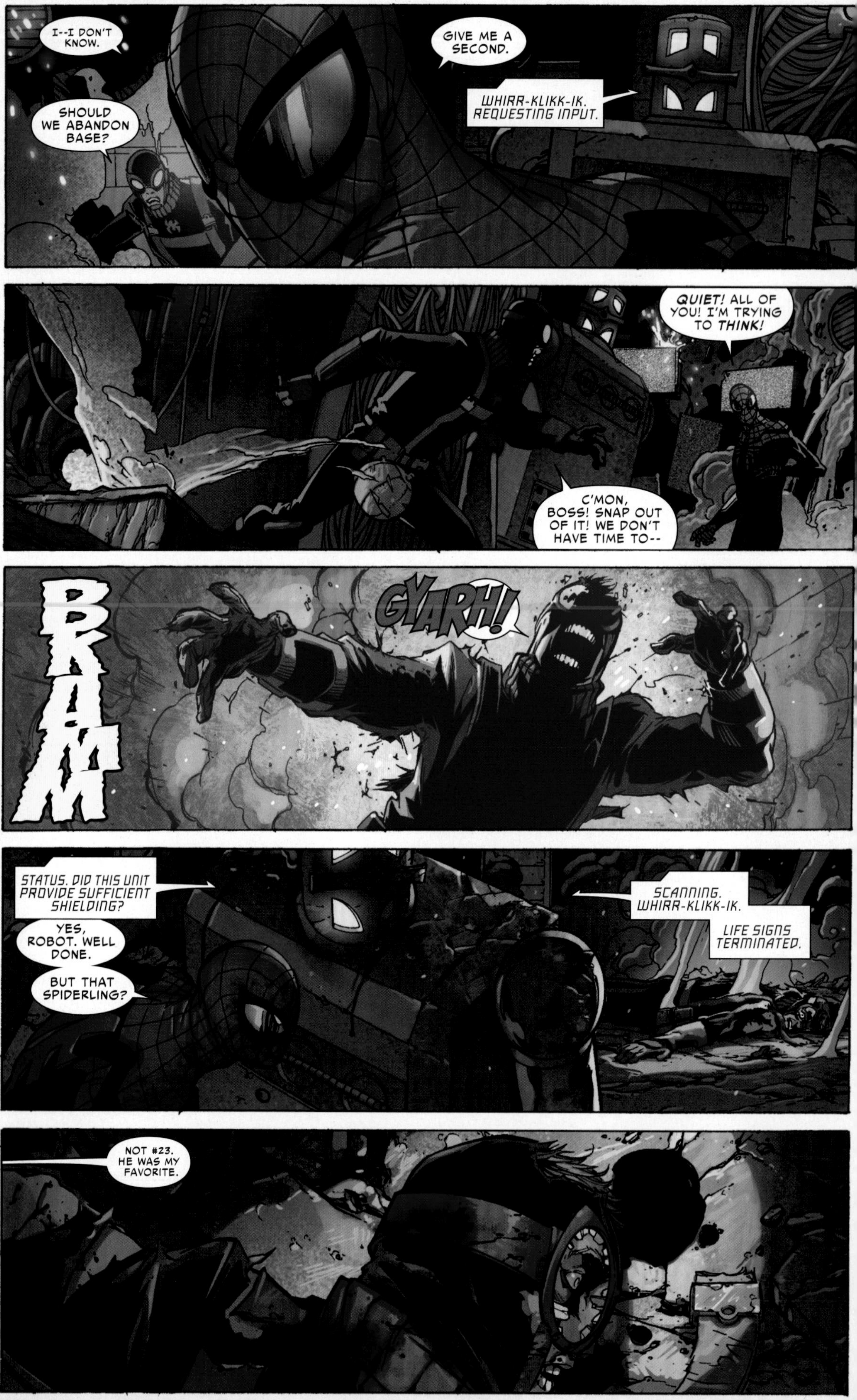
I--I DON'T KNOW.
SHOULD WE ABANDON BASE?
GIVE ME A SECOND.
WHIRR-KLIKK-IK. REQUESTING INPUT.
QUIET! ALL OF YOU! I'M TRYING TO THINK!
C'MON, BOSS! SNAP OUT OF IT! WE DON'T HAVE TIME TO--
BRAAM
GYARH!
STATUS. DID THIS UNIT PROVIDE SUFFICIENT SHIELDING?
YES, ROBOT. WELL DONE.
BUT THAT SPIDERLING?
SCANNING. WHIRR-KLIKK-IK.
LIFE SIGNS TERMINATED.
NOT #23. HE WAS MY FAVORITE.

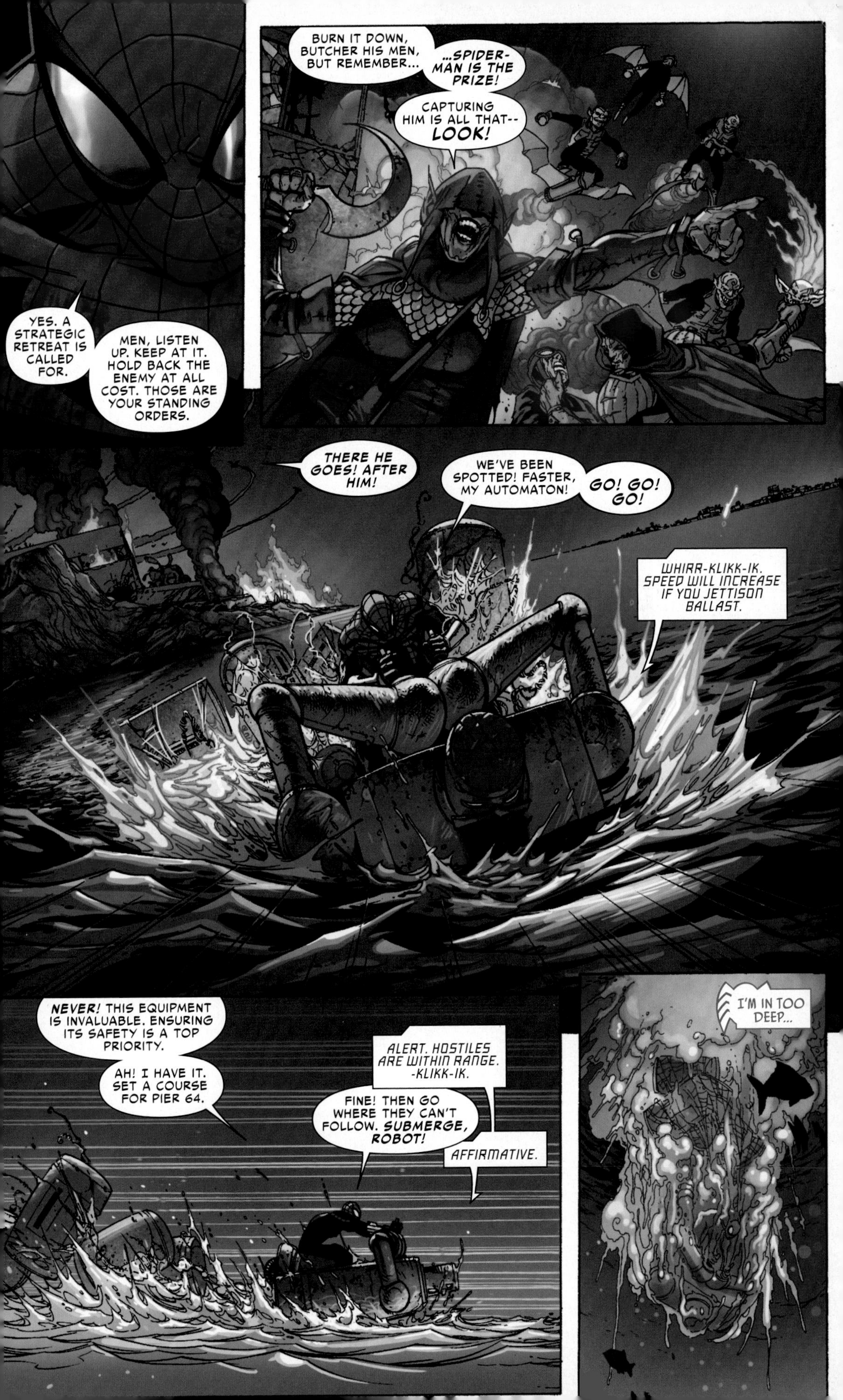
YES. A STRATEGIC RETREAT IS CALLED FOR.
MEN, LISTEN UP. KEEP AT IT. HOLD BACK THE ENEMY AT ALL COST. THOSE ARE YOUR STANDING ORDERS.
BURN IT DOWN, BUTCHER HIS MEN, BUT REMEMBER...
...SPIDER-MAN IS THE PRIZE!
CAPTURING HIM IS ALL THAT-- LOOK!
THERE HE GOES! AFTER HIM!
WE'VE BEEN SPOTTED! FASTER, MY AUTOMATON!
GO! GO! GO!
WHIRR-KLIKK-IK. SPEED WILL INCREASE IF YOU JETTISON BALLAST.
NEVER! THIS EQUIPMENT IS INVALUABLE. ENSURING ITS SAFETY IS A TOP PRIORITY.
AH! I HAVE IT. SET A COURSE FOR PIER 64.
ALERT. HOSTILES ARE WITHIN RANGE. -KLIKK-IK.
FINE! THEN GO WHERE THEY CAN'T FOLLOW. SUBMERGE, ROBOT!
AFFIRMATIVE.
I'M IN TOO DEEP...

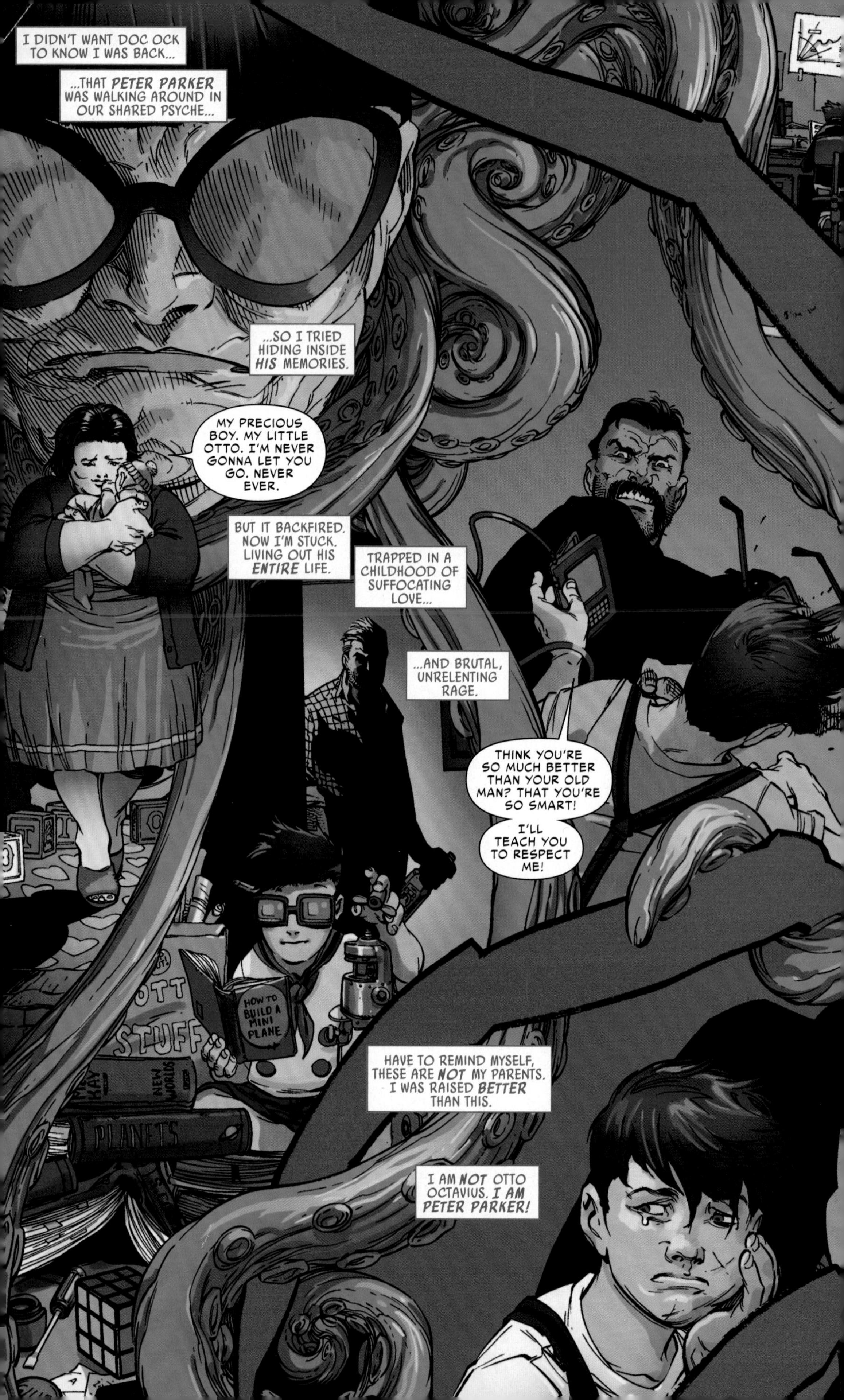
I DIDN'T WANT DOC OCK TO KNOW I WAS BACK...
...THAT PETER PARKER WAS WALKING AROUND IN OUR SHARED PSYCHE...
...SO I TRIED HIDING INSIDE HIS MEMORIES.
MY PRECIOUS BOY. MY LITTLE OTTO. I'M NEVER GONNA LET YOU GO. NEVER EVER.
BUT IT BACKFIRED. NOW I'M STUCK. LIVING OUT HIS ENTIRE LIFE.
TRAPPED IN A CHILDHOOD OF SUFFOCATING LOVE...
...AND BRUTAL, UNRELENTING RAGE.
THINK YOU'RE SO MUCH BETTER THAN YOUR OLD MAN? THAT YOU'RE SO SMART!
I'LL TEACH YOU TO RESPECT ME!
HOW TO BUILD A MINI PLANE
OTT STUFF
NEW WORLDS
PLANETS
HAVE TO REMIND MYSELF, THESE ARE NOT MY PARENTS. I WAS RAISED BETTER THAN THIS.
I AM NOT OTTO OCTAVIUS. I AM PETER PARKER!

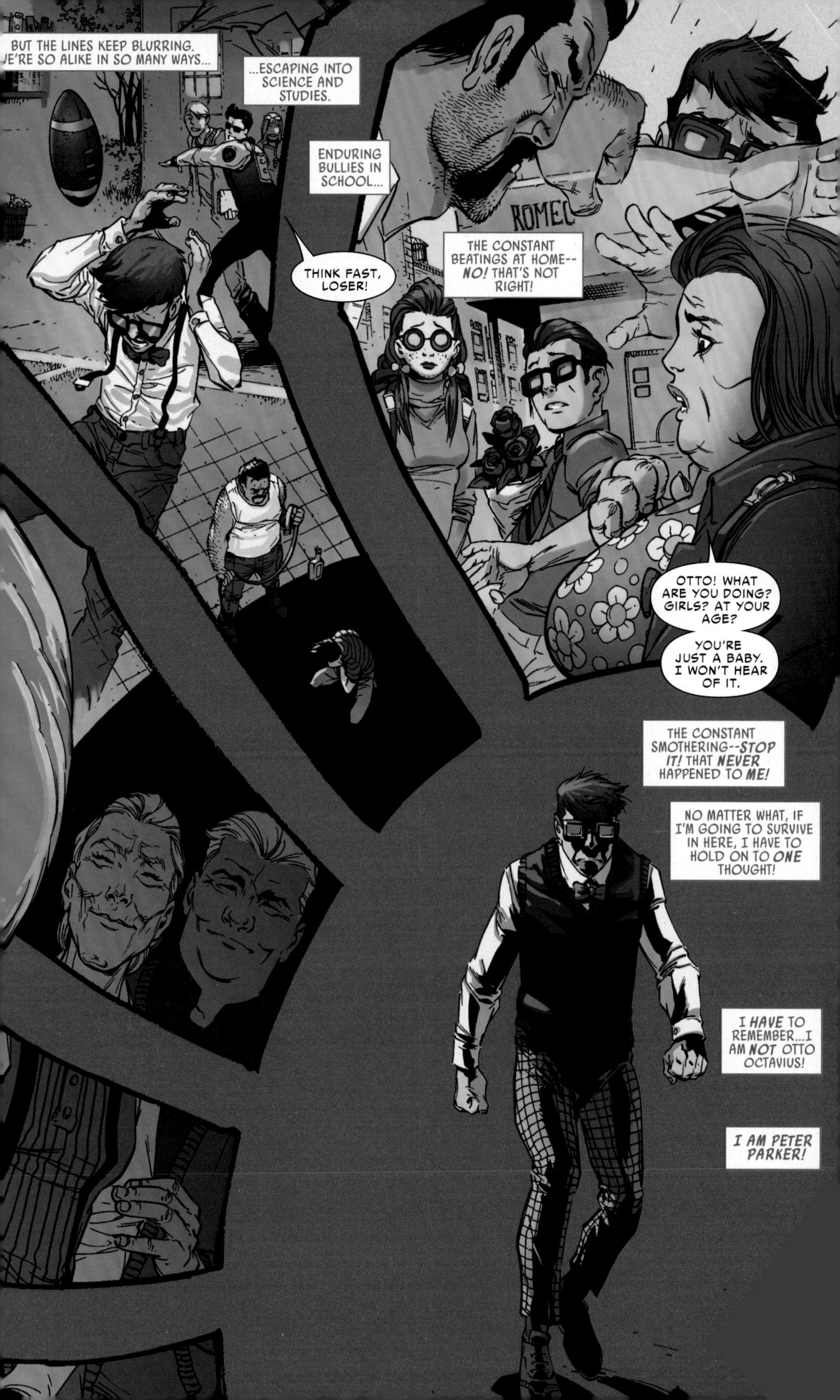

BUT THE LINES KEEP BLURRING. WE'RE SO ALIKE IN SO MANY WAYS...
...ESCAPING INTO SCIENCE AND STUDIES.
ENDURING BULLIES IN SCHOOL...
THINK FAST, LOSER!
ROMEO
THE CONSTANT BEATINGS AT HOME-- NO! THAT'S NOT RIGHT!
OTTO! WHAT ARE YOU DOING? GIRLS? AT YOUR AGE?
YOU'RE JUST A BABY. I WON'T HEAR OF IT.
THE CONSTANT SMOTHERING--STOP IT! THAT NEVER HAPPENED TO ME!
NO MATTER WHAT, IF I'M GOING TO SURVIVE IN HERE, I HAVE TO HOLD ON TO ONE THOUGHT!
I HAVE TO REMEMBER...I AM NOT OTTO OCTAVIUS!
I AM PETER PARKER!

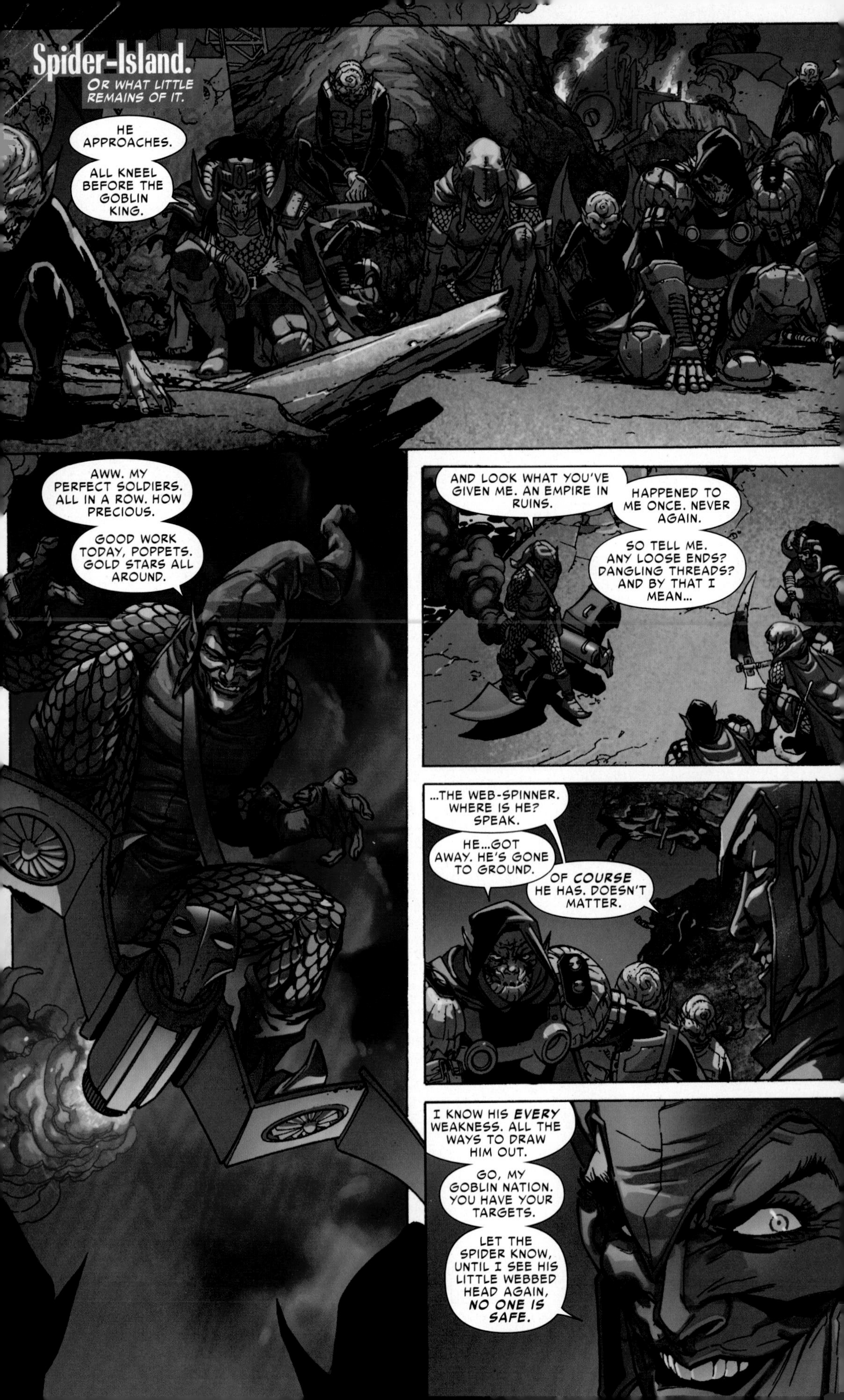
Spider-Island.
OR WHAT LITTLE REMAINS OF IT.
HE APPROACHES.
ALL KNEEL BEFORE THE GOBLIN KING.
AWW. MY PERFECT SOLDIERS. ALL IN A ROW. HOW PRECIOUS.
GOOD WORK TODAY, POPPETS. GOLD STARS ALL AROUND.
AND LOOK WHAT YOU'VE GIVEN ME. AN EMPIRE IN RUINS.
HAPPENED TO ME ONCE. NEVER AGAIN.
SO TELL ME. ANY LOOSE ENDS? DANGLING THREADS? AND BY THAT I MEAN...
...THE WEB-SPINNER. WHERE IS HE? SPEAK.
HE...GOT AWAY. HE'S GONE TO GROUND.
OF COURSE HE HAS. DOESN'T MATTER.
I KNOW HIS EVERY WEAKNESS. ALL THE WAYS TO DRAW HIM OUT.
GO, MY GOBLIN NATION. YOU HAVE YOUR TARGETS.
LET THE SPIDER KNOW, UNTIL I SEE HIS LITTLE WEBBED HEAD AGAIN, NO ONE IS SAFE.

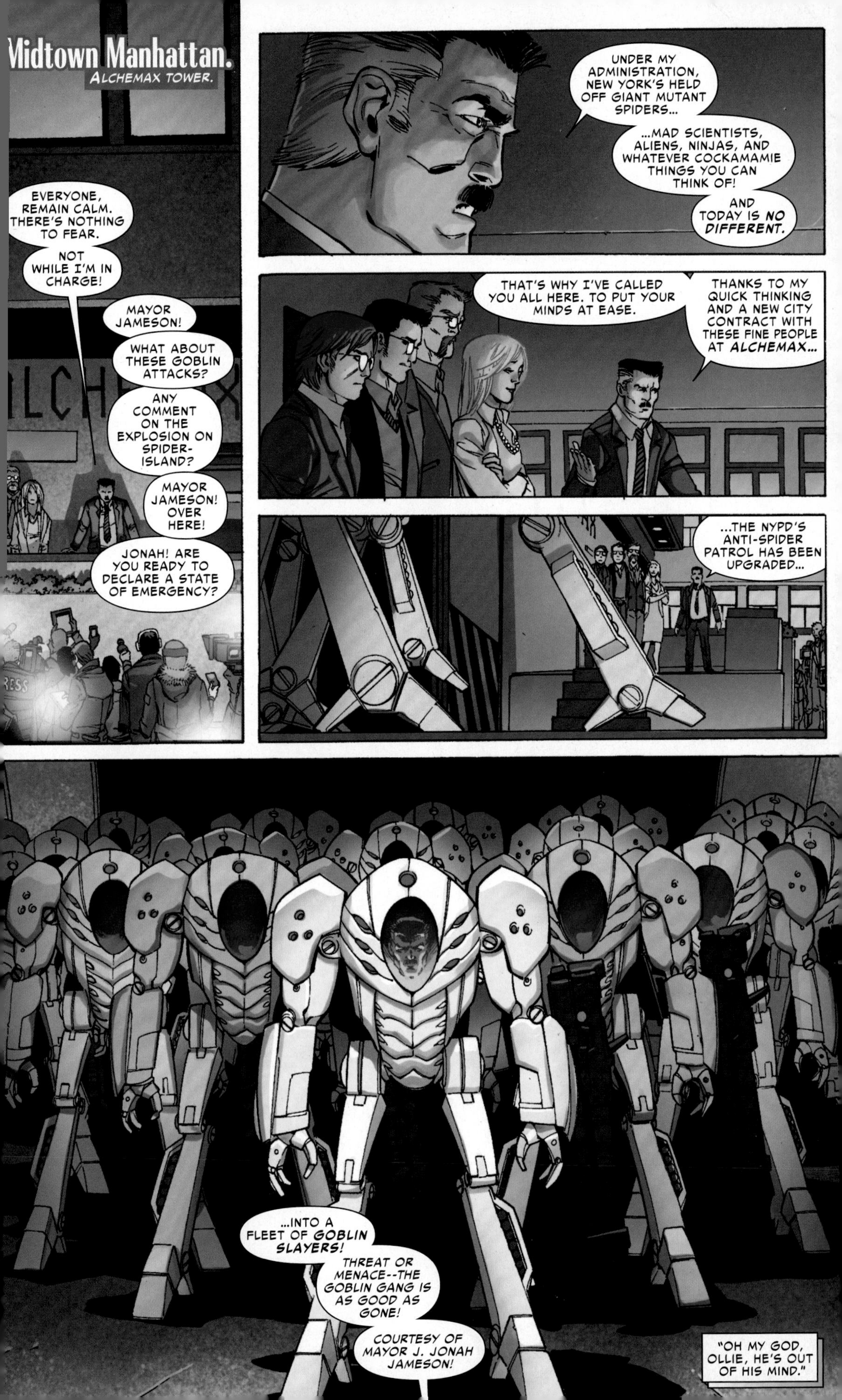

Midtown Manhattan.
ALCHEMAX TOWER.
EVERYONE, REMAIN CALM. THERE'S NOTHING TO FEAR.
NOT WHILE I'M IN CHARGE!
MAYOR JAMESON!
WHAT ABOUT THESE GOBLIN ATTACKS?
ANY COMMENT ON THE EXPLOSION ON SPIDER-ISLAND?
MAYOR JAMESON! OVER HERE!
JONAH! ARE YOU READY TO DECLARE A STATE OF EMERGENCY?
UNDER MY ADMINISTRATION, NEW YORK'S HELD OFF GIANT MUTANT SPIDERS...
...MAD SCIENTISTS, ALIENS, NINJAS, AND WHATEVER COCKAMAMIE THINGS YOU CAN THINK OF!
AND TODAY IS NO DIFFERENT.
THAT'S WHY I'VE CALLED YOU ALL HERE. TO PUT YOUR MINDS AT EASE.
THANKS TO MY QUICK THINKING AND A NEW CITY CONTRACT WITH THESE FINE PEOPLE AT ALCHEMAX...
...THE NYPD'S ANTI-SPIDER PATROL HAS BEEN UPGRADED...
...INTO A FLEET OF GOBLIN SLAYERS!
THREAT OR MENACE--THE GOBLIN GANG IS AS GOOD AS GONE!
COURTESY OF MAYOR J. JONAH JAMESON!
"OH MY GOD, OLLIE, HE'S OUT OF HIS MIND."

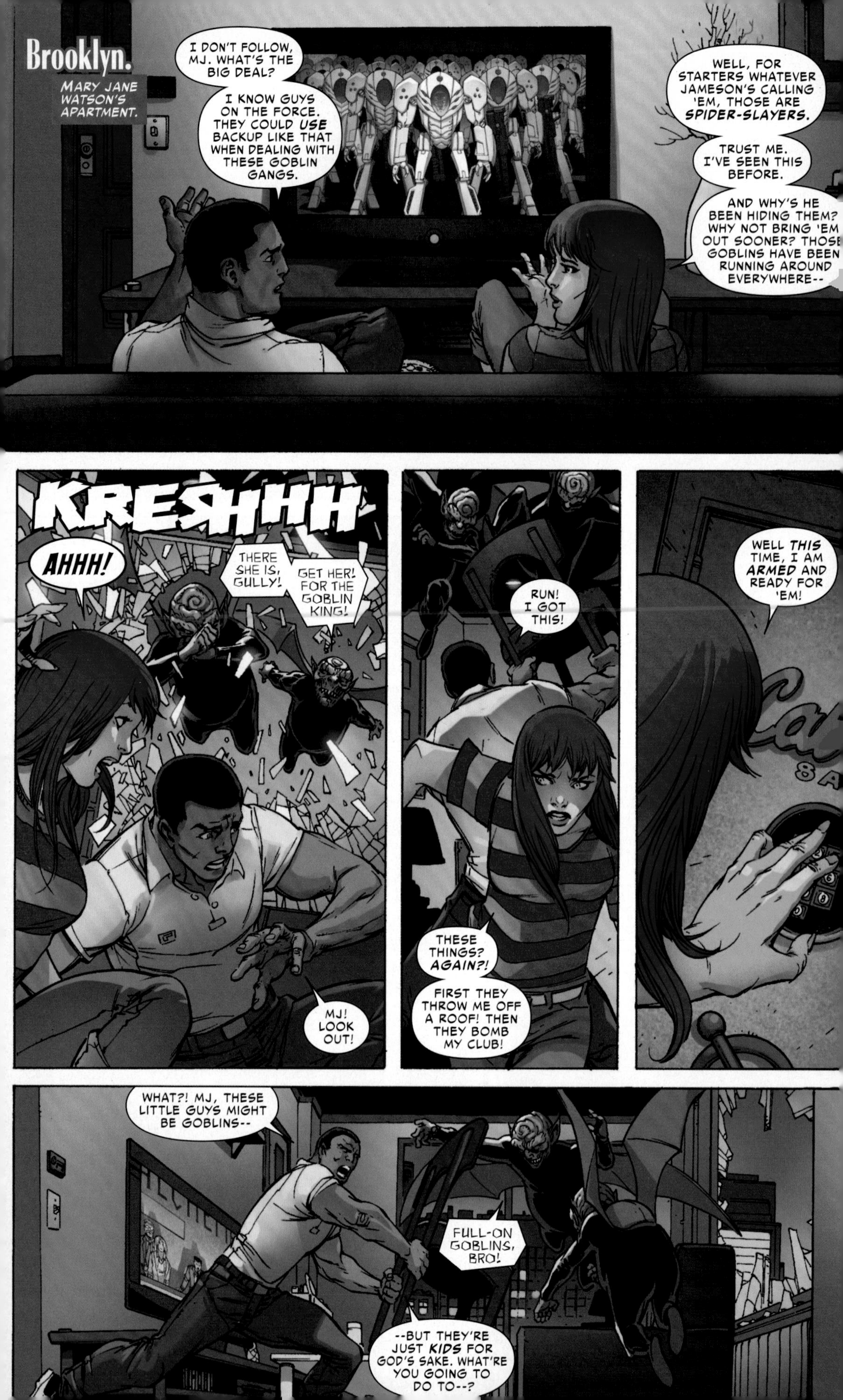

Brooklyn.
MARY JANE WATSON'S APARTMENT.
I DON'T FOLLOW, MJ. WHAT'S THE BIG DEAL?
I KNOW GUYS ON THE FORCE. THEY COULD USE BACKUP LIKE THAT WHEN DEALING WITH THESE GOBLIN GANGS.
WELL, FOR STARTERS WHATEVER JAMESON'S CALLING 'EM, THOSE ARE SPIDER-SLAYERS.
TRUST ME. I'VE SEEN THIS BEFORE.
AND WHY'S HE BEEN HIDING THEM? WHY NOT BRING 'EM OUT SOONER? THOSE GOBLINS HAVE BEEN RUNNING AROUND EVERYWHERE--
KRESHHH
AHHH!
THERE SHE IS, GULLY!
GET HER! FOR THE GOBLIN KING!
MJ! LOOK OUT!
RUN! I GOT THIS!
THESE THINGS? AGAIN?!
FIRST THEY THROW ME OFF A ROOF! THEN THEY BOMB MY CLUB!
WELL THIS TIME, I AM ARMED AND READY FOR 'EM!
WHAT?! MJ, THESE LITTLE GUYS MIGHT BE GOBLINS--
FULL-ON GOBLINS, BRO!
--BUT THEY'RE JUST KIDS FOR GOD'S SAKE. WHAT'RE YOU GOING TO DO TO--?

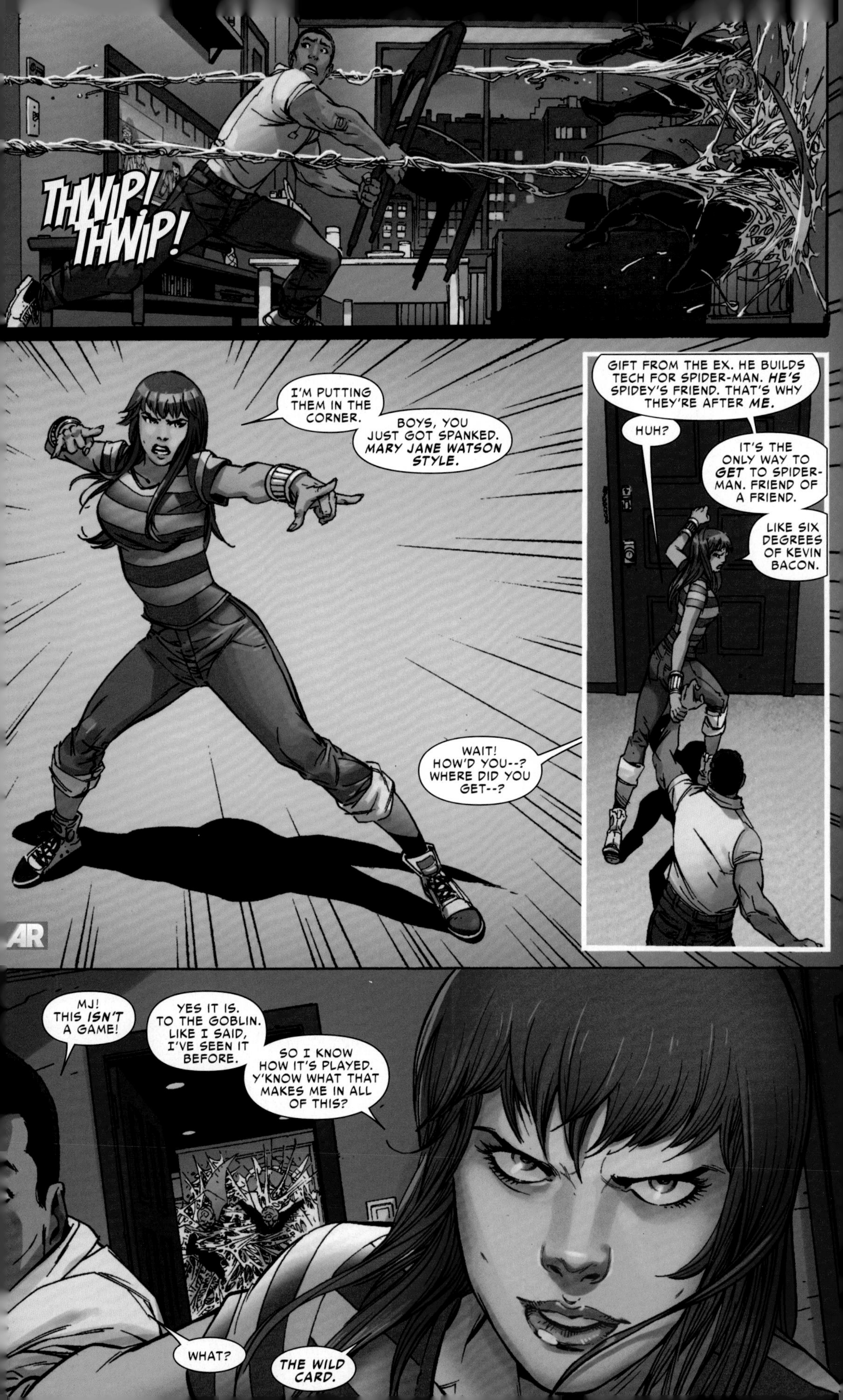
THWIP! THWIP!
I'M PUTTING THEM IN THE CORNER.
BOYS, YOU JUST GOT SPANKED. MARY JANE WATSON STYLE.
WAIT! HOW'D YOU--? WHERE DID YOU GET--?
GIFT FROM THE EX. HE BUILDS TECH FOR SPIDER-MAN. HE'S SPIDEY'S FRIEND. THAT'S WHY THEY'RE AFTER ME.
HUH?
IT'S THE ONLY WAY TO GET TO SPIDER-MAN. FRIEND OF A FRIEND.
LIKE SIX DEGREES OF KEVIN BACON.
AR
MJ! THIS ISN'T A GAME!
YES IT IS. TO THE GOBLIN. LIKE I SAID, I'VE SEEN IT BEFORE.
SO I KNOW HOW IT'S PLAYED. Y'KNOW WHAT THAT MAKES ME IN ALL OF THIS?
WHAT?
THE WILD CARD.

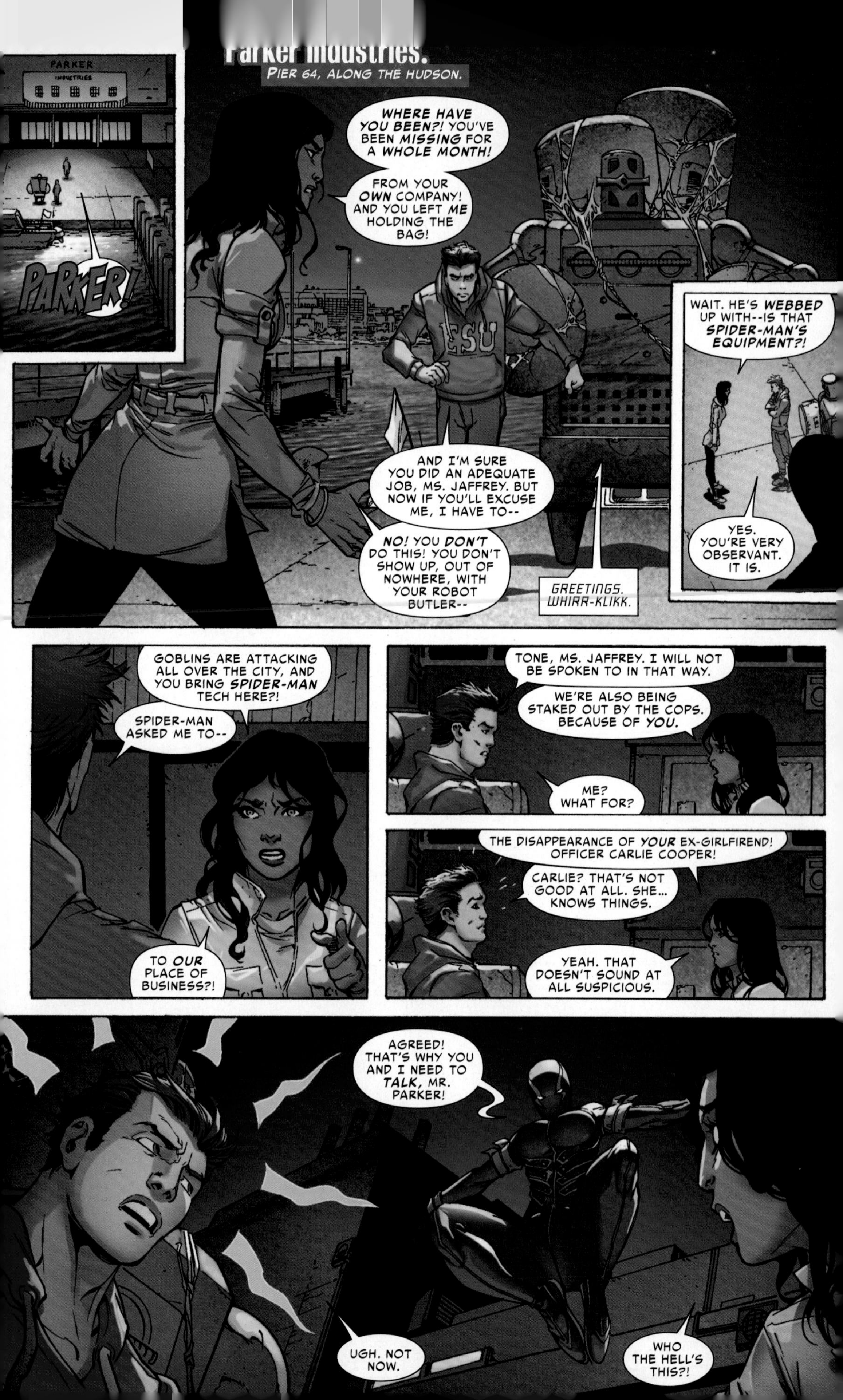
Parker Industries.
PIER 64, ALONG THE HUDSON.
PARKER INDUSTRIES
PARKER!
WHERE HAVE YOU BEEN?! YOU'VE BEEN MISSING FOR A WHOLE MONTH!
FROM YOUR OWN COMPANY! AND YOU LEFT ME HOLDING THE BAG!
AND I'M SURE YOU DID AN ADEQUATE JOB, MS. JAFFREY. BUT NOW IF YOU'LL EXCUSE ME, I HAVE TO--
NO! YOU DON'T DO THIS! YOU DON'T SHOW UP, OUT OF NOWHERE, WITH YOUR ROBOT BUTLER--
GREETINGS. WHIRR-KLIKK.
WAIT. HE'S WEBBED UP WITH--IS THAT SPIDER-MAN'S EQUIPMENT?!
YES. YOU'RE VERY OBSERVANT. IT IS.
GOBLINS ARE ATTACKING ALL OVER THE CITY, AND YOU BRING SPIDER-MAN TECH HERE?!
SPIDER-MAN ASKED ME TO--
TO OUR PLACE OF BUSINESS?!
TONE, MS. JAFFREY. I WILL NOT BE SPOKEN TO IN THAT WAY.
WE'RE ALSO BEING STAKED OUT BY THE COPS. BECAUSE OF YOU.
ME? WHAT FOR?
THE DISAPPEARANCE OF YOUR EX-GIRLFIREND! OFFICER CARLIE COOPER!
CARLIE? THAT'S NOT GOOD AT ALL. SHE... KNOWS THINGS.
YEAH. THAT DOESN'T SOUND AT ALL SUSPICIOUS.
AGREED! THAT'S WHY YOU AND I NEED TO TALK, MR. PARKER!
UGH. NOT NOW.
WHO THE HELL'S THIS?!

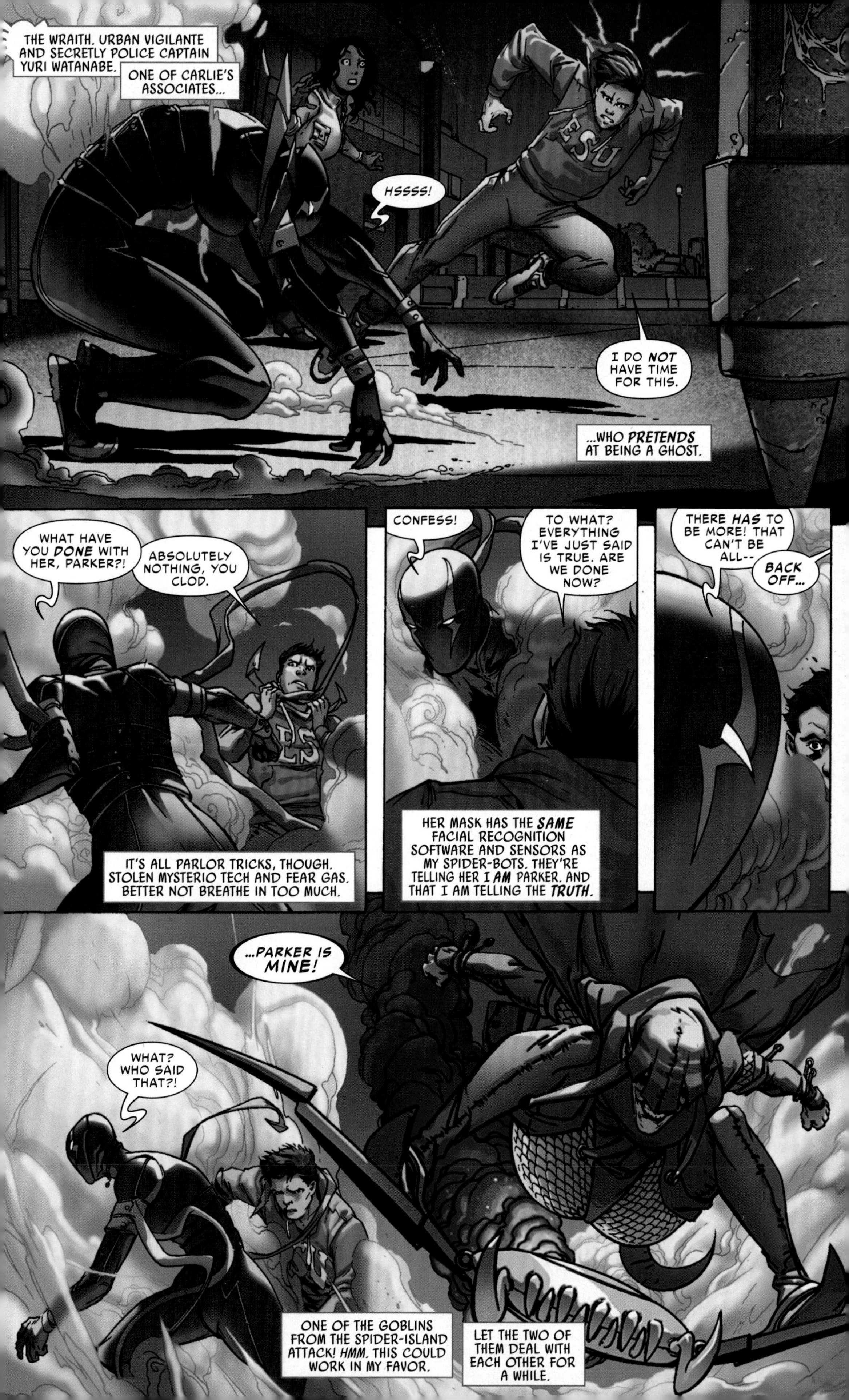
THE WRAITH. URBAN VIGILANTE AND SECRETLY POLICE CAPTAIN YURI WATANABE.
ONE OF CARLIE'S ASSOCIATES...
HSSSS!
I DO NOT HAVE TIME FOR THIS.
...WHO PRETENDS AT BEING A GHOST.
WHAT HAVE YOU DONE WITH HER, PARKER?!
ABSOLUTELY NOTHING, YOU CLOD.
IT'S ALL PARLOR TRICKS, THOUGH. STOLEN MYSTERIO TECH AND FEAR GAS. BETTER NOT BREATHE IN TOO MUCH.
CONFESS!
TO WHAT? EVERYTHING I'VE JUST SAID IS TRUE. ARE WE DONE NOW?
HER MASK HAS THE SAME FACIAL RECOGNITION SOFTWARE AND SENSORS AS MY SPIDER-BOTS. THEY'RE TELLING HER I AM PARKER. AND THAT I AM TELLING THE TRUTH.
THERE HAS TO BE MORE! THAT CAN'T BE ALL--
BACK OFF...
...PARKER IS MINE!
WHAT? WHO SAID THAT?!
ONE OF THE GOBLINS FROM THE SPIDER-ISLAND ATTACK! HMM. THIS COULD WORK IN MY FAVOR.
LET THE TWO OF THEM DEAL WITH EACH OTHER FOR A WHILE.

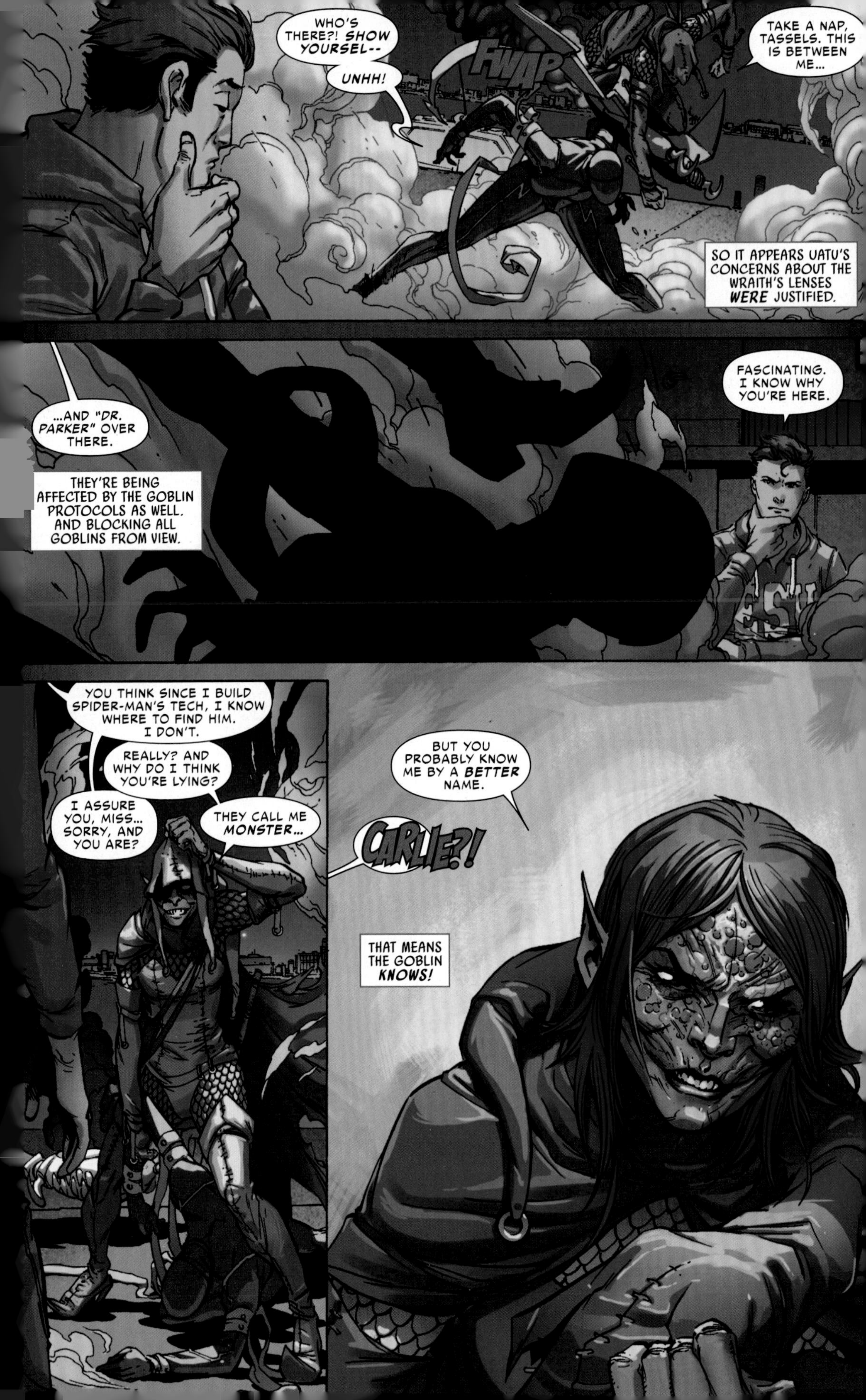
WHO'S THERE?! SHOW YOURSEL--
UNHH!
FWAP
TAKE A NAP, TASSELS. THIS IS BETWEEN ME...
SO IT APPEARS UATU'S CONCERNS ABOUT THE WRAITH'S LENSES WERE JUSTIFIED.
...AND "DR. PARKER" OVER THERE.
THEY'RE BEING AFFECTED BY THE GOBLIN PROTOCOLS AS WELL. AND BLOCKING ALL GOBLINS FROM VIEW.
FASCINATING. I KNOW WHY YOU'RE HERE.
YOU THINK SINCE I BUILD SPIDER-MAN'S TECH, I KNOW WHERE TO FIND HIM. I DON'T.
REALLY? AND WHY DO I THINK YOU'RE LYING?
I ASSURE YOU, MISS... SORRY, AND YOU ARE?
THEY CALL ME MONSTER...
BUT YOU PROBABLY KNOW ME BY A BETTER NAME.
CARLIE?!
THAT MEANS THE GOBLIN KNOWS!

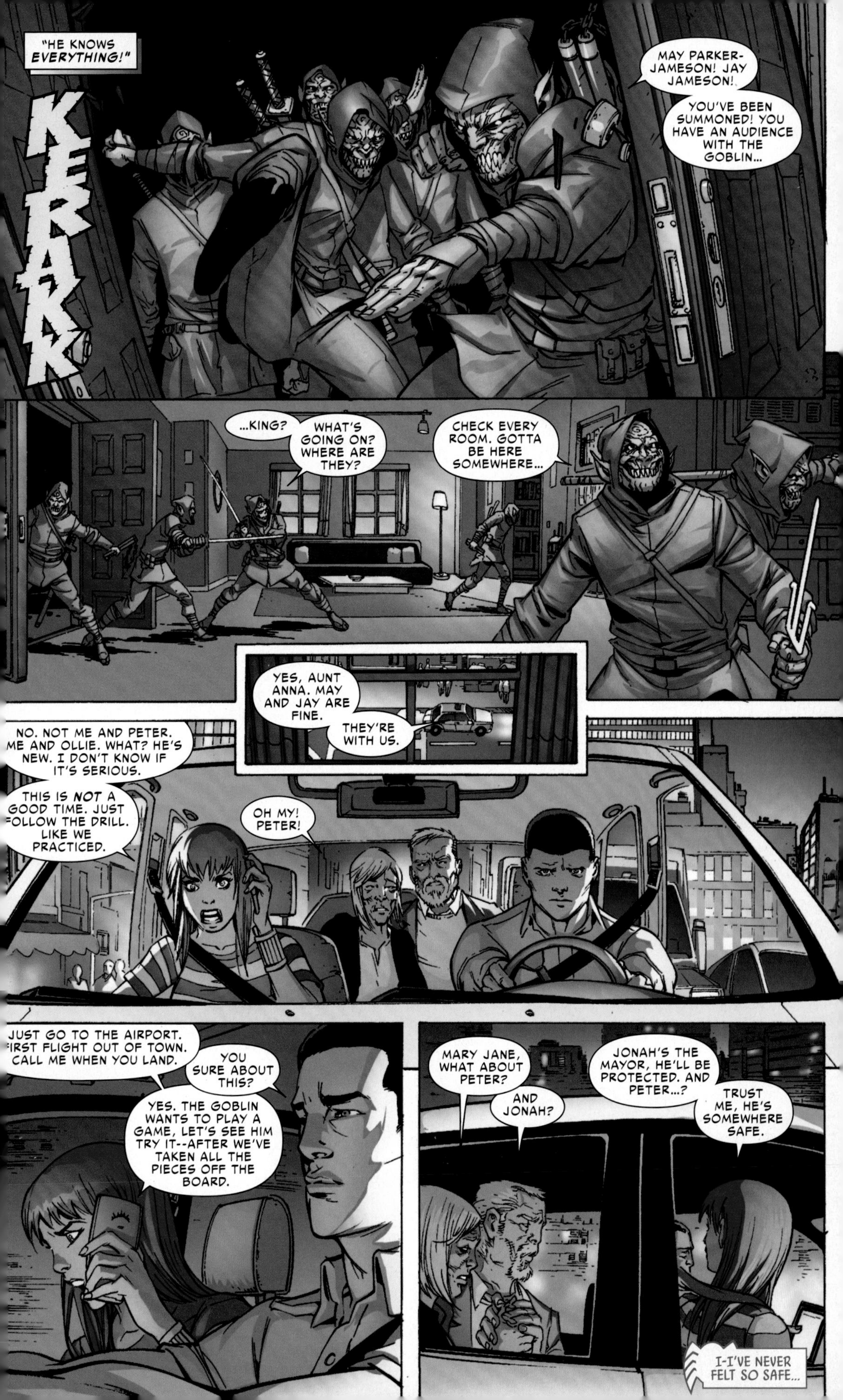
"HE KNOWS EVERYTHING!"
KERAK
MAY PARKER-JAMESON! JAY JAMESON!
YOU'VE BEEN SUMMONED! YOU HAVE AN AUDIENCE WITH THE GOBLIN...
...KING?
WHAT'S GOING ON? WHERE ARE THEY?
CHECK EVERY ROOM. GOTTA BE HERE SOMEWHERE...
YES, AUNT ANNA. MAY AND JAY ARE FINE.
THEY'RE WITH US.
NO. NOT ME AND PETER. ME AND OLLIE. WHAT? HE'S NEW. I DON'T KNOW IF IT'S SERIOUS.
THIS IS NOT A GOOD TIME. JUST FOLLOW THE DRILL. LIKE WE PRACTICED.
OH MY! PETER!
JUST GO TO THE AIRPORT. FIRST FLIGHT OUT OF TOWN. CALL ME WHEN YOU LAND.
YOU SURE ABOUT THIS?
YES. THE GOBLIN WANTS TO PLAY A GAME, LET'S SEE HIM TRY IT--AFTER WE'VE TAKEN ALL THE PIECES OFF THE BOARD.
MARY JANE, WHAT ABOUT PETER?
AND JONAH?
JONAH'S THE MAYOR, HE'LL BE PROTECTED. AND PETER...?
TRUST ME, HE'S SOMEWHERE SAFE.
I-I'VE NEVER FELT SO SAFE...

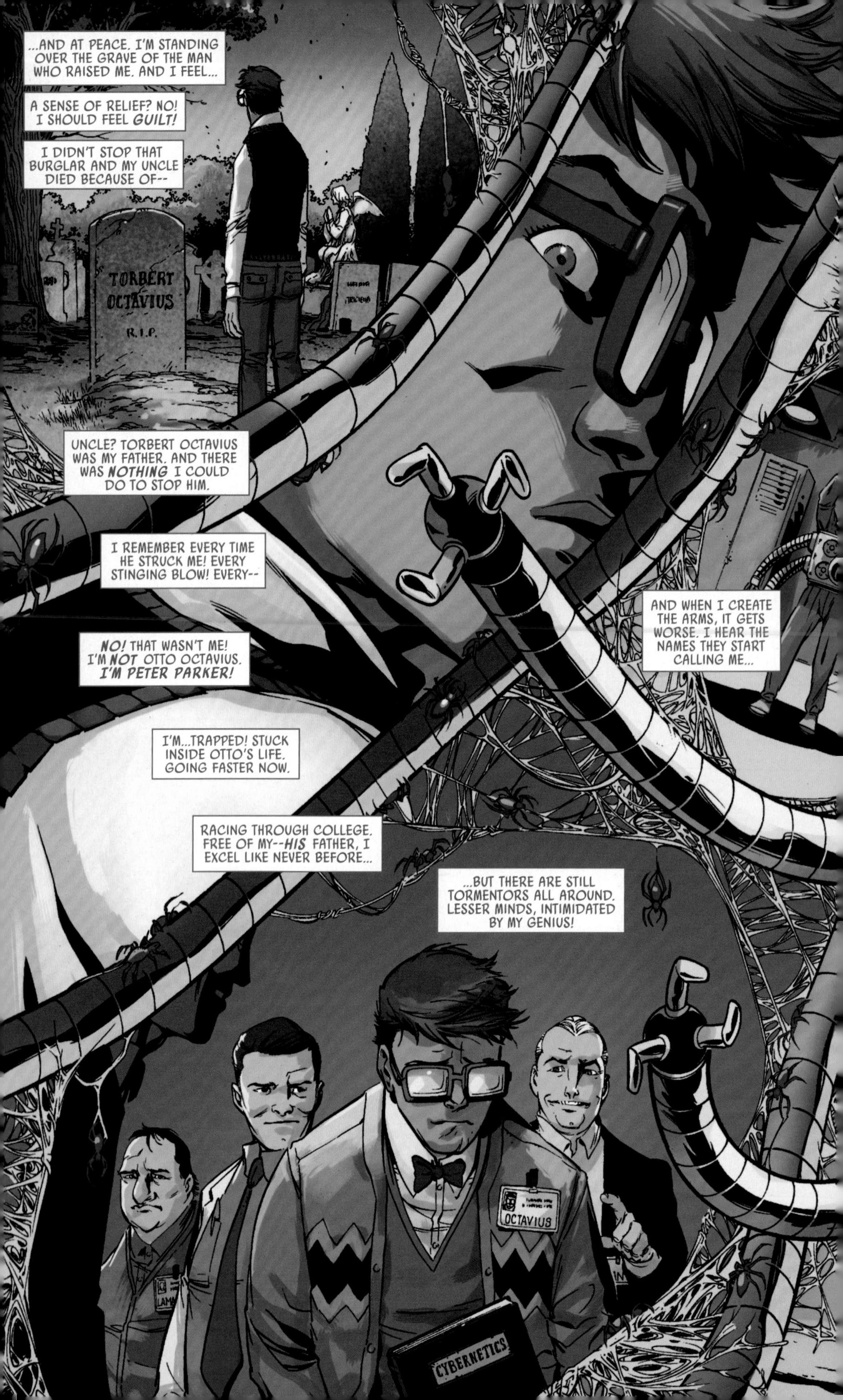
...AND AT PEACE. I'M STANDING OVER THE GRAVE OF THE MAN WHO RAISED ME. AND I FEEL...
A SENSE OF RELIEF? NO! I SHOULD FEEL GUILT!
I DIDN'T STOP THAT BURGLAR AND MY UNCLE DIED BECAUSE OF--
TORBERT OCTAVIUS R.I.P.
UNCLE? TORBERT OCTAVIUS WAS MY FATHER. AND THERE WAS NOTHING I COULD DO TO STOP HIM.
I REMEMBER EVERY TIME HE STRUCK ME! EVERY STINGING BLOW! EVERY--
NO! THAT WASN'T ME! I'M NOT OTTO OCTAVIUS. I'M PETER PARKER!
AND WHEN I CREATE THE ARMS, IT GETS WORSE. I HEAR THE NAMES THEY START CALLING ME...
I'M...TRAPPED! STUCK INSIDE OTTO'S LIFE. GOING FASTER NOW.
RACING THROUGH COLLEGE. FREE OF MY--HIS FATHER, I EXCEL LIKE NEVER BEFORE...
...BUT THERE ARE STILL TORMENTORS ALL AROUND. LESSER MINDS, INTIMIDATED BY MY GENIUS!
OCTAVIUS
CYBERNETICS

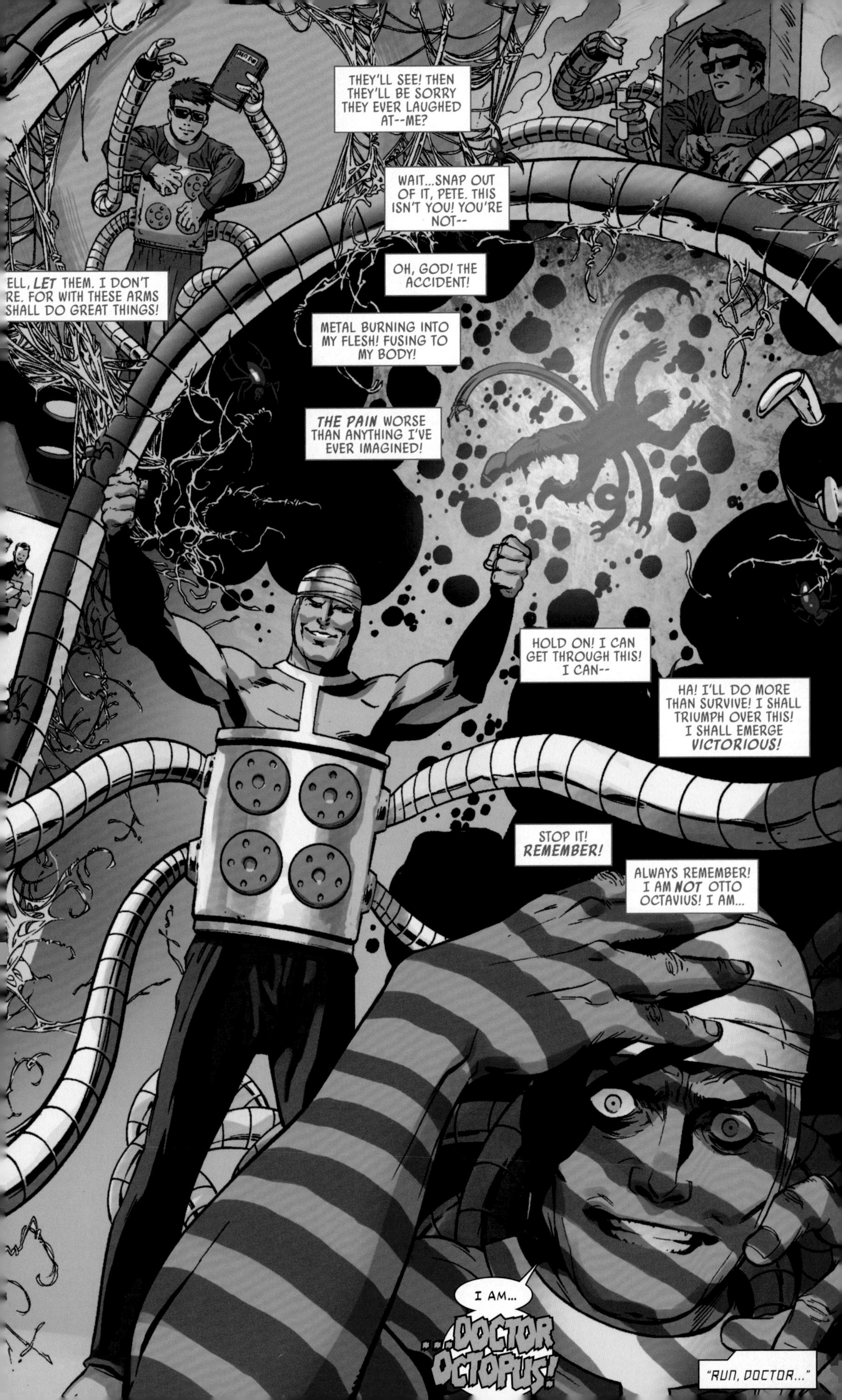
THEY'LL SEE! THEN THEY'LL BE SORRY THEY EVER LAUGHED AT--ME?
WAIT...SNAP OUT OF IT, PETE. THIS ISN'T YOU! YOU'RE NOT--
ELL, LET THEM. I DON'T RE. FOR WITH THESE ARMS SHALL DO GREAT THINGS!
OH, GOD! THE ACCIDENT!
METAL BURNING INTO MY FLESH! FUSING TO MY BODY!
THE PAIN WORSE THAN ANYTHING I'VE EVER IMAGINED!
HOLD ON! I CAN GET THROUGH THIS! I CAN--
HA! I'LL DO MORE THAN SURVIVE! I SHALL TRIUMPH OVER THIS! I SHALL EMERGE VICTORIOUS!
STOP IT! REMEMBER!
ALWAYS REMEMBER! I AM NOT OTTO OCTAVIUS! I AM...
I AM...
...DOCTOR OCTOPUS!
"RUN, DOCTOR..."

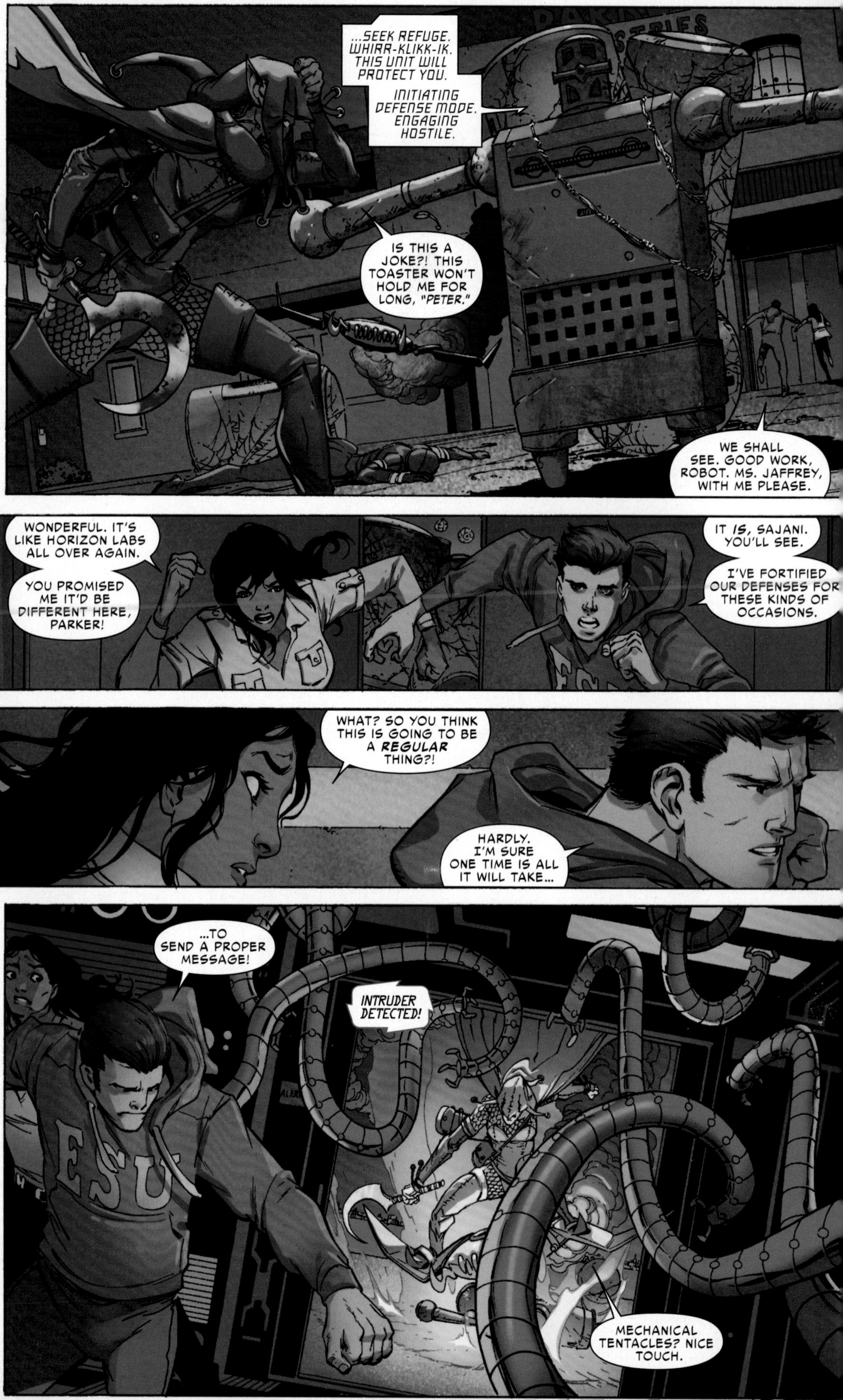
...SEEK REFUGE. WHIRR-KLIKK-IK. THIS UNIT WILL PROTECT YOU.
INITIATING DEFENSE MODE. ENGAGING HOSTILE.
IS THIS A JOKE?! THIS TOASTER WON'T HOLD ME FOR LONG, "PETER."
WE SHALL SEE. GOOD WORK, ROBOT. MS. JAFFREY, WITH ME PLEASE.
WONDERFUL. IT'S LIKE HORIZON LABS ALL OVER AGAIN.
YOU PROMISED ME IT'D BE DIFFERENT HERE, PARKER!
IT IS, SAJANI. YOU'LL SEE.
I'VE FORTIFIED OUR DEFENSES FOR THESE KINDS OF OCCASIONS.
WHAT? SO YOU THINK THIS IS GOING TO BE A REGULAR THING?!
HARDLY. I'M SURE ONE TIME IS ALL IT WILL TAKE...
...TO SEND A PROPER MESSAGE!
INTRUDER DETECTED!
MECHANICAL TENTACLES? NICE TOUCH.

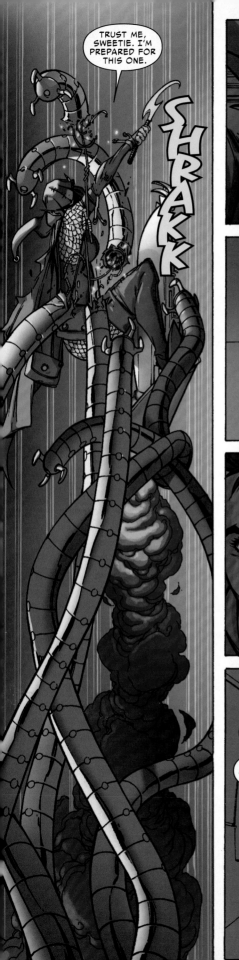

TRUST ME, SWEETIE. I'M PREPARED FOR THIS ONE.

SHRAKK

THIS IS ME, REMEMBER? AND I KNOW ALL YOUR SECRETS. HA HA HA!

AND APPARENTLY YOU WANT TO BE A LITTLE CHATTY ABOUT THEM. SAJANI! IN THERE! NOW!

PARKER?! WHAT ARE YOU--?

THAT WOMAN'S MY EX. SOMETHING TELLS ME, IF WE SPLIT UP...

...I'M THE ONE SHE'LL FOLLOW.

TOO TRUE, "PETEY." YOU KNOW ME, ALL I EVER WANTED FROM YOU...

...WAS MORE ALONE TIME!

THIS IS A DISASTER!

TESTROOM

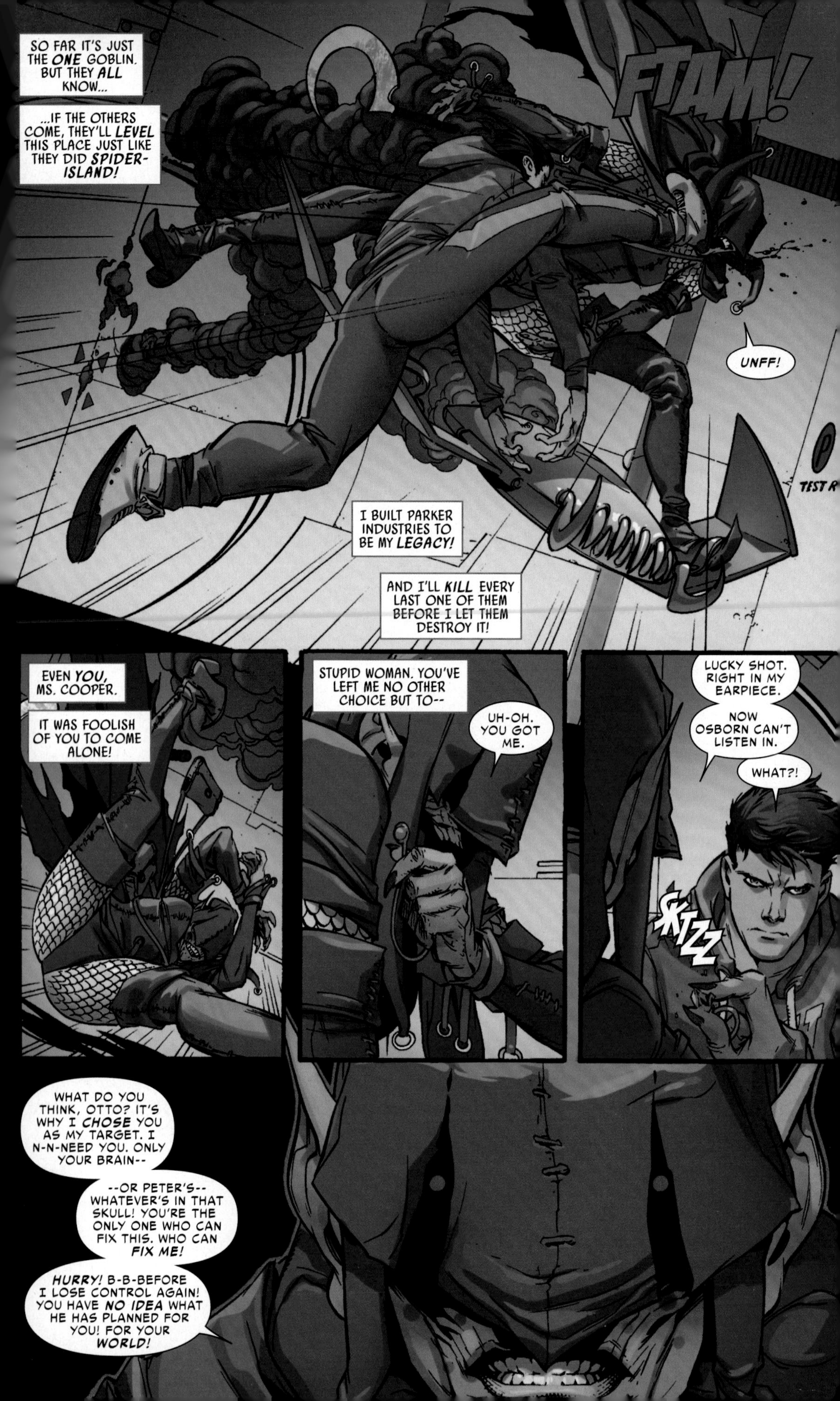

SO FAR IT'S JUST THE ONE GOBLIN. BUT THEY ALL KNOW...
...IF THE OTHERS COME, THEY'LL LEVEL THIS PLACE JUST LIKE THEY DID SPIDER-ISLAND!
FTAM!
UNFF!
I BUILT PARKER INDUSTRIES TO BE MY LEGACY!
AND I'LL KILL EVERY LAST ONE OF THEM BEFORE I LET THEM DESTROY IT!
EVEN YOU, MS. COOPER.
IT WAS FOOLISH OF YOU TO COME ALONE!
STUPID WOMAN. YOU'VE LEFT ME NO OTHER CHOICE BUT TO--
UH-OH. YOU GOT ME.
LUCKY SHOT. RIGHT IN MY EARPIECE.
NOW OSBORN CAN'T LISTEN IN.
WHAT?!
SKTZZ
WHAT DO YOU THINK, OTTO? IT'S WHY I CHOSE YOU AS MY TARGET. I N-N-NEED YOU. ONLY YOUR BRAIN--
--OR PETER'S--WHATEVER'S IN THAT SKULL! YOU'RE THE ONLY ONE WHO CAN FIX THIS. WHO CAN FIX ME!
HURRY! B-B-BEFORE I LOSE CONTROL AGAIN! YOU HAVE NO IDEA WHAT HE HAS PLANNED FOR YOU! FOR YOUR WORLD!

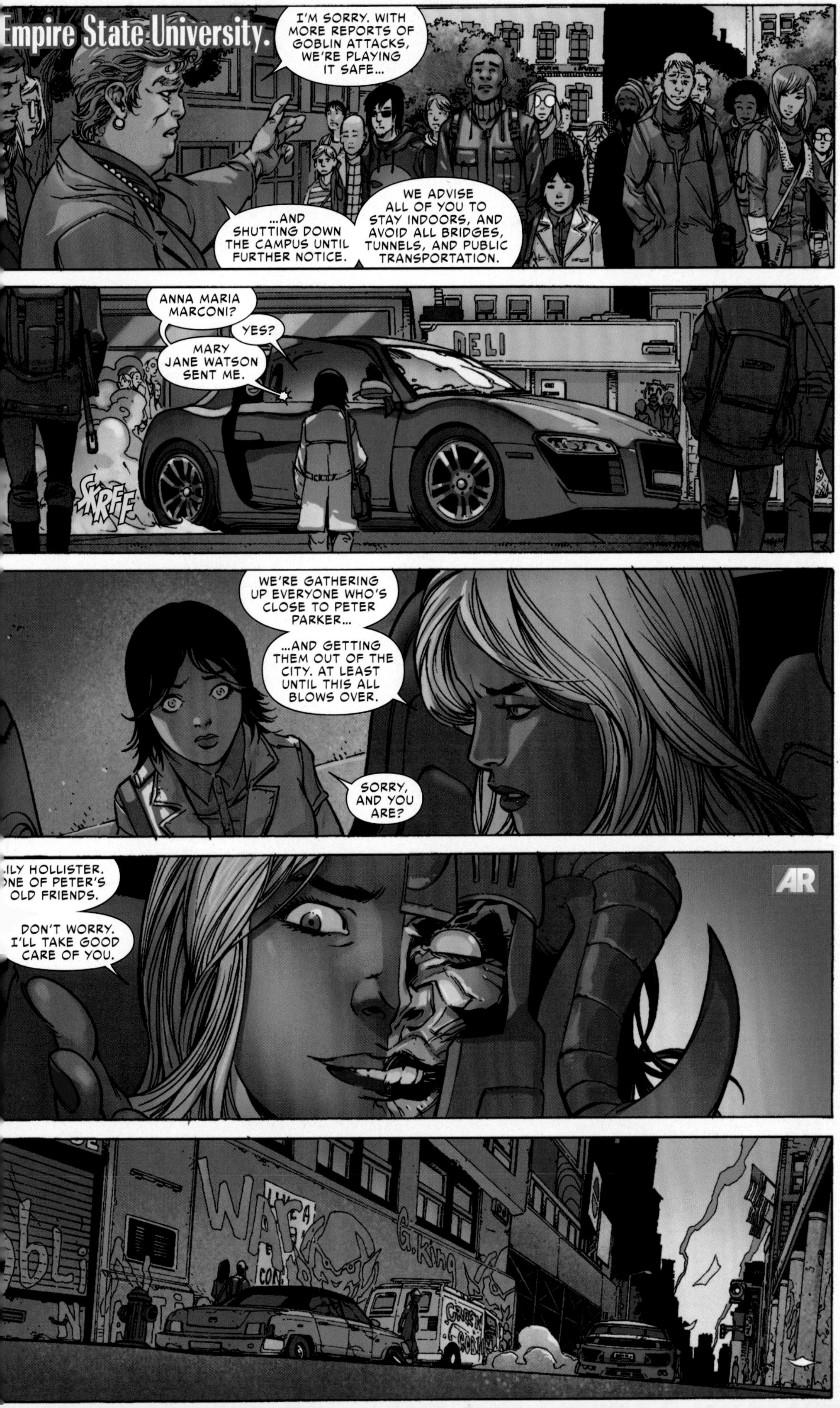
Empire State University.
I'M SORRY. WITH MORE REPORTS OF GOBLIN ATTACKS, WE'RE PLAYING IT SAFE...
...AND SHUTTING DOWN THE CAMPUS UNTIL FURTHER NOTICE.
WE ADVISE ALL OF YOU TO STAY INDOORS, AND AVOID ALL BRIDGES, TUNNELS, AND PUBLIC TRANSPORTATION.
ANNA MARIA MARCONI?
YES?
MARY JANE WATSON SENT ME.
DELI
SKRFF
WE'RE GATHERING UP EVERYONE WHO'S CLOSE TO PETER PARKER...
...AND GETTING THEM OUT OF THE CITY. AT LEAST UNTIL THIS ALL BLOWS OVER.
SORRY, AND YOU ARE?
ILY HOLLISTER. NE OF PETER'S OLD FRIENDS.
DON'T WORRY. I'LL TAKE GOOD CARE OF YOU.
G. King

29

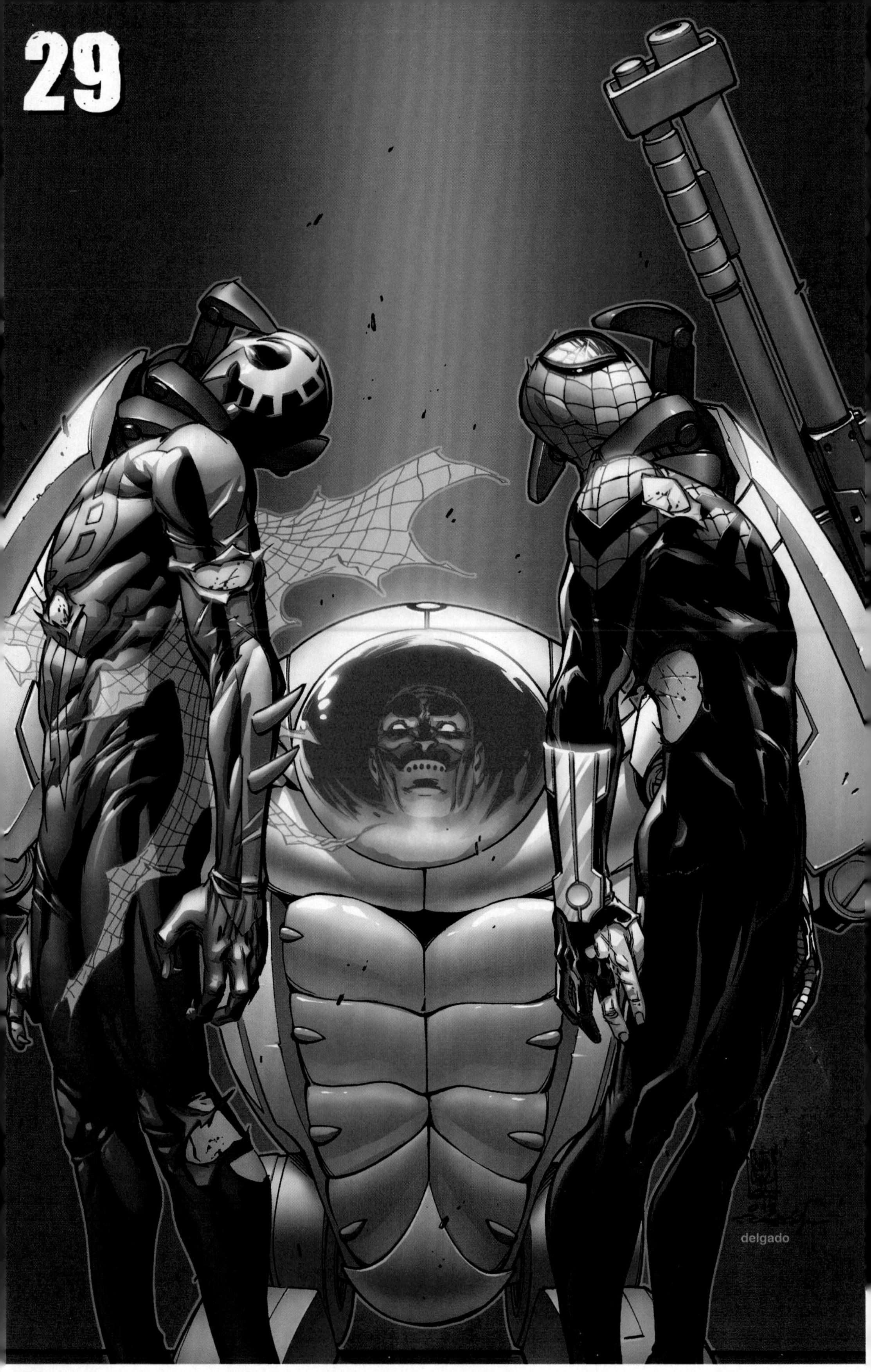
delgado

LEGS OUT FROM UNDER YOU

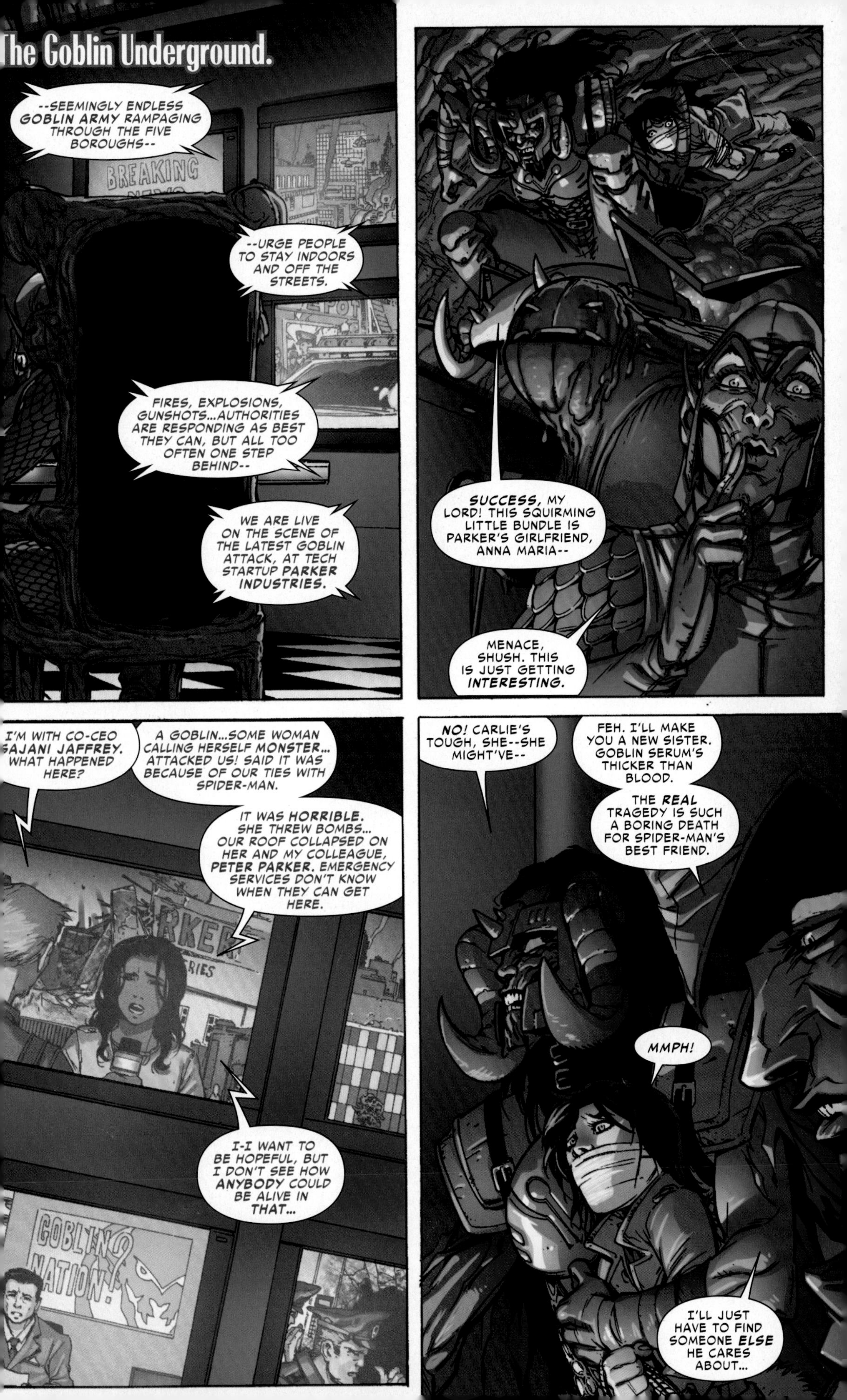
The Goblin Underground.
--SEEMINGLY ENDLESS GOBLIN ARMY RAMPAGING THROUGH THE FIVE BOROUGHS--
BREAKING
--URGE PEOPLE TO STAY INDOORS AND OFF THE STREETS.
FIRES, EXPLOSIONS, GUNSHOTS...AUTHORITIES ARE RESPONDING AS BEST THEY CAN, BUT ALL TOO OFTEN ONE STEP BEHIND--
WE ARE LIVE ON THE SCENE OF THE LATEST GOBLIN ATTACK, AT TECH STARTUP PARKER INDUSTRIES.
SUCCESS, MY LORD! THIS SQUIRMING LITTLE BUNDLE IS PARKER'S GIRLFRIEND, ANNA MARIA--
MENACE, SHUSH. THIS IS JUST GETTING INTERESTING.
I'M WITH CO-CEO SAJANI JAFFREY. WHAT HAPPENED HERE?
A GOBLIN...SOME WOMAN CALLING HERSELF MONSTER... ATTACKED US! SAID IT WAS BECAUSE OF OUR TIES WITH SPIDER-MAN.
IT WAS HORRIBLE. SHE THREW BOMBS... OUR ROOF COLLAPSED ON HER AND MY COLLEAGUE, PETER PARKER. EMERGENCY SERVICES DON'T KNOW WHEN THEY CAN GET HERE.
I-I WANT TO BE HOPEFUL, BUT I DON'T SEE HOW ANYBODY COULD BE ALIVE IN THAT...
GOBLIN NATION!
NO! CARLIE'S TOUGH, SHE--SHE MIGHT'VE--
FEH. I'LL MAKE YOU A NEW SISTER. GOBLIN SERUM'S THICKER THAN BLOOD.
THE REAL TRAGEDY IS SUCH A BORING DEATH FOR SPIDER-MAN'S BEST FRIEND.
MMPH!
I'LL JUST HAVE TO FIND SOMEONE ELSE HE CARES ABOUT...

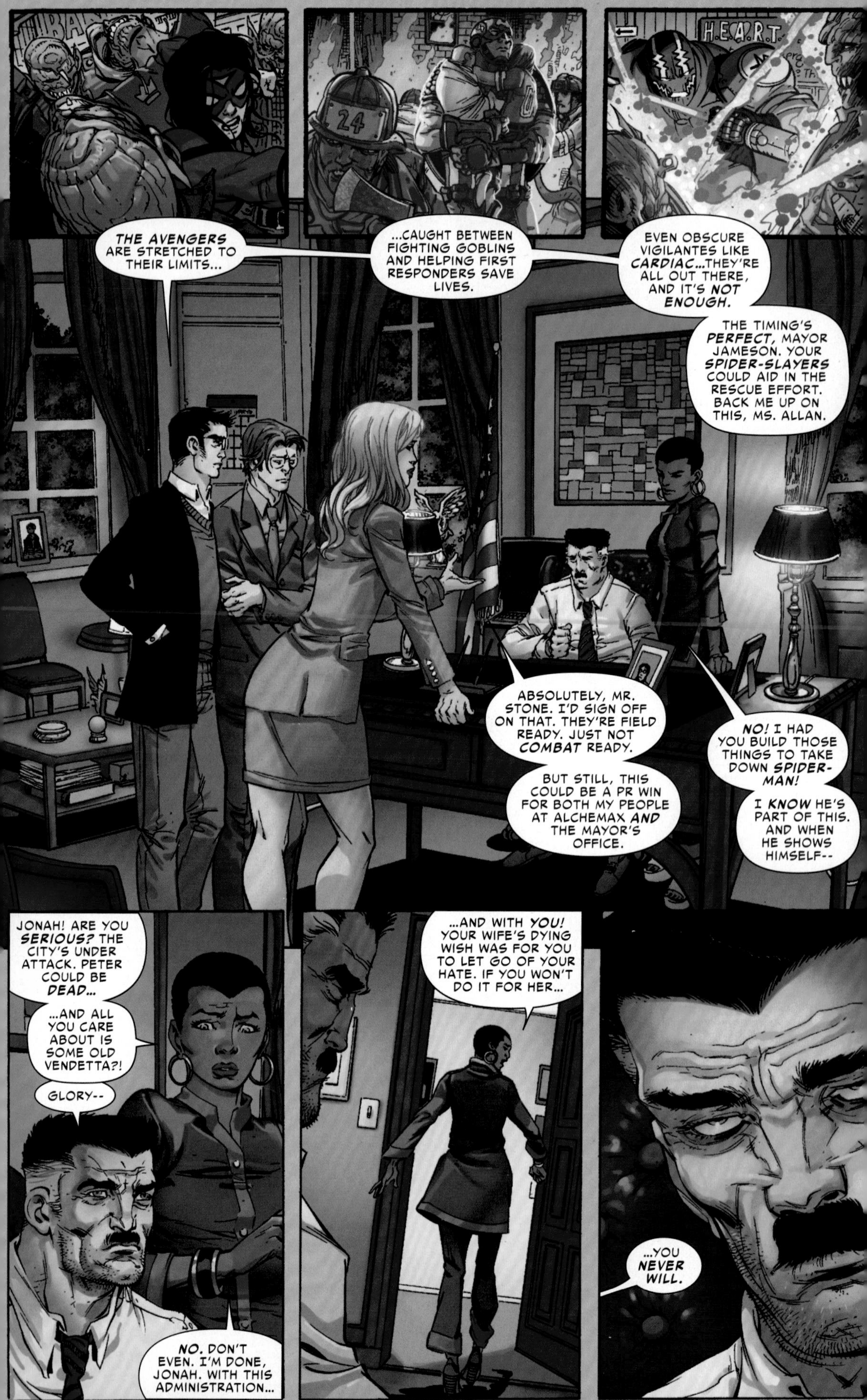
THE AVENGERS ARE STRETCHED TO THEIR LIMITS...
...CAUGHT BETWEEN FIGHTING GOBLINS AND HELPING FIRST RESPONDERS SAVE LIVES.
EVEN OBSCURE VIGILANTES LIKE CARDIAC...THEY'RE ALL OUT THERE, AND IT'S NOT ENOUGH.
THE TIMING'S PERFECT, MAYOR JAMESON. YOUR SPIDER-SLAYERS COULD AID IN THE RESCUE EFFORT. BACK ME UP ON THIS, MS. ALLAN.
ABSOLUTELY, MR. STONE. I'D SIGN OFF ON THAT. THEY'RE FIELD READY. JUST NOT COMBAT READY.
BUT STILL, THIS COULD BE A PR WIN FOR BOTH MY PEOPLE AT ALCHEMAX AND THE MAYOR'S OFFICE.
NO! I HAD YOU BUILD THOSE THINGS TO TAKE DOWN SPIDER-MAN!
I KNOW HE'S PART OF THIS. AND WHEN HE SHOWS HIMSELF--
JONAH! ARE YOU SERIOUS? THE CITY'S UNDER ATTACK. PETER COULD BE DEAD...
...AND ALL YOU CARE ABOUT IS SOME OLD VENDETTA?!
GLORY--
NO. DON'T EVEN. I'M DONE, JONAH. WITH THIS ADMINISTRATION...
...AND WITH YOU! YOUR WIFE'S DYING WISH WAS FOR YOU TO LET GO OF YOUR HATE. IF YOU WON'T DO IT FOR HER...
...YOU NEVER WILL.

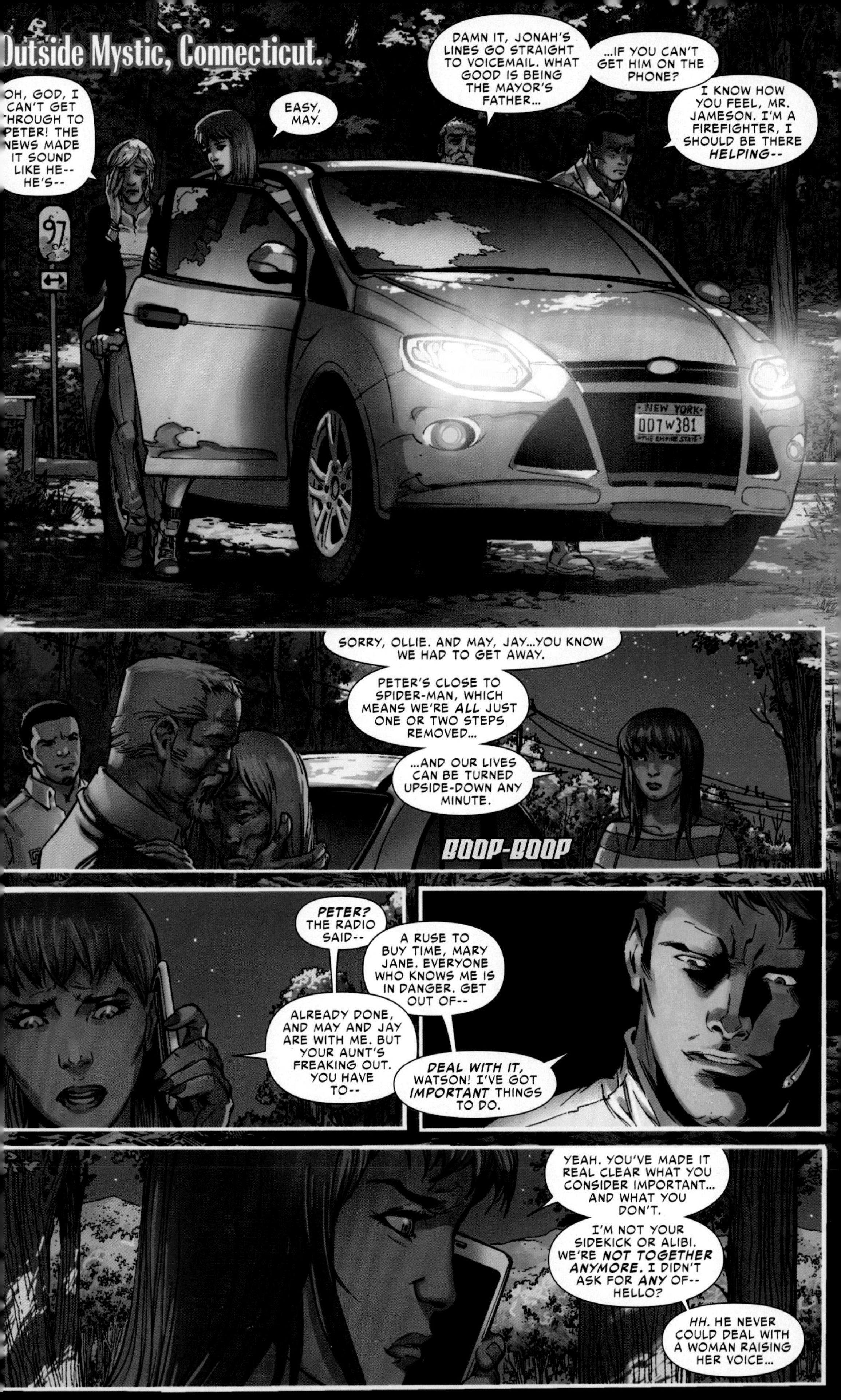
Outside Mystic, Connecticut.
OH, GOD, I CAN'T GET THROUGH TO PETER! THE NEWS MADE IT SOUND LIKE HE-- HE'S--
EASY, MAY.
DAMN IT, JONAH'S LINES GO STRAIGHT TO VOICEMAIL. WHAT GOOD IS BEING THE MAYOR'S FATHER...
...IF YOU CAN'T GET HIM ON THE PHONE?
I KNOW HOW YOU FEEL, MR. JAMESON. I'M A FIREFIGHTER, I SHOULD BE THERE HELPING--
97
NEW YORK
007 W381
THE EMPIRE STATE
SORRY, OLLIE. AND MAY, JAY...YOU KNOW WE HAD TO GET AWAY.
PETER'S CLOSE TO SPIDER-MAN, WHICH MEANS WE'RE ALL JUST ONE OR TWO STEPS REMOVED...
...AND OUR LIVES CAN BE TURNED UPSIDE-DOWN ANY MINUTE.
BOOP-BOOP
PETER? THE RADIO SAID--
A RUSE TO BUY TIME, MARY JANE. EVERYONE WHO KNOWS ME IS IN DANGER. GET OUT OF--
ALREADY DONE, AND MAY AND JAY ARE WITH ME. BUT YOUR AUNT'S FREAKING OUT. YOU HAVE TO--
DEAL WITH IT, WATSON! I'VE GOT IMPORTANT THINGS TO DO.
YEAH. YOU'VE MADE IT REAL CLEAR WHAT YOU CONSIDER IMPORTANT... AND WHAT YOU DON'T.
I'M NOT YOUR SIDEKICK OR ALIBI. WE'RE NOT TOGETHER ANYMORE. I DIDN'T ASK FOR ANY OF-- HELLO?
HH. HE NEVER COULD DEAL WITH A WOMAN RAISING HER VOICE...

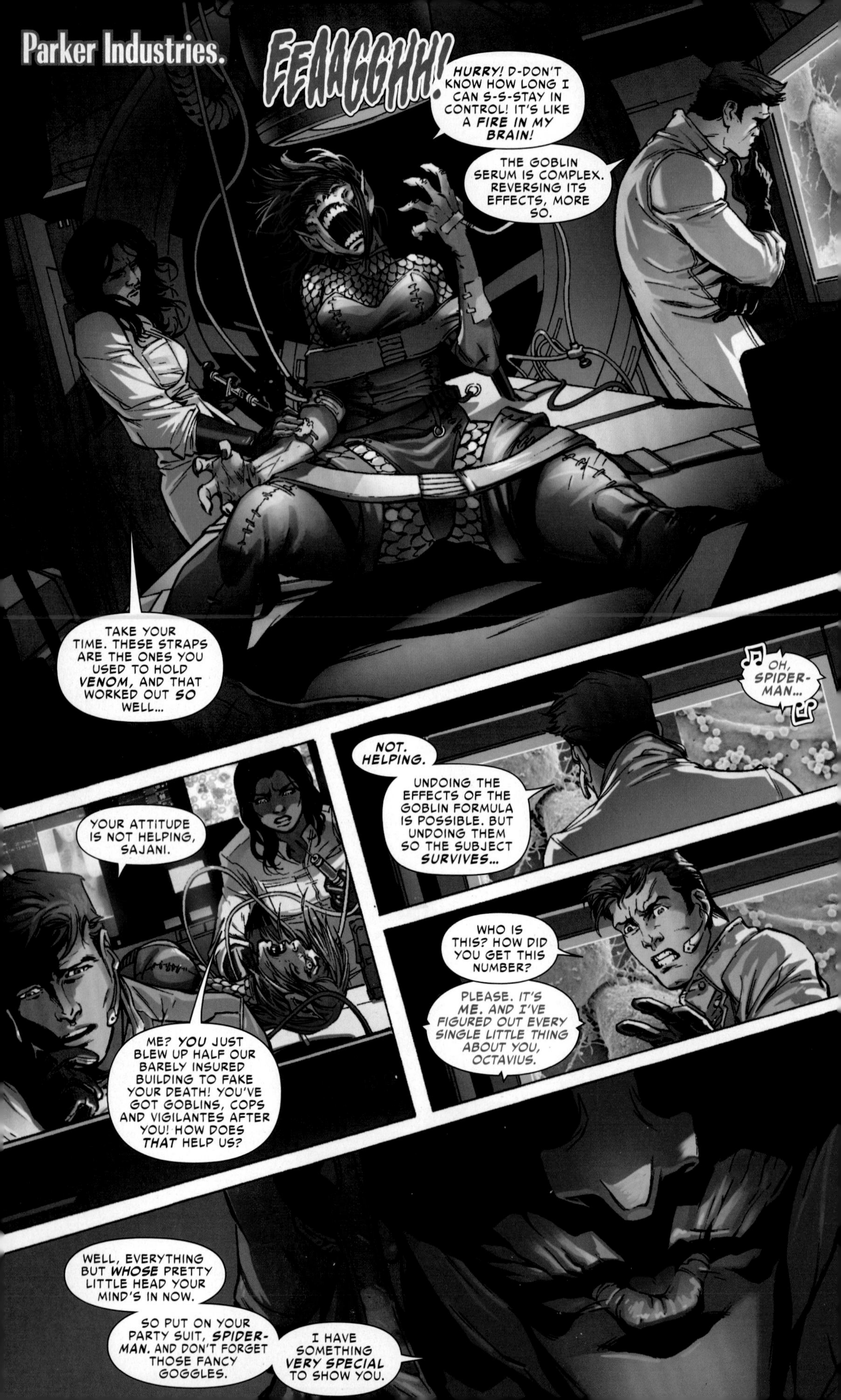
Parker Industries.
EEAAGGHH!
HURRY! D-DON'T KNOW HOW LONG I CAN S-S-STAY IN CONTROL! IT'S LIKE A FIRE IN MY BRAIN!
THE GOBLIN SERUM IS COMPLEX. REVERSING ITS EFFECTS, MORE SO.
TAKE YOUR TIME. THESE STRAPS ARE THE ONES YOU USED TO HOLD VENOM, AND THAT WORKED OUT SO WELL...
YOUR ATTITUDE IS NOT HELPING, SAJANI.
ME? YOU JUST BLEW UP HALF OUR BARELY INSURED BUILDING TO FAKE YOUR DEATH! YOU'VE GOT GOBLINS, COPS AND VIGILANTES AFTER YOU! HOW DOES THAT HELP US?
NOT. HELPING.
UNDOING THE EFFECTS OF THE GOBLIN FORMULA IS POSSIBLE. BUT UNDOING THEM SO THE SUBJECT SURVIVES...
OH, SPIDER-MAN...
WHO IS THIS? HOW DID YOU GET THIS NUMBER?
PLEASE. IT'S ME. AND I'VE FIGURED OUT EVERY SINGLE LITTLE THING ABOUT YOU, OCTAVIUS.
WELL, EVERYTHING BUT WHOSE PRETTY LITTLE HEAD YOUR MIND'S IN NOW.
SO PUT ON YOUR PARTY SUIT, SPIDER-MAN. AND DON'T FORGET THOSE FANCY GOGGLES.
I HAVE SOMETHING VERY SPECIAL TO SHOW YOU.

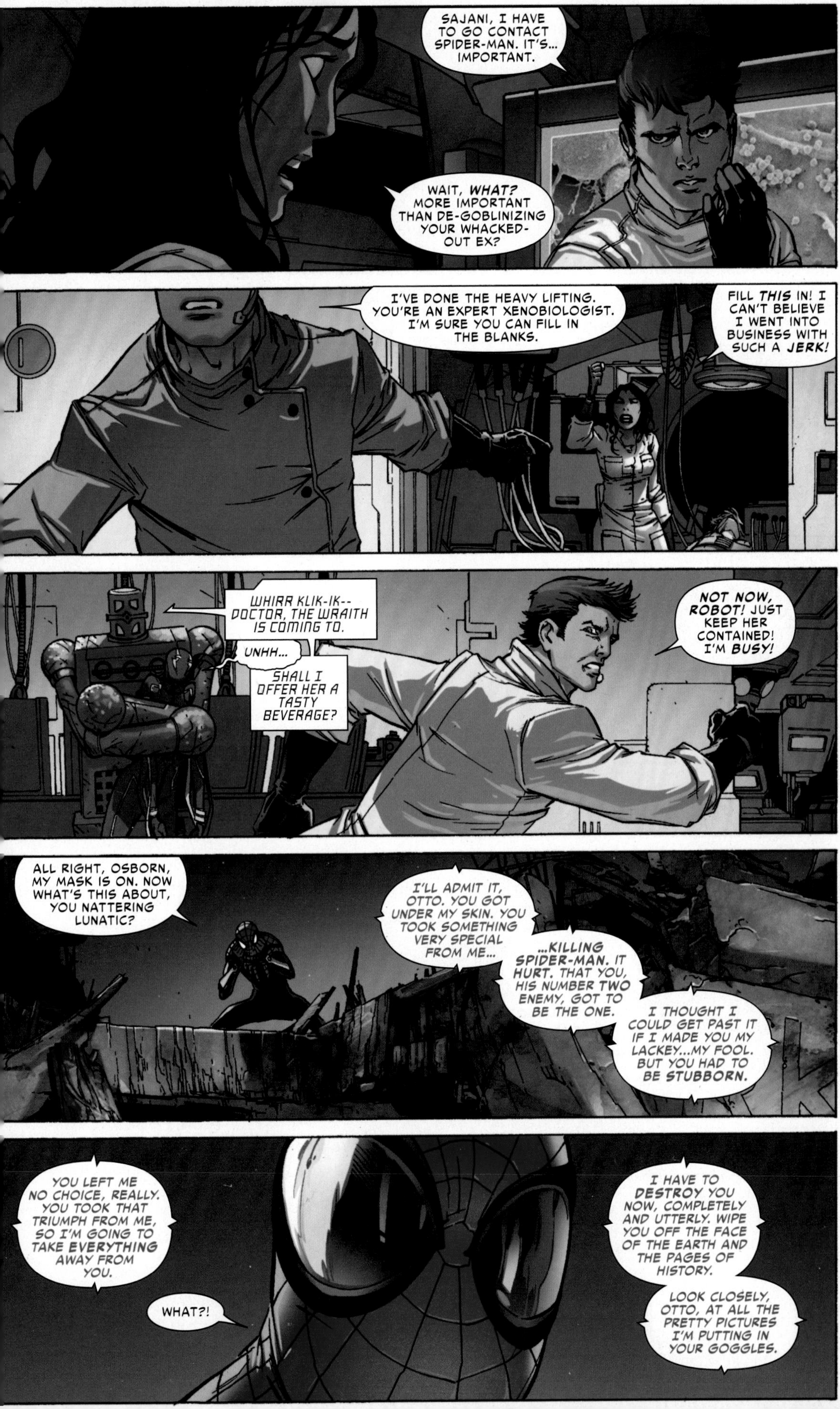
SAJANI, I HAVE TO GO CONTACT SPIDER-MAN. IT'S... IMPORTANT.
WAIT, WHAT? MORE IMPORTANT THAN DE-GOBLINIZING YOUR WHACKED-OUT EX?
I'VE DONE THE HEAVY LIFTING. YOU'RE AN EXPERT XENOBIOLOGIST. I'M SURE YOU CAN FILL IN THE BLANKS.
FILL THIS IN! I CAN'T BELIEVE I WENT INTO BUSINESS WITH SUCH A JERK!
WHIRR KLIK-IK-- DOCTOR, THE WRAITH IS COMING TO.
UNHH...
SHALL I OFFER HER A TASTY BEVERAGE?
NOT NOW, ROBOT! JUST KEEP HER CONTAINED! I'M BUSY!
ALL RIGHT, OSBORN, MY MASK IS ON. NOW WHAT'S THIS ABOUT, YOU NATTERING LUNATIC?
I'LL ADMIT IT, OTTO. YOU GOT UNDER MY SKIN. YOU TOOK SOMETHING VERY SPECIAL FROM ME...
...KILLING SPIDER-MAN. IT HURT. THAT YOU, HIS NUMBER TWO ENEMY, GOT TO BE THE ONE.
I THOUGHT I COULD GET PAST IT IF I MADE YOU MY LACKEY...MY FOOL. BUT YOU HAD TO BE STUBBORN.
YOU LEFT ME NO CHOICE, REALLY. YOU TOOK THAT TRIUMPH FROM ME, SO I'M GOING TO TAKE EVERYTHING AWAY FROM YOU.
WHAT?!
I HAVE TO DESTROY YOU NOW, COMPLETELY AND UTTERLY. WIPE YOU OFF THE FACE OF THE EARTH AND THE PAGES OF HISTORY.
LOOK CLOSELY, OTTO, AT ALL THE PRETTY PICTURES I'M PUTTING IN YOUR GOGGLES.

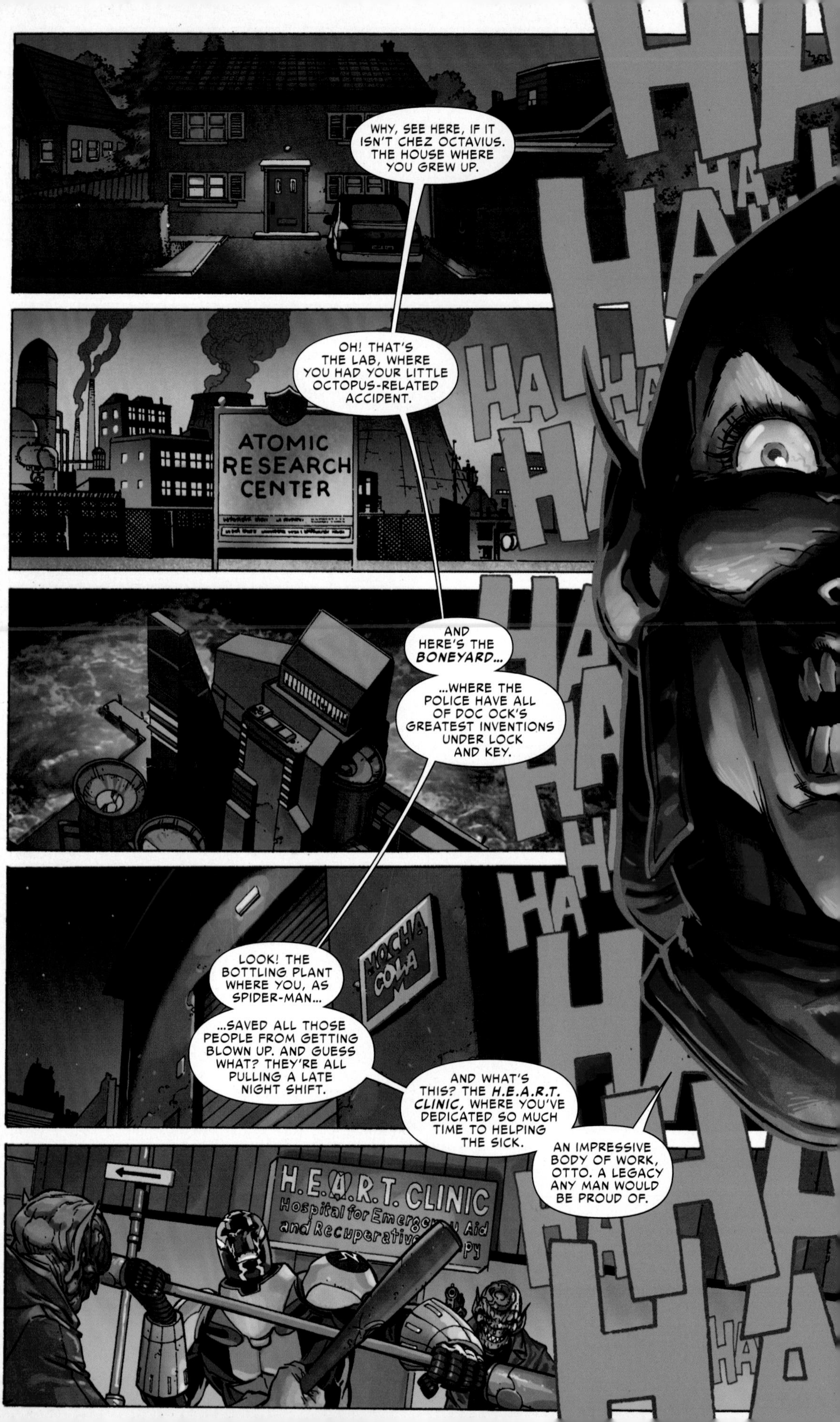

WHY, SEE HERE, IF IT ISN'T CHEZ OCTAVIUS. THE HOUSE WHERE YOU GREW UP.
OH! THAT'S THE LAB, WHERE YOU HAD YOUR LITTLE OCTOPUS-RELATED ACCIDENT.
ATOMIC RESEARCH CENTER
AND HERE'S THE *BONEYARD...*
...WHERE THE POLICE HAVE ALL OF DOC OCK'S GREATEST INVENTIONS UNDER LOCK AND KEY.
LOOK! THE BOTTLING PLANT WHERE YOU, AS SPIDER-MAN...
...SAVED ALL THOSE PEOPLE FROM GETTING BLOWN UP. AND GUESS WHAT? THEY'RE ALL PULLING A LATE NIGHT SHIFT.
MOCHA COLA
AND WHAT'S THIS? THE *H.E.A.R.T. CLINIC,* WHERE YOU'VE DEDICATED SO MUCH TIME TO HELPING THE SICK.
AN IMPRESSIVE BODY OF WORK, OTTO. A LEGACY ANY MAN WOULD BE PROUD OF.
H.E.A.R.T. CLINIC
HAHAHAHA

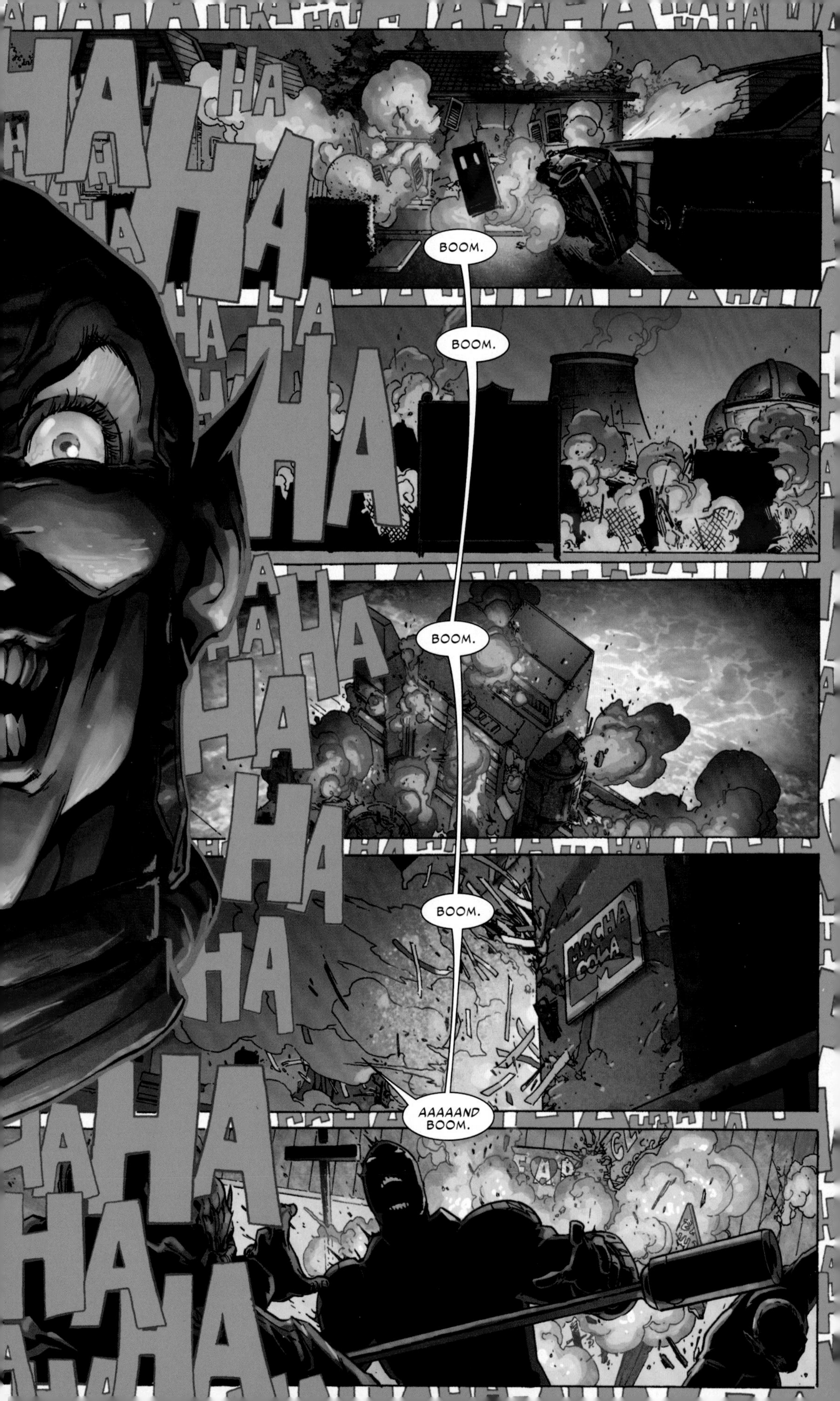
HA HA HA HA HA HA HA HA
BOOM.
BOOM.
BOOM.
BOOM.
AAAAAND BOOM.
MOCHA COLA

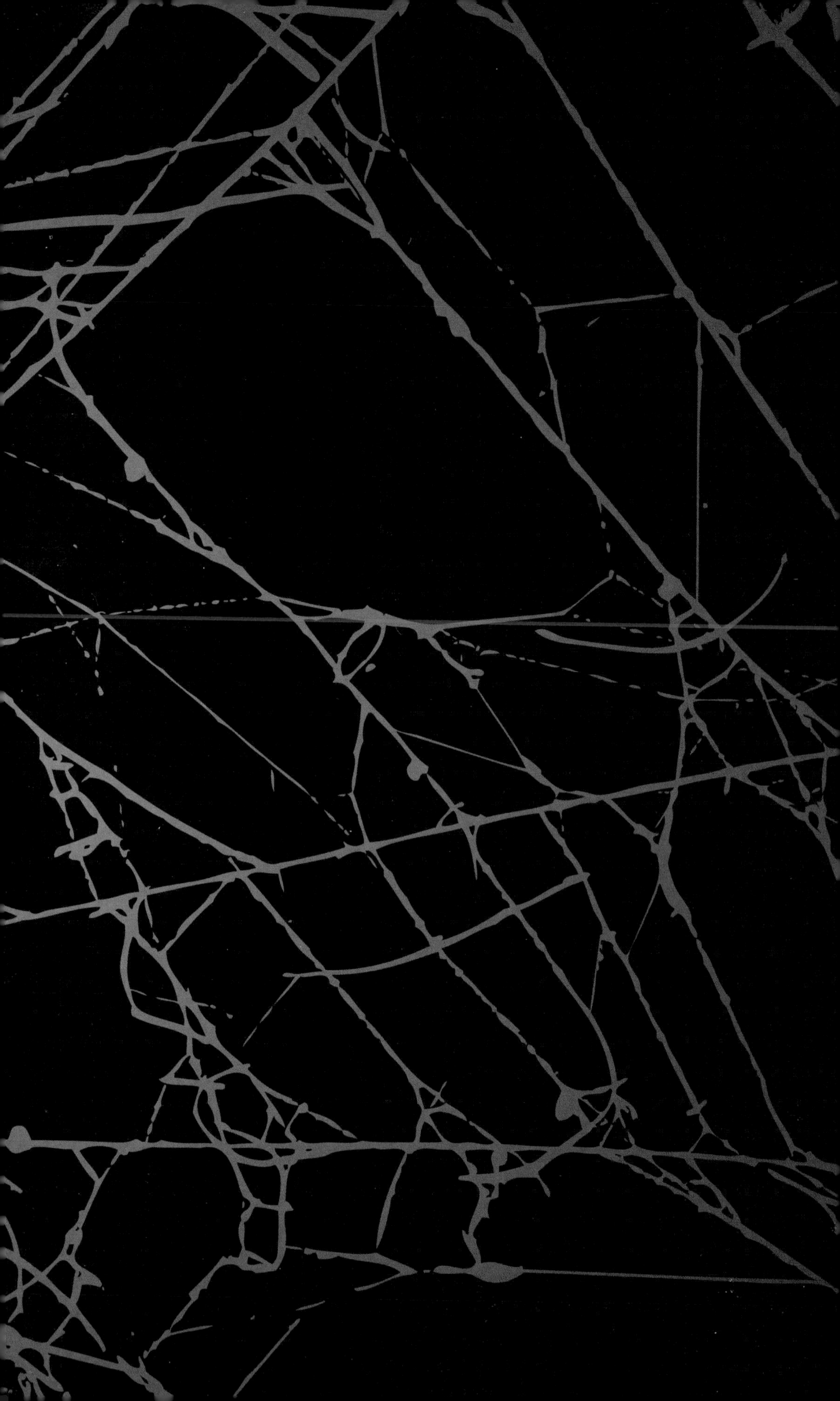

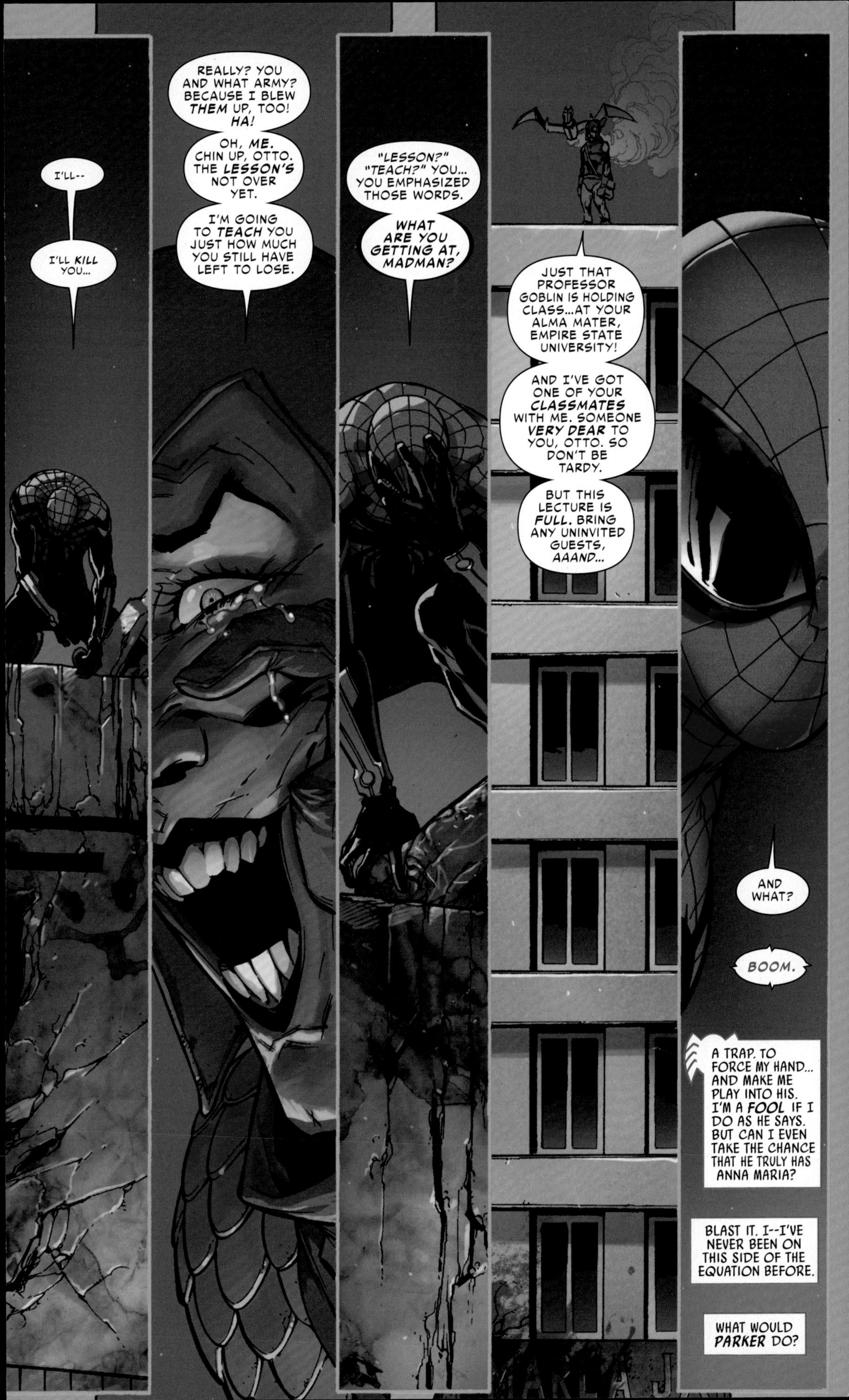
I'LL--
I'LL KILL YOU...
REALLY? YOU AND WHAT ARMY? BECAUSE I BLEW THEM UP, TOO! HA!
OH, ME. CHIN UP, OTTO. THE LESSON'S NOT OVER YET.
I'M GOING TO TEACH YOU JUST HOW MUCH YOU STILL HAVE LEFT TO LOSE.
"LESSON?" "TEACH?" YOU... YOU EMPHASIZED THOSE WORDS.
WHAT ARE YOU GETTING AT, MADMAN?
JUST THAT PROFESSOR GOBLIN IS HOLDING CLASS...AT YOUR ALMA MATER, EMPIRE STATE UNIVERSITY!
AND I'VE GOT ONE OF YOUR CLASSMATES WITH ME. SOMEONE VERY DEAR TO YOU, OTTO. SO DON'T BE TARDY.
BUT THIS LECTURE IS FULL. BRING ANY UNINVITED GUESTS, AAAND...
AND WHAT?
BOOM.
A TRAP. TO FORCE MY HAND... AND MAKE ME PLAY INTO HIS. I'M A FOOL IF I DO AS HE SAYS. BUT CAN I EVEN TAKE THE CHANCE THAT HE TRULY HAS ANNA MARIA?
BLAST IT. I--I'VE NEVER BEEN ON THIS SIDE OF THE EQUATION BEFORE.
WHAT WOULD PARKER DO?

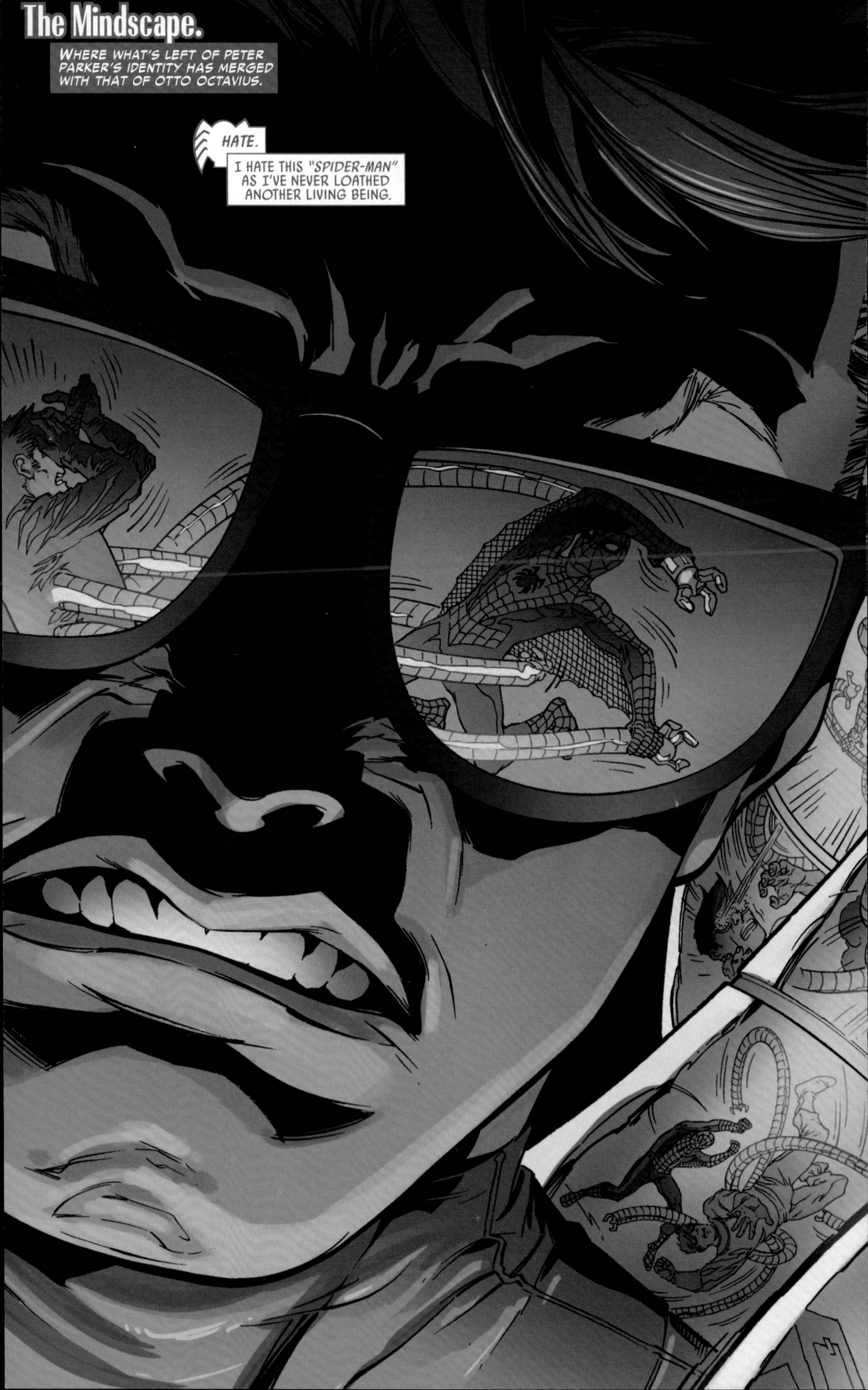
The Mindscape.
WHERE WHAT'S LEFT OF PETER PARKER'S IDENTITY HAS MERGED WITH THAT OF OTTO OCTAVIUS.
HATE.
I HATE THIS "SPIDER-MAN" AS I'VE NEVER LOATHED ANOTHER LIVING BEING.

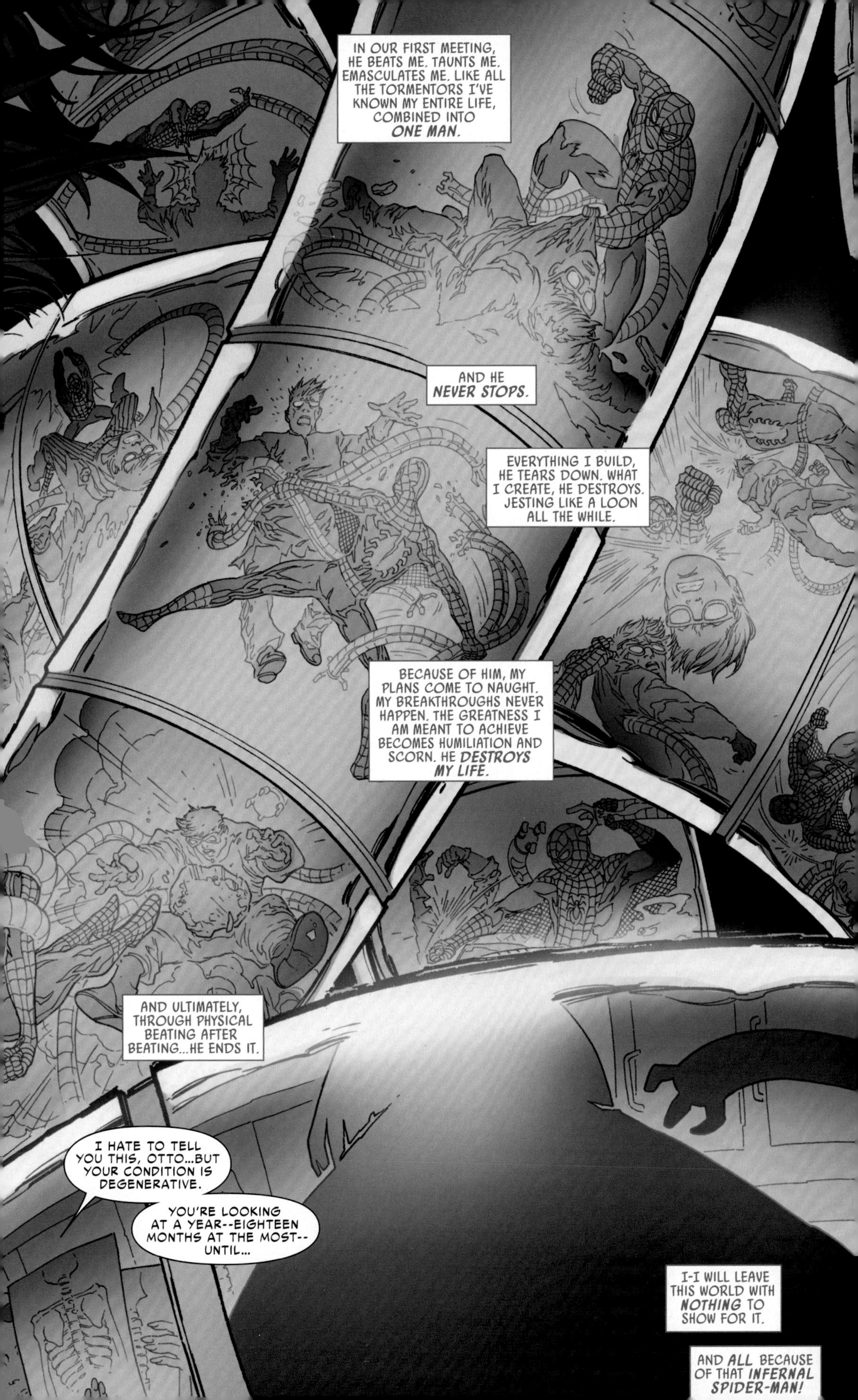
IN OUR FIRST MEETING, HE BEATS ME. TAUNTS ME. EMASCULATES ME. LIKE ALL THE TORMENTORS I'VE KNOWN MY ENTIRE LIFE, COMBINED INTO ONE MAN.
AND HE NEVER STOPS.
EVERYTHING I BUILD, HE TEARS DOWN. WHAT I CREATE, HE DESTROYS. JESTING LIKE A LOON ALL THE WHILE.
BECAUSE OF HIM, MY PLANS COME TO NAUGHT. MY BREAKTHROUGHS NEVER HAPPEN. THE GREATNESS I AM MEANT TO ACHIEVE BECOMES HUMILIATION AND SCORN. HE DESTROYS MY LIFE.
AND ULTIMATELY, THROUGH PHYSICAL BEATING AFTER BEATING...HE ENDS IT.
I HATE TO TELL YOU THIS, OTTO...BUT YOUR CONDITION IS DEGENERATIVE.
YOU'RE LOOKING AT A YEAR--EIGHTEEN MONTHS AT THE MOST--UNTIL...
I-I WILL LEAVE THIS WORLD WITH NOTHING TO SHOW FOR IT.
AND ALL BECAUSE OF THAT INFERNAL SPIDER-MAN!

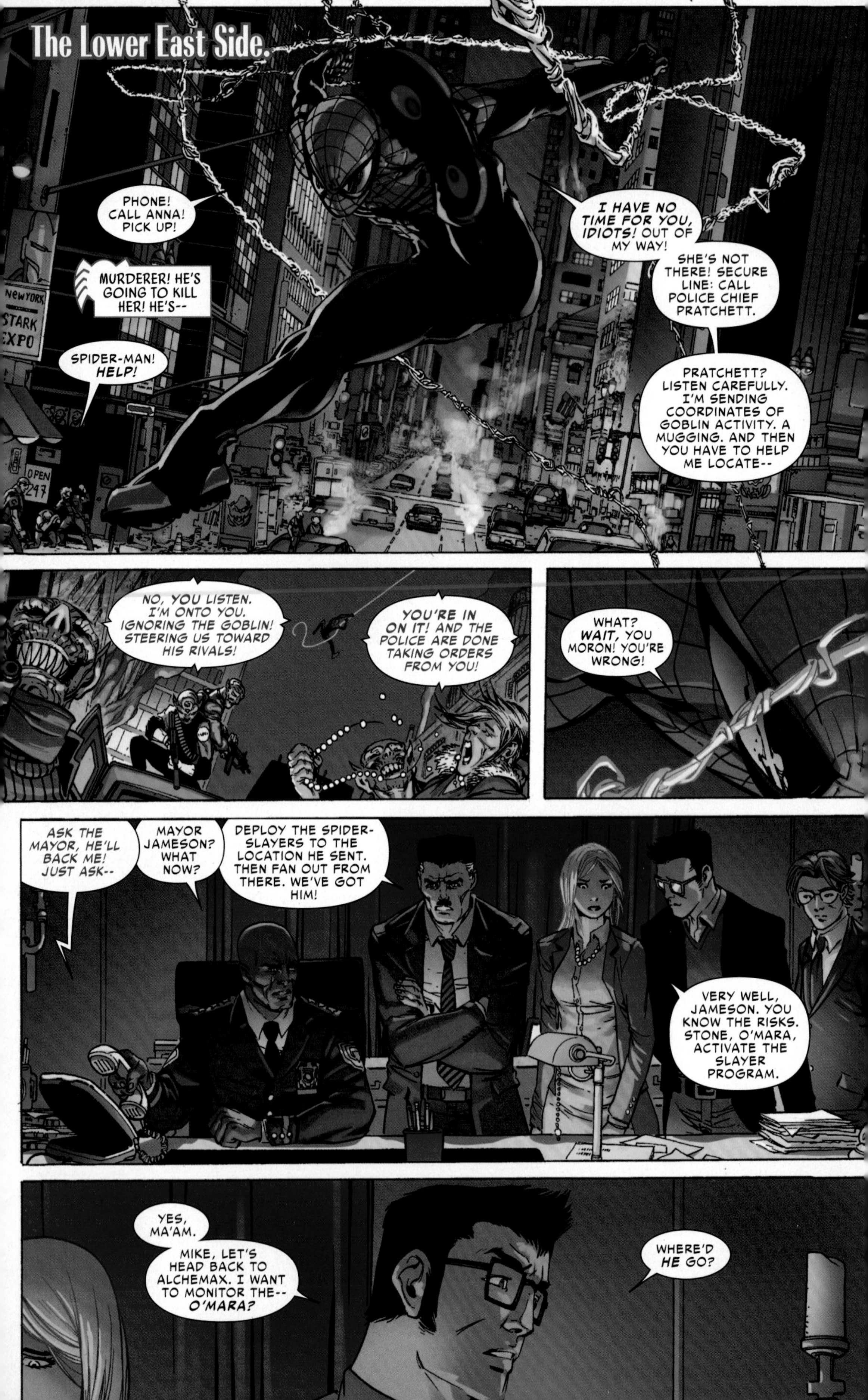
The Lower East Side.
PHONE! CALL ANNA! PICK UP!
MURDERER! HE'S GOING TO KILL HER! HE'S--
SPIDER-MAN! HELP!
I HAVE NO TIME FOR YOU, IDIOTS! OUT OF MY WAY!
SHE'S NOT THERE! SECURE LINE: CALL POLICE CHIEF PRATCHETT.
PRATCHETT? LISTEN CAREFULLY. I'M SENDING COORDINATES OF GOBLIN ACTIVITY. A MUGGING. AND THEN YOU HAVE TO HELP ME LOCATE--
NO, YOU LISTEN. I'M ONTO YOU. IGNORING THE GOBLIN! STEERING US TOWARD HIS RIVALS!
YOU'RE IN ON IT! AND THE POLICE ARE DONE TAKING ORDERS FROM YOU!
WHAT? WAIT, YOU MORON! YOU'RE WRONG!
ASK THE MAYOR, HE'LL BACK ME! JUST ASK--
MAYOR JAMESON? WHAT NOW?
DEPLOY THE SPIDER-SLAYERS TO THE LOCATION HE SENT. THEN FAN OUT FROM THERE. WE'VE GOT HIM!
VERY WELL, JAMESON. YOU KNOW THE RISKS. STONE, O'MARA, ACTIVATE THE SLAYER PROGRAM.
YES, MA'AM.
MIKE, LET'S HEAD BACK TO ALCHEMAX. I WANT TO MONITOR THE-- O'MARA?
WHERE'D HE GO?

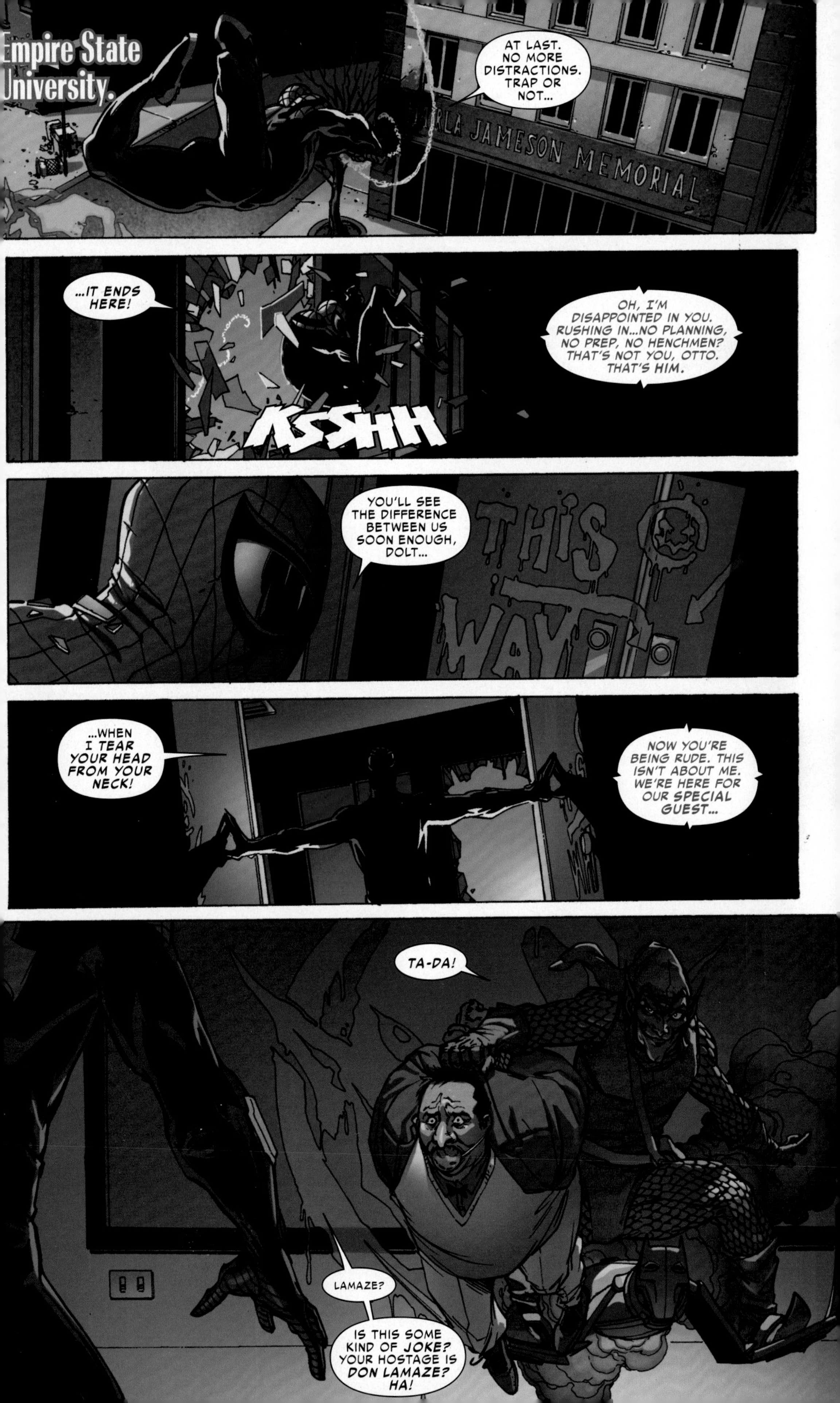

Empire State University.
AT LAST. NO MORE DISTRACTIONS. TRAP OR NOT...
...RLA JAMESON MEMORIAL
...IT ENDS HERE!
OH, I'M DISAPPOINTED IN YOU. RUSHING IN...NO PLANNING, NO PREP, NO HENCHMEN? THAT'S NOT YOU, OTTO. THAT'S HIM.
KSSHH
YOU'LL SEE THE DIFFERENCE BETWEEN US SOON ENOUGH, DOLT...
THIS WAY
...WHEN I TEAR YOUR HEAD FROM YOUR NECK!
NOW YOU'RE BEING RUDE. THIS ISN'T ABOUT ME. WE'RE HERE FOR OUR SPECIAL GUEST...
TA-DA!
LAMAZE?
IS THIS SOME KIND OF JOKE? YOUR HOSTAGE IS DON LAMAZE? HA!

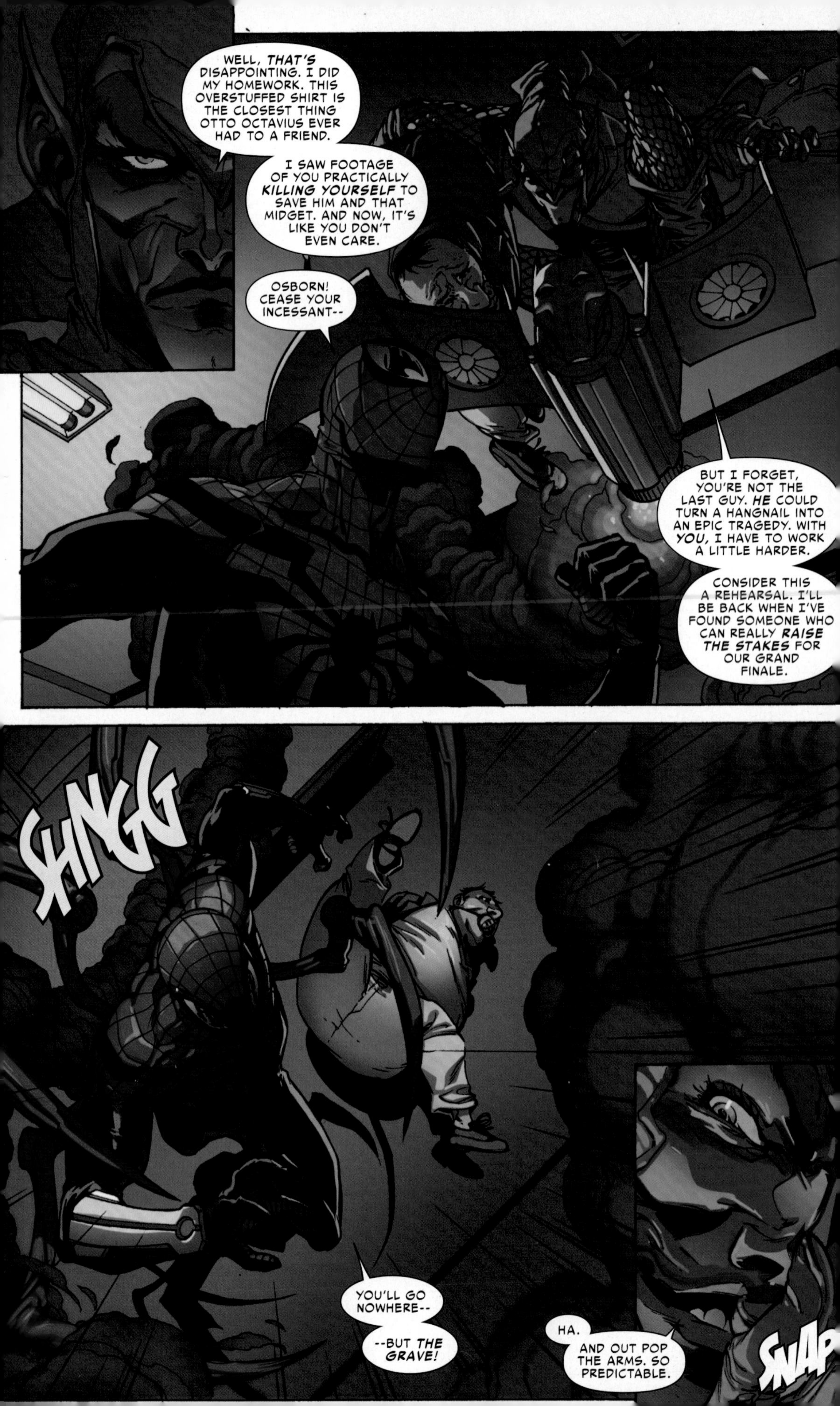
WELL, THAT'S DISAPPOINTING. I DID MY HOMEWORK. THIS OVERSTUFFED SHIRT IS THE CLOSEST THING OTTO OCTAVIUS EVER HAD TO A FRIEND.
I SAW FOOTAGE OF YOU PRACTICALLY KILLING YOURSELF TO SAVE HIM AND THAT MIDGET. AND NOW, IT'S LIKE YOU DON'T EVEN CARE.
OSBORN! CEASE YOUR INCESSANT--
BUT I FORGET, YOU'RE NOT THE LAST GUY. HE COULD TURN A HANGNAIL INTO AN EPIC TRAGEDY. WITH YOU, I HAVE TO WORK A LITTLE HARDER.
CONSIDER THIS A REHEARSAL. I'LL BE BACK WHEN I'VE FOUND SOMEONE WHO CAN REALLY RAISE THE STAKES FOR OUR GRAND FINALE.
SHNGG
YOU'LL GO NOWHERE--
--BUT THE GRAVE!
HA.
AND OUT POP THE ARMS. SO PREDICTABLE.
SNAP

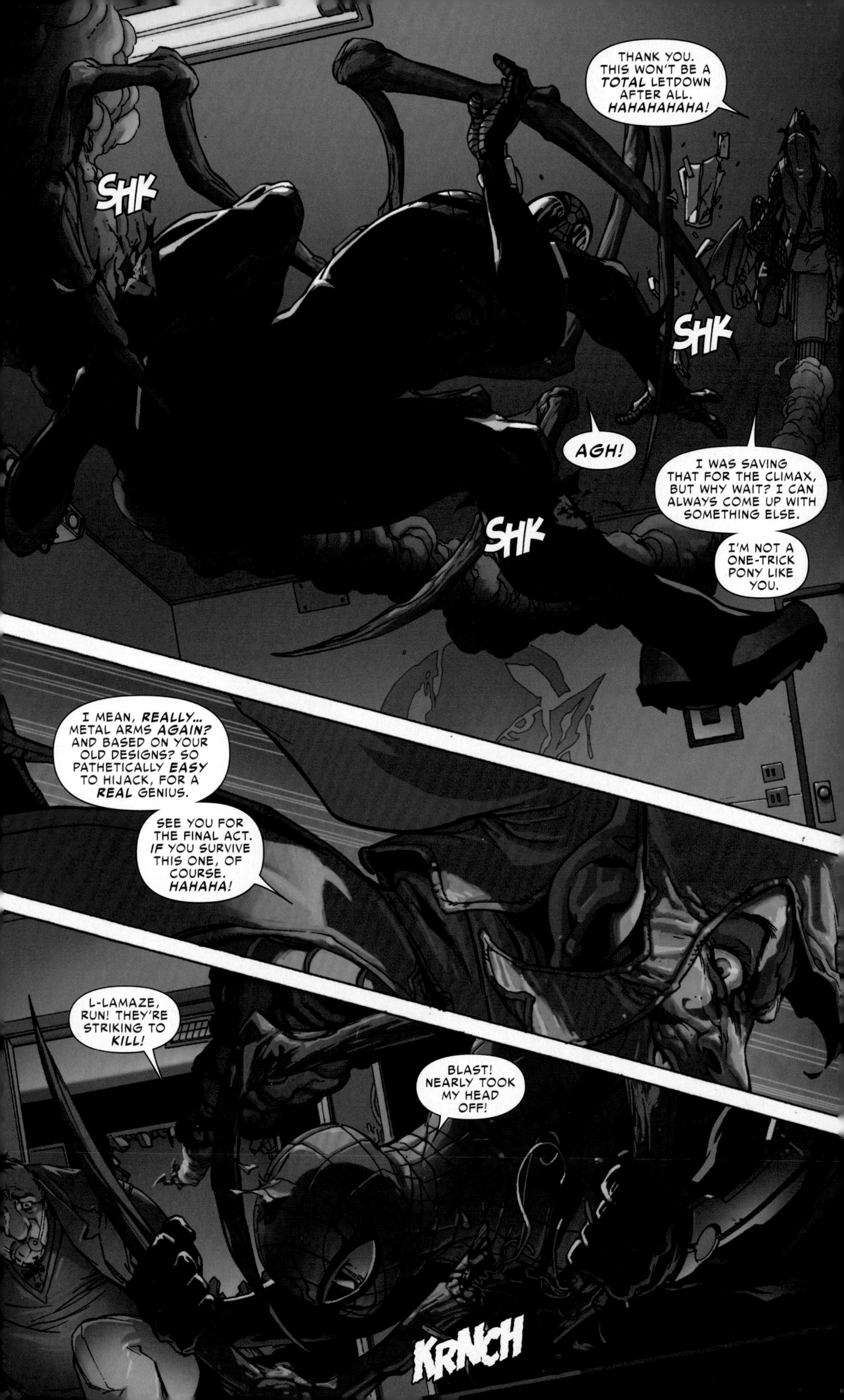
THANK YOU. THIS WON'T BE A TOTAL LETDOWN AFTER ALL. HAHAHAHAHA!
SHK
SHK
AGH!
I WAS SAVING THAT FOR THE CLIMAX, BUT WHY WAIT? I CAN ALWAYS COME UP WITH SOMETHING ELSE.
SHK
I'M NOT A ONE-TRICK PONY LIKE YOU.
I MEAN, REALLY... METAL ARMS AGAIN? AND BASED ON YOUR OLD DESIGNS? SO PATHETICALLY EASY TO HIJACK, FOR A REAL GENIUS.
SEE YOU FOR THE FINAL ACT. IF YOU SURVIVE THIS ONE, OF COURSE. HAHAHA!
L-LAMAZE, RUN! THEY'RE STRIKING TO KILL!
BLAST! NEARLY TOOK MY HEAD OFF!
KRNCH

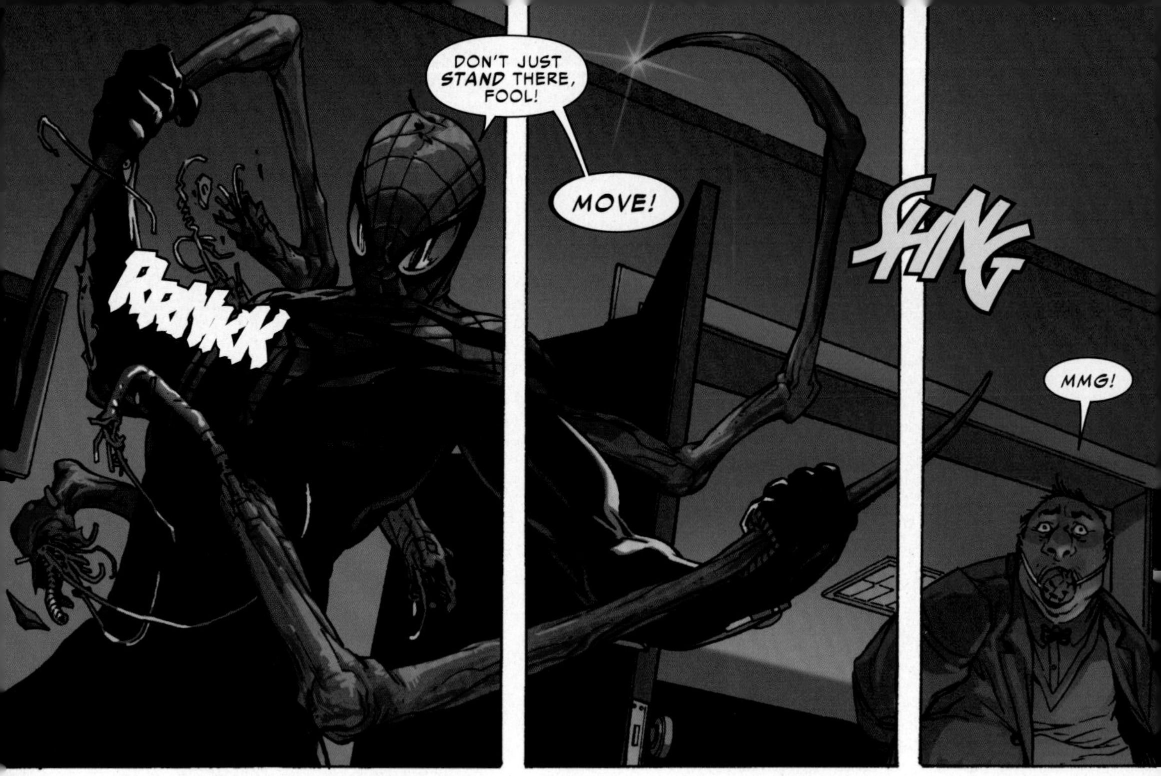
DON'T JUST STAND THERE, FOOL!
MOVE!
SHING
MMG!

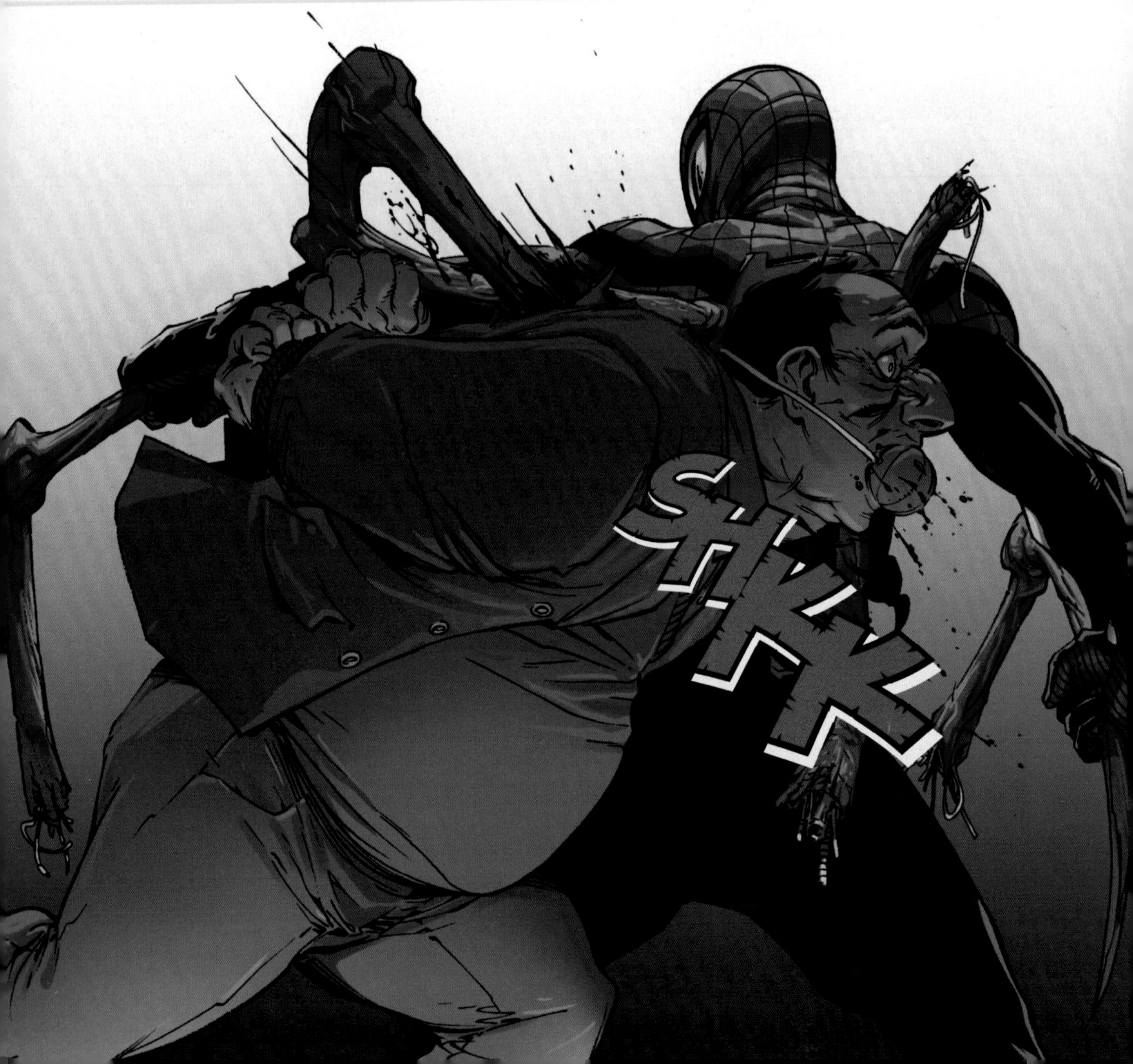
SHK

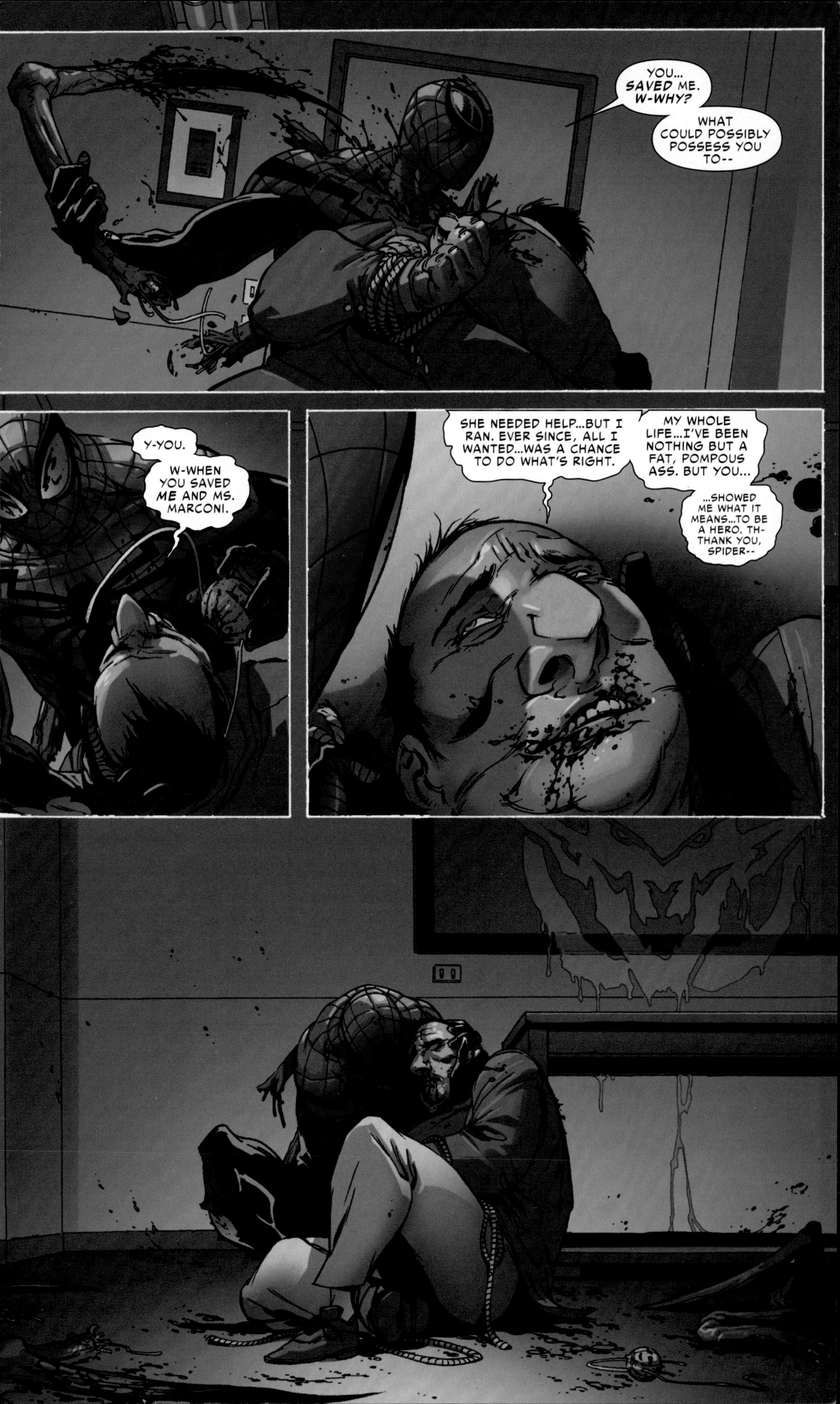
YOU... SAVED ME. W-WHY?
WHAT COULD POSSIBLY POSSESS YOU TO--
Y-YOU.
W-WHEN YOU SAVED ME AND MS. MARCONI.
SHE NEEDED HELP...BUT I RAN. EVER SINCE, ALL I WANTED...WAS A CHANCE TO DO WHAT'S RIGHT.
MY WHOLE LIFE...I'VE BEEN NOTHING BUT A FAT, POMPOUS ASS. BUT YOU...
...SHOWED ME WHAT IT MEANS...TO BE A HERO. TH-THANK YOU, SPIDER--

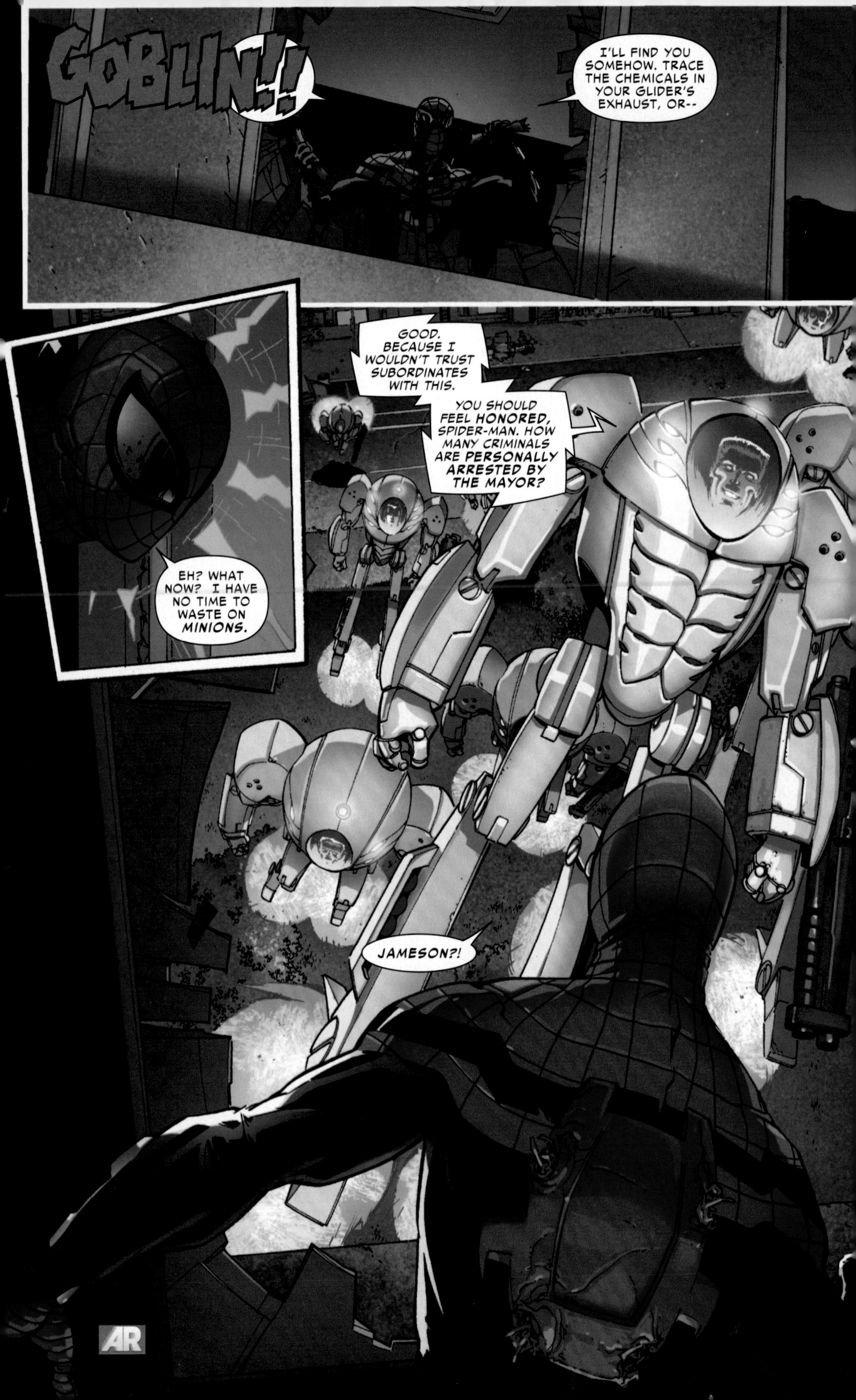
GOBLIN!!
I'LL FIND YOU SOMEHOW. TRACE THE CHEMICALS IN YOUR GLIDER'S EXHAUST, OR--
EH? WHAT NOW? I HAVE NO TIME TO WASTE ON MINIONS.
GOOD. BECAUSE I WOULDN'T TRUST SUBORDINATES WITH THIS.
YOU SHOULD FEEL HONORED, SPIDER-MAN. HOW MANY CRIMINALS ARE PERSONALLY ARRESTED BY THE MAYOR?
JAMESON?!
AR

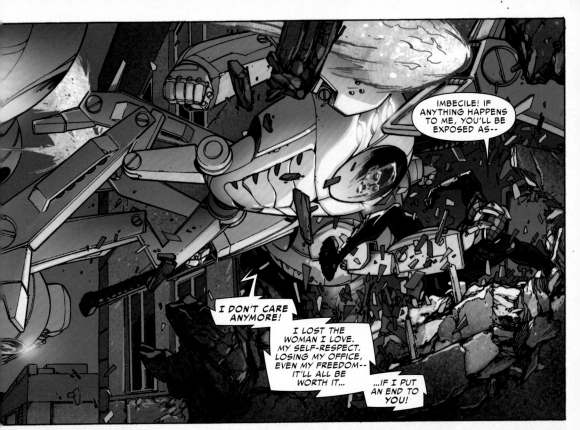

IMBECILE! IF ANYTHING HAPPENS TO ME, YOU'LL BE EXPOSED AS--

I DON'T CARE ANYMORE!

I LOST THE WOMAN I LOVE. MY SELF-RESPECT. LOSING MY OFFICE, EVEN MY FREEDOM-- IT'LL ALL BE WORTH IT...

...IF I PUT AN END TO YOU!

WITH SPIDER-SLAYERS? I COULD DISMANTLE THESE TOYS IN MY SLEEP. I'LL --

NGGH!

STRONGER THAN YOU REMEMBERED, AREN'T THEY? LIGHT-YEARS AHEAD OF THE OLD ONES.

POWERFUL ENOUGH TO TEAR YOU LIMB FROM--

ZWOOOOooo

SHUT DOWN? HOW--

THAT WOULD BE ME, BIT-HEAD.

I REMEMBER YOU. THE SPIDER-MAN OF 2099. WHY ARE YOU STILL IN THIS TIMELINE?

BE GLAD I AM. THOSE THINGS WOULD'VE SLAGGED YOU IF I HADN'T SHUT 'EM OFF. LET'S JUST SAY I HAVE AN IN.*

*NAMELY, AS "MICHAEL O'MARA," SPIDEY 2099 HELPED BUILD THEM! -EDIFYIN' ELLIE

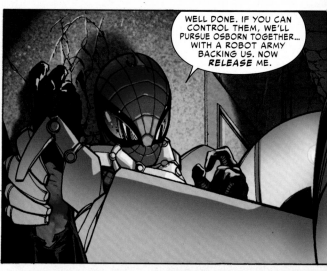

WELL DONE. IF YOU CAN CONTROL THEM, WE'LL PURSUE OSBORN TOGETHER... WITH A ROBOT ARMY BACKING US. NOW *RELEASE* ME.

MAYBE LATER. I'VE GOT SOME *QUESTIONS* FIRST.

AND YOU'RE NOT GOING *ANYWHERE* UNTIL YOU ANSWER THEM.

YOU FOOL, WE DON'T HAVE *TIME* FOR THIS!

ACTUALLY, I'VE GOT *DECADES.* I DON'T BELONG HERE... AND I'M NOT SURE *YOU* DO, EITHER.

SOMETHING'S WRONG WITH HISTORY... WITH *YOU.* YOU'RE ACTING *TOTALLY DIFFERENT* FROM THE GUY YOU'RE SUPPOSED TO BE.

AND UNTIL YOU TELL ME WHAT THE SHOCK IS GOING ON, *NOBODY MOVES!*

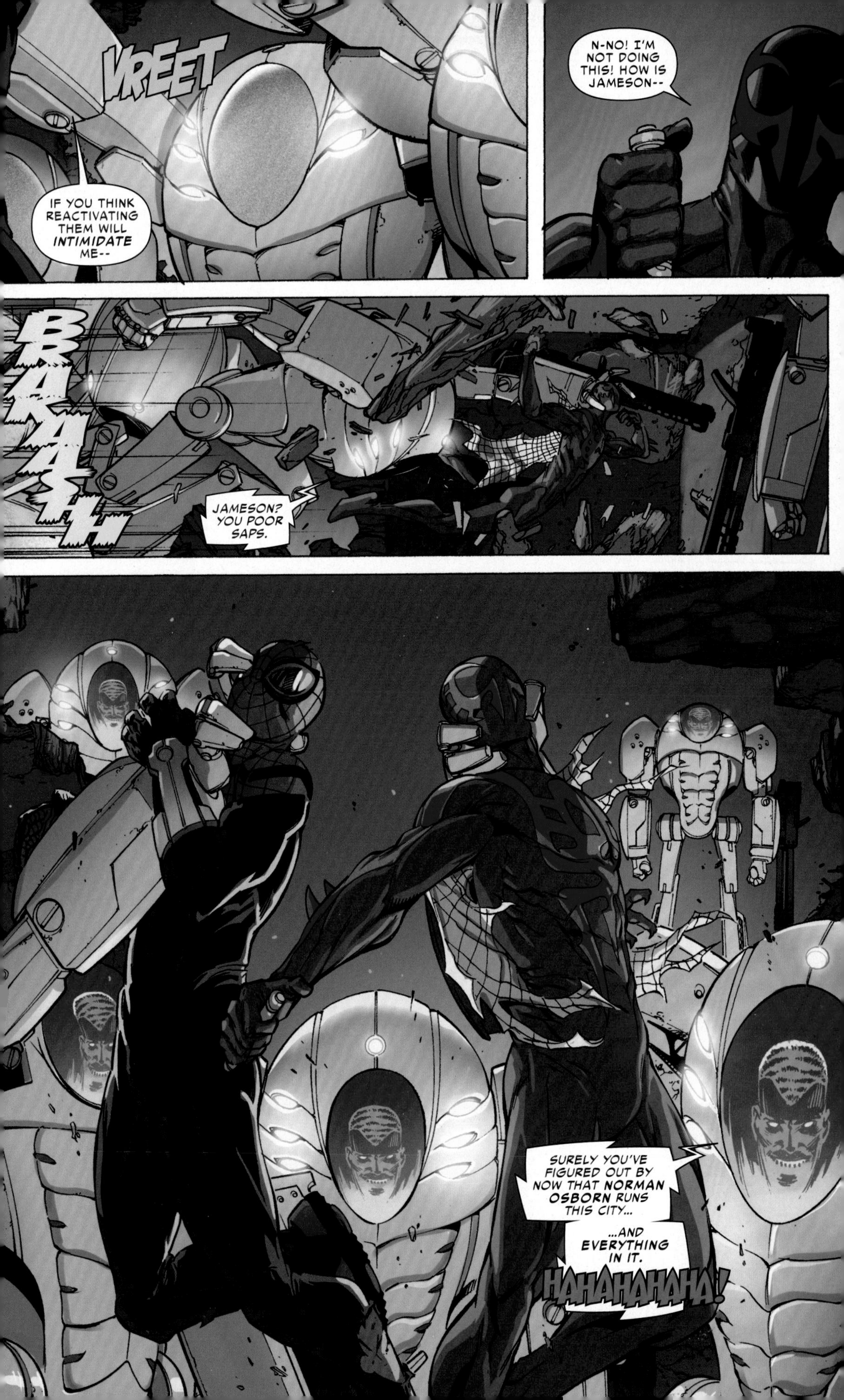
VREET
IF YOU THINK REACTIVATING THEM WILL INTIMIDATE ME--
N-NO! I'M NOT DOING THIS! HOW IS JAMESON--
BRAKASHH
JAMESON? YOU POOR SAPS.
SURELY YOU'VE FIGURED OUT BY NOW THAT NORMAN OSBORN RUNS THIS CITY...
...AND EVERYTHING IN IT.
HAHAHAHAHA!

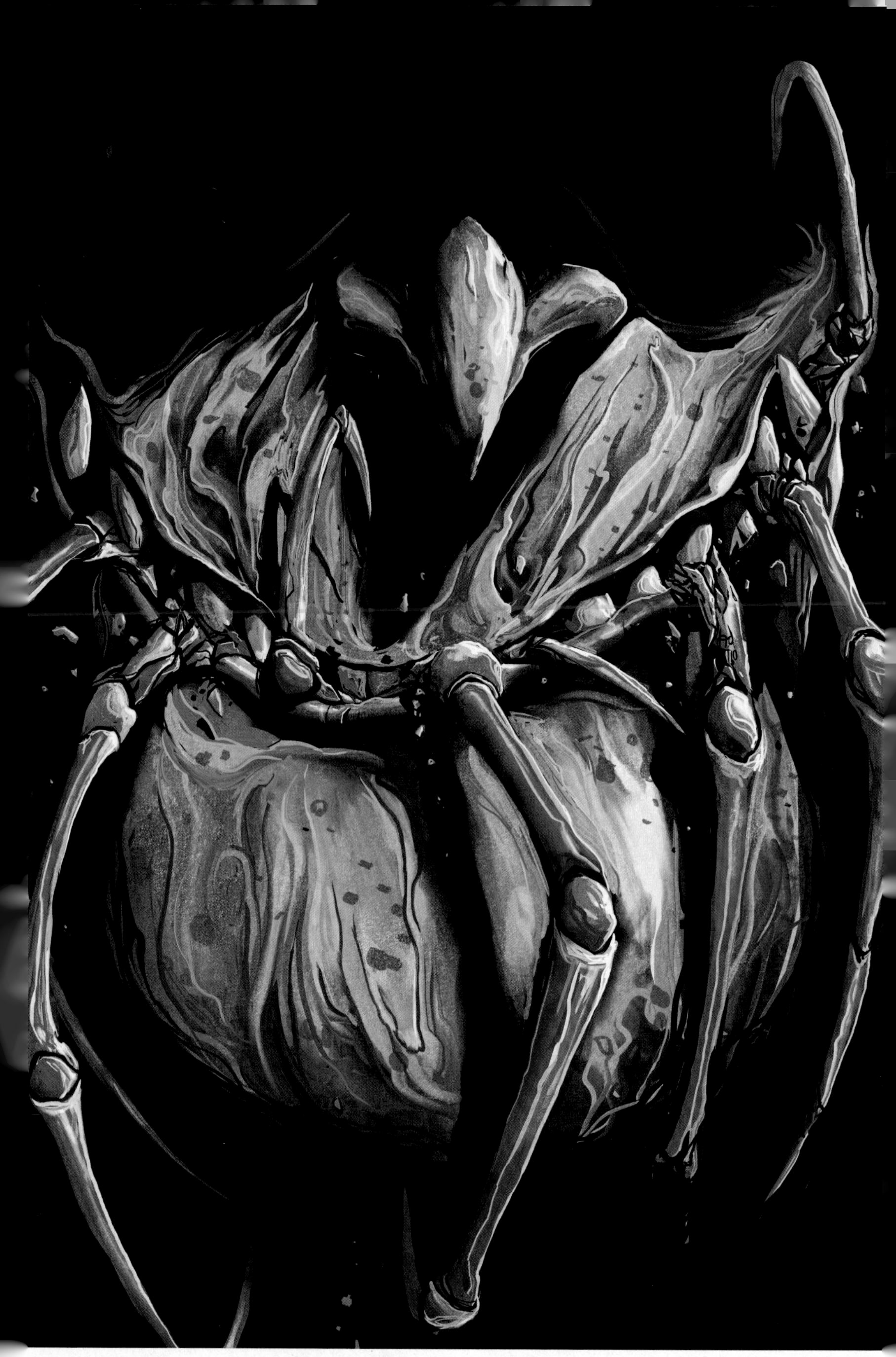

SUPERIOR SPIDER-MAN ANNUAL 2

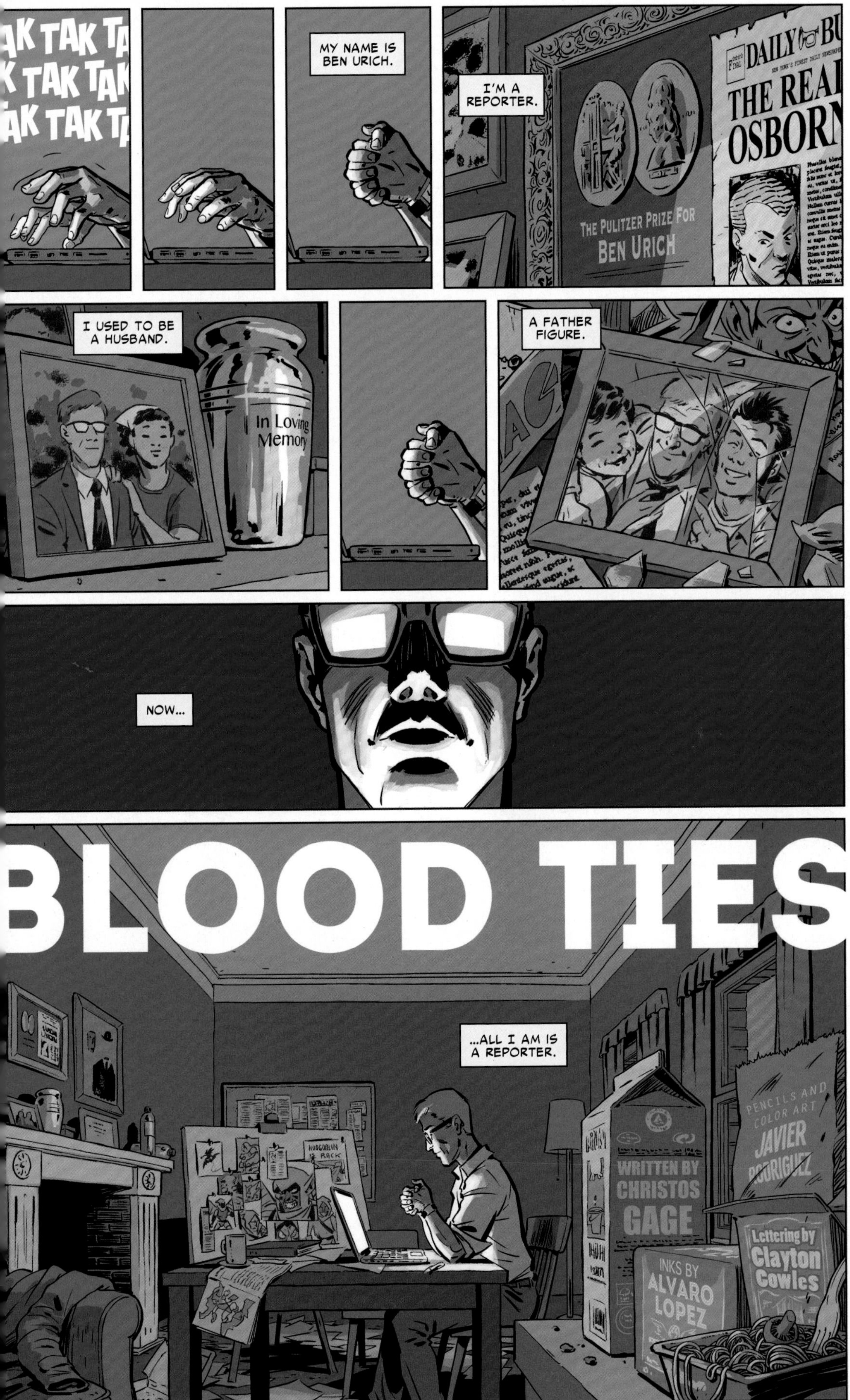
TAK TAK TAK
TAK TAK TAK
TAK TAK TAK
MY NAME IS BEN URICH.
I'M A REPORTER.
THE PULITZER PRIZE FOR BEN URICH
DAILY BU
THE REAL OSBORN
I USED TO BE A HUSBAND.
In Loving Memory
A FATHER FIGURE.
NOW...
BLOOD TIES
...ALL I AM IS A REPORTER.
HOBGOBLIN IS BACK
WRITTEN BY CHRISTOS GAGE
PENCILS AND COLOR ART JAVIER RODRIGUEZ
INKS BY ALVARO LOPEZ
Lettering by Clayton Cowles

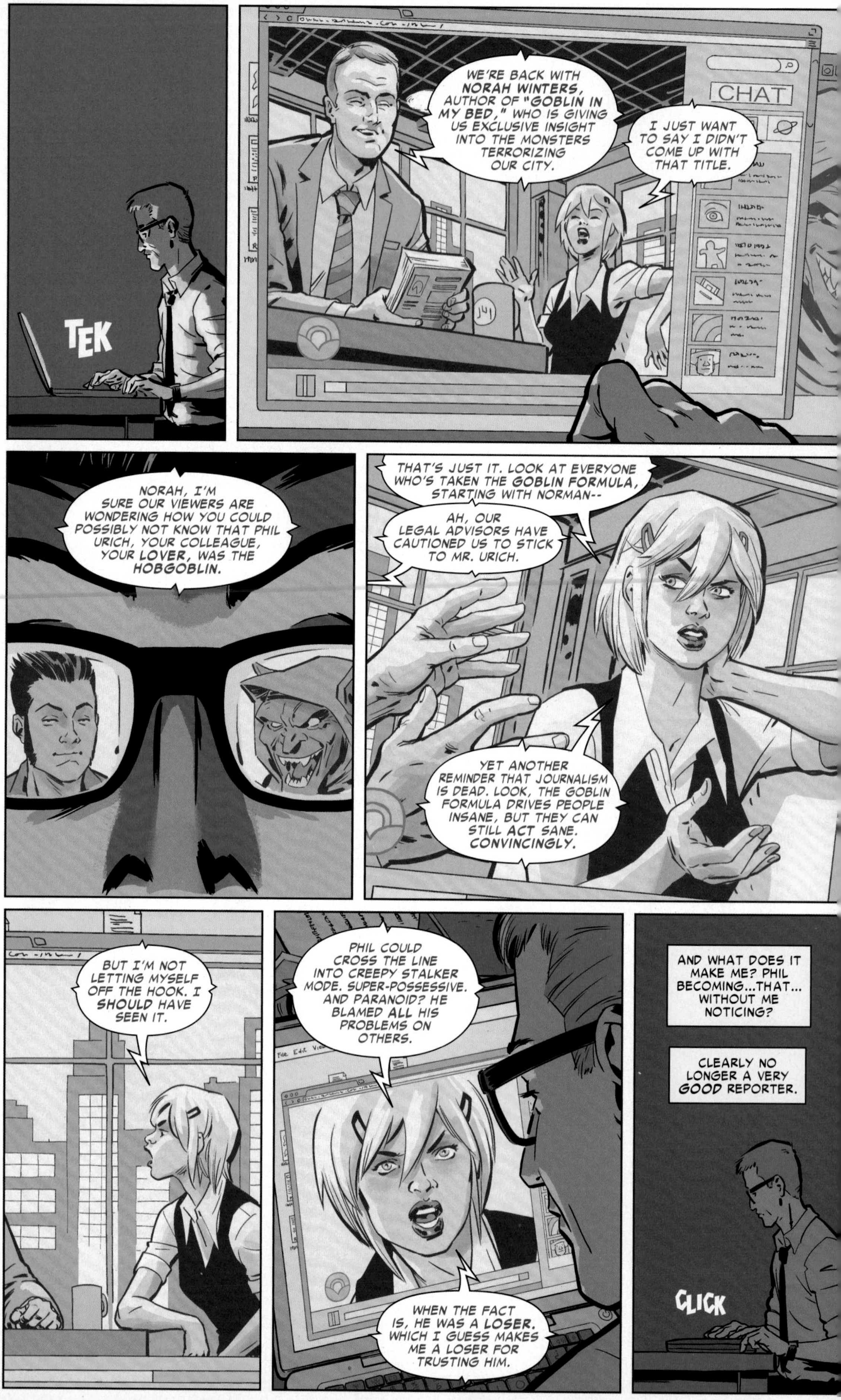
TEK
WE'RE BACK WITH NORAH WINTERS, AUTHOR OF "GOBLIN IN MY BED," WHO IS GIVING US EXCLUSIVE INSIGHT INTO THE MONSTERS TERRORIZING OUR CITY.
I JUST WANT TO SAY I DIDN'T COME UP WITH THAT TITLE.
CHAT
NORAH, I'M SURE OUR VIEWERS ARE WONDERING HOW YOU COULD POSSIBLY NOT KNOW THAT PHIL URICH, YOUR COLLEAGUE, YOUR LOVER, WAS THE HOBGOBLIN.
THAT'S JUST IT. LOOK AT EVERYONE WHO'S TAKEN THE GOBLIN FORMULA, STARTING WITH NORMAN--
AH, OUR LEGAL ADVISORS HAVE CAUTIONED US TO STICK TO MR. URICH.
YET ANOTHER REMINDER THAT JOURNALISM IS DEAD. LOOK, THE GOBLIN FORMULA DRIVES PEOPLE INSANE, BUT THEY CAN STILL ACT SANE. CONVINCINGLY.
BUT I'M NOT LETTING MYSELF OFF THE HOOK. I SHOULD HAVE SEEN IT.
PHIL COULD CROSS THE LINE INTO CREEPY STALKER MODE. SUPER-POSSESSIVE. AND PARANOID? HE BLAMED ALL HIS PROBLEMS ON OTHERS.
WHEN THE FACT IS, HE WAS A LOSER. WHICH I GUESS MAKES ME A LOSER FOR TRUSTING HIM.
AND WHAT DOES IT MAKE ME? PHIL BECOMING...THAT... WITHOUT ME NOTICING?
CLEARLY NO LONGER A VERY GOOD REPORTER.
CLICK

I'M THE GUY WHO FIGURED OUT WHO *DAREDEVIL* REALLY IS. WHO *EXPOSED* NORMAN OSBORN.

BUT MY OWN *NEPHEW* WAS A CRIMINAL, AN ENFORCER FOR THE *KINGPIN*, AND I DIDN'T HAVE A CLUE? I'VE BEEN DEALING WITH A LOT, BUT THAT'S *INEXCUSABLE.*

I OWE IT TO PHIL TO FIND OUT HOW THIS HAPPENED. AND WHETHER THERE'S ANY CHANCE OF--

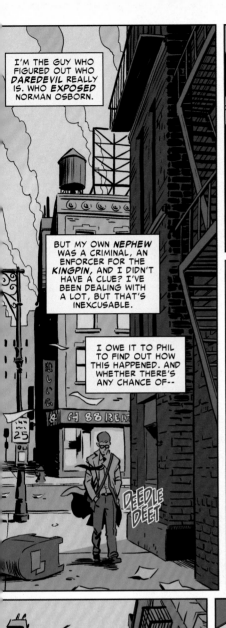

DEEDLE DEET

URICH.

BEN, THANK GOD. THIS IS MARY JANE WATSON. I'VE BEEN TRYING TO GET THROUGH TO ROBBIE, BUT I DON'T THINK THEY'RE TAKING ME SERIOUSLY AT THE BUGLE.

SLOW DOWN. WHAT'S GOING ON?

THE *GREEN GOBLIN'S* COMING AFTER ANYONE CLOSE TO SPIDER-MAN...*AND* PETER PARKER. I'M GETTING OUT OF TOWN WITH MAY AND JAY JAMESON.

YOU SHOULD DO THE SAME. PLEASE, WARN ROBBIE ROBERTSON...AND ANYONE ELSE AT THE *DAILY BUGLE* YOU THINK MIGHT BE A TARGET.

I WILL. BE CAREFUL.

YOU TOO. THANKS, BEN.

I'M SO GLAD YOU'RE OKAY.

DON'T TURN AROUND.

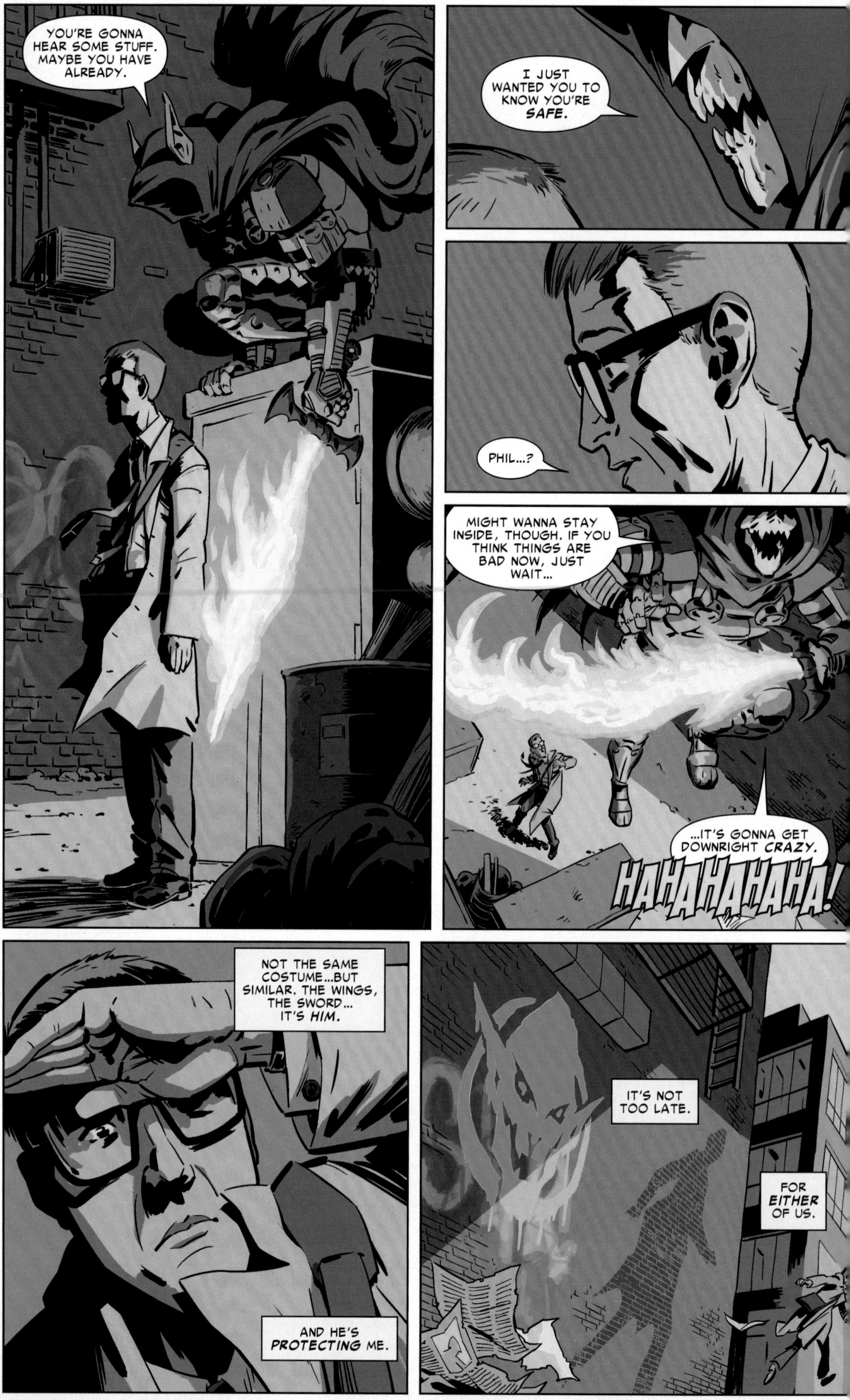

YOU'RE GONNA HEAR SOME STUFF. MAYBE YOU HAVE ALREADY.
I JUST WANTED YOU TO KNOW YOU'RE SAFE.
PHIL...?
MIGHT WANNA STAY INSIDE, THOUGH. IF YOU THINK THINGS ARE BAD NOW, JUST WAIT...
...IT'S GONNA GET DOWNRIGHT CRAZY.
HAHAHAHAHA!
NOT THE SAME COSTUME...BUT SIMILAR. THE WINGS, THE SWORD... IT'S HIM.
AND HE'S PROTECTING ME.
IT'S NOT TOO LATE.
FOR EITHER OF US.

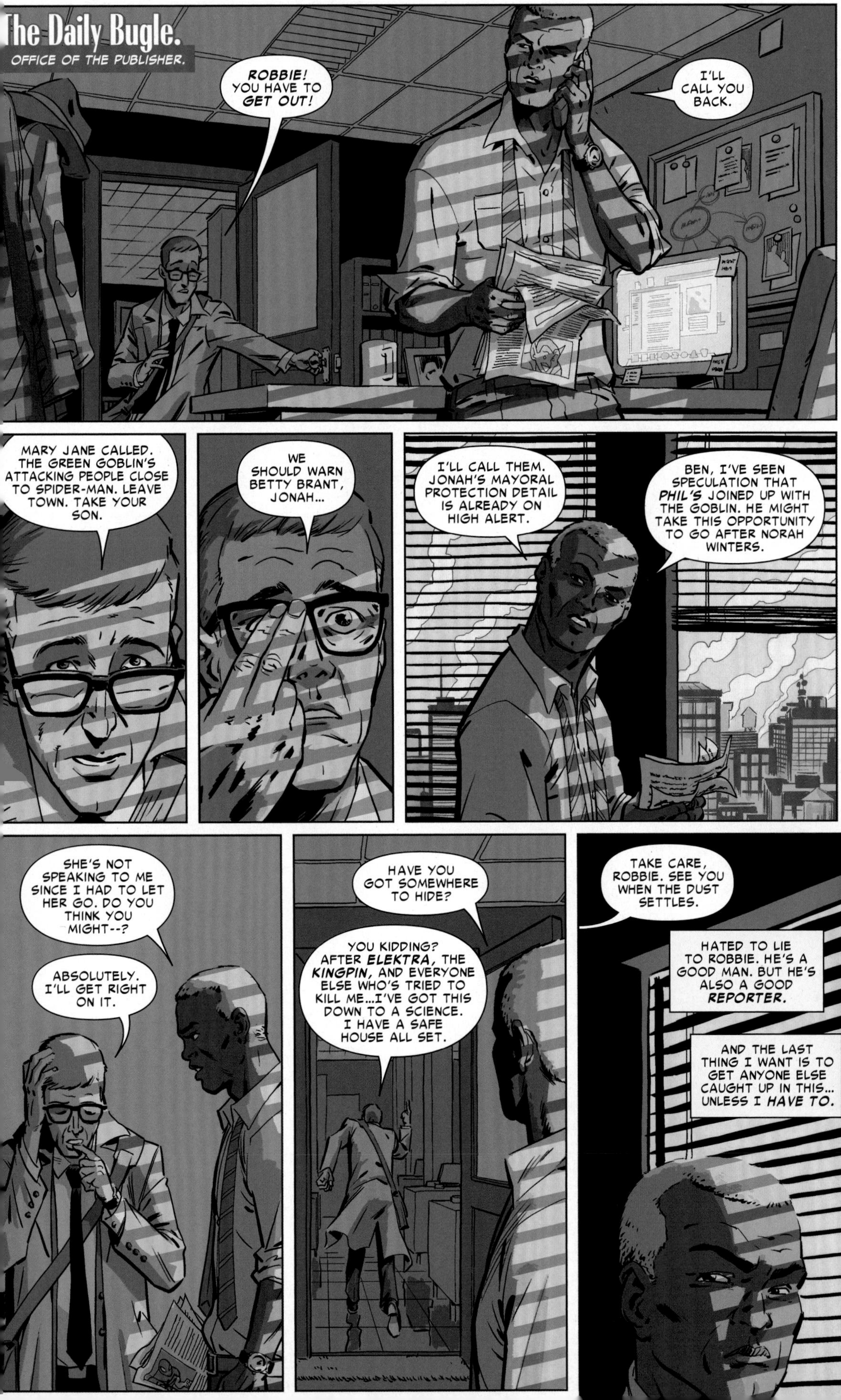

The Daily Bugle.
OFFICE OF THE PUBLISHER.
ROBBIE! YOU HAVE TO GET OUT!
I'LL CALL YOU BACK.
MARY JANE CALLED. THE GREEN GOBLIN'S ATTACKING PEOPLE CLOSE TO SPIDER-MAN. LEAVE TOWN. TAKE YOUR SON.
WE SHOULD WARN BETTY BRANT, JONAH...
I'LL CALL THEM. JONAH'S MAYORAL PROTECTION DETAIL IS ALREADY ON HIGH ALERT.
BEN, I'VE SEEN SPECULATION THAT PHIL'S JOINED UP WITH THE GOBLIN. HE MIGHT TAKE THIS OPPORTUNITY TO GO AFTER NORAH WINTERS.
SHE'S NOT SPEAKING TO ME SINCE I HAD TO LET HER GO. DO YOU THINK YOU MIGHT--?
ABSOLUTELY. I'LL GET RIGHT ON IT.
HAVE YOU GOT SOMEWHERE TO HIDE?
YOU KIDDING? AFTER ELEKTRA, THE KINGPIN, AND EVERYONE ELSE WHO'S TRIED TO KILL ME...I'VE GOT THIS DOWN TO A SCIENCE. I HAVE A SAFE HOUSE ALL SET.
TAKE CARE, ROBBIE. SEE YOU WHEN THE DUST SETTLES.
HATED TO LIE TO ROBBIE. HE'S A GOOD MAN. BUT HE'S ALSO A GOOD REPORTER.
AND THE LAST THING I WANT IS TO GET ANYONE ELSE CAUGHT UP IN THIS... UNLESS I HAVE TO.

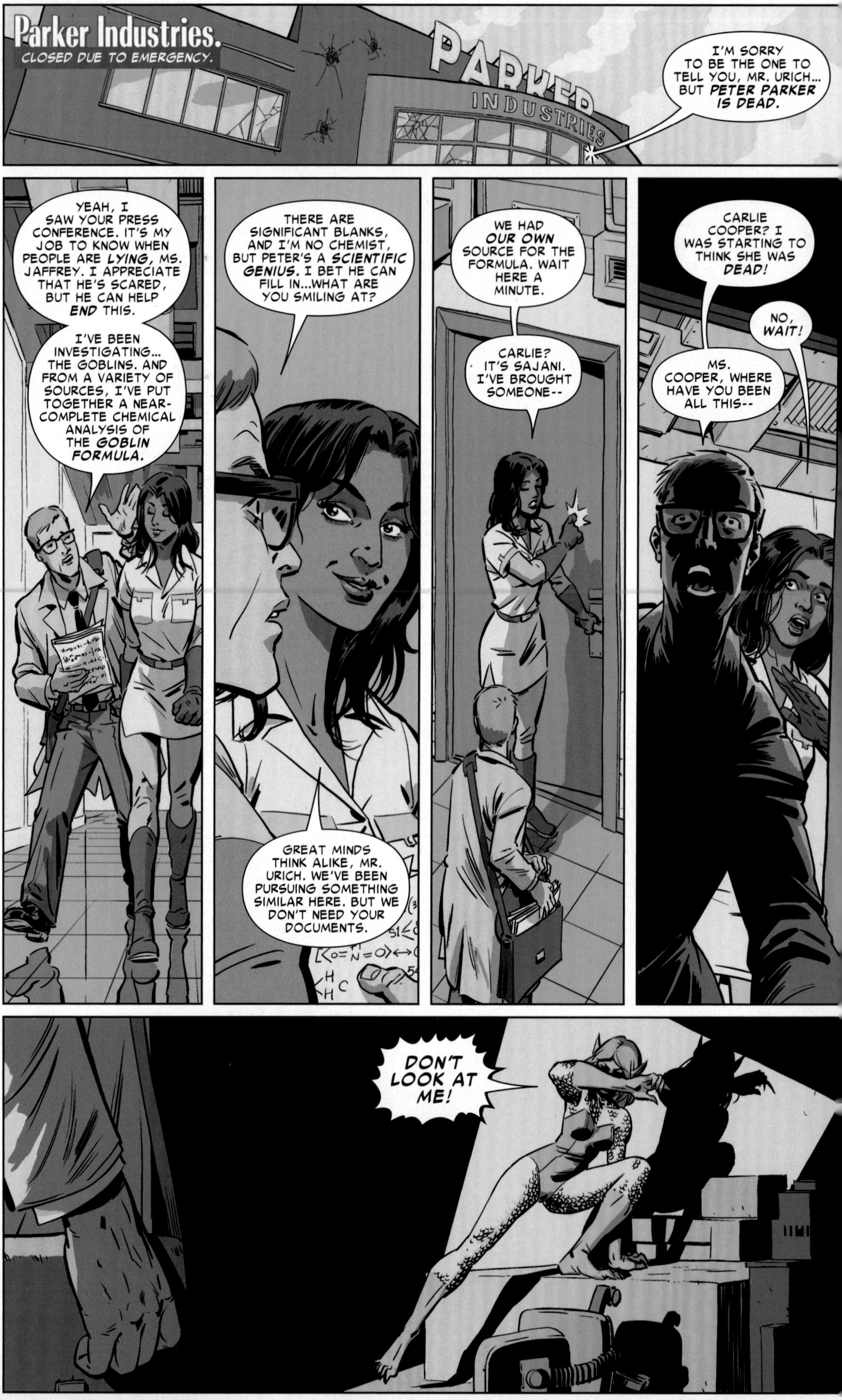
Parker Industries.
CLOSED DUE TO EMERGENCY.
PARKER INDUSTRIES
I'M SORRY TO BE THE ONE TO TELL YOU, MR. URICH... BUT PETER PARKER IS DEAD.
YEAH, I SAW YOUR PRESS CONFERENCE. IT'S MY JOB TO KNOW WHEN PEOPLE ARE LYING, MS. JAFFREY. I APPRECIATE THAT HE'S SCARED, BUT HE CAN HELP END THIS.
I'VE BEEN INVESTIGATING... THE GOBLINS. AND FROM A VARIETY OF SOURCES, I'VE PUT TOGETHER A NEAR-COMPLETE CHEMICAL ANALYSIS OF THE GOBLIN FORMULA.
THERE ARE SIGNIFICANT BLANKS, AND I'M NO CHEMIST, BUT PETER'S A SCIENTIFIC GENIUS. I BET HE CAN FILL IN...WHAT ARE YOU SMILING AT?
GREAT MINDS THINK ALIKE, MR. URICH. WE'VE BEEN PURSUING SOMETHING SIMILAR HERE. BUT WE DON'T NEED YOUR DOCUMENTS.
WE HAD OUR OWN SOURCE FOR THE FORMULA. WAIT HERE A MINUTE.
CARLIE? IT'S SAJANI. I'VE BROUGHT SOMEONE--
CARLIE COOPER? I WAS STARTING TO THINK SHE WAS DEAD!
NO, WAIT!
MS. COOPER, WHERE HAVE YOU BEEN ALL THIS--
DON'T LOOK AT ME!

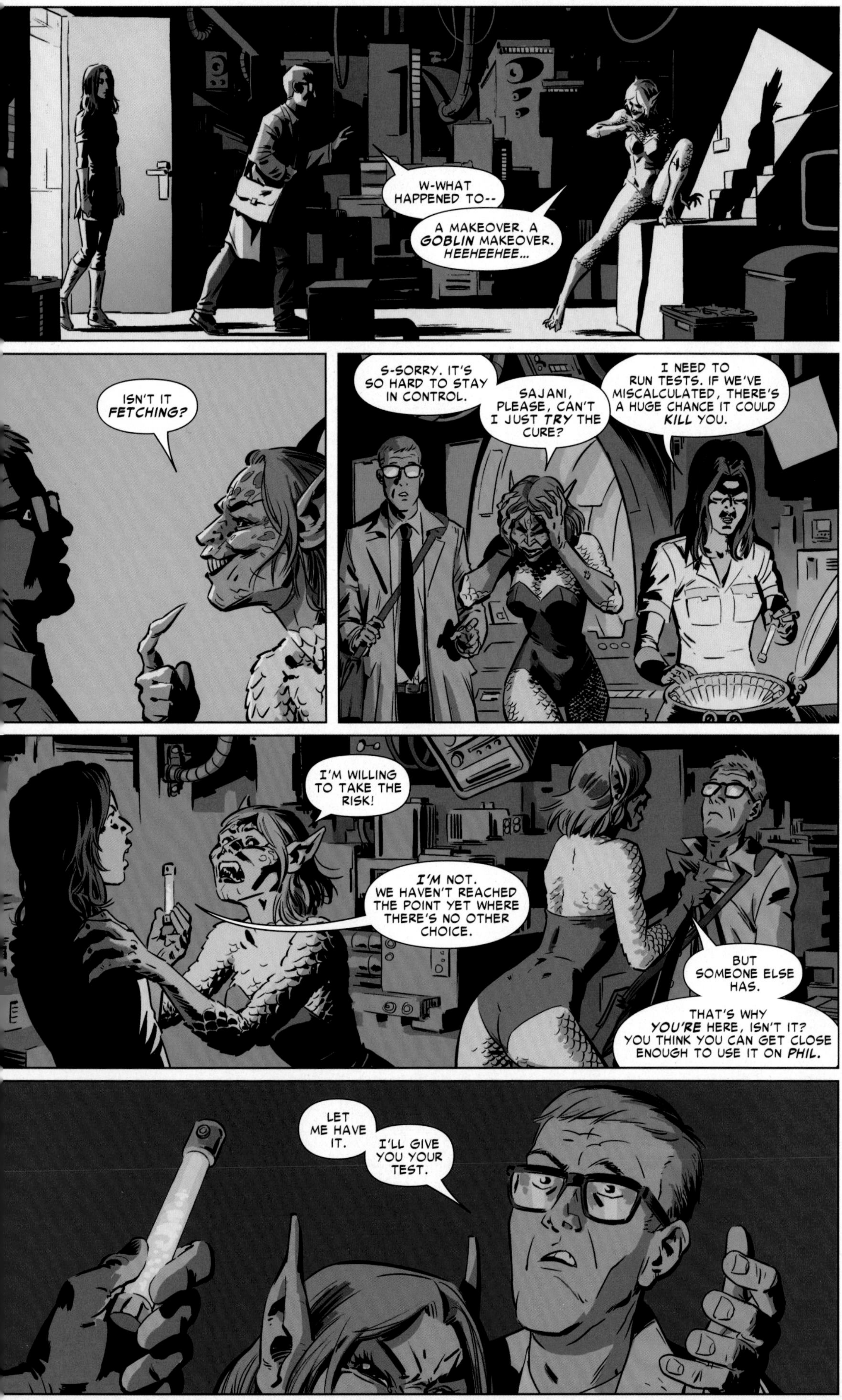
W-WHAT HAPPENED TO--
A MAKEOVER. A GOBLIN MAKEOVER. HEEHEEHEE...
ISN'T IT FETCHING?
S-SORRY. IT'S SO HARD TO STAY IN CONTROL.
SAJANI, PLEASE, CAN'T I JUST TRY THE CURE?
I NEED TO RUN TESTS. IF WE'VE MISCALCULATED, THERE'S A HUGE CHANCE IT COULD KILL YOU.
I'M WILLING TO TAKE THE RISK!
I'M NOT. WE HAVEN'T REACHED THE POINT YET WHERE THERE'S NO OTHER CHOICE.
BUT SOMEONE ELSE HAS.
THAT'S WHY YOU'RE HERE, ISN'T IT? YOU THINK YOU CAN GET CLOSE ENOUGH TO USE IT ON PHIL.
LET ME HAVE IT.
I'LL GIVE YOU YOUR TEST.

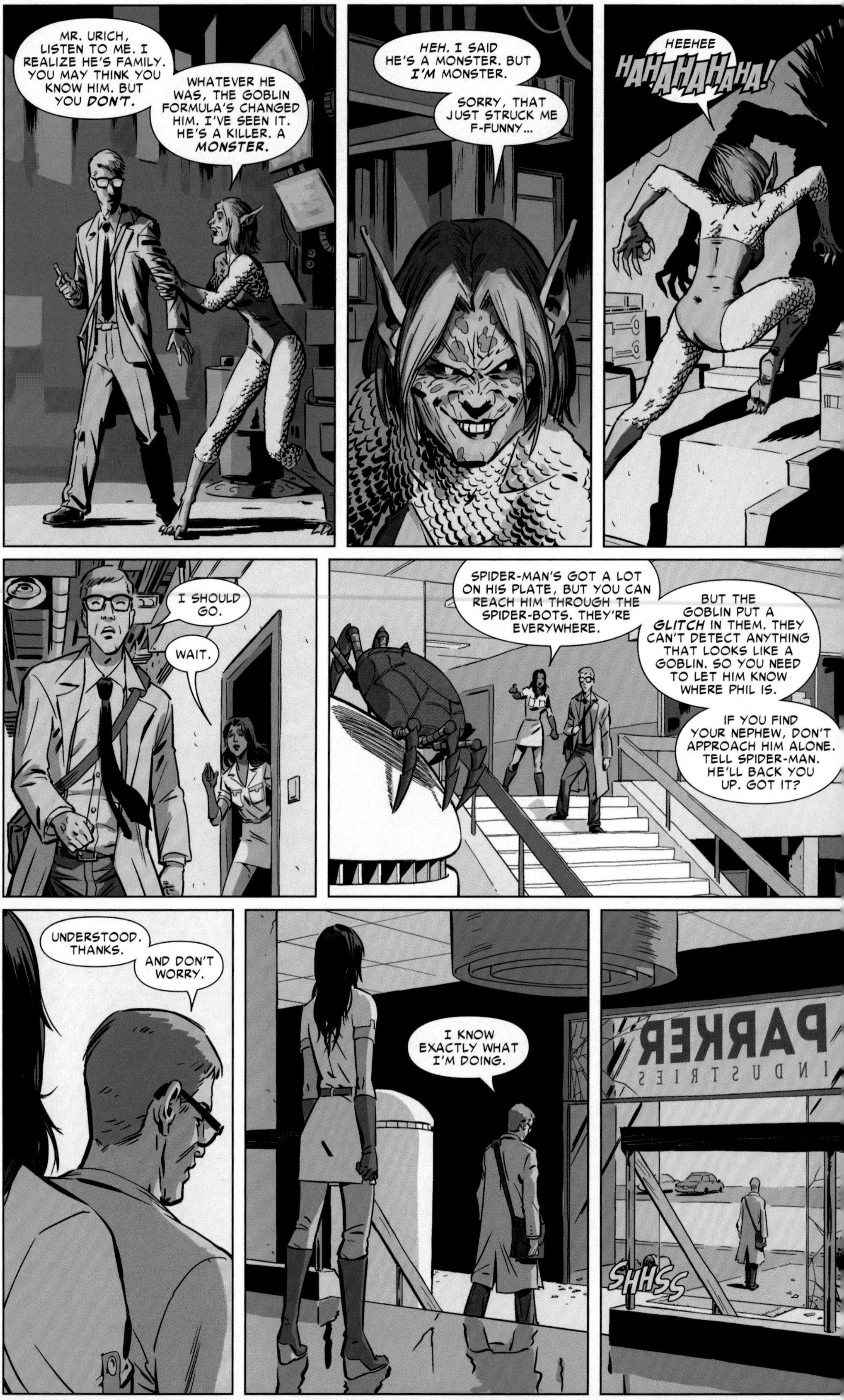
MR. URICH, LISTEN TO ME. I REALIZE HE'S FAMILY. YOU MAY THINK YOU KNOW HIM. BUT YOU DON'T.
WHATEVER HE WAS, THE GOBLIN FORMULA'S CHANGED HIM. I'VE SEEN IT. HE'S A KILLER. A MONSTER.
HEH. I SAID HE'S A MONSTER. BUT I'M MONSTER.
SORRY, THAT JUST STRUCK ME F-FUNNY...
HEEHEE
HAHAHAHAHA!
I SHOULD GO.
WAIT.
SPIDER-MAN'S GOT A LOT ON HIS PLATE, BUT YOU CAN REACH HIM THROUGH THE SPIDER-BOTS. THEY'RE EVERYWHERE.
BUT THE GOBLIN PUT A GLITCH IN THEM. THEY CAN'T DETECT ANYTHING THAT LOOKS LIKE A GOBLIN. SO YOU NEED TO LET HIM KNOW WHERE PHIL IS.
IF YOU FIND YOUR NEPHEW, DON'T APPROACH HIM ALONE. TELL SPIDER-MAN. HE'LL BACK YOU UP. GOT IT?
UNDERSTOOD. THANKS.
AND DON'T WORRY.
I KNOW EXACTLY WHAT I'M DOING.
SHHSS

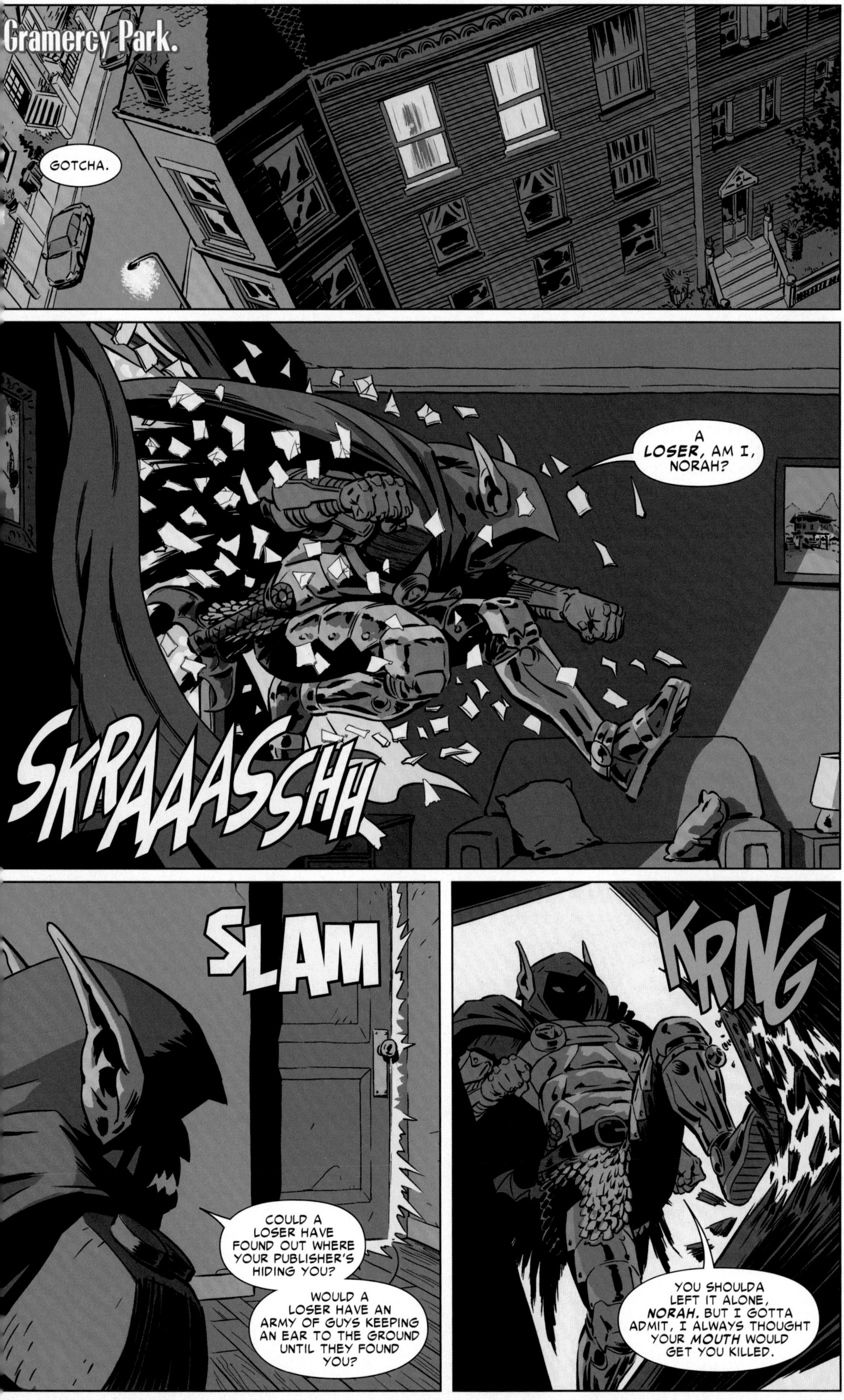
Gramercy Park.
GOTCHA.
A LOSER, AM I, NORAH?
SKRAAASSHH
SLAM
COULD A LOSER HAVE FOUND OUT WHERE YOUR PUBLISHER'S HIDING YOU?
WOULD A LOSER HAVE AN ARMY OF GUYS KEEPING AN EAR TO THE GROUND UNTIL THEY FOUND YOU?
KRNG
YOU SHOULDA LEFT IT ALONE, NORAH. BUT I GOTTA ADMIT, I ALWAYS THOUGHT YOUR MOUTH WOULD GET YOU KILLED.

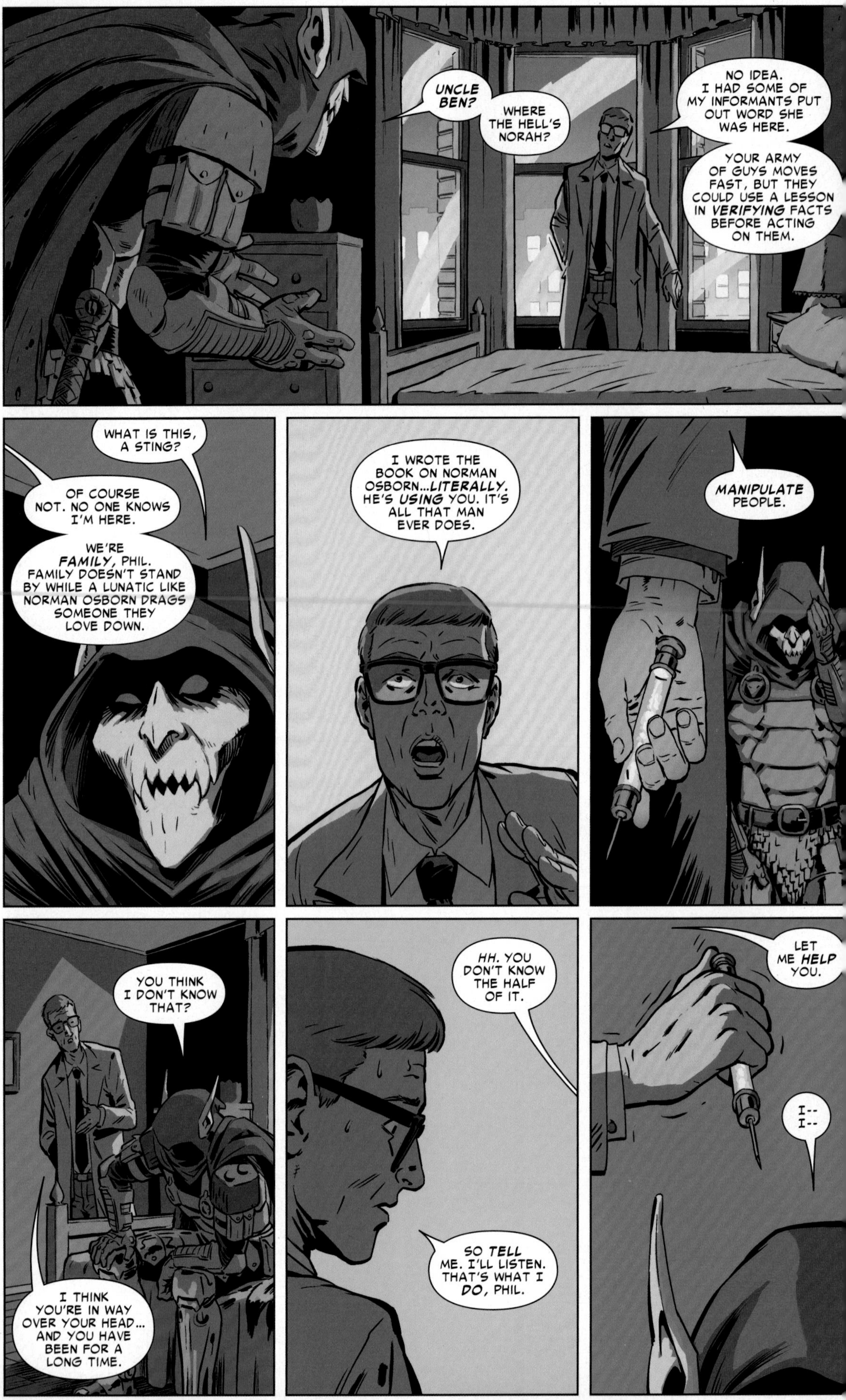
UNCLE BEN?
WHERE THE HELL'S NORAH?
NO IDEA. I HAD SOME OF MY INFORMANTS PUT OUT WORD SHE WAS HERE.
YOUR ARMY OF GUYS MOVES FAST, BUT THEY COULD USE A LESSON IN VERIFYING FACTS BEFORE ACTING ON THEM.
WHAT IS THIS, A STING?
OF COURSE NOT. NO ONE KNOWS I'M HERE.
WE'RE FAMILY, PHIL. FAMILY DOESN'T STAND BY WHILE A LUNATIC LIKE NORMAN OSBORN DRAGS SOMEONE THEY LOVE DOWN.
I WROTE THE BOOK ON NORMAN OSBORN...LITERALLY. HE'S USING YOU. IT'S ALL THAT MAN EVER DOES.
MANIPULATE PEOPLE.
YOU THINK I DON'T KNOW THAT?
I THINK YOU'RE IN WAY OVER YOUR HEAD... AND YOU HAVE BEEN FOR A LONG TIME.
HH. YOU DON'T KNOW THE HALF OF IT.
SO TELL ME. I'LL LISTEN. THAT'S WHAT I DO, PHIL.
LET ME HELP YOU.
I-- I--

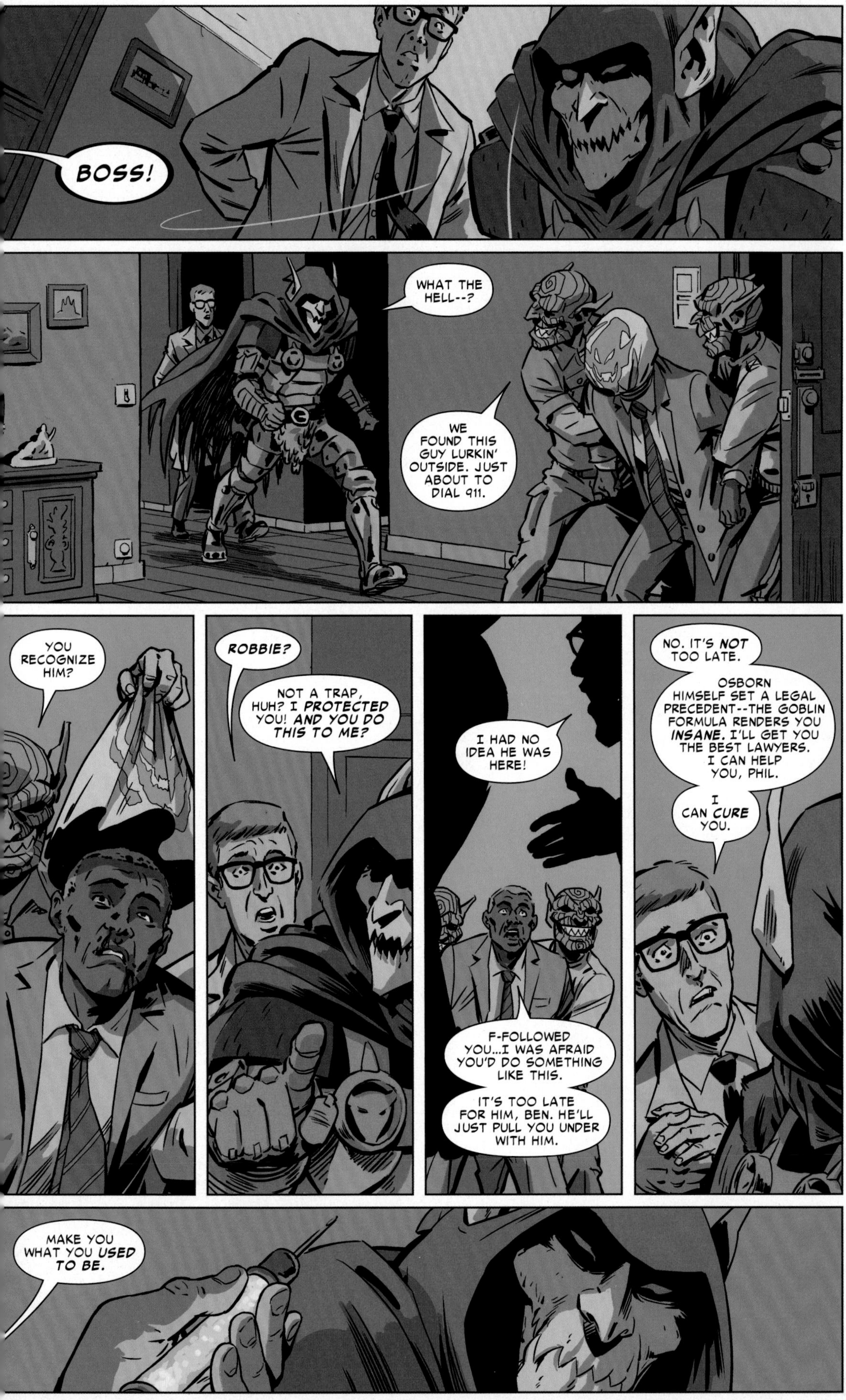
BOSS!
WHAT THE HELL--?
WE FOUND THIS GUY LURKIN' OUTSIDE. JUST ABOUT TO DIAL 911.
YOU RECOGNIZE HIM?
ROBBIE?
NOT A TRAP, HUH? I PROTECTED YOU! AND YOU DO THIS TO ME?
I HAD NO IDEA HE WAS HERE!
F-FOLLOWED YOU...I WAS AFRAID YOU'D DO SOMETHING LIKE THIS.
IT'S TOO LATE FOR HIM, BEN. HE'LL JUST PULL YOU UNDER WITH HIM.
NO. IT'S NOT TOO LATE.
OSBORN HIMSELF SET A LEGAL PRECEDENT--THE GOBLIN FORMULA RENDERS YOU INSANE. I'LL GET YOU THE BEST LAWYERS. I CAN HELP YOU, PHIL.
I CAN CURE YOU.
MAKE YOU WHAT YOU USED TO BE.

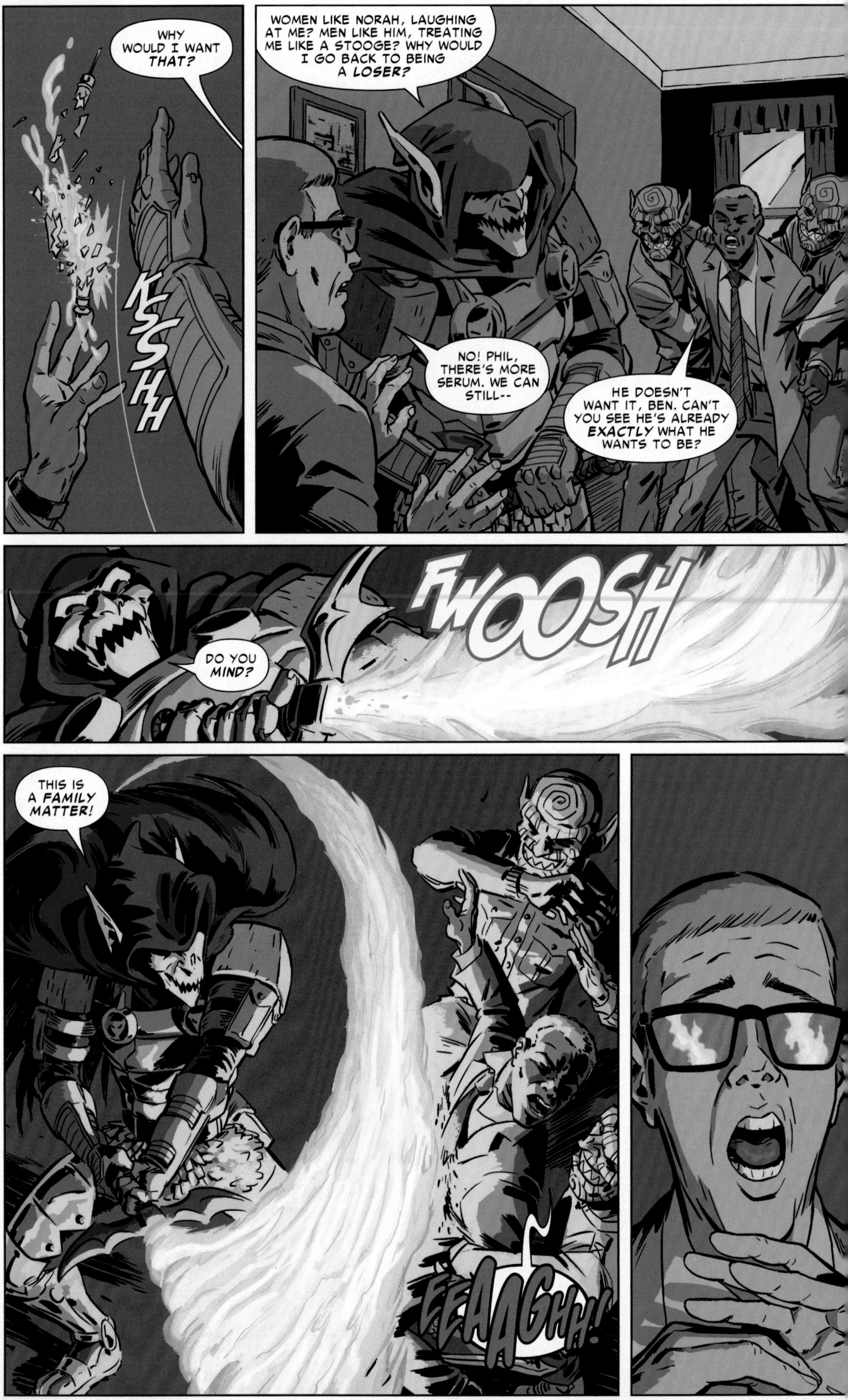

WHY WOULD I WANT THAT?
KSSHH
WOMEN LIKE NORAH, LAUGHING AT ME? MEN LIKE HIM, TREATING ME LIKE A STOOGE? WHY WOULD I GO BACK TO BEING A LOSER?
NO! PHIL, THERE'S MORE SERUM. WE CAN STILL--
HE DOESN'T WANT IT, BEN. CAN'T YOU SEE HE'S ALREADY EXACTLY WHAT HE WANTS TO BE?
FWOOSH
DO YOU MIND?
THIS IS A FAMILY MATTER!
EEAAGHH!

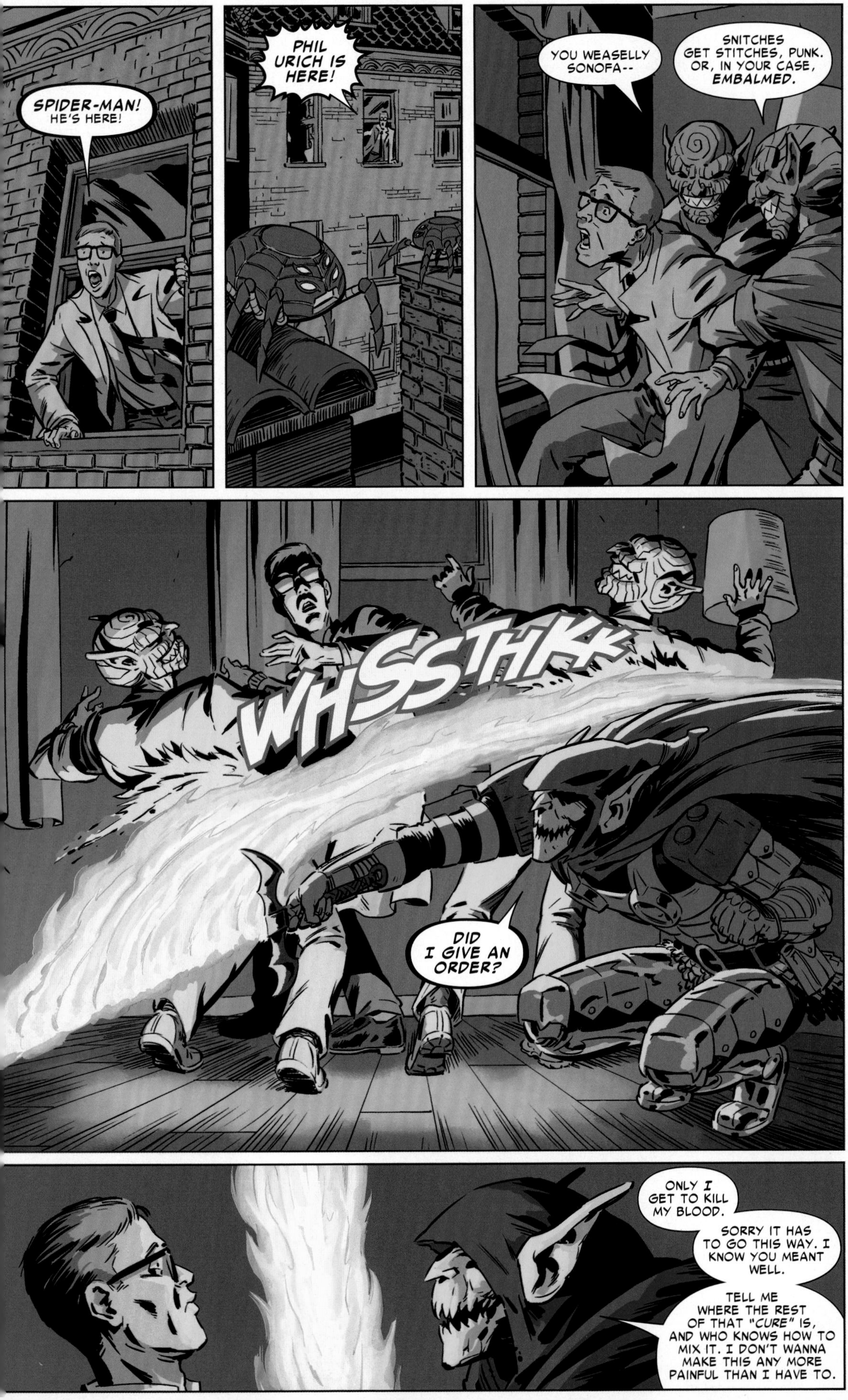
SPIDER-MAN! HE'S HERE!
PHIL URICH IS HERE!
YOU WEASELLY SONOFA--
SNITCHES GET STITCHES, PUNK. OR, IN YOUR CASE, EMBALMED.
WHSSTHKK
DID I GIVE AN ORDER?
ONLY I GET TO KILL MY BLOOD.
SORRY IT HAS TO GO THIS WAY. I KNOW YOU MEANT WELL.
TELL ME WHERE THE REST OF THAT "CURE" IS, AND WHO KNOWS HOW TO MIX IT. I DON'T WANNA MAKE THIS ANY MORE PAINFUL THAN I HAVE TO.

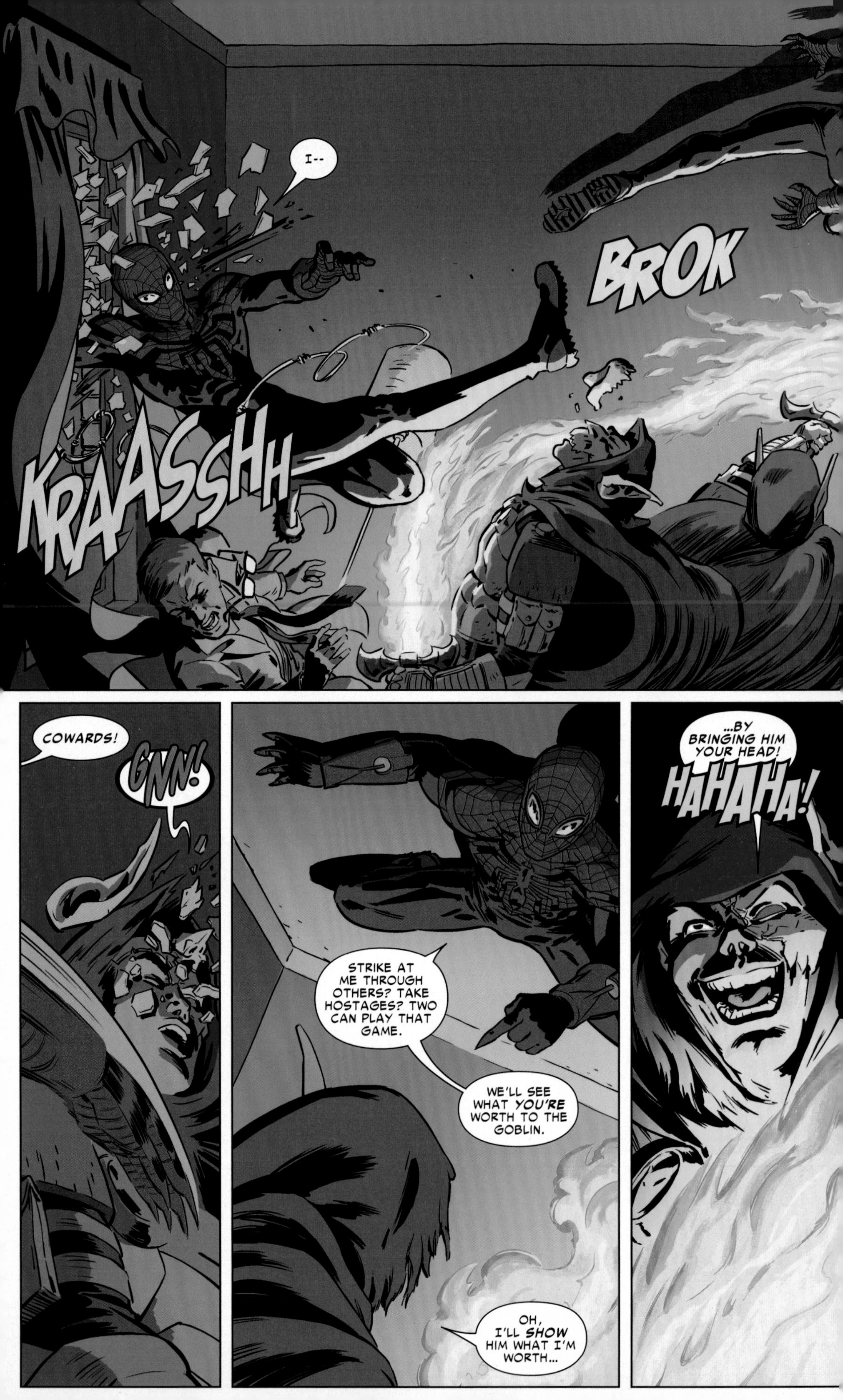
I--
BROK
KRAASSHH
COWARDS!
GNN!
STRIKE AT ME THROUGH OTHERS? TAKE HOSTAGES? TWO CAN PLAY THAT GAME.
WE'LL SEE WHAT *YOU'RE* WORTH TO THE GOBLIN.
OH, I'LL *SHOW* HIM WHAT I'M WORTH...
...BY BRINGING HIM YOUR HEAD!
HAHAHA!

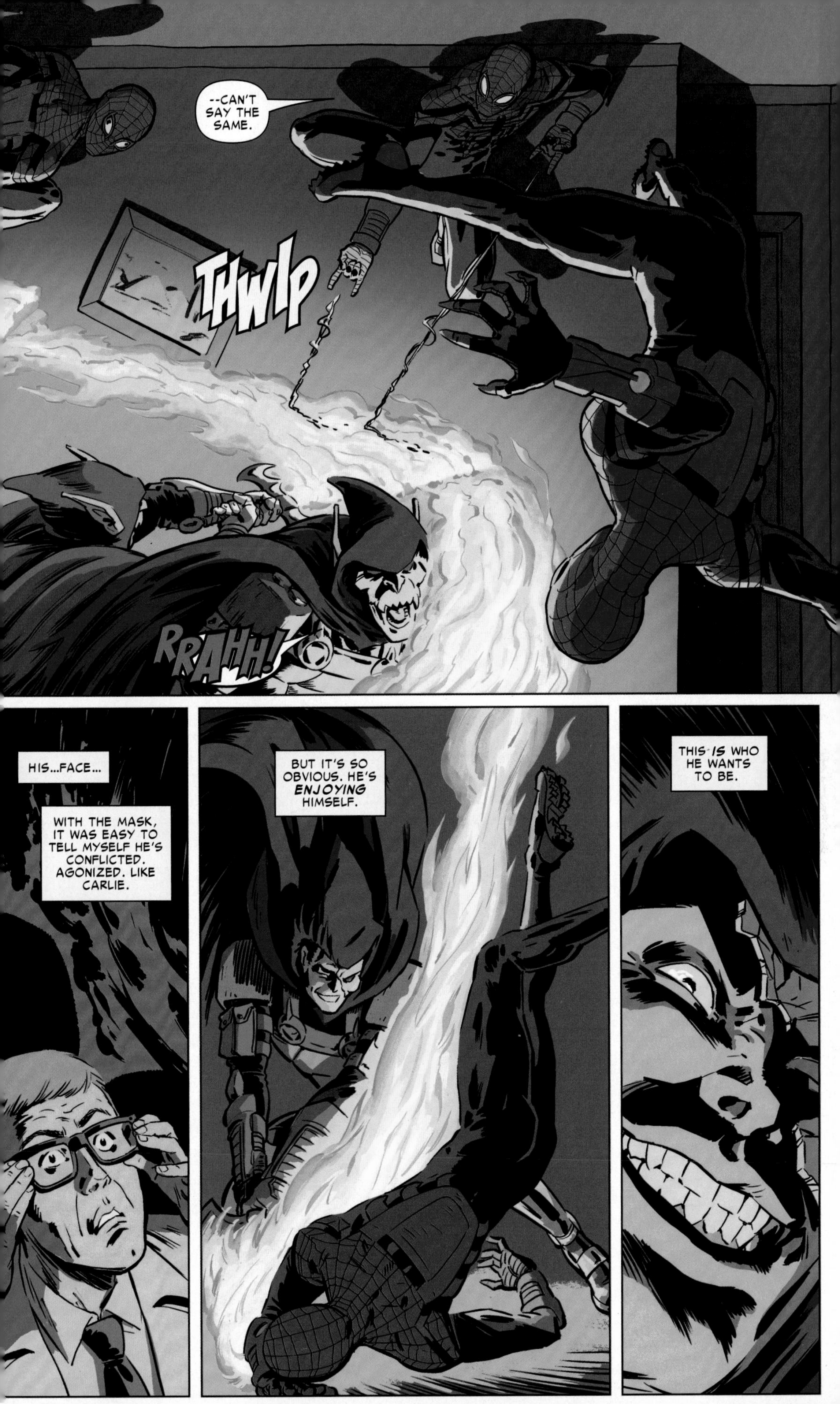

--CAN'T SAY THE SAME.
THWIP
RRAHH!
HIS...FACE...
WITH THE MASK, IT WAS EASY TO TELL MYSELF HE'S CONFLICTED. AGONIZED. LIKE CARLIE.
BUT IT'S SO OBVIOUS. HE'S ENJOYING HIMSELF.
THIS IS WHO HE WANTS TO BE.

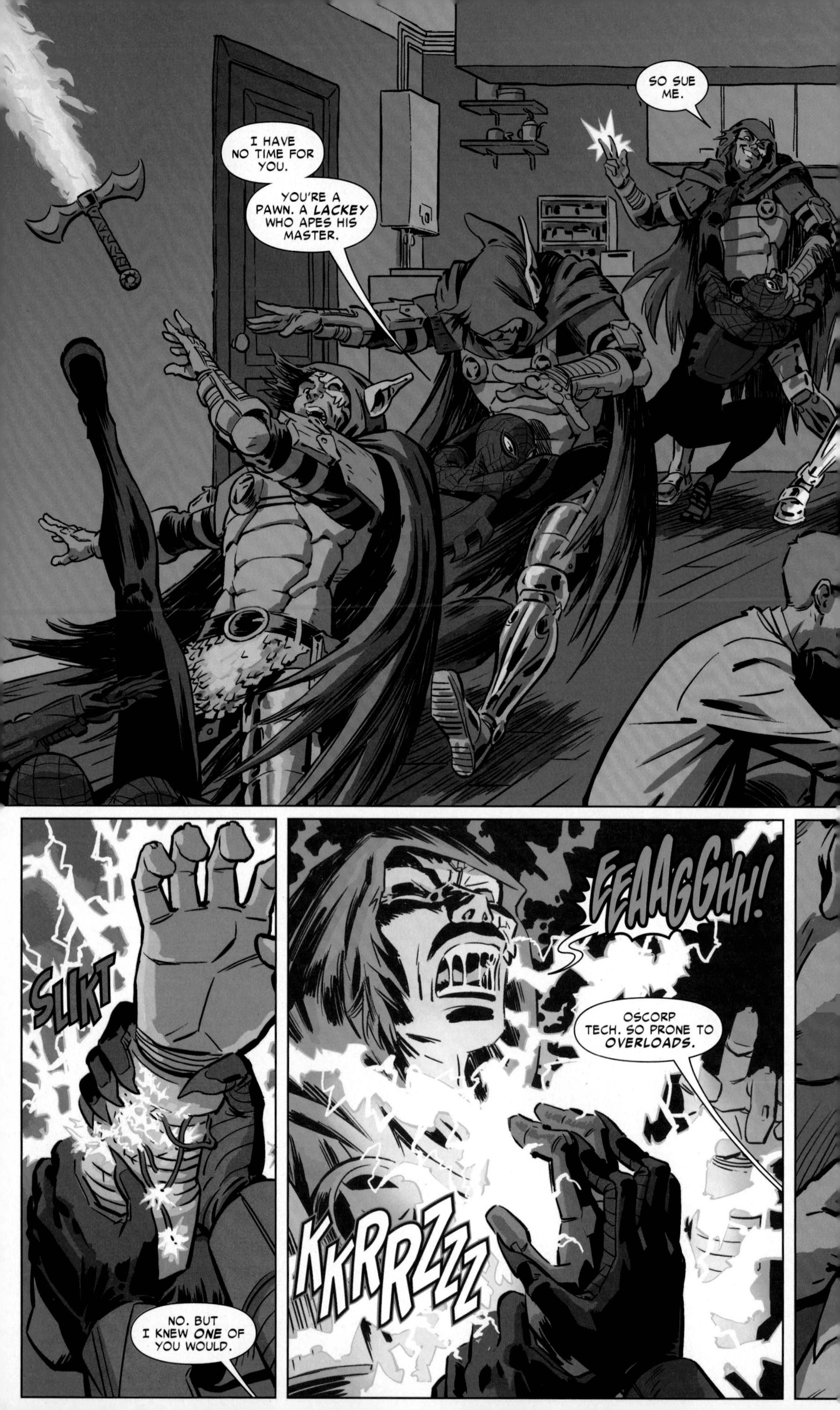

SO SUE ME.
I HAVE NO TIME FOR YOU.
YOU'RE A PAWN. A LACKEY WHO APES HIS MASTER.
SLIKT
NO. BUT I KNEW ONE OF YOU WOULD.
EEAAGGHH!
OSCORP TECH. SO PRONE TO OVERLOADS.
KKRRZZZ

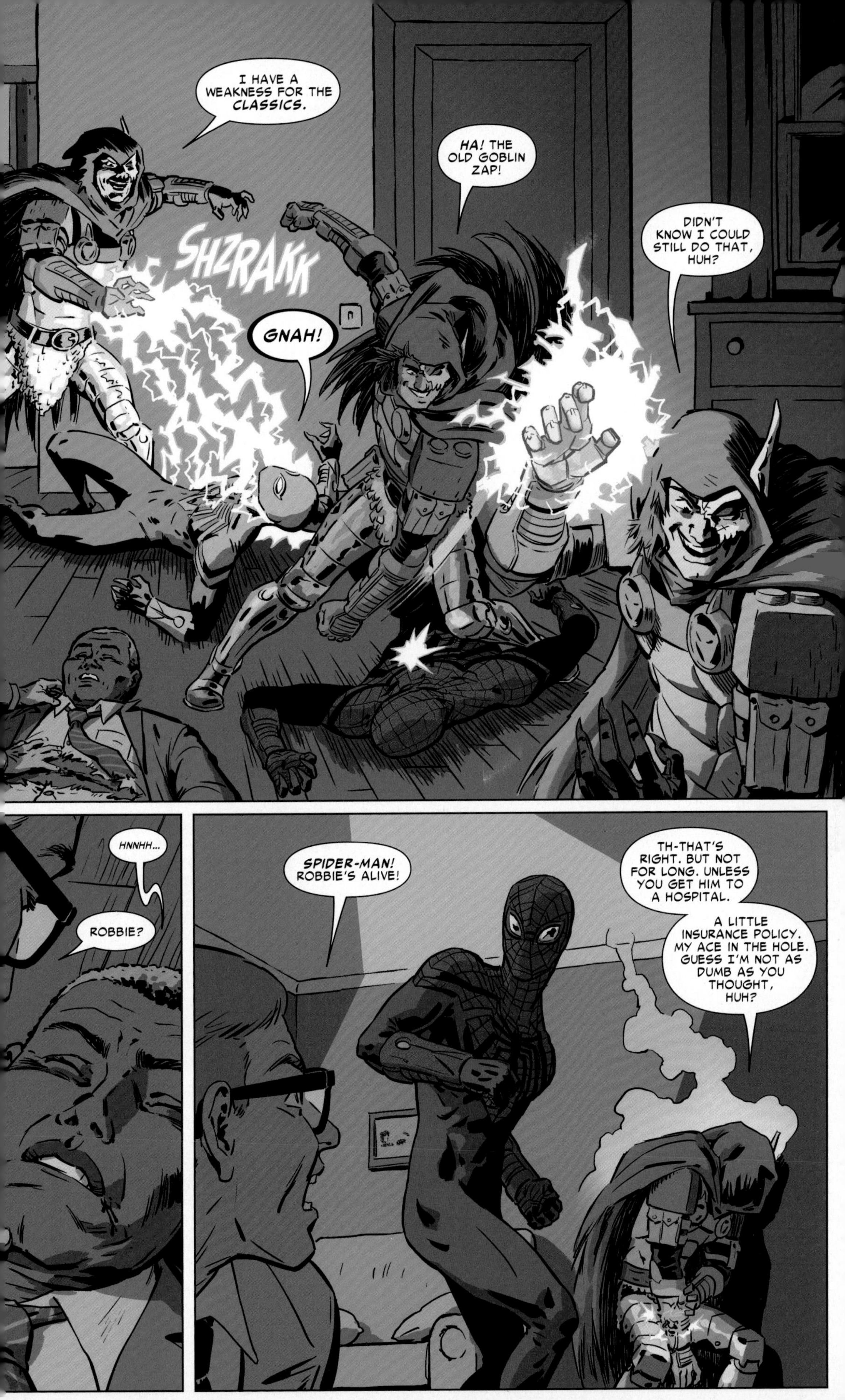
I HAVE A WEAKNESS FOR THE CLASSICS.
SHZRAKK
GNAH!
HA! THE OLD GOBLIN ZAP!
DIDN'T KNOW I COULD STILL DO THAT, HUH?
HNNHH...
ROBBIE?
SPIDER-MAN! ROBBIE'S ALIVE!
TH-THAT'S RIGHT. BUT NOT FOR LONG. UNLESS YOU GET HIM TO A HOSPITAL.
A LITTLE INSURANCE POLICY. MY ACE IN THE HOLE. GUESS I'M NOT AS DUMB AS YOU THOUGHT, HUH?

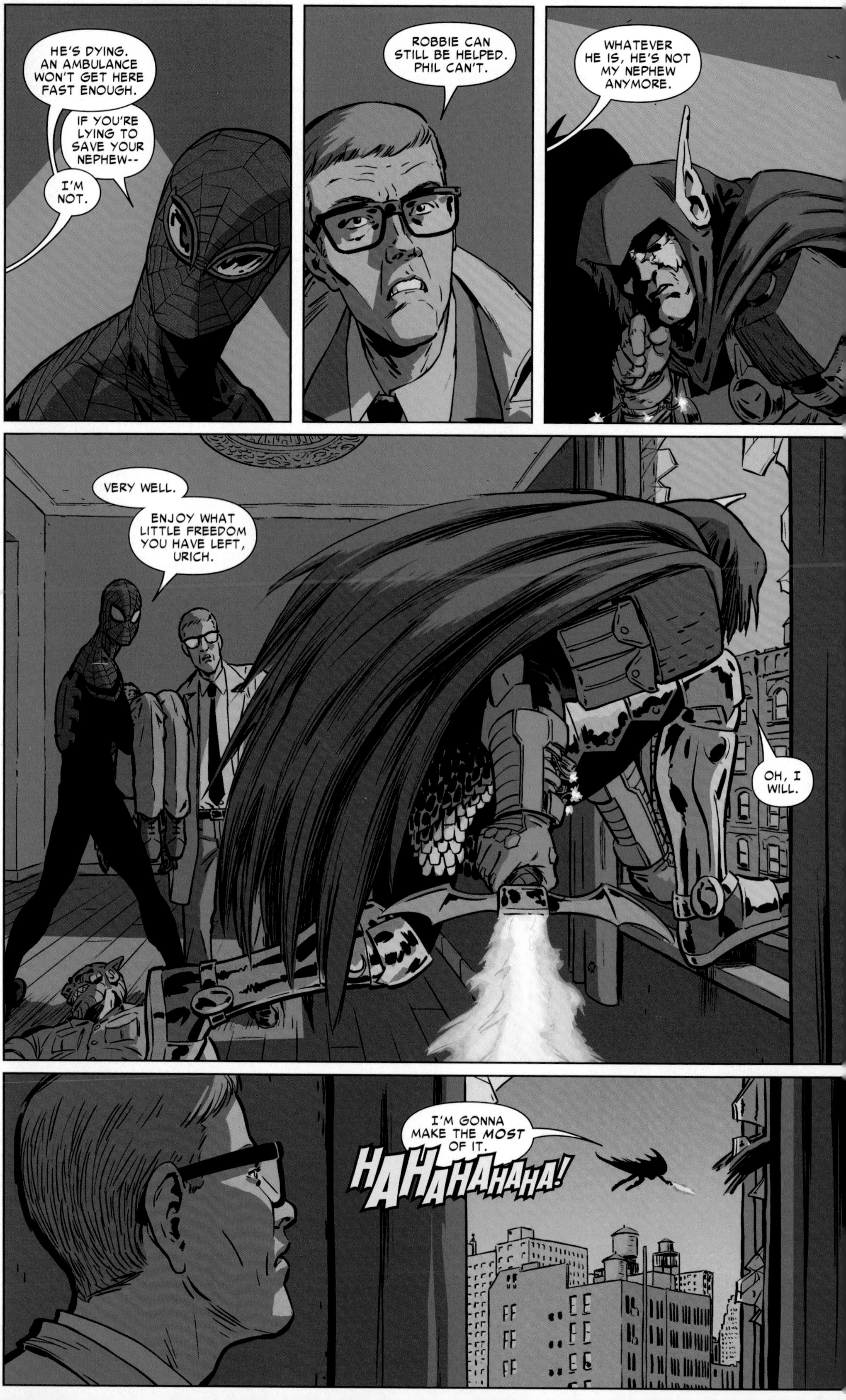
HE'S DYING. AN AMBULANCE WON'T GET HERE FAST ENOUGH.
IF YOU'RE LYING TO SAVE YOUR NEPHEW--
I'M NOT.
ROBBIE CAN STILL BE HELPED. PHIL CAN'T.
WHATEVER HE IS, HE'S NOT MY NEPHEW ANYMORE.
VERY WELL.
ENJOY WHAT LITTLE FREEDOM YOU HAVE LEFT, URICH.
OH, I WILL.
I'M GONNA MAKE THE MOST OF IT.
HAHAHAHAHAHA!

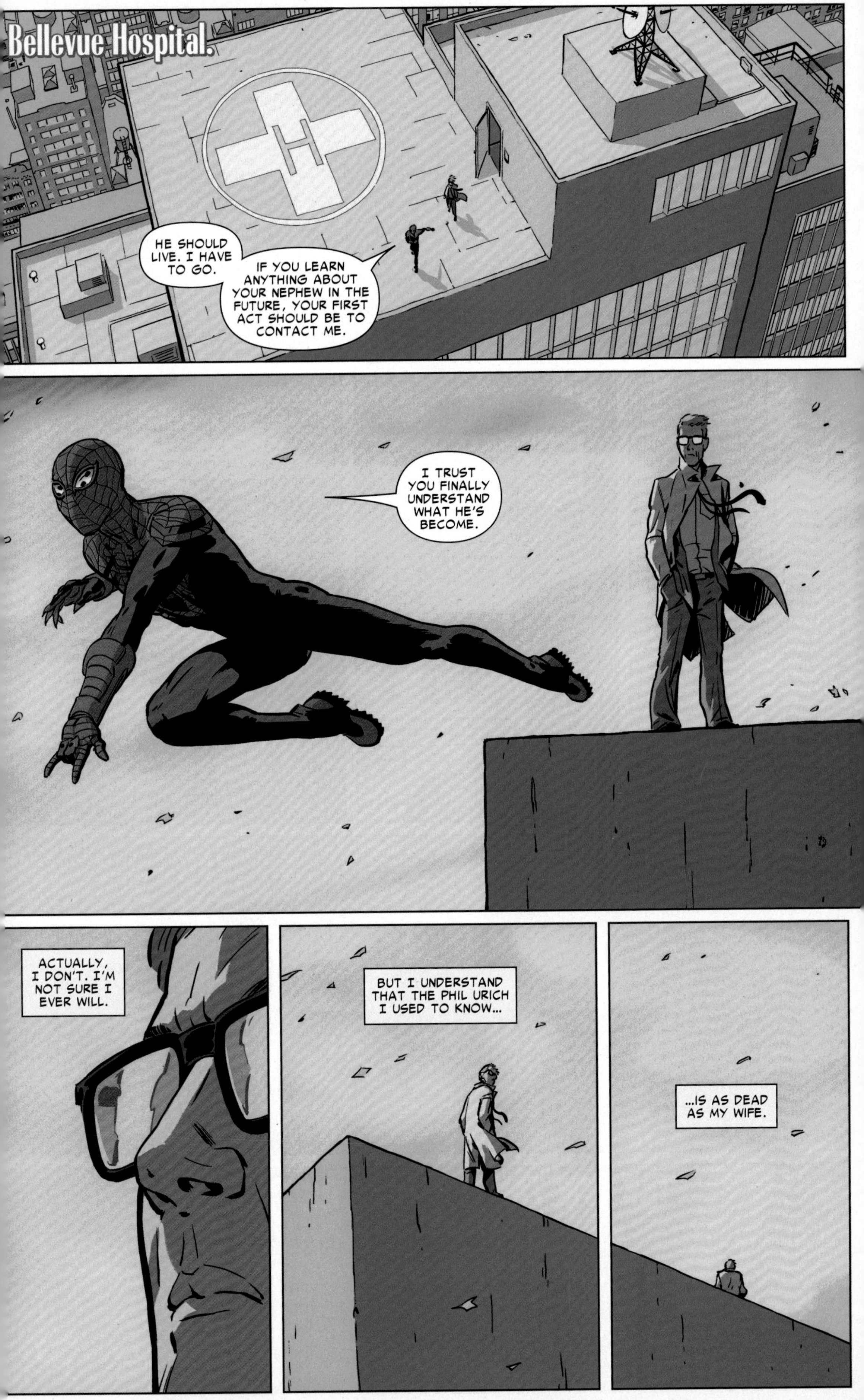
Bellevue Hospital.
HE SHOULD LIVE. I HAVE TO GO.
IF YOU LEARN ANYTHING ABOUT YOUR NEPHEW IN THE FUTURE, YOUR FIRST ACT SHOULD BE TO CONTACT ME.
I TRUST YOU FINALLY UNDERSTAND WHAT HE'S BECOME.
ACTUALLY, I DON'T. I'M NOT SURE I EVER WILL.
BUT I UNDERSTAND THAT THE PHIL URICH I USED TO KNOW...
...IS AS DEAD AS MY WIFE.

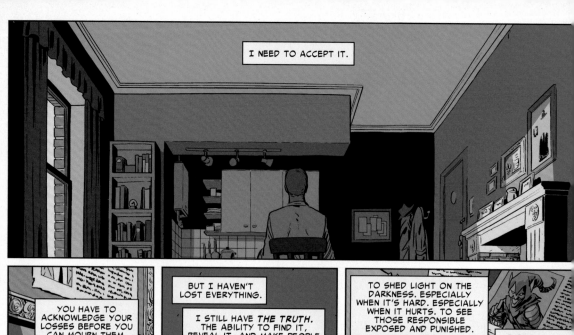

I NEED TO ACCEPT IT.

YOU HAVE TO ACKNOWLEDGE YOUR LOSSES BEFORE YOU CAN MOURN THEM.

BUT I HAVEN'T LOST EVERYTHING.

I STILL HAVE *THE TRUTH*. THE ABILITY TO FIND IT, REVEAL IT, AND MAKE PEOPLE UNDERSTAND IT.

TO SHED LIGHT ON THE DARKNESS. ESPECIALLY WHEN IT'S HARD. ESPECIALLY WHEN IT HURTS. TO SEE THOSE RESPONSIBLE EXPOSED AND PUNISHED.

I OWE IT TO THE MAN PHIL ONCE WAS. AND TO MYSELF.

MY NAME IS BEN URICH.

TAK TAK TAK TAK TAK TAK TAK

AND I'M A REPORTER.

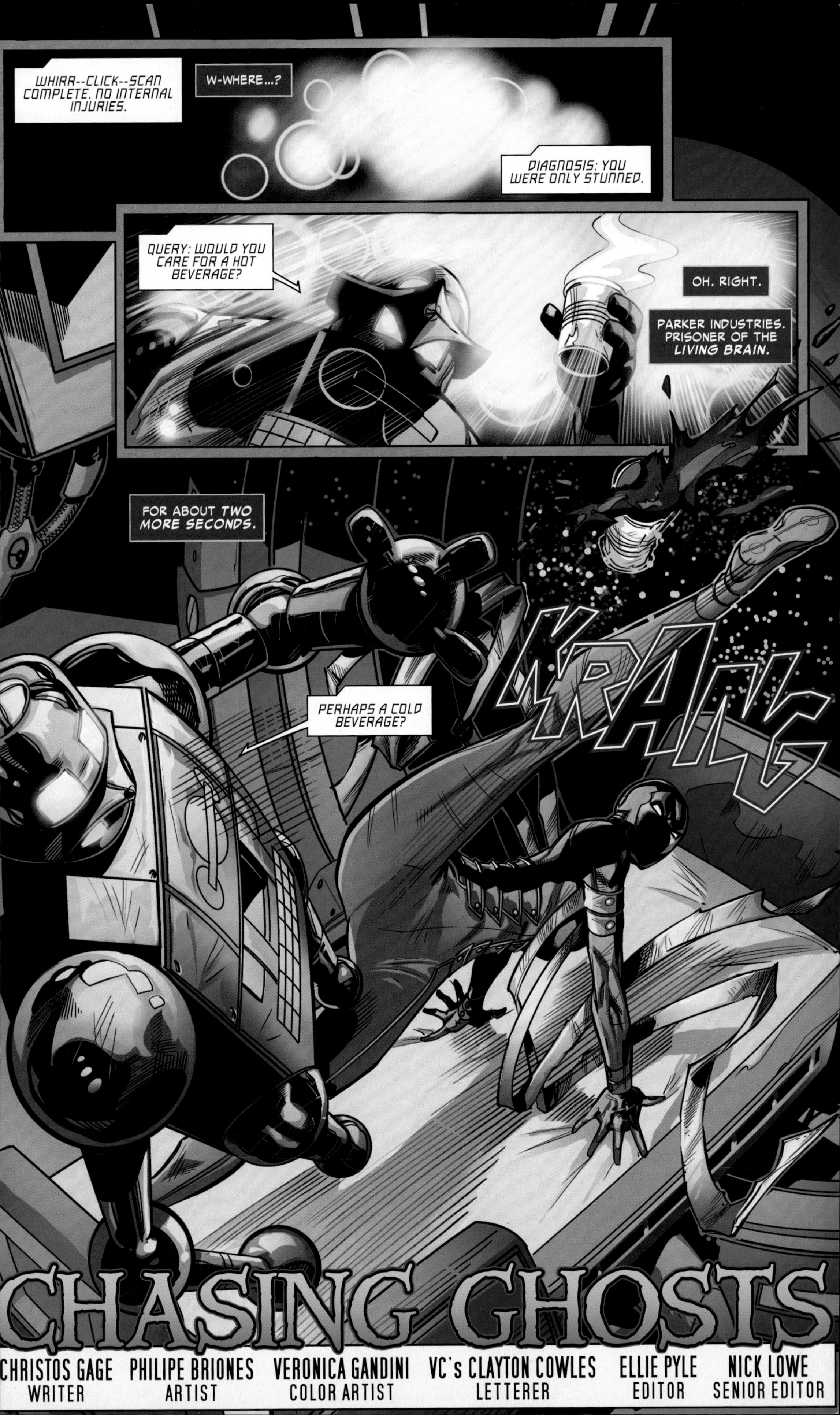
WHIRR--CLICK--SCAN COMPLETE. NO INTERNAL INJURIES.
W-WHERE...?
DIAGNOSIS: YOU WERE ONLY STUNNED.
QUERY: WOULD YOU CARE FOR A HOT BEVERAGE?
OH. RIGHT.
PARKER INDUSTRIES. PRISONER OF THE LIVING BRAIN.
FOR ABOUT TWO MORE SECONDS.
KRANG
PERHAPS A COLD BEVERAGE?
CHASING GHOSTS
CHRISTOS GAGE WRITER
PHILIPE BRIONES ARTIST
VERONICA GANDINI COLOR ARTIST
VC's CLAYTON COWLES LETTERER
ELLIE PYLE EDITOR
NICK LOWE SENIOR EDITOR

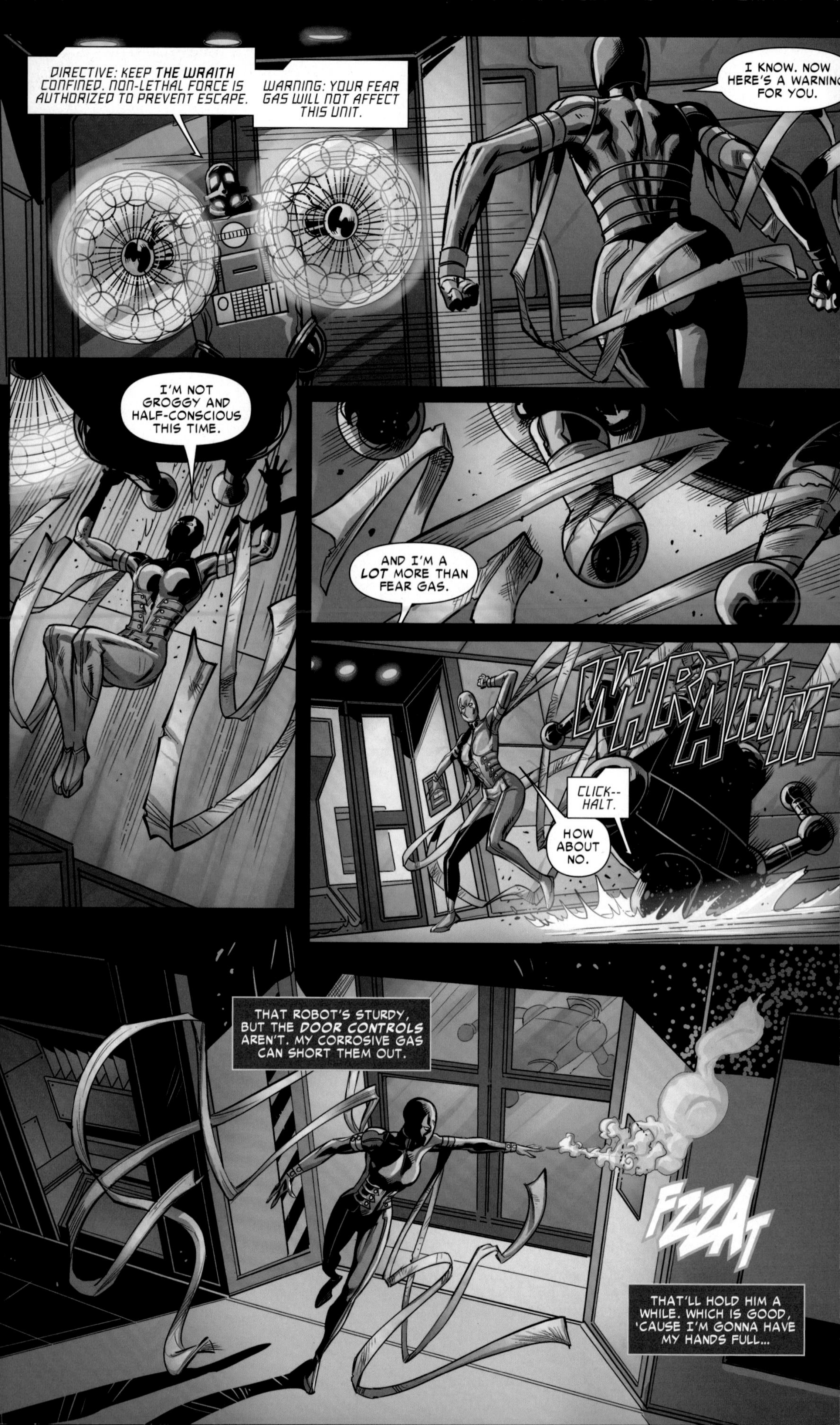
DIRECTIVE: KEEP THE WRAITH CONFINED. NON-LETHAL FORCE IS AUTHORIZED TO PREVENT ESCAPE.
WARNING: YOUR FEAR GAS WILL NOT AFFECT THIS UNIT.
I KNOW. NOW HERE'S A WARNING FOR YOU.
I'M NOT GROGGY AND HALF-CONSCIOUS THIS TIME.
AND I'M A LOT MORE THAN FEAR GAS.
WHRAMM
CLICK-- HALT.
HOW ABOUT NO.
THAT ROBOT'S STURDY, BUT THE DOOR CONTROLS AREN'T. MY CORROSIVE GAS CAN SHORT THEM OUT.
FZZAT
THAT'LL HOLD HIM A WHILE. WHICH IS GOOD, 'CAUSE I'M GONNA HAVE MY HANDS FULL...

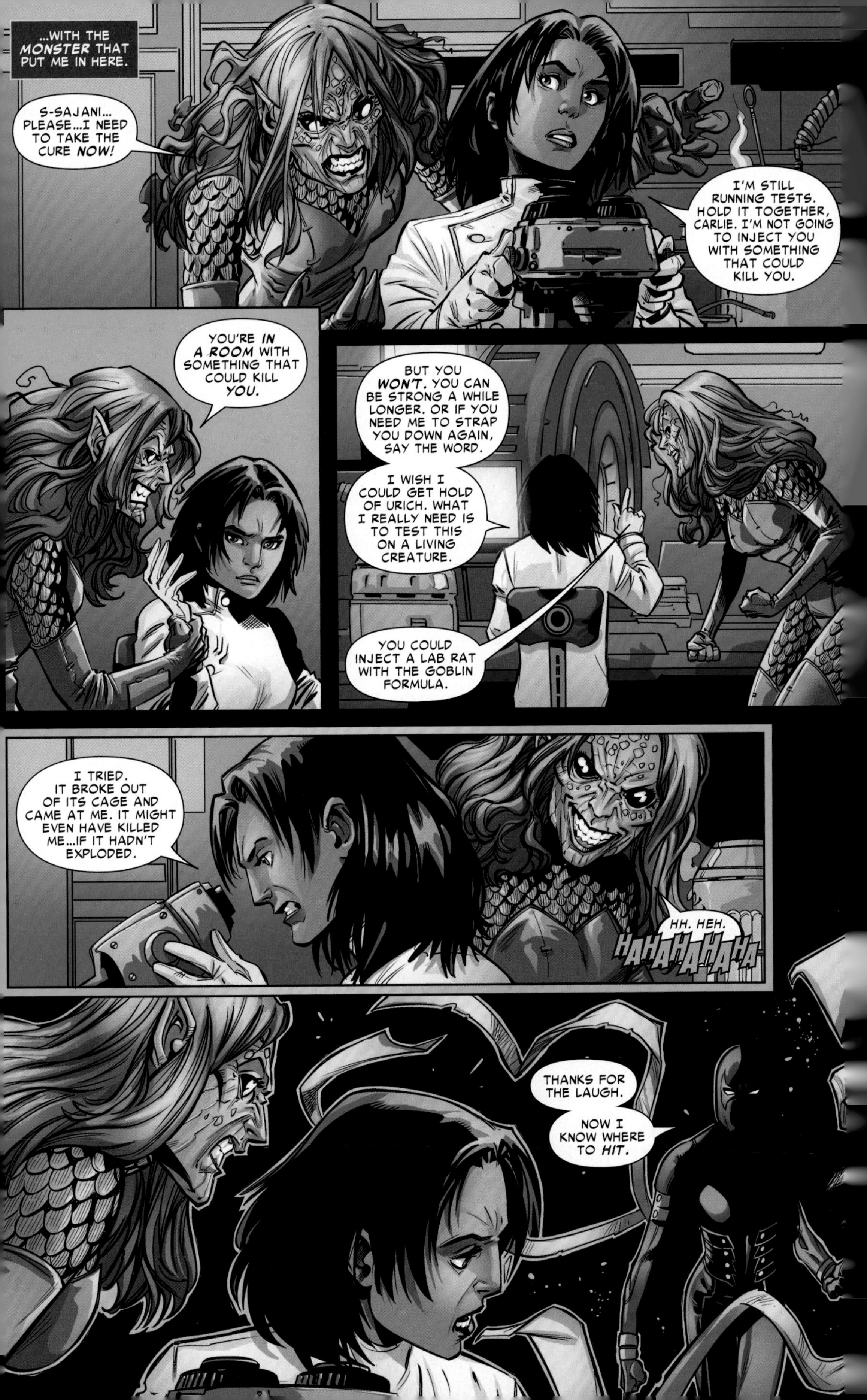
...WITH THE MONSTER THAT PUT ME IN HERE.
S-SAJANI... PLEASE...I NEED TO TAKE THE CURE NOW!
I'M STILL RUNNING TESTS. HOLD IT TOGETHER, CARLIE. I'M NOT GOING TO INJECT YOU WITH SOMETHING THAT COULD KILL YOU.
YOU'RE IN A ROOM WITH SOMETHING THAT COULD KILL YOU.
BUT YOU WON'T. YOU CAN BE STRONG A WHILE LONGER. OR IF YOU NEED ME TO STRAP YOU DOWN AGAIN, SAY THE WORD.
I WISH I COULD GET HOLD OF URICH. WHAT I REALLY NEED IS TO TEST THIS ON A LIVING CREATURE.
YOU COULD INJECT A LAB RAT WITH THE GOBLIN FORMULA.
I TRIED. IT BROKE OUT OF ITS CAGE AND CAME AT ME. IT MIGHT EVEN HAVE KILLED ME...IF IT HADN'T EXPLODED.
HH. HEH.
HAHAHAHAHA
THANKS FOR THE LAUGH.
NOW I KNOW WHERE TO HIT.

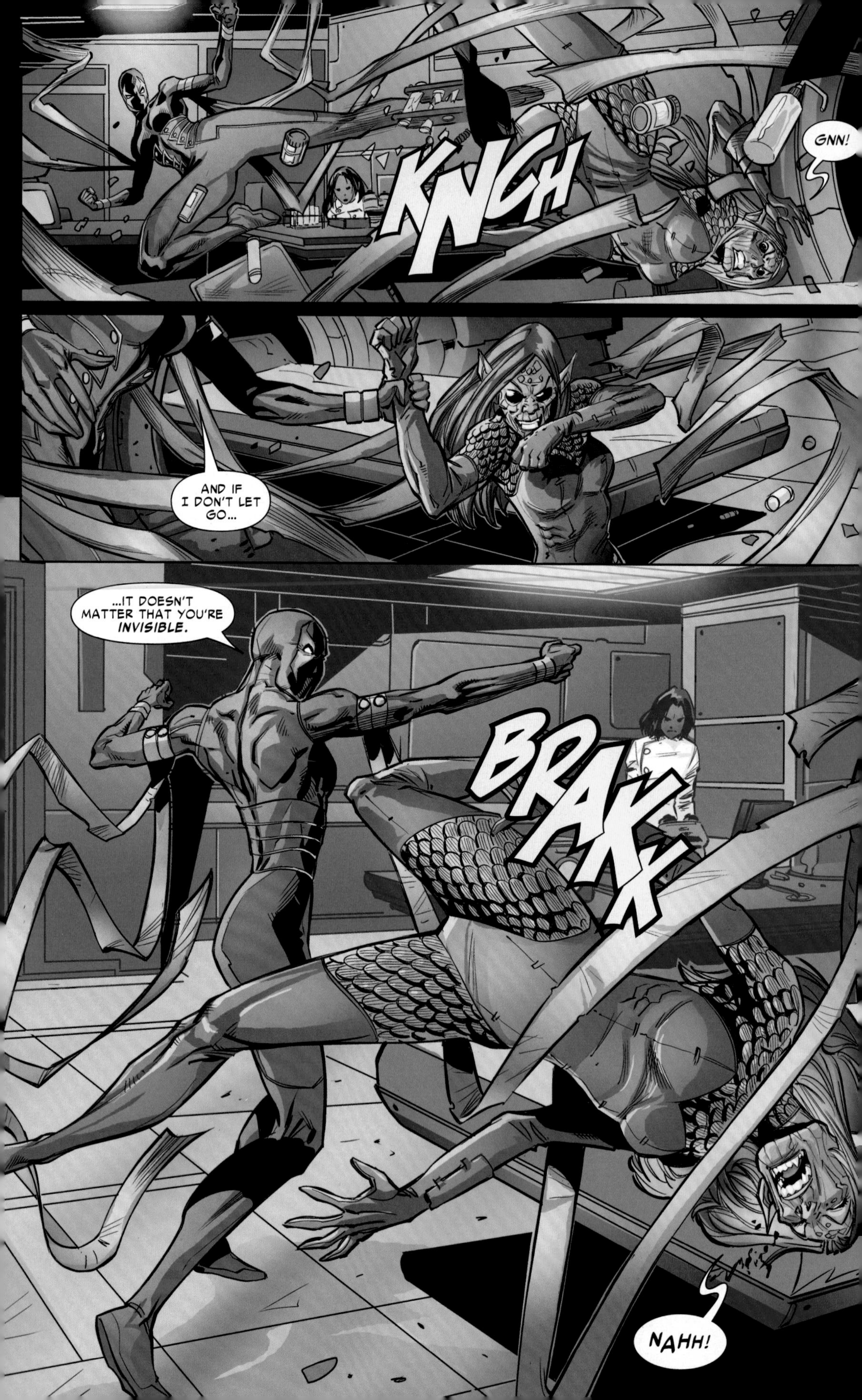
KNCH
GNN!
AND IF I DON'T LET GO...
...IT DOESN'T MATTER THAT YOU'RE *INVISIBLE.*
BRAKK
NAHH!

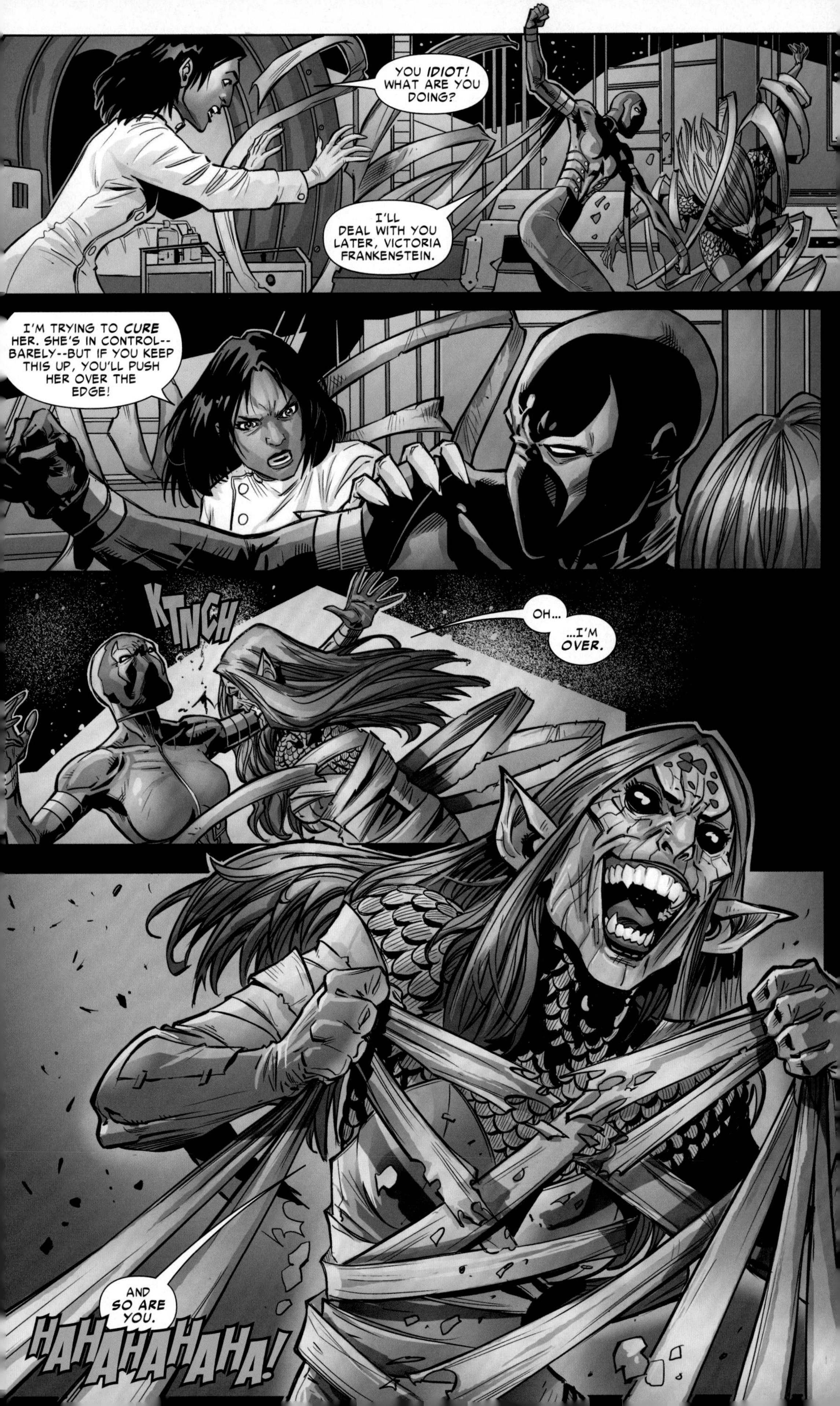
YOU IDIOT! WHAT ARE YOU DOING?
I'LL DEAL WITH YOU LATER, VICTORIA FRANKENSTEIN.
I'M TRYING TO CURE HER. SHE'S IN CONTROL-- BARELY--BUT IF YOU KEEP THIS UP, YOU'LL PUSH HER OVER THE EDGE!
KTNCH
OH...
...I'M OVER.
AND SO ARE YOU.
HAHAHAHAHA!

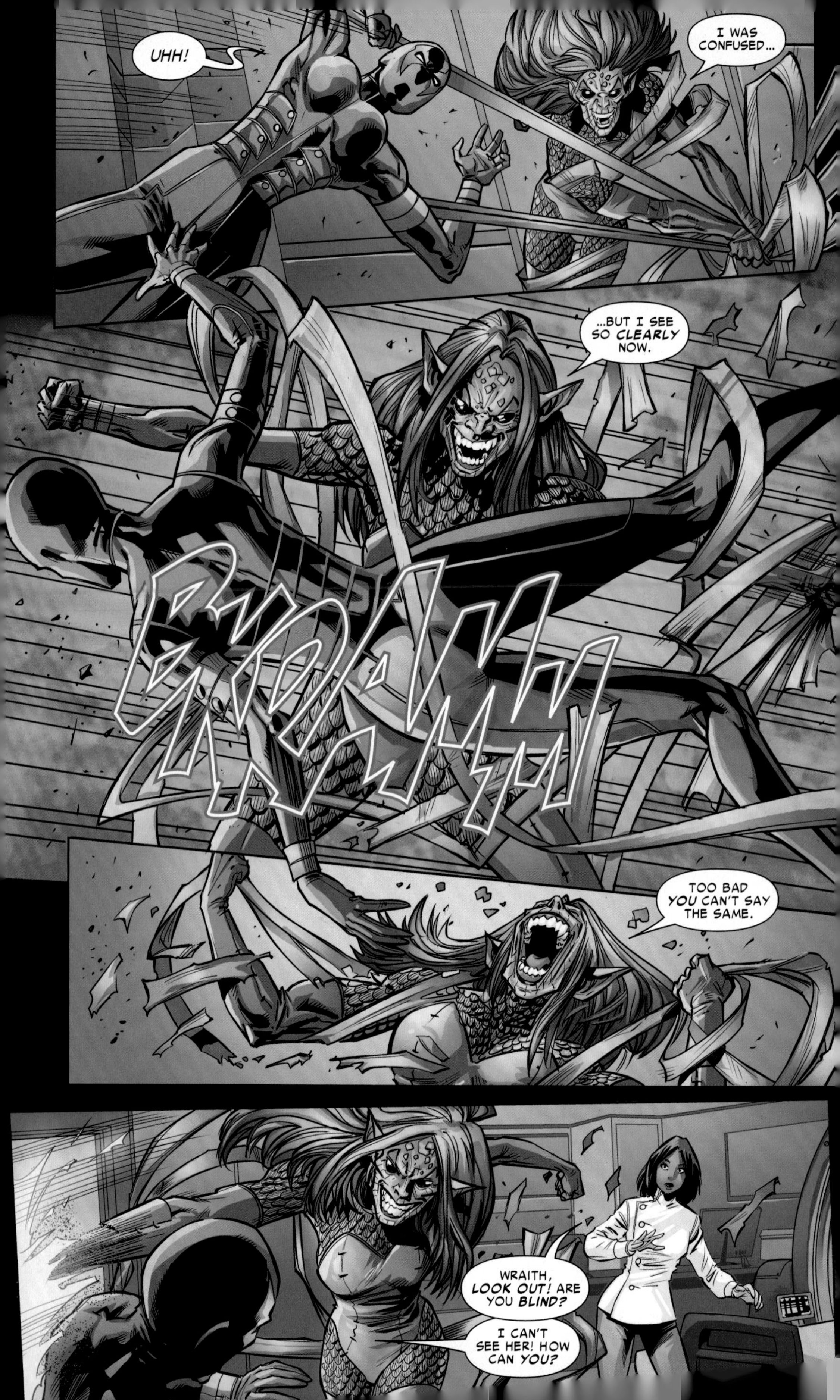
UHH!
I WAS CONFUSED...
...BUT I SEE SO CLEARLY NOW.
TOO BAD YOU CAN'T SAY THE SAME.
WRAITH, LOOK OUT! ARE YOU BLIND?
I CAN'T SEE HER! HOW CAN YOU?

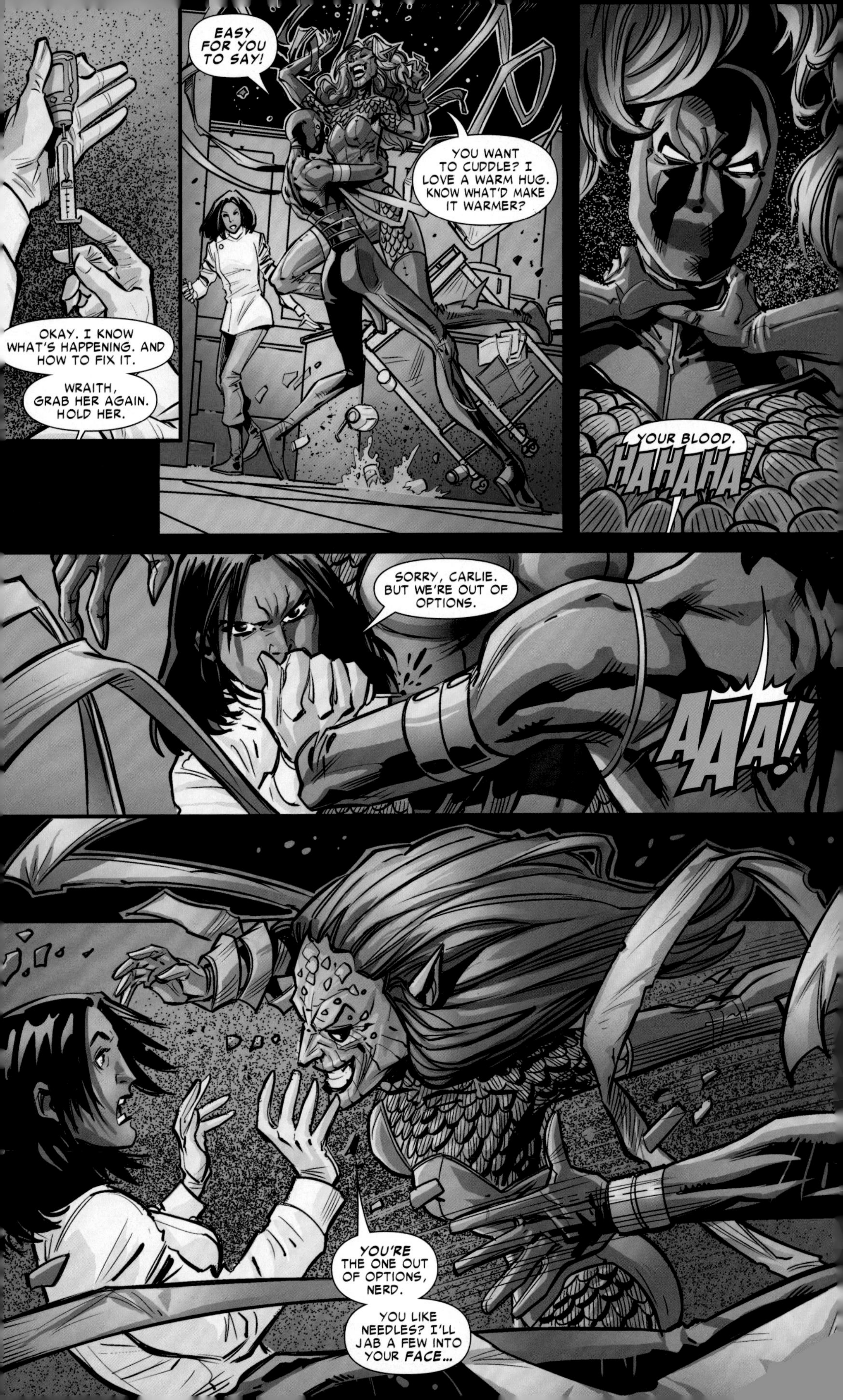

OKAY. I KNOW WHAT'S HAPPENING. AND HOW TO FIX IT.
WRAITH, GRAB HER AGAIN. HOLD HER.
EASY FOR YOU TO SAY!
YOU WANT TO CUDDLE? I LOVE A WARM HUG. KNOW WHAT'D MAKE IT WARMER?
YOUR BLOOD.
HAHAHA!
SORRY, CARLIE. BUT WE'RE OUT OF OPTIONS.
AAA!
YOU'RE THE ONE OUT OF OPTIONS, NERD.
YOU LIKE NEEDLES? I'LL JAB A FEW INTO YOUR FACE...

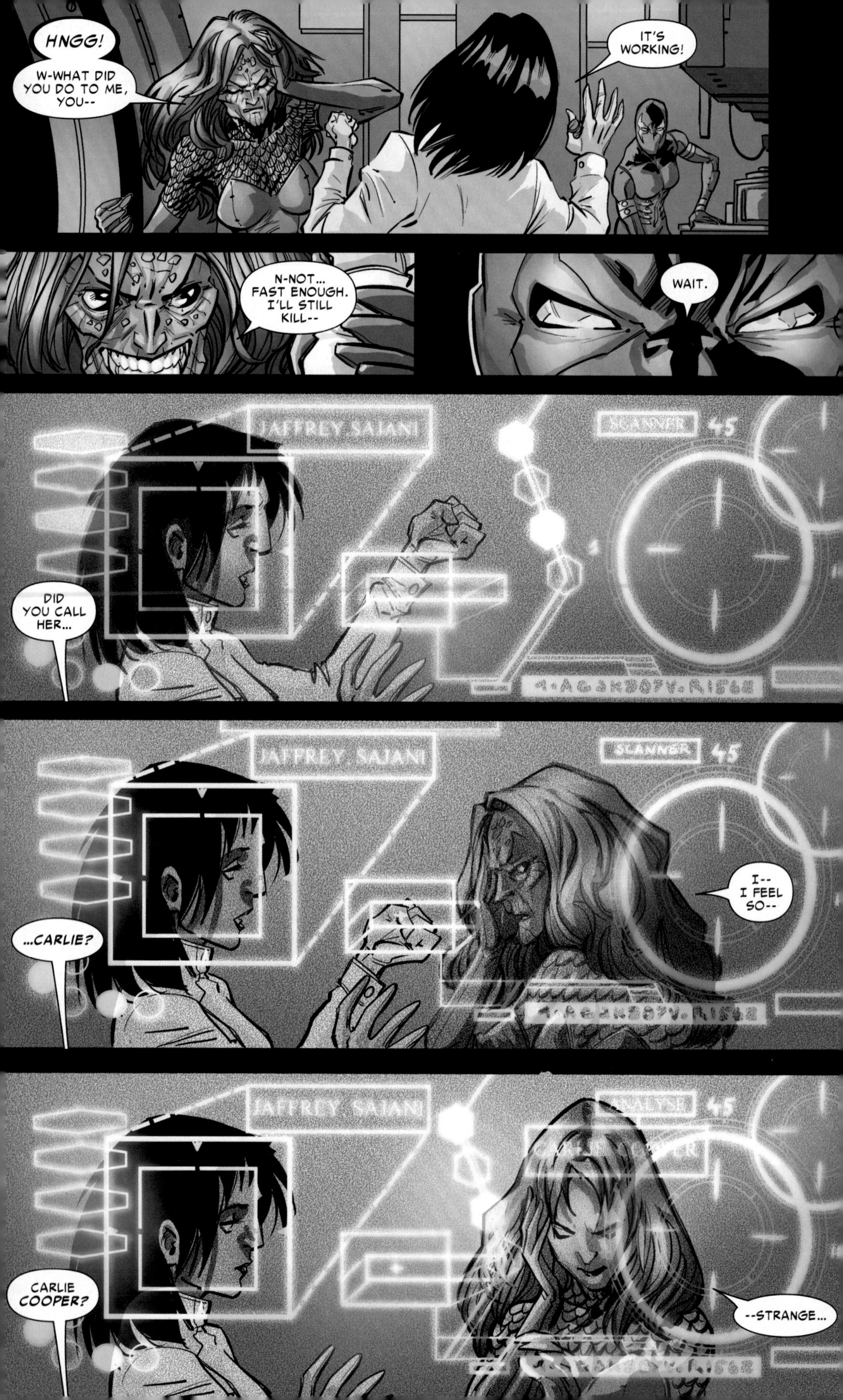
HNGG!
W-WHAT DID YOU DO TO ME, YOU--
IT'S WORKING!
N-NOT... FAST ENOUGH. I'LL STILL KILL--
WAIT.
JAFFREY SAJANI
SCANNER
45
DID YOU CALL HER...
JAFFREY SAJANI
SCANNER
45
...CARLIE?
I-- I FEEL SO--
JAFFREY SAJANI
ANALYSE
45
CARLIE COOPER?
--STRANGE...

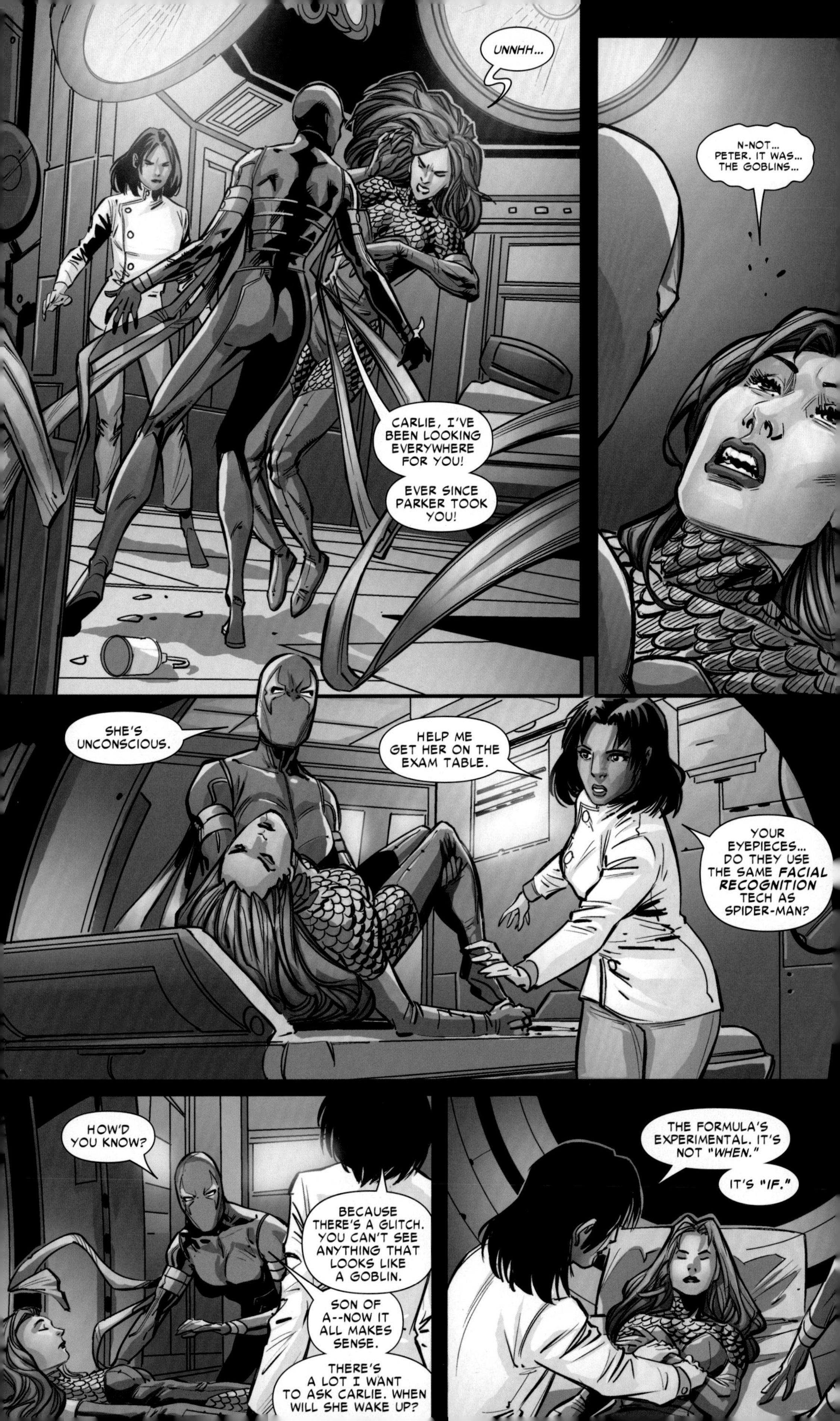
UNNHH...
N-NOT... PETER. IT WAS... THE GOBLINS...
CARLIE, I'VE BEEN LOOKING EVERYWHERE FOR YOU!
EVER SINCE PARKER TOOK YOU!
SHE'S UNCONSCIOUS.
HELP ME GET HER ON THE EXAM TABLE.
YOUR EYEPIECES... DO THEY USE THE SAME *FACIAL RECOGNITION* TECH AS SPIDER-MAN?
HOW'D YOU KNOW?
BECAUSE THERE'S A GLITCH. YOU CAN'T SEE ANYTHING THAT LOOKS LIKE A GOBLIN.
SON OF A--NOW IT ALL MAKES SENSE.
THERE'S A LOT I WANT TO ASK CARLIE. WHEN WILL SHE WAKE UP?
THE FORMULA'S EXPERIMENTAL. IT'S NOT "*WHEN.*"
IT'S "*IF.*"

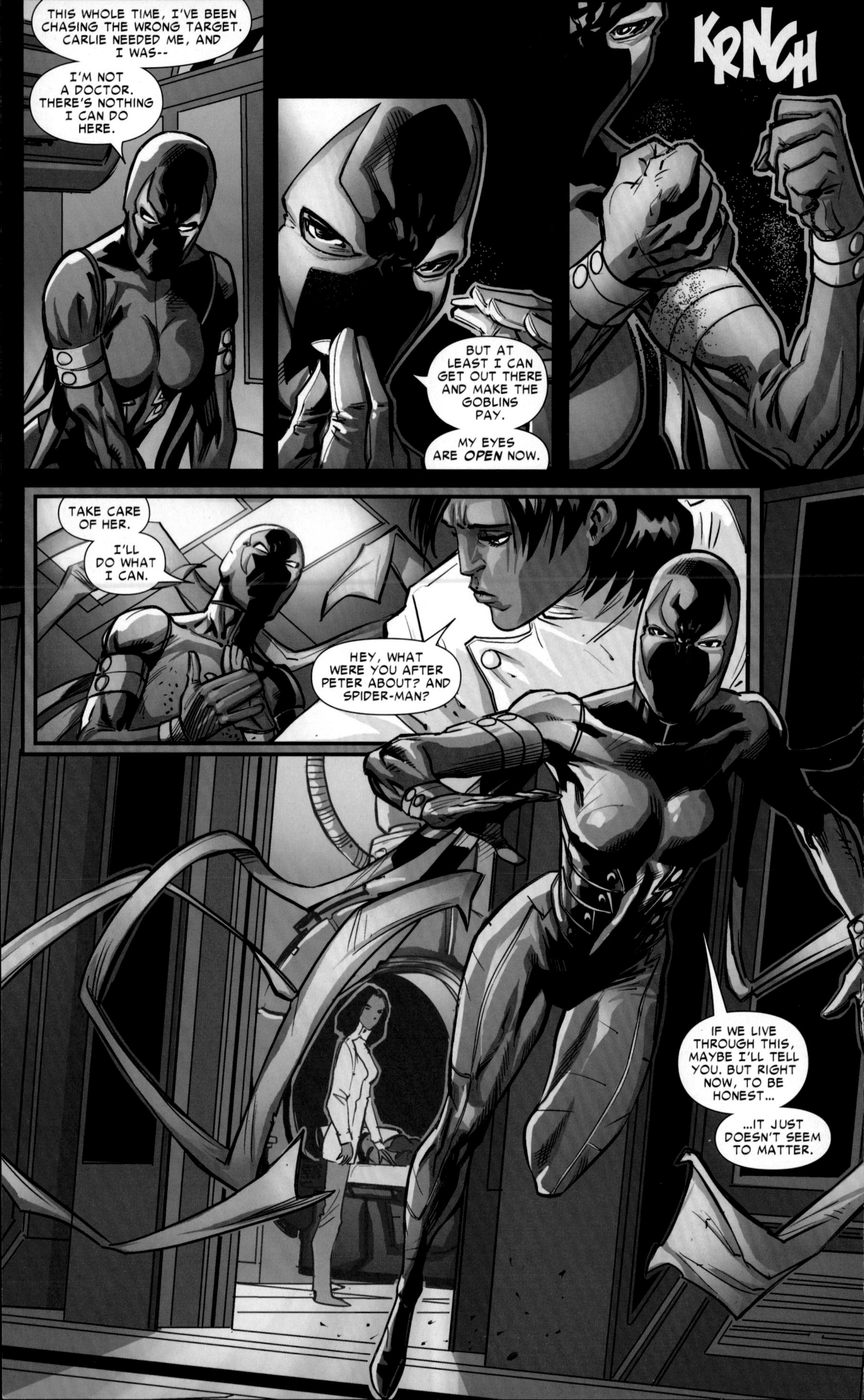
THIS WHOLE TIME, I'VE BEEN CHASING THE WRONG TARGET. CARLIE NEEDED ME, AND I WAS--
I'M NOT A DOCTOR. THERE'S NOTHING I CAN DO HERE.
BUT AT LEAST I CAN GET OUT THERE AND MAKE THE GOBLINS PAY.
MY EYES ARE *OPEN* NOW.
KRNCH
TAKE CARE OF HER.
I'LL DO WHAT I CAN.
HEY, WHAT WERE YOU AFTER PETER ABOUT? AND SPIDER-MAN?
IF WE LIVE THROUGH THIS, MAYBE I'LL TELL YOU. BUT RIGHT NOW, TO BE HONEST...
...IT JUST DOESN'T SEEM TO MATTER.

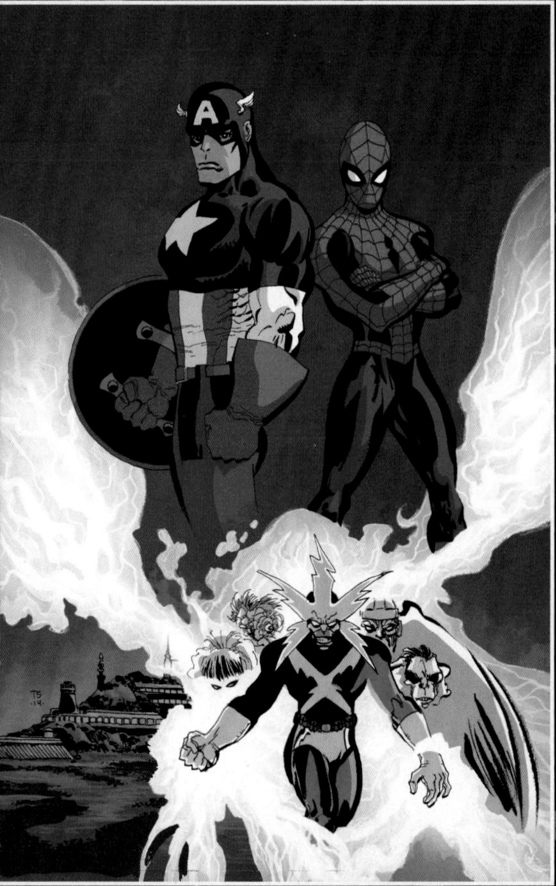

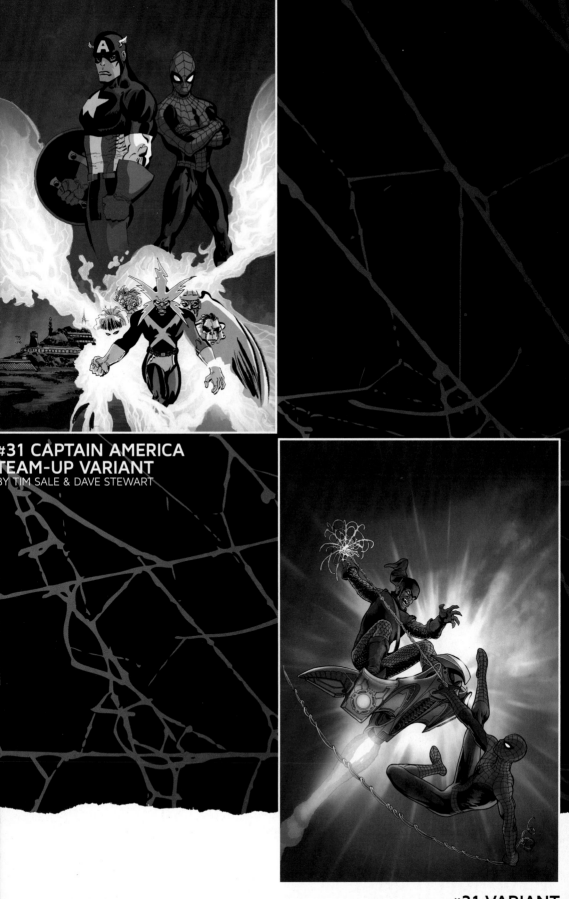

#31 CAPTAIN AMERICA
TEAM-UP VARIANT
BY TIM SALE & DAVE STEWART

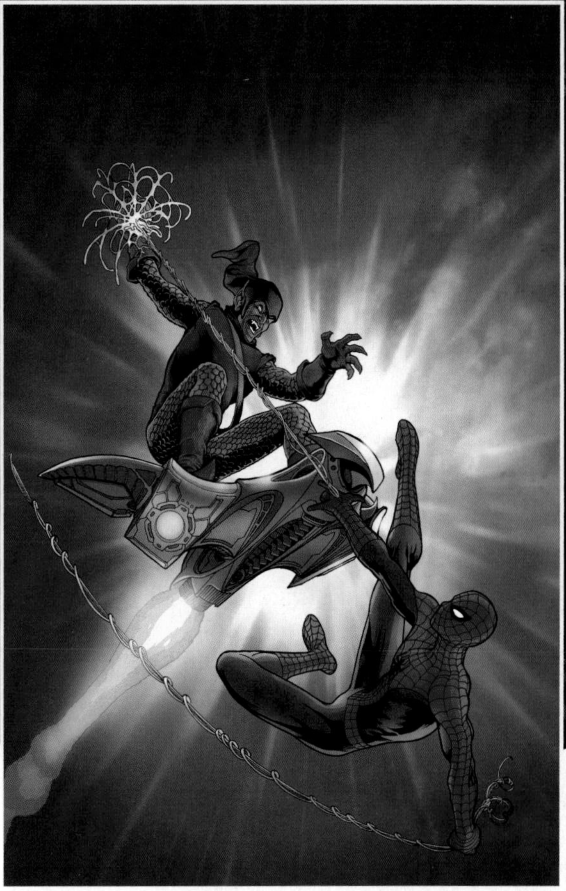

#31 VARIANT
BY KEVIN MAGUIRE & JAMES CAMPBELL

30

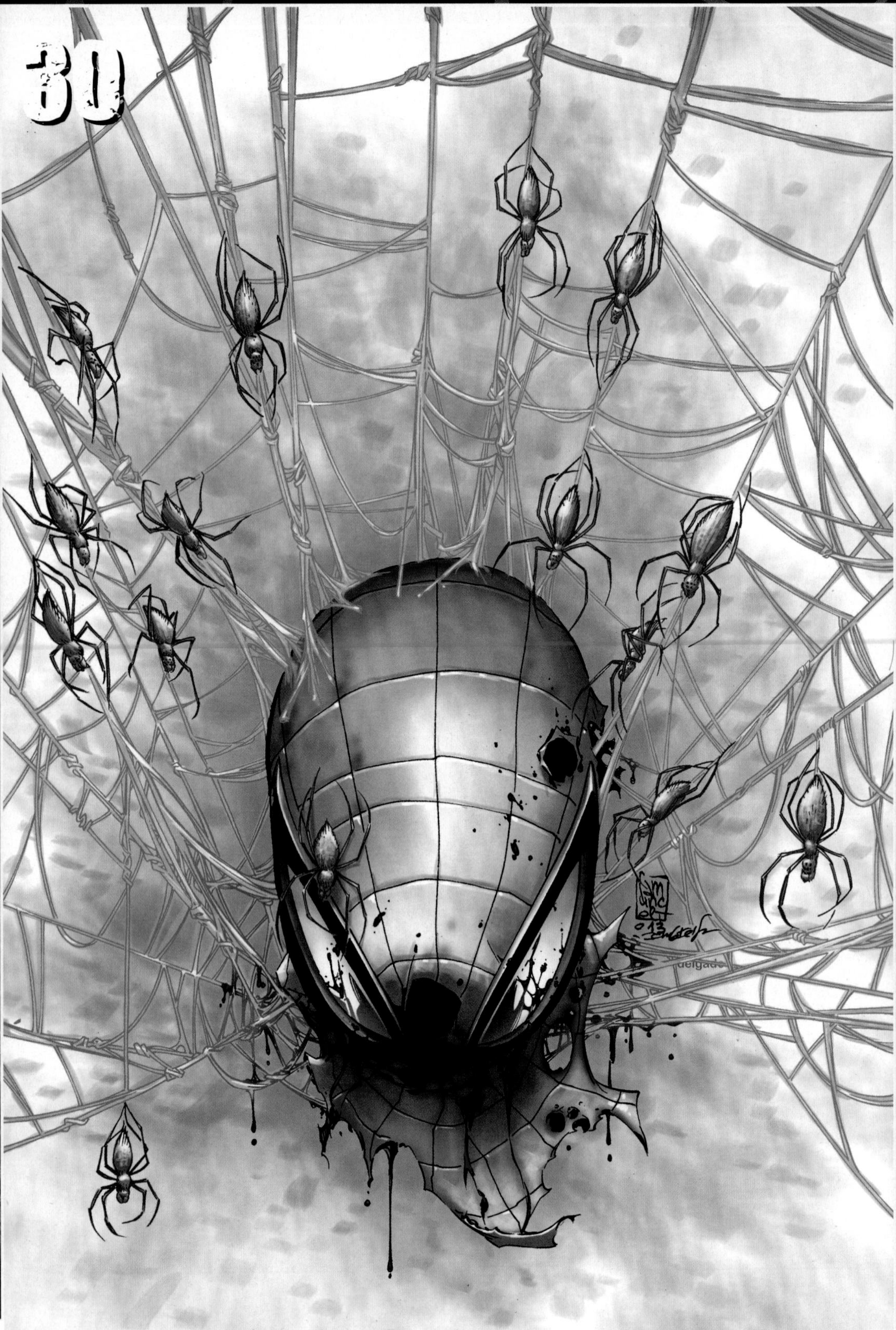

A TROUBLED SOUL

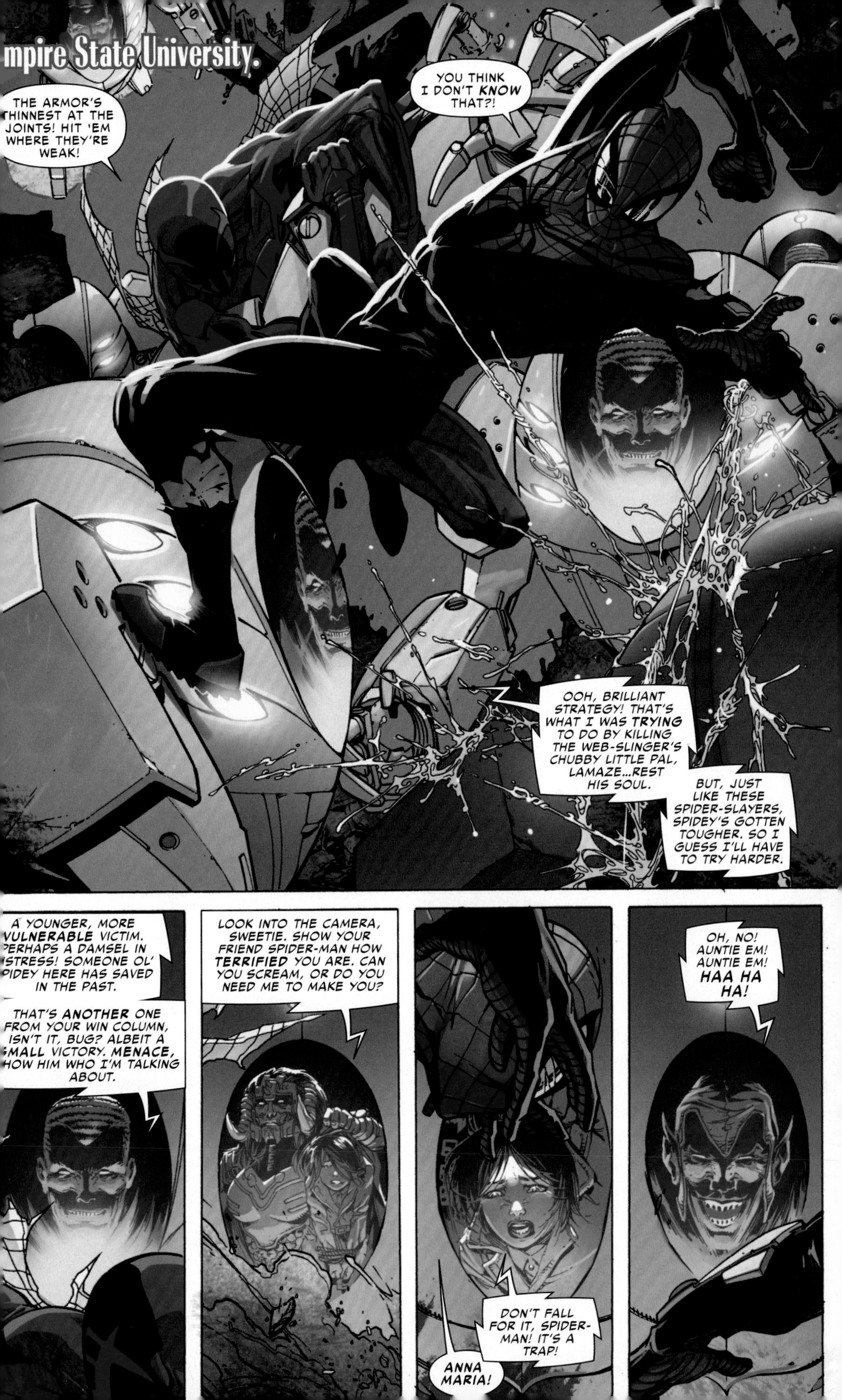

mpire State University.
THE ARMOR'S THINNEST AT THE JOINTS! HIT 'EM WHERE THEY'RE WEAK!
YOU THINK I DON'T KNOW THAT?!
OOH, BRILLIANT STRATEGY! THAT'S WHAT I WAS TRYING TO DO BY KILLING THE WEB-SLINGER'S CHUBBY LITTLE PAL, LAMAZE...REST HIS SOUL.
BUT, JUST LIKE THESE SPIDER-SLAYERS, SPIDEY'S GOTTEN TOUGHER. SO I GUESS I'LL HAVE TO TRY HARDER.
A YOUNGER, MORE VULNERABLE VICTIM. PERHAPS A DAMSEL IN DISTRESS! SOMEONE OL' SPIDEY HERE HAS SAVED IN THE PAST.
THAT'S ANOTHER ONE FROM YOUR WIN COLUMN, ISN'T IT, BUG? ALBEIT A SMALL VICTORY. MENACE, SHOW HIM WHO I'M TALKING ABOUT.
LOOK INTO THE CAMERA, SWEETIE. SHOW YOUR FRIEND SPIDER-MAN HOW TERRIFIED YOU ARE. CAN YOU SCREAM, OR DO YOU NEED ME TO MAKE YOU?
DON'T FALL FOR IT, SPIDER-MAN! IT'S A TRAP!
ANNA MARIA!
OH, NO! AUNTIE EM! AUNTIE EM! HAA HA HA!

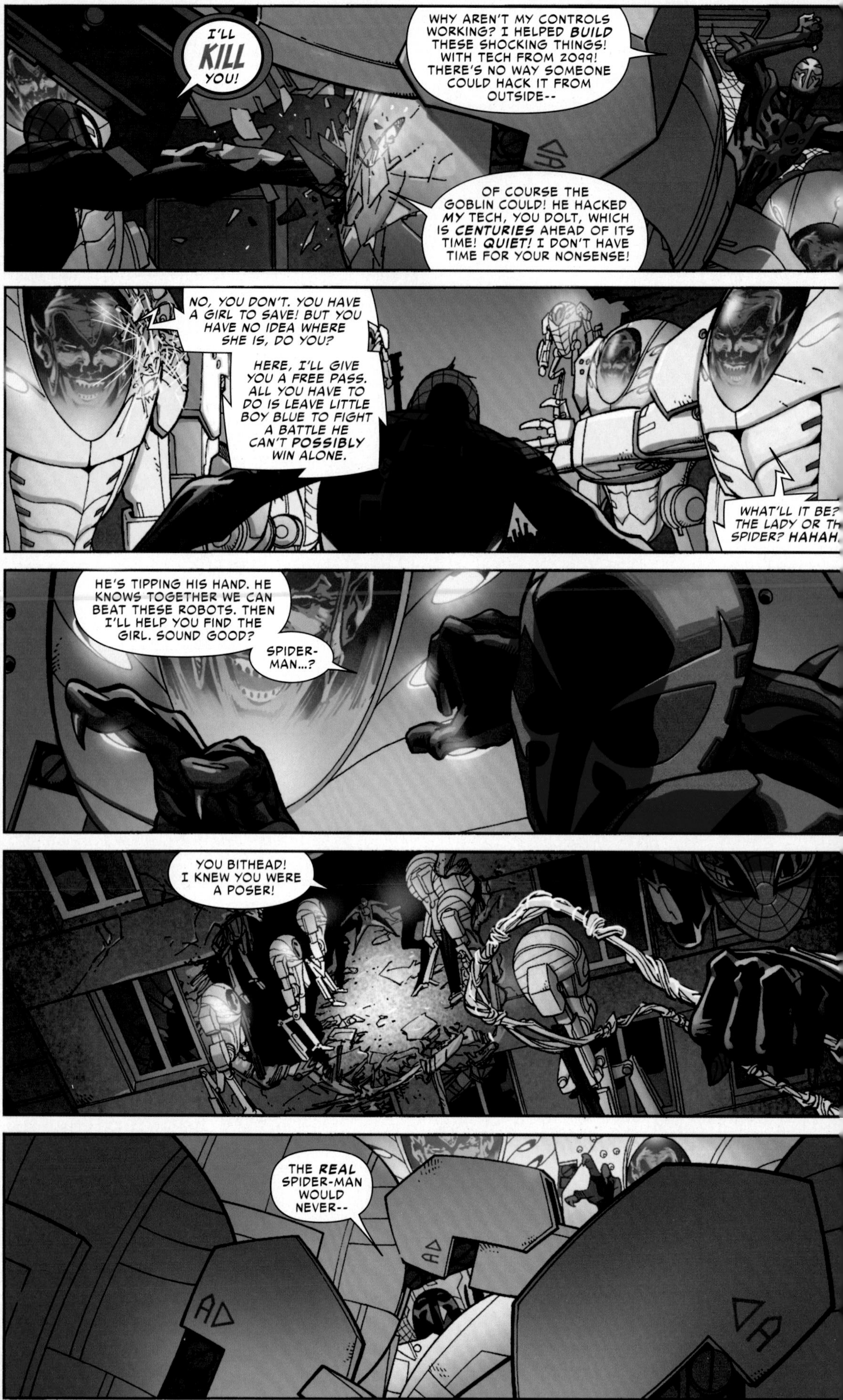
I'LL KILL YOU!
WHY AREN'T MY CONTROLS WORKING? I HELPED BUILD THESE SHOCKING THINGS! WITH TECH FROM 2099! THERE'S NO WAY SOMEONE COULD HACK IT FROM OUTSIDE--
OF COURSE THE GOBLIN COULD! HE HACKED MY TECH, YOU DOLT, WHICH IS CENTURIES AHEAD OF ITS TIME! QUIET! I DON'T HAVE TIME FOR YOUR NONSENSE!
NO, YOU DON'T. YOU HAVE A GIRL TO SAVE! BUT YOU HAVE NO IDEA WHERE SHE IS, DO YOU?
HERE, I'LL GIVE YOU A FREE PASS. ALL YOU HAVE TO DO IS LEAVE LITTLE BOY BLUE TO FIGHT A BATTLE HE CAN'T POSSIBLY WIN ALONE.
WHAT'LL IT BE? THE LADY OR TH SPIDER? HAHAH
HE'S TIPPING HIS HAND. HE KNOWS TOGETHER WE CAN BEAT THESE ROBOTS. THEN I'LL HELP YOU FIND THE GIRL. SOUND GOOD?
SPIDER-MAN...?
YOU BITHEAD! I KNEW YOU WERE A POSER!
THE REAL SPIDER-MAN WOULD NEVER--

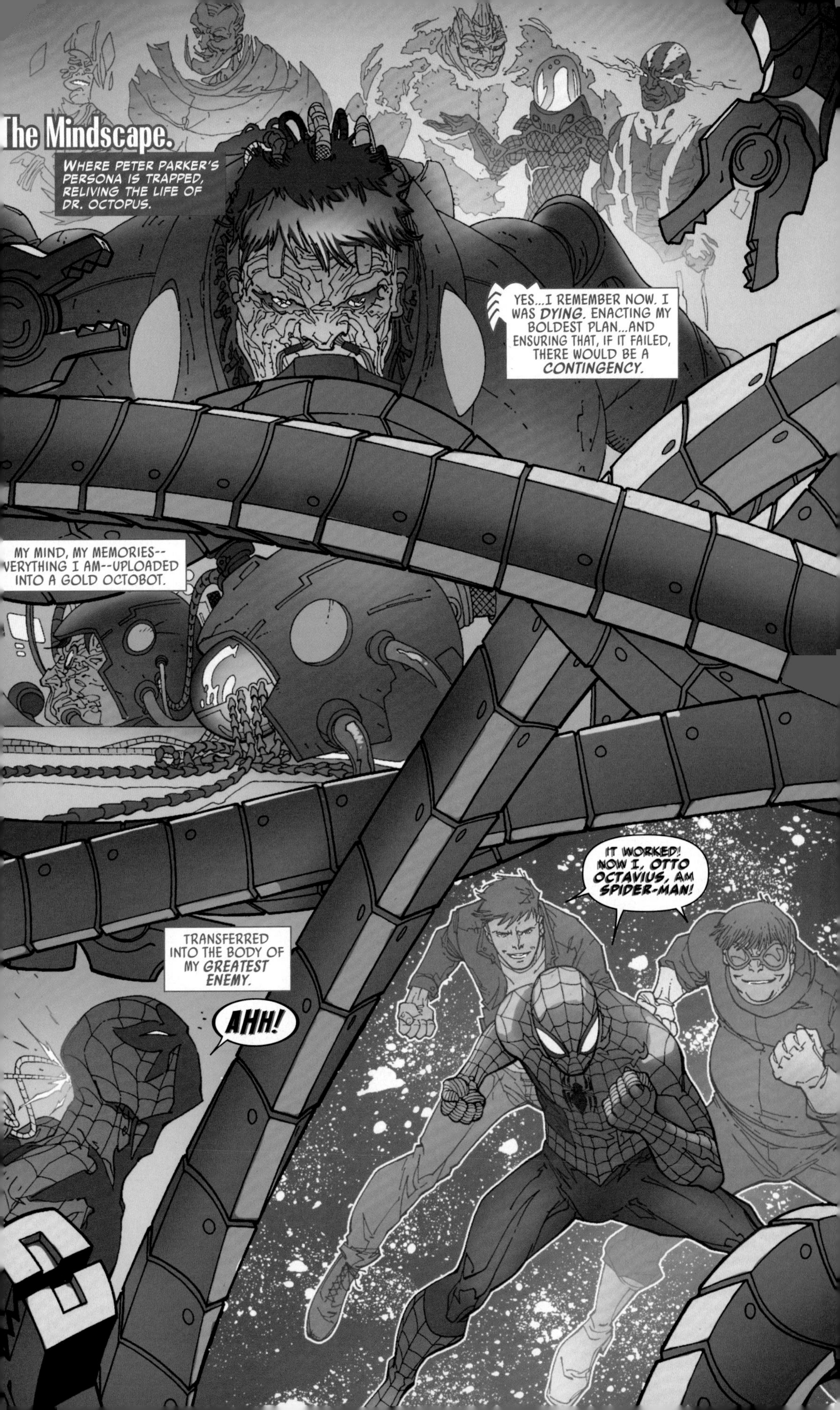
The Mindscape.
WHERE PETER PARKER'S PERSONA IS TRAPPED, RELIVING THE LIFE OF DR. OCTOPUS.
YES...I REMEMBER NOW. I WAS DYING. ENACTING MY BOLDEST PLAN...AND ENSURING THAT, IF IT FAILED, THERE WOULD BE A CONTINGENCY.
MY MIND, MY MEMORIES--EVERYTHING I AM--UPLOADED INTO A GOLD OCTOBOT.
TRANSFERRED INTO THE BODY OF MY GREATEST ENEMY.
AHH!
IT WORKED! NOW I, OTTO OCTAVIUS, AM SPIDER-MAN!

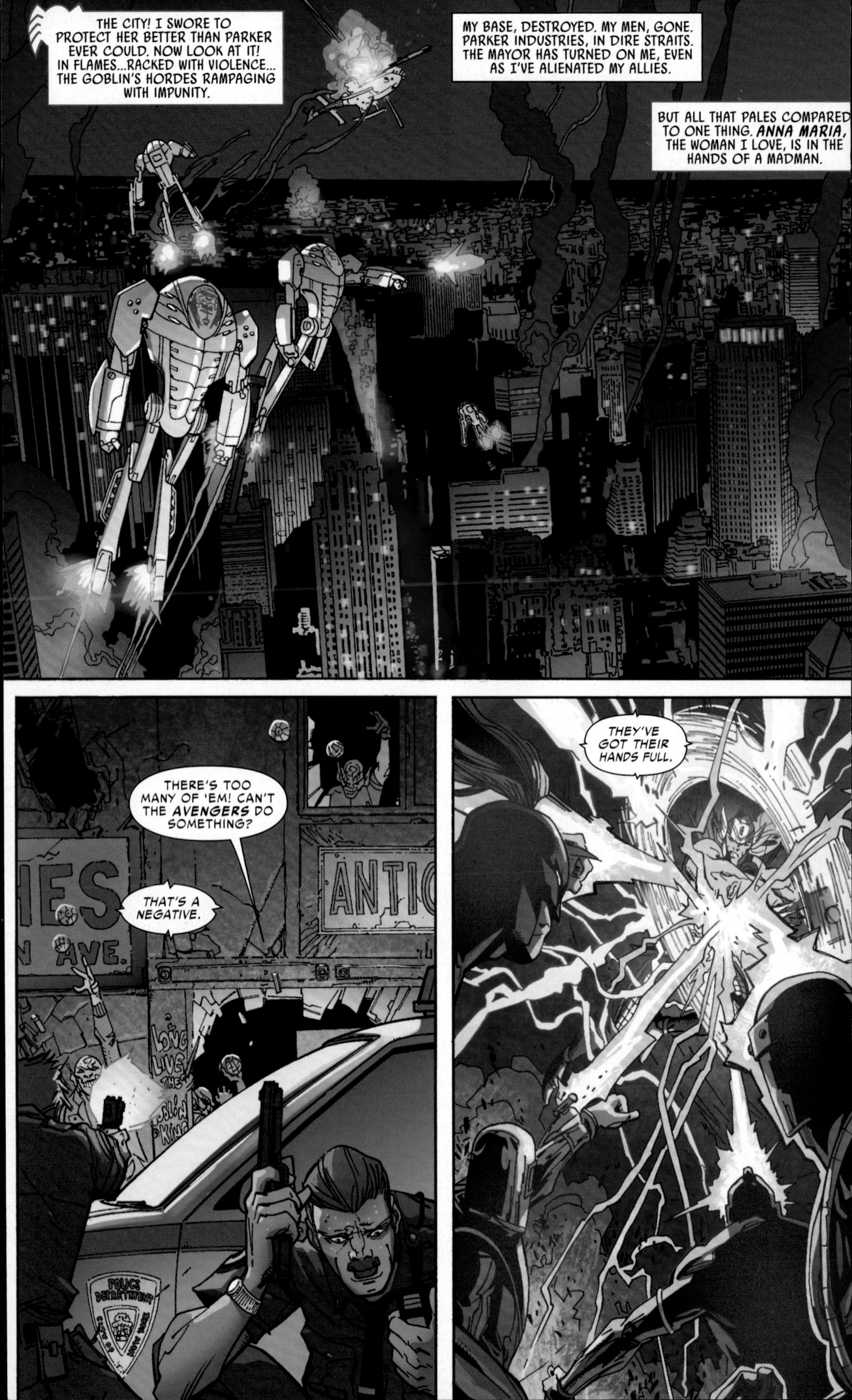
THE CITY! I SWORE TO PROTECT HER BETTER THAN PARKER EVER COULD. NOW LOOK AT IT! IN FLAMES...RACKED WITH VIOLENCE... THE GOBLIN'S HORDES RAMPAGING WITH IMPUNITY.
MY BASE, DESTROYED. MY MEN, GONE. PARKER INDUSTRIES, IN DIRE STRAITS. THE MAYOR HAS TURNED ON ME, EVEN AS I'VE ALIENATED MY ALLIES.
BUT ALL THAT PALES COMPARED TO ONE THING. ANNA MARIA, THE WOMAN I LOVE, IS IN THE HANDS OF A MADMAN.
HES
AVE.
ANTIC
THERE'S TOO MANY OF 'EM! CAN'T THE AVENGERS DO SOMETHING?
THAT'S A NEGATIVE.
THEY'VE GOT THEIR HANDS FULL.

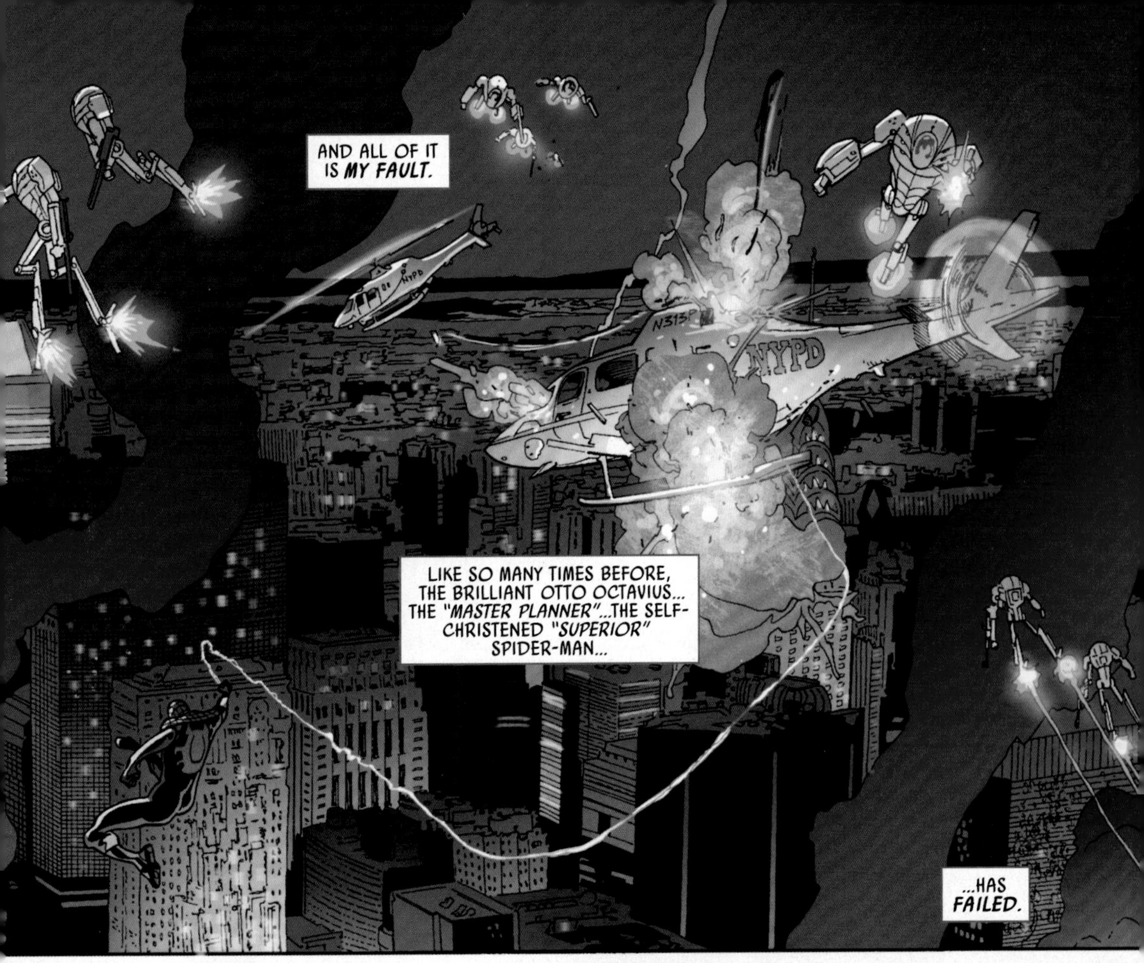
AND ALL OF IT IS MY FAULT.
LIKE SO MANY TIMES BEFORE, THE BRILLIANT OTTO OCTAVIUS... THE "MASTER PLANNER"...THE SELF-CHRISTENED "SUPERIOR" SPIDER-MAN...
...HAS FAILED.

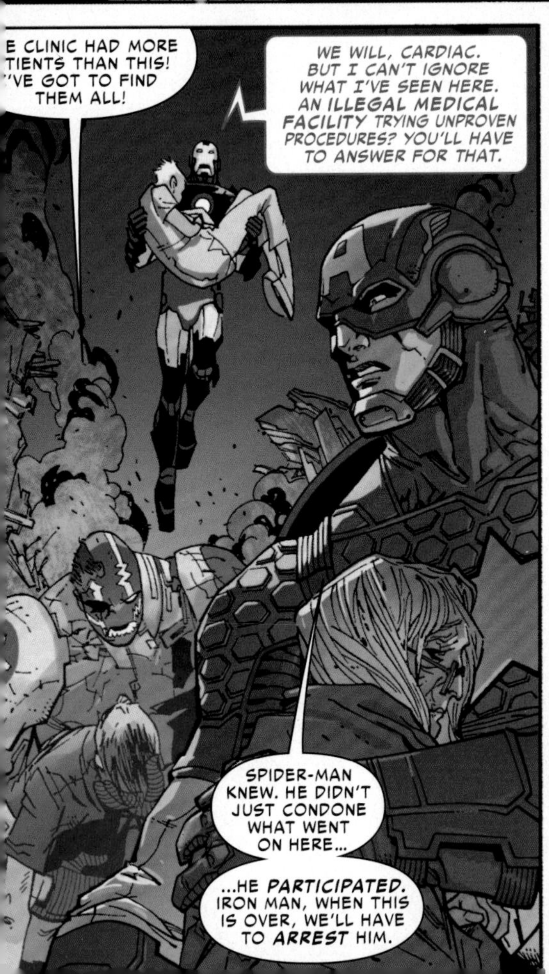
E CLINIC HAD MORE TIENTS THAN THIS! 'VE GOT TO FIND THEM ALL!
WE WILL, CARDIAC. BUT I CAN'T IGNORE WHAT I'VE SEEN HERE. AN ILLEGAL MEDICAL FACILITY TRYING UNPROVEN PROCEDURES? YOU'LL HAVE TO ANSWER FOR THAT.
SPIDER-MAN KNEW. HE DIDN'T JUST CONDONE WHAT WENT ON HERE...
...HE PARTICIPATED. IRON MAN, WHEN THIS IS OVER, WE'LL HAVE TO ARREST HIM.

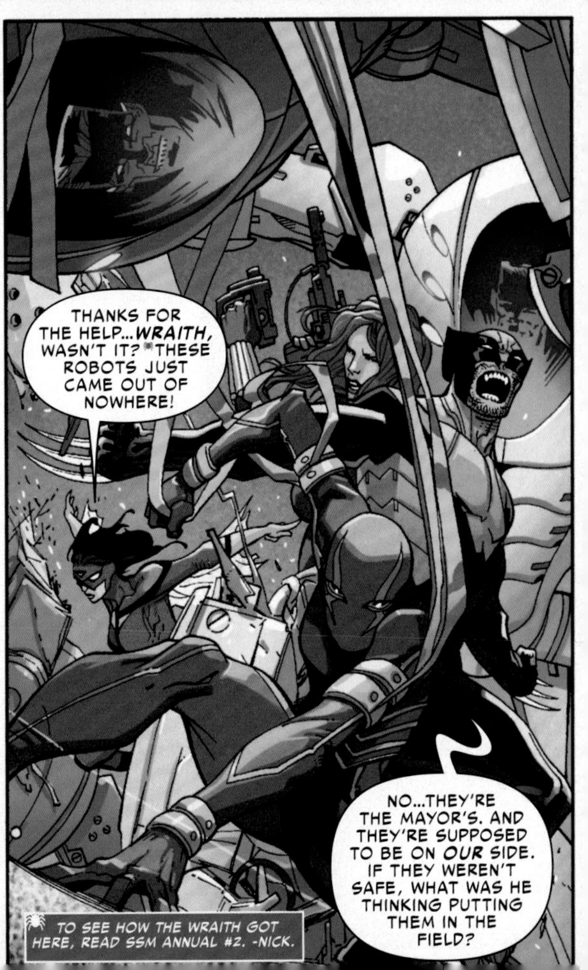
THANKS FOR THE HELP...WRAITH, WASN'T IT?* THESE ROBOTS JUST CAME OUT OF NOWHERE!
NO...THEY'RE THE MAYOR'S. AND THEY'RE SUPPOSED TO BE ON OUR SIDE. IF THEY WEREN'T SAFE, WHAT WAS HE THINKING PUTTING THEM IN THE FIELD?
*TO SEE HOW THE WRAITH GOT HERE, READ SSM ANNUAL #2. -NICK.

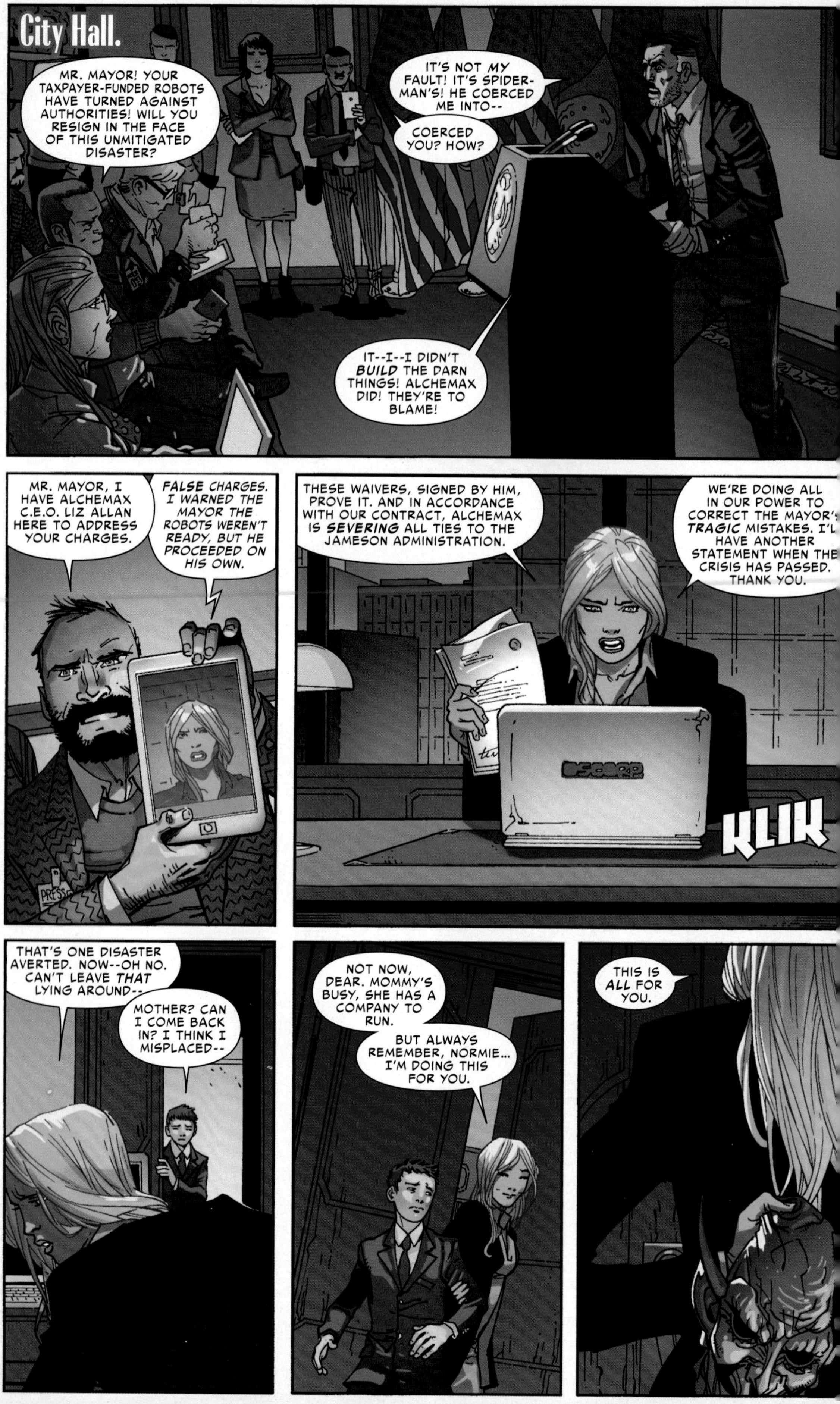
City Hall.
MR. MAYOR! YOUR TAXPAYER-FUNDED ROBOTS HAVE TURNED AGAINST AUTHORITIES! WILL YOU RESIGN IN THE FACE OF THIS UNMITIGATED DISASTER?
IT'S NOT MY FAULT! IT'S SPIDER-MAN'S! HE COERCED ME INTO--
COERCED YOU? HOW?
IT--I--I DIDN'T BUILD THE DARN THINGS! ALCHEMAX DID! THEY'RE TO BLAME!
MR. MAYOR, I HAVE ALCHEMAX C.E.O. LIZ ALLAN HERE TO ADDRESS YOUR CHARGES.
FALSE CHARGES. I WARNED THE MAYOR THE ROBOTS WEREN'T READY, BUT HE PROCEEDED ON HIS OWN.
PRESS
THESE WAIVERS, SIGNED BY HIM, PROVE IT. AND IN ACCORDANCE WITH OUR CONTRACT, ALCHEMAX IS SEVERING ALL TIES TO THE JAMESON ADMINISTRATION.
WE'RE DOING ALL IN OUR POWER TO CORRECT THE MAYOR'S TRAGIC MISTAKES. I'LL HAVE ANOTHER STATEMENT WHEN THE CRISIS HAS PASSED. THANK YOU.
KLIK
THAT'S ONE DISASTER AVERTED. NOW--OH NO. CAN'T LEAVE THAT LYING AROUND--
MOTHER? CAN I COME BACK IN? I THINK I MISPLACED--
NOT NOW, DEAR. MOMMY'S BUSY, SHE HAS A COMPANY TO RUN.
BUT ALWAYS REMEMBER, NORMIE... I'M DOING THIS FOR YOU.
THIS IS ALL FOR YOU.

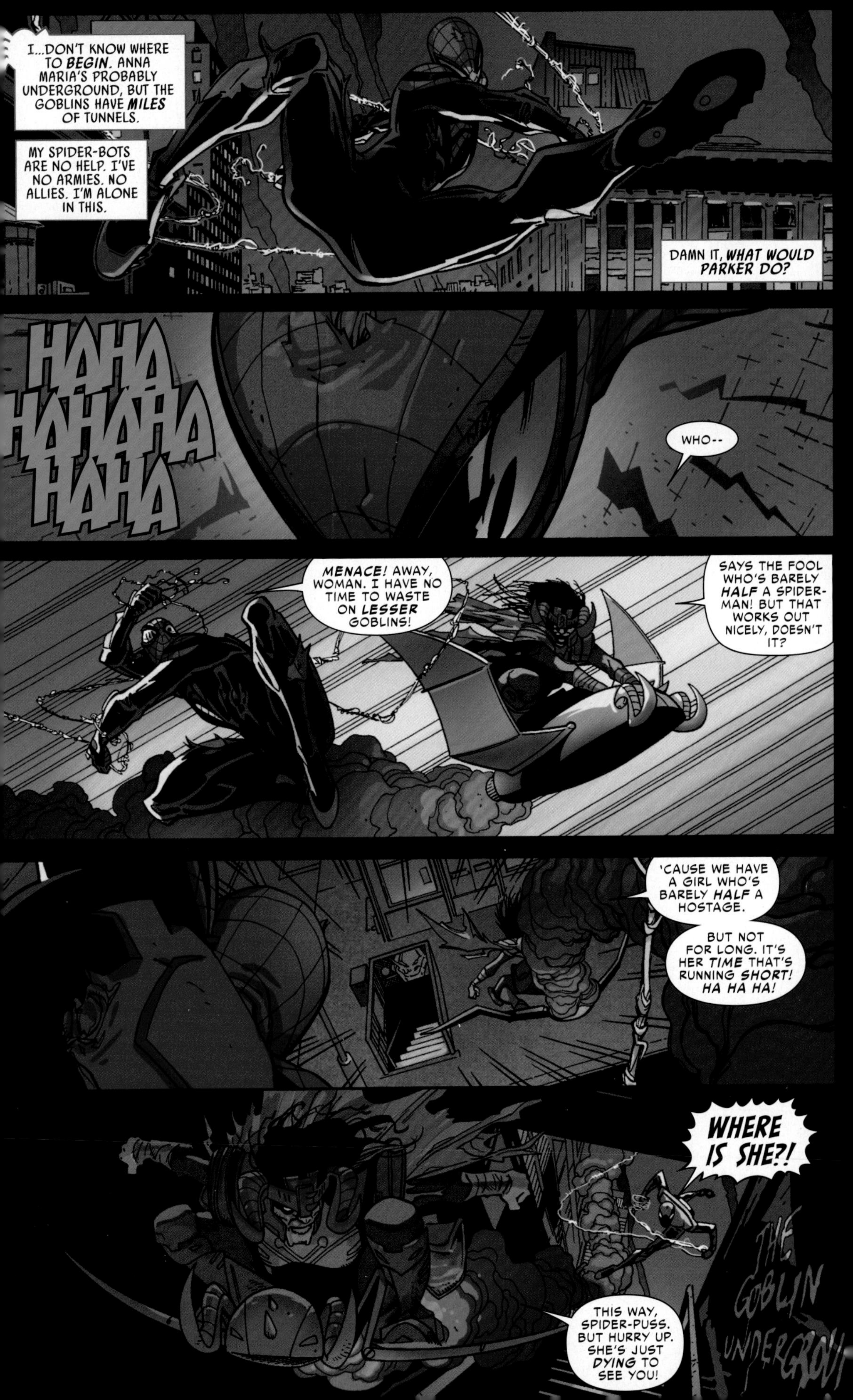

I...DON'T KNOW WHERE TO BEGIN. ANNA MARIA'S PROBABLY UNDERGROUND, BUT THE GOBLINS HAVE MILES OF TUNNELS.
MY SPIDER-BOTS ARE NO HELP. I'VE NO ARMIES. NO ALLIES. I'M ALONE IN THIS.
DAMN IT, WHAT WOULD PARKER DO?
HAHA HAHAHA HAHA
WHO--
MENACE! AWAY, WOMAN. I HAVE NO TIME TO WASTE ON LESSER GOBLINS!
SAYS THE FOOL WHO'S BARELY HALF A SPIDER-MAN! BUT THAT WORKS OUT NICELY, DOESN'T IT?
'CAUSE WE HAVE A GIRL WHO'S BARELY HALF A HOSTAGE.
BUT NOT FOR LONG. IT'S HER TIME THAT'S RUNNING SHORT! HA HA HA!
WHERE IS SHE?!
THIS WAY, SPIDER-PUSS. BUT HURRY UP. SHE'S JUST DYING TO SEE YOU!

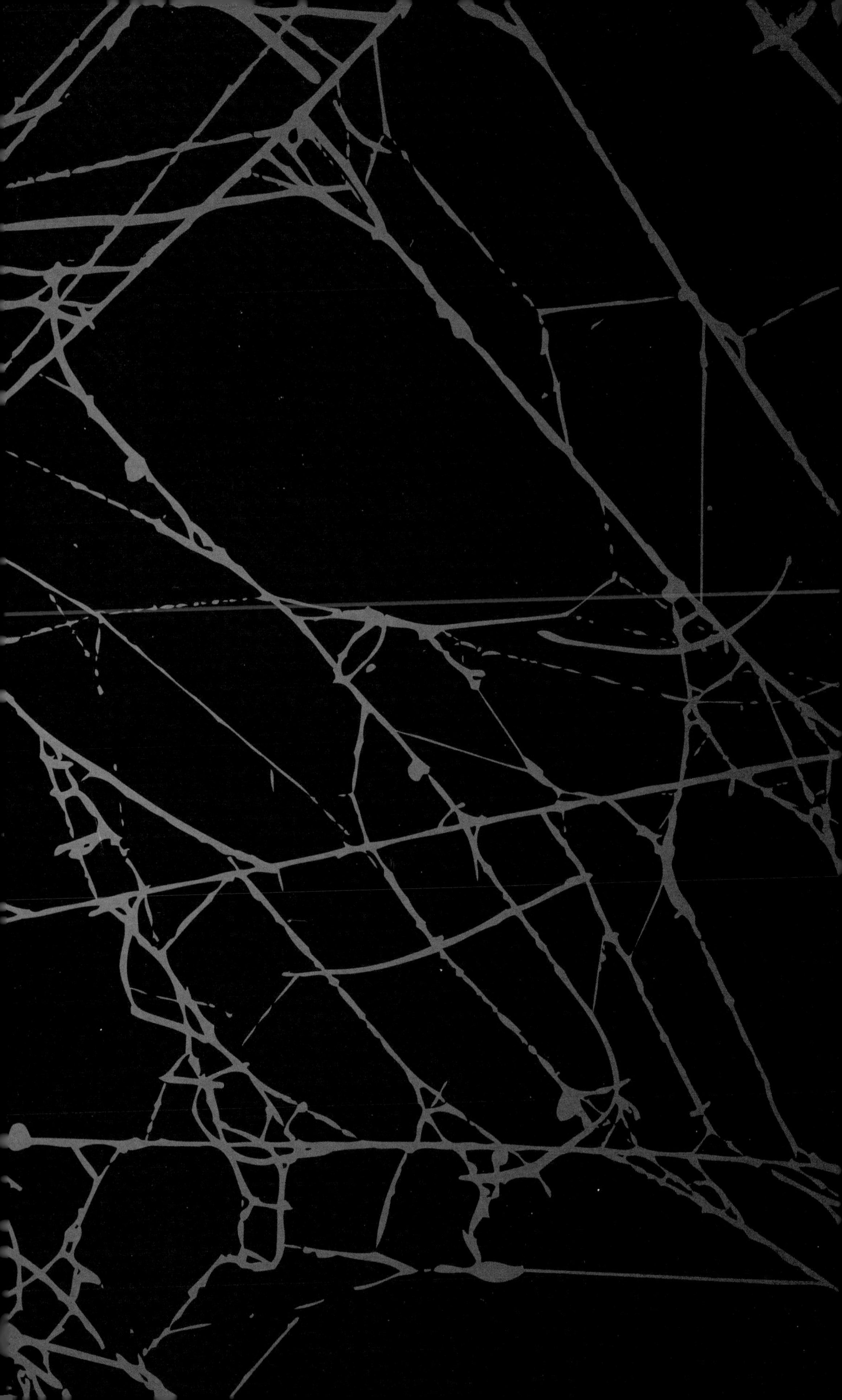

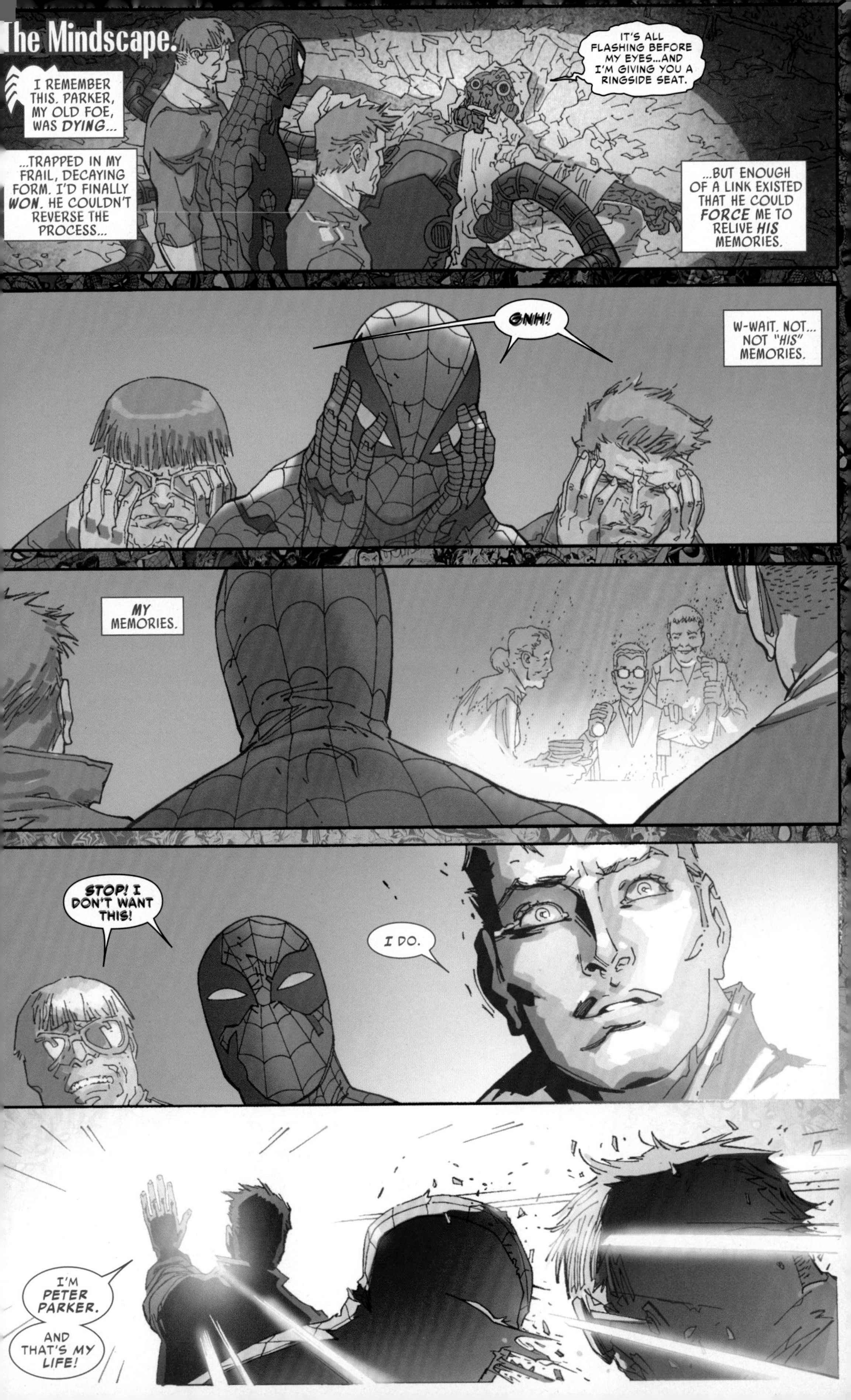

The Mindscape.
I REMEMBER THIS. PARKER, MY OLD FOE, WAS DYING...
...TRAPPED IN MY FRAIL, DECAYING FORM. I'D FINALLY WON. HE COULDN'T REVERSE THE PROCESS...
IT'S ALL FLASHING BEFORE MY EYES...AND I'M GIVING YOU A RINGSIDE SEAT.
...BUT ENOUGH OF A LINK EXISTED THAT HE COULD FORCE ME TO RELIVE HIS MEMORIES.
GNH!
W-WAIT. NOT... NOT "HIS" MEMORIES.
MY MEMORIES.
STOP! I DON'T WANT THIS!
I DO.
I'M PETER PARKER.
AND THAT'S MY LIFE!

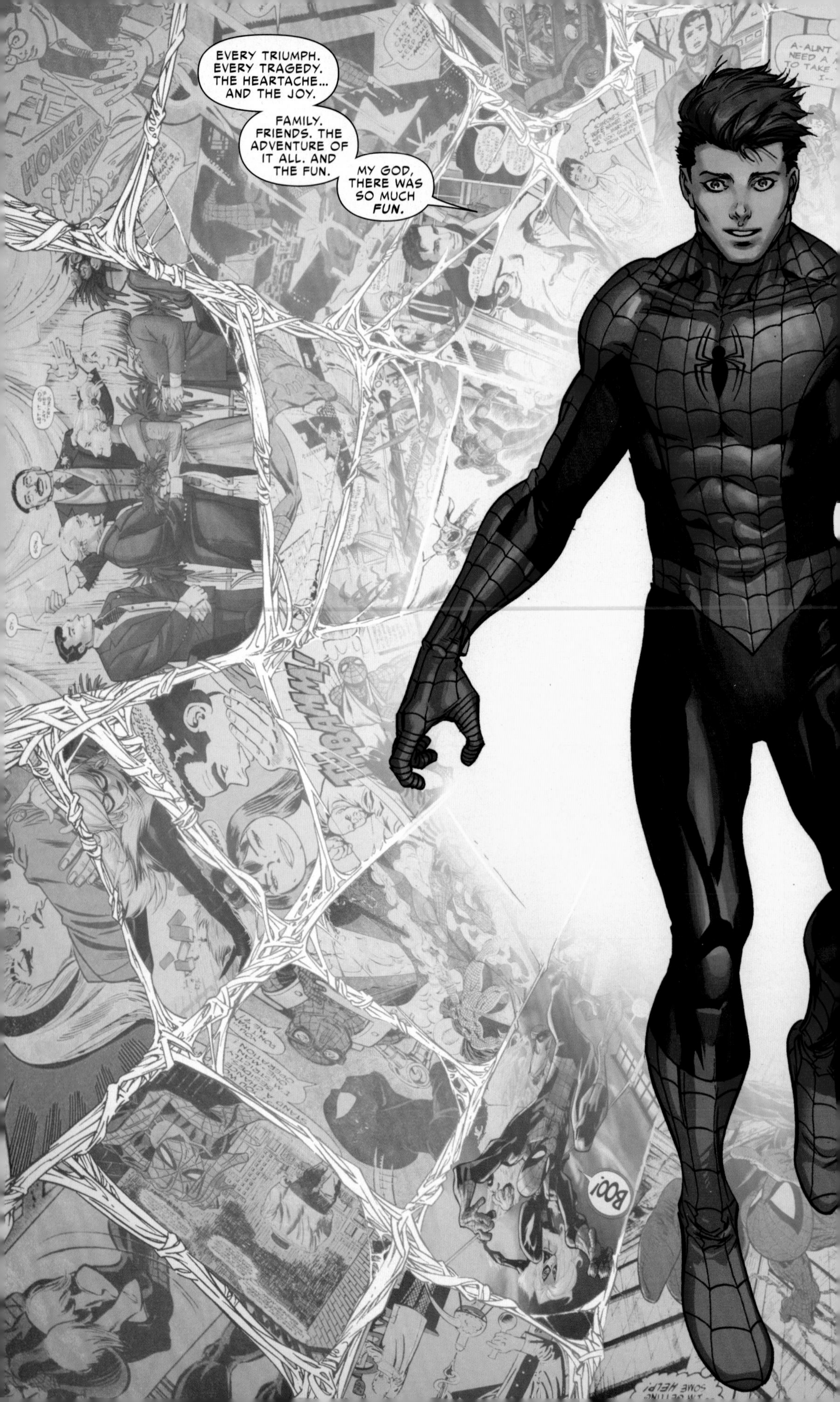

EVERY TRIUMPH. EVERY TRAGEDY. THE HEARTACHE... AND THE JOY.
FAMILY. FRIENDS. THE ADVENTURE OF IT ALL. AND THE FUN.
MY GOD, THERE WAS SO MUCH *FUN.*

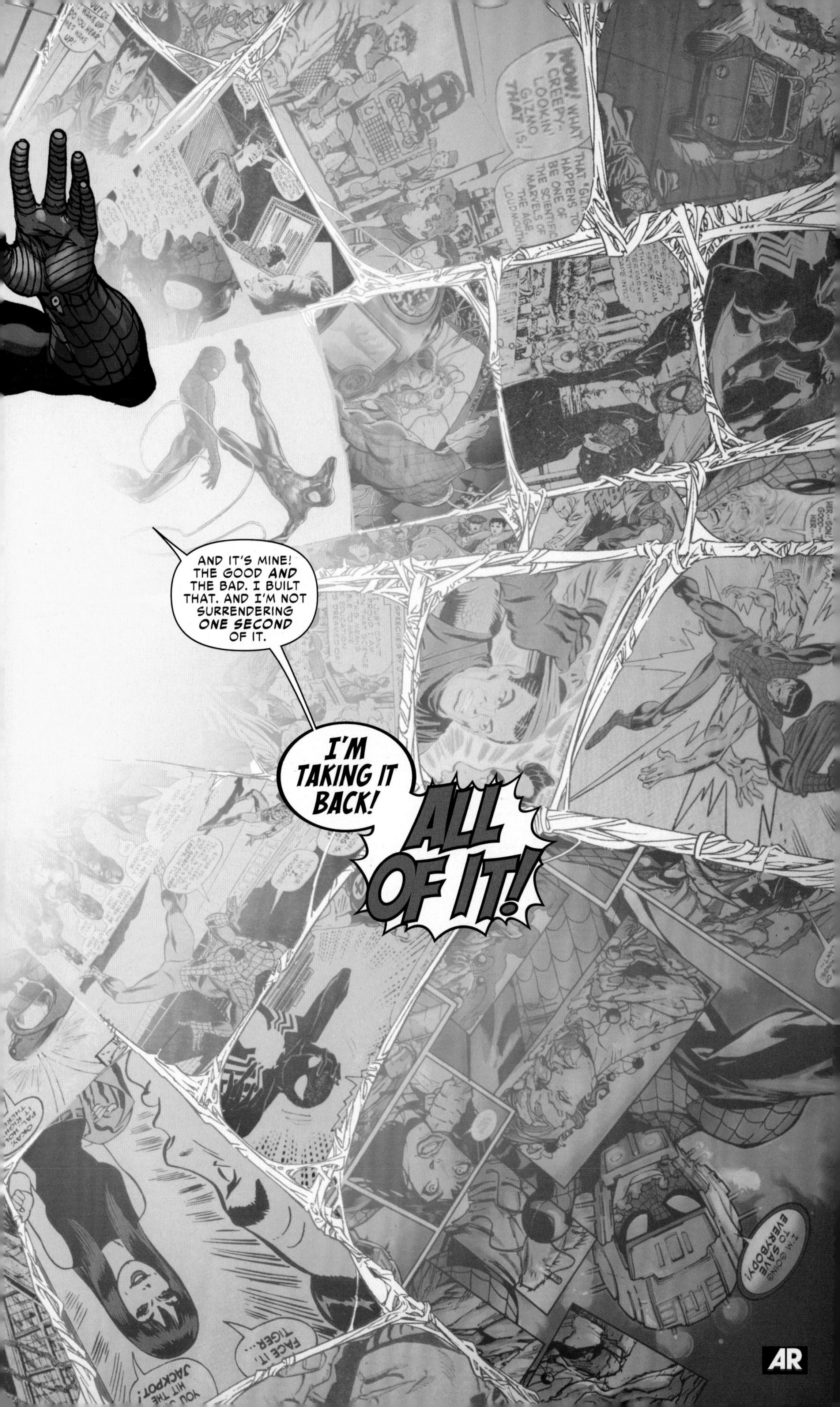
AND IT'S MINE! THE GOOD *AND* THE BAD. I BUILT THAT. AND I'M NOT SURRENDERING *ONE SECOND* OF IT.
I'M TAKING IT BACK!
ALL OF IT!

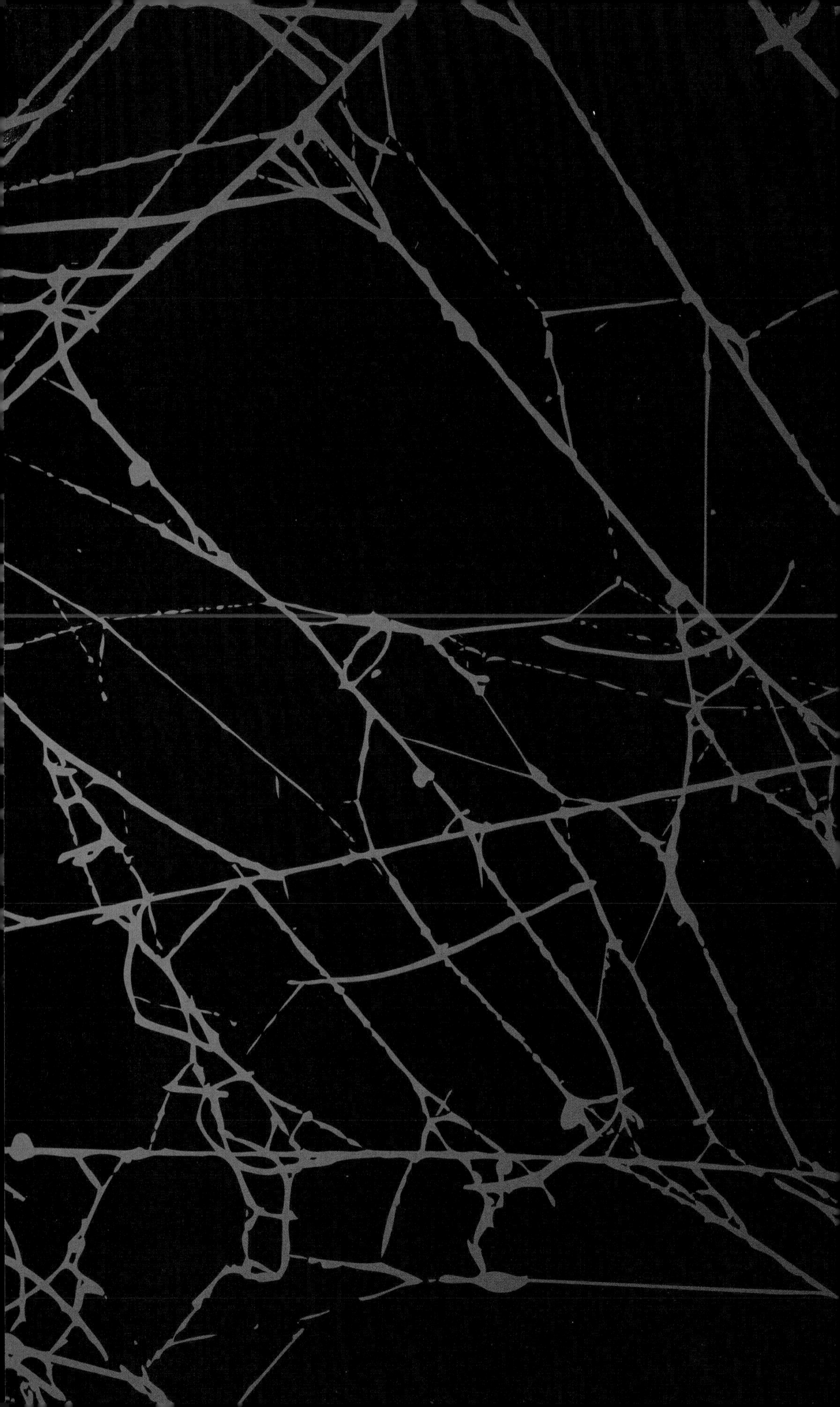

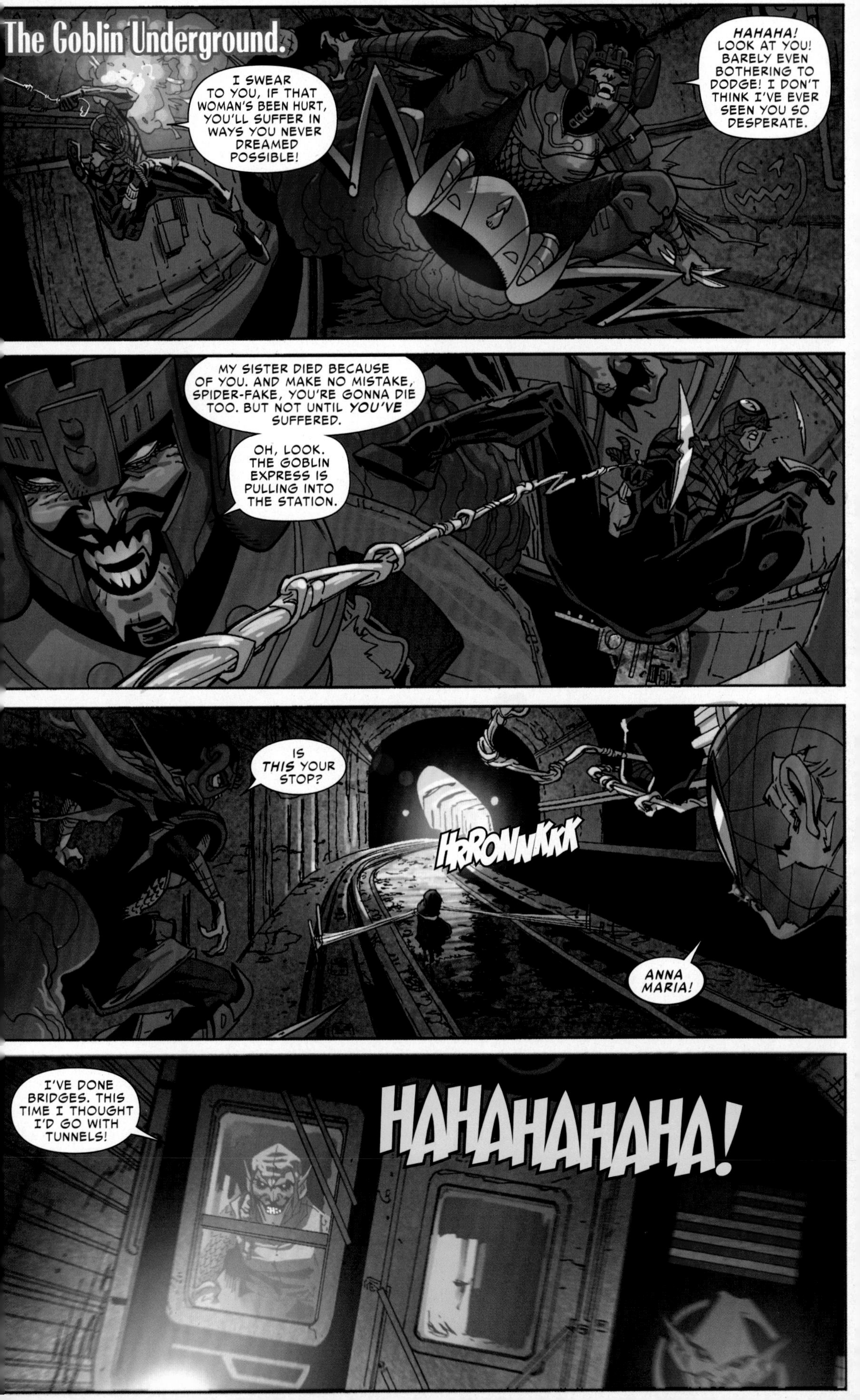

The Goblin Underground.
I SWEAR TO YOU, IF THAT WOMAN'S BEEN HURT, YOU'LL SUFFER IN WAYS YOU NEVER DREAMED POSSIBLE!
HAHAHA! LOOK AT YOU! BARELY EVEN BOTHERING TO DODGE! I DON'T THINK I'VE EVER SEEN YOU SO DESPERATE.
MY SISTER DIED BECAUSE OF YOU. AND MAKE NO MISTAKE, SPIDER-FAKE, YOU'RE GONNA DIE TOO. BUT NOT UNTIL YOU'VE SUFFERED.
OH, LOOK. THE GOBLIN EXPRESS IS PULLING INTO THE STATION.
IS THIS YOUR STOP?
HRRONNKKK
ANNA MARIA!
I'VE DONE BRIDGES. THIS TIME I THOUGHT I'D GO WITH TUNNELS!
HAHAHAHAHA!

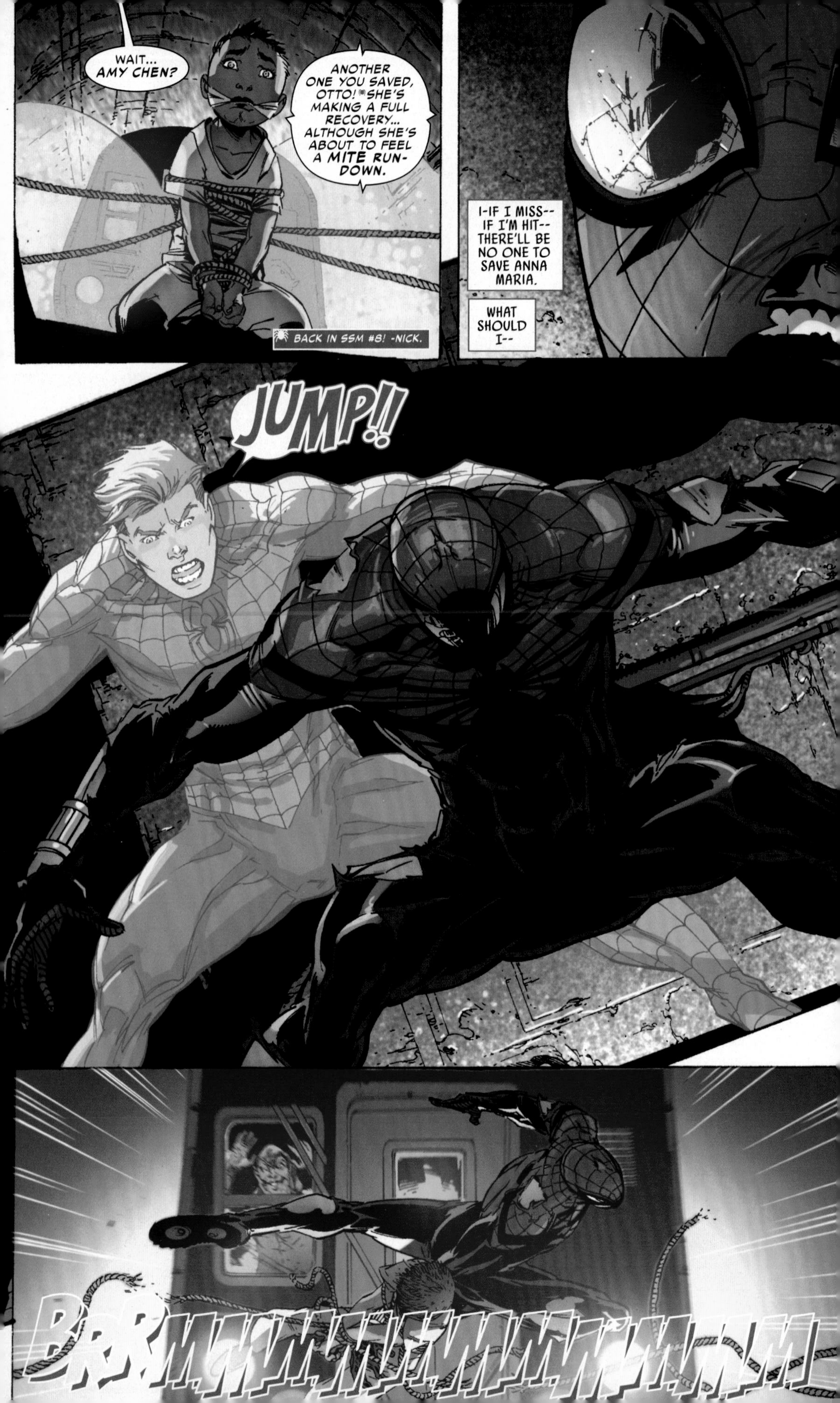

WAIT... AMY CHEN?
ANOTHER ONE YOU SAVED, OTTO!* SHE'S MAKING A FULL RECOVERY... ALTHOUGH SHE'S ABOUT TO FEEL A MITE RUN-DOWN.
*BACK IN SSM #8! -NICK.
I-IF I MISS-- IF I'M HIT-- THERE'LL BE NO ONE TO SAVE ANNA MARIA.
WHAT SHOULD I--
JUMP!!
BRRMMMMMMMMMMMMMMM

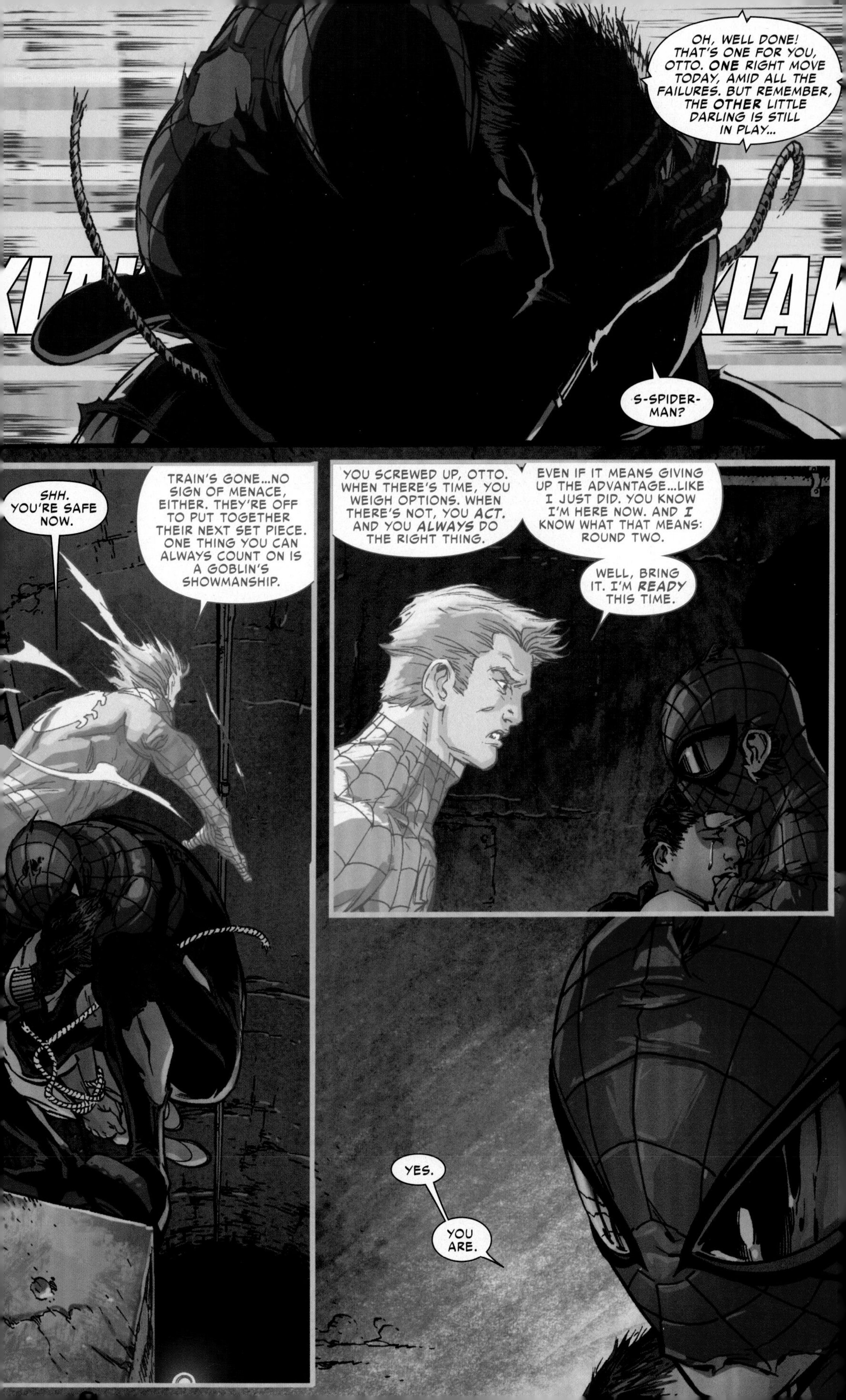
OH, WELL DONE! THAT'S ONE FOR YOU, OTTO. ONE RIGHT MOVE TODAY, AMID ALL THE FAILURES. BUT REMEMBER, THE OTHER LITTLE DARLING IS STILL IN PLAY...
KLAK
KLAK
S-SPIDER-MAN?
SHH. YOU'RE SAFE NOW.
TRAIN'S GONE...NO SIGN OF MENACE, EITHER. THEY'RE OFF TO PUT TOGETHER THEIR NEXT SET PIECE. ONE THING YOU CAN ALWAYS COUNT ON IS A GOBLIN'S SHOWMANSHIP.
YOU SCREWED UP, OTTO. WHEN THERE'S TIME, YOU WEIGH OPTIONS. WHEN THERE'S NOT, YOU ACT. AND YOU ALWAYS DO THE RIGHT THING.
EVEN IF IT MEANS GIVING UP THE ADVANTAGE...LIKE I JUST DID. YOU KNOW I'M HERE NOW. AND I KNOW WHAT THAT MEANS: ROUND TWO.
WELL, BRING IT. I'M READY THIS TIME.
YES.
YOU ARE.

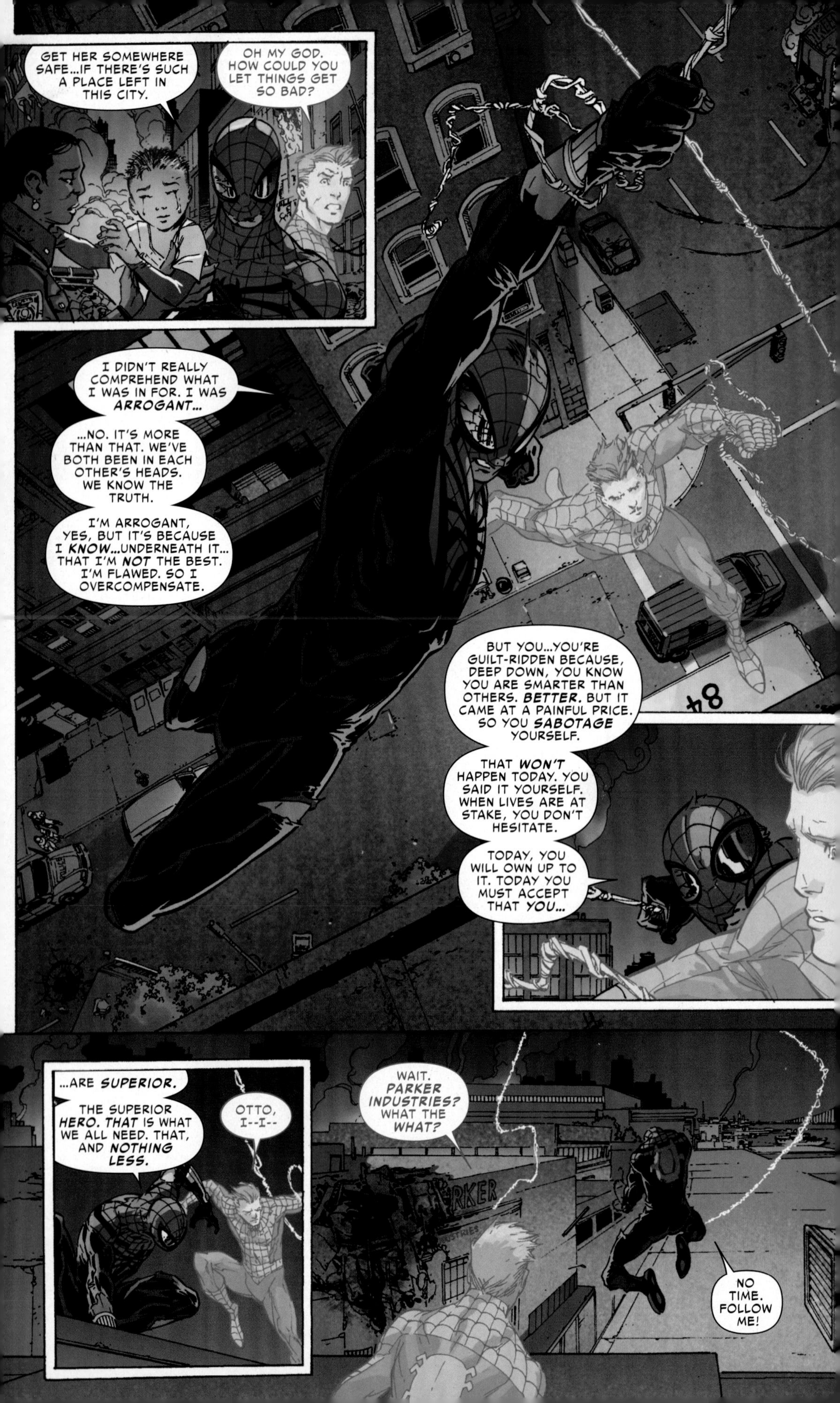

GET HER SOMEWHERE SAFE...IF THERE'S SUCH A PLACE LEFT IN THIS CITY.
OH MY GOD. HOW COULD YOU LET THINGS GET SO BAD?
I DIDN'T REALLY COMPREHEND WHAT I WAS IN FOR. I WAS ARROGANT...
...NO. IT'S MORE THAN THAT. WE'VE BOTH BEEN IN EACH OTHER'S HEADS. WE KNOW THE TRUTH.
I'M ARROGANT, YES, BUT IT'S BECAUSE I KNOW...UNDERNEATH IT... THAT I'M NOT THE BEST. I'M FLAWED. SO I OVERCOMPENSATE.
BUT YOU...YOU'RE GUILT-RIDDEN BECAUSE, DEEP DOWN, YOU KNOW YOU ARE SMARTER THAN OTHERS. BETTER. BUT IT CAME AT A PAINFUL PRICE. SO YOU SABOTAGE YOURSELF.
THAT WON'T HAPPEN TODAY. YOU SAID IT YOURSELF. WHEN LIVES ARE AT STAKE, YOU DON'T HESITATE.
TODAY, YOU WILL OWN UP TO IT. TODAY YOU MUST ACCEPT THAT YOU...
...ARE SUPERIOR.
THE SUPERIOR HERO. THAT IS WHAT WE ALL NEED. THAT, AND NOTHING LESS.
OTTO, I--I--
WAIT. PARKER INDUSTRIES? WHAT THE WHAT?
NO TIME. FOLLOW ME!

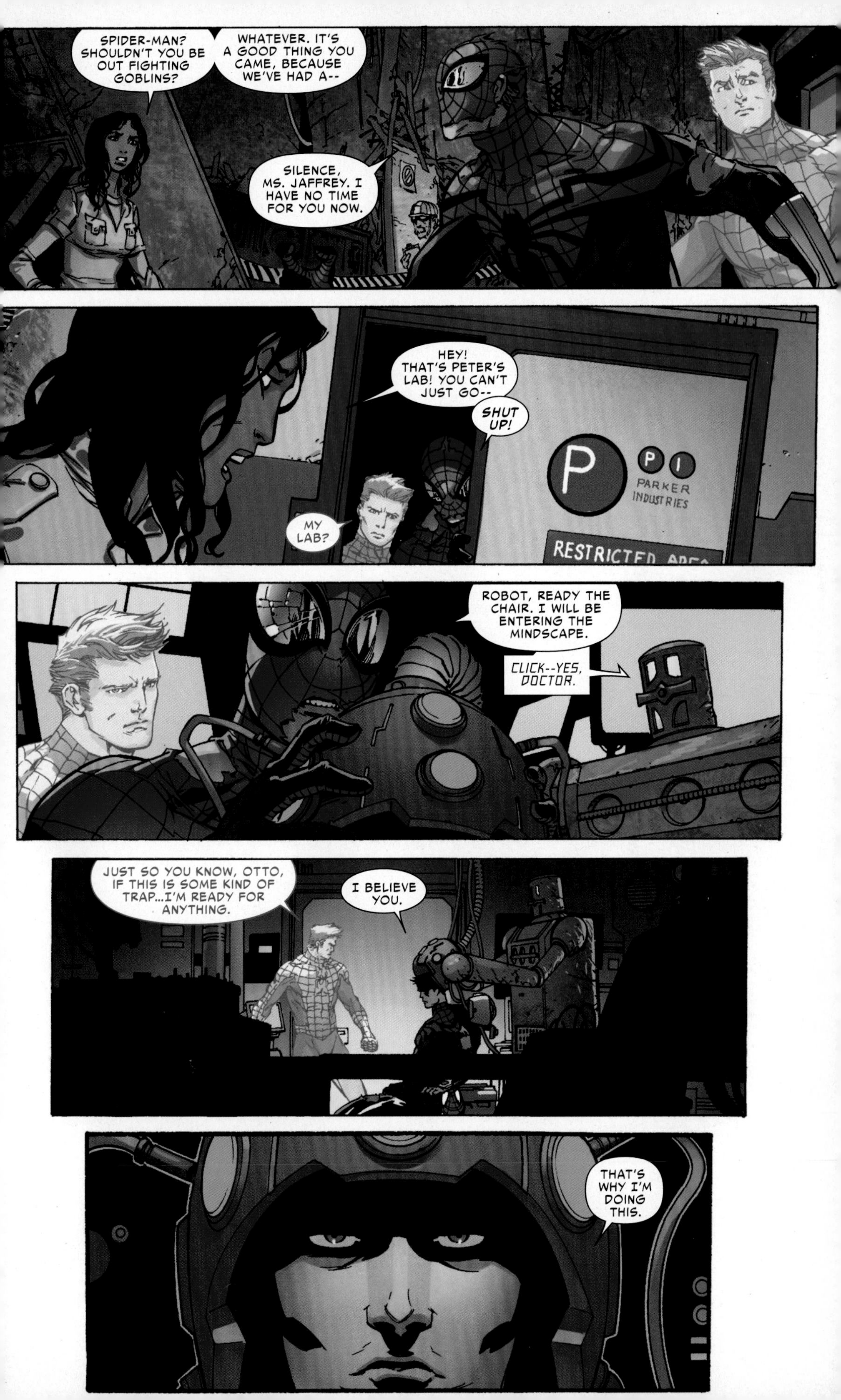

SPIDER-MAN? SHOULDN'T YOU BE OUT FIGHTING GOBLINS?
WHATEVER. IT'S A GOOD THING YOU CAME, BECAUSE WE'VE HAD A--
SILENCE, MS. JAFFREY. I HAVE NO TIME FOR YOU NOW.
HEY! THAT'S PETER'S LAB! YOU CAN'T JUST GO--
SHUT UP!
MY LAB?
PARKER INDUSTRIES
ROBOT, READY THE CHAIR. I WILL BE ENTERING THE MINDSCAPE.
CLICK--YES, DOCTOR.
JUST SO YOU KNOW, OTTO, IF THIS IS SOME KIND OF TRAP...I'M READY FOR ANYTHING.
I BELIEVE YOU.
THAT'S WHY I'M DOING THIS.

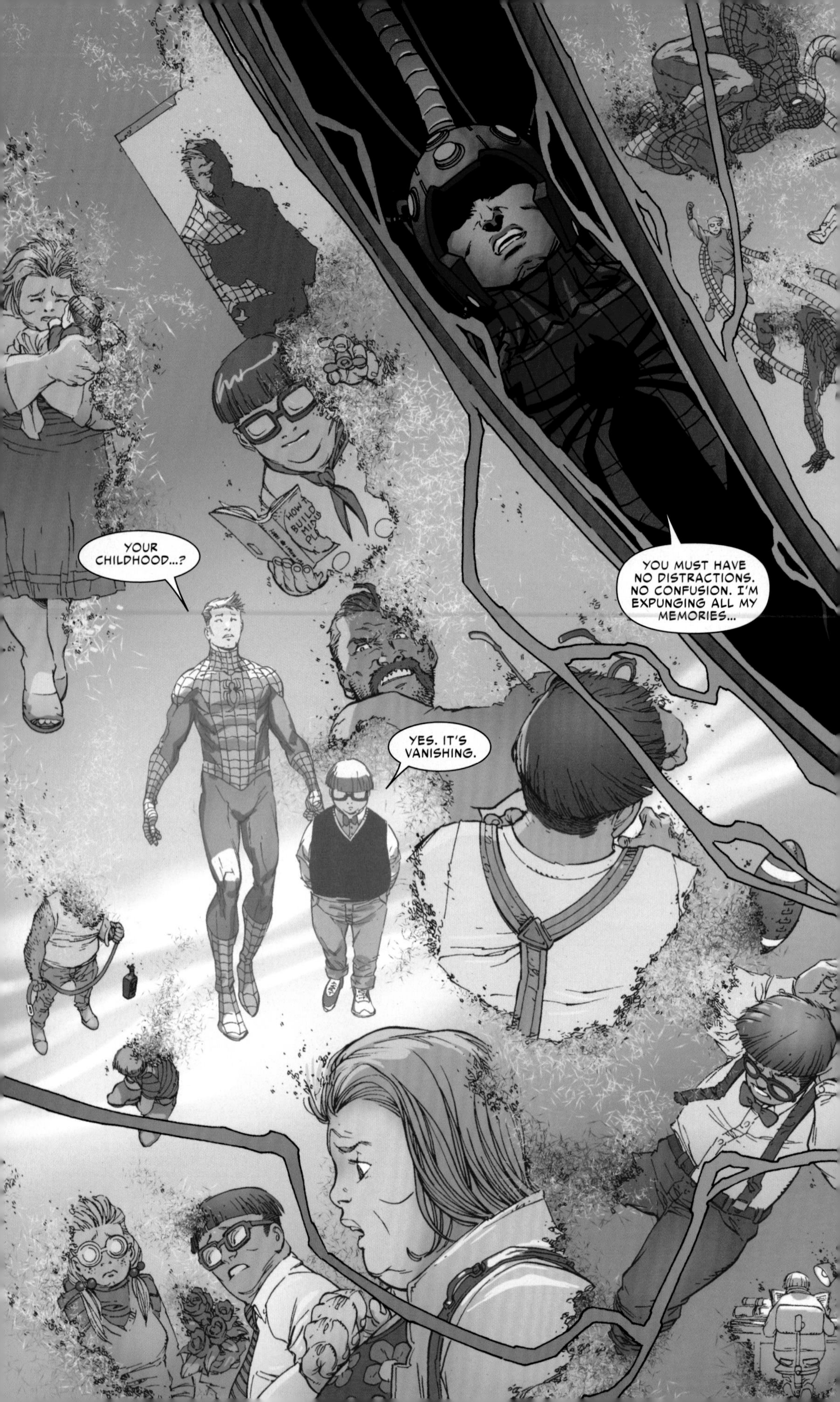
YOU MUST HAVE NO DISTRACTIONS. NO CONFUSION. I'M EXPUNGING ALL MY MEMORIES...
YOUR CHILDHOOD...?
YES. IT'S VANISHING.

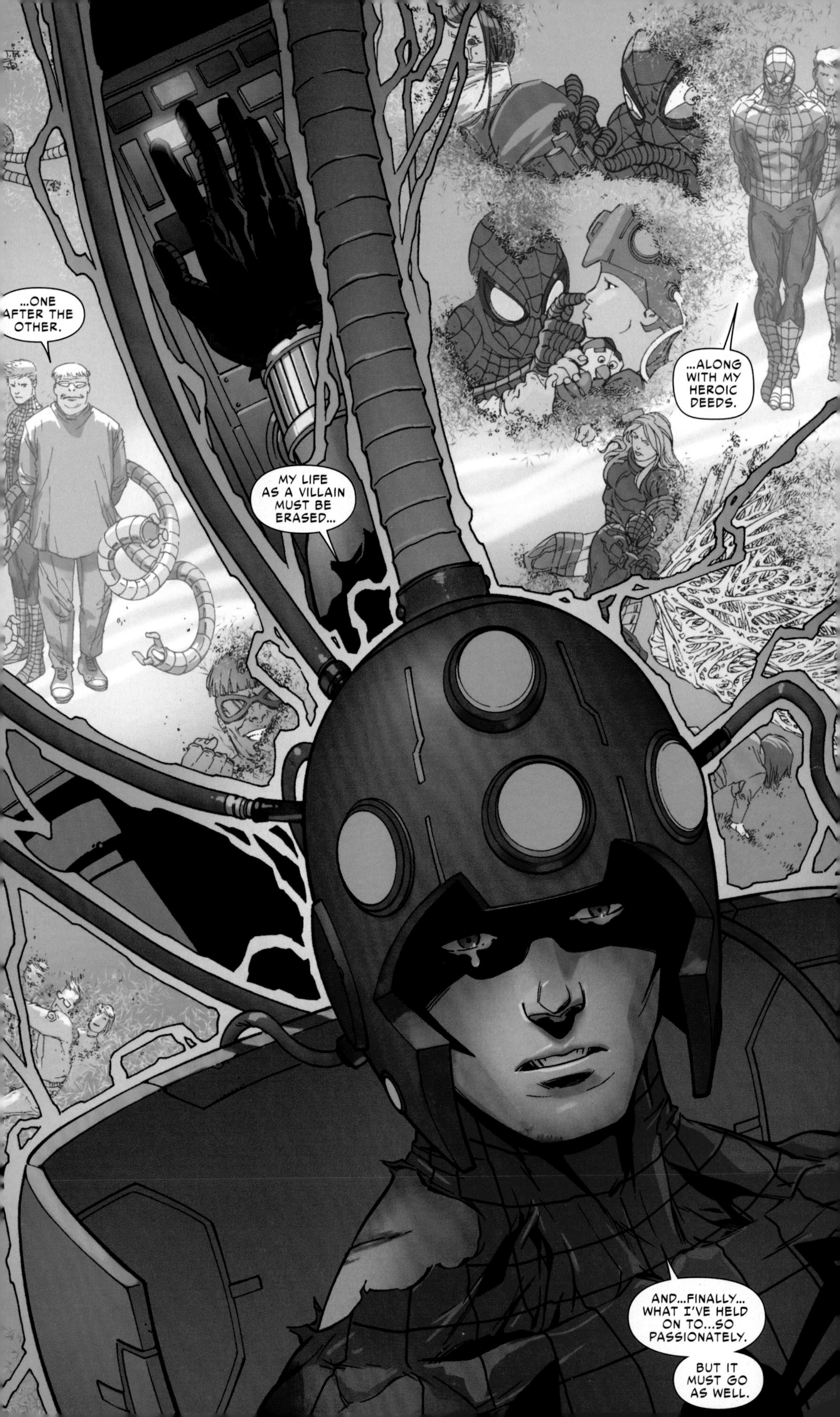
...ONE AFTER THE OTHER.
MY LIFE AS A VILLAIN MUST BE ERASED...
...ALONG WITH MY HEROIC DEEDS.
AND...FINALLY... WHAT I'VE HELD ON TO...SO PASSIONATELY.
BUT IT MUST GO AS WELL.

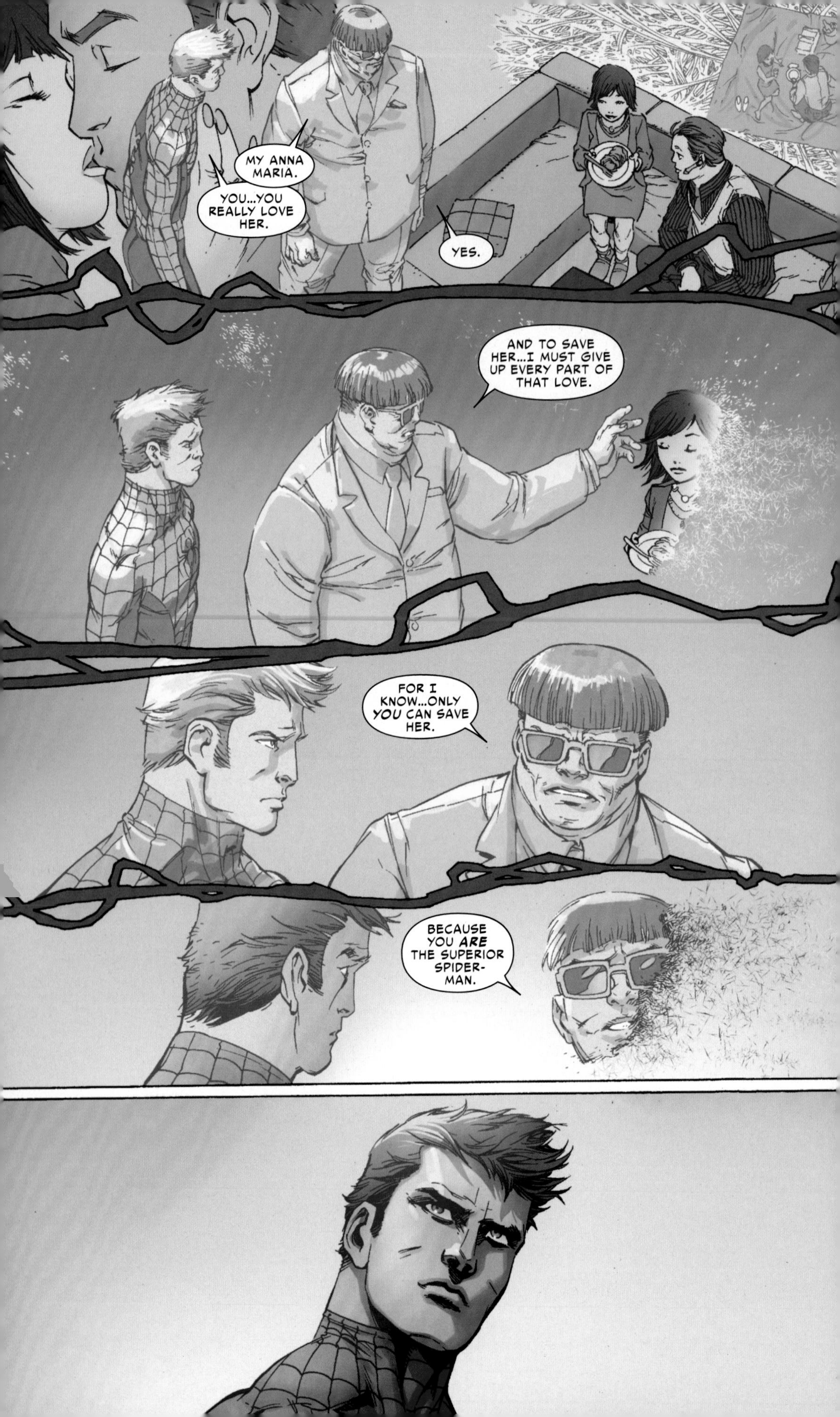
MY ANNA MARIA.
YOU...YOU REALLY LOVE HER.
YES.
AND TO SAVE HER...I MUST GIVE UP EVERY PART OF THAT LOVE.
FOR I KNOW...ONLY *YOU* CAN SAVE HER.
BECAUSE YOU ***ARE*** THE SUPERIOR SPIDER-MAN.

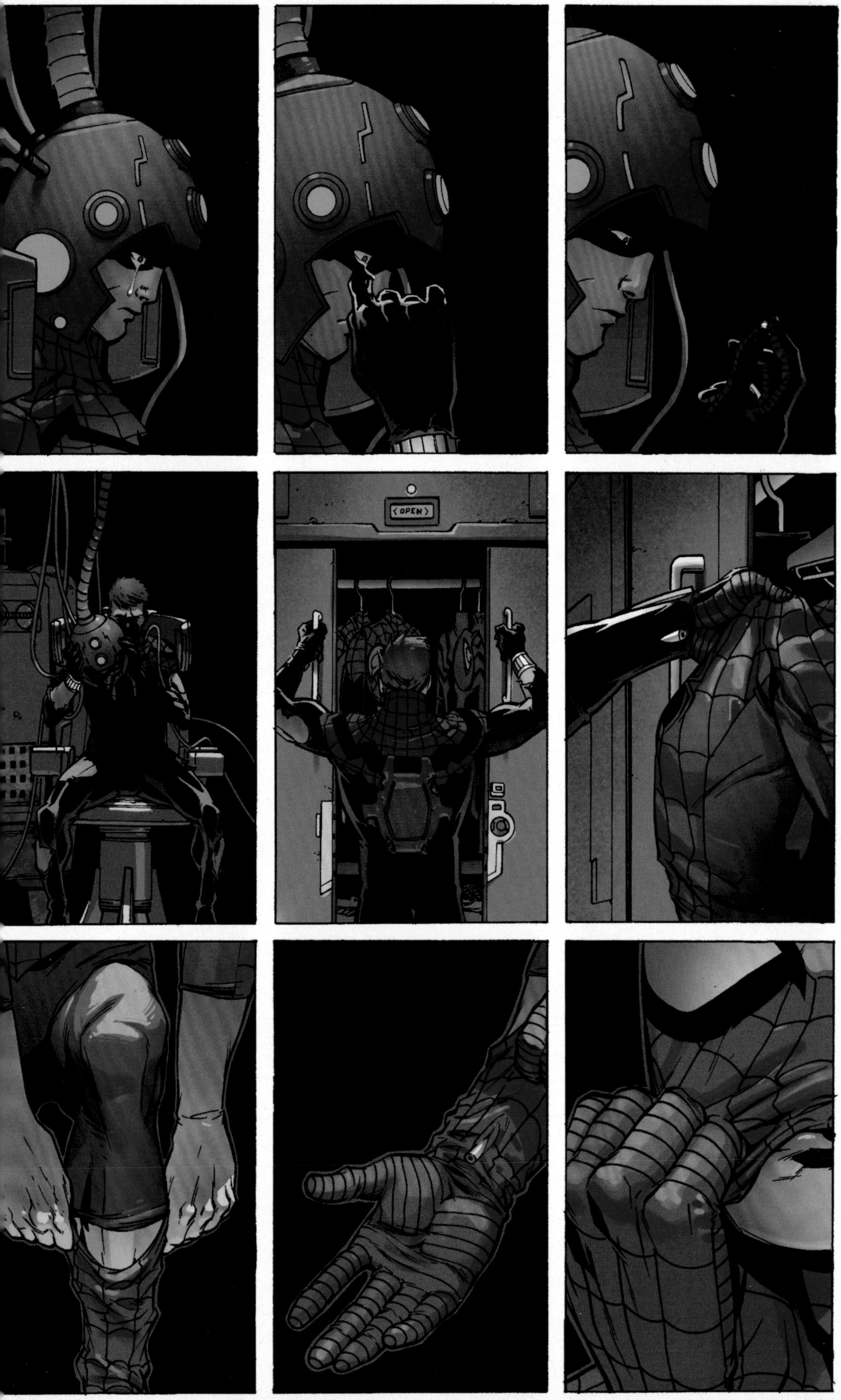
OPEN

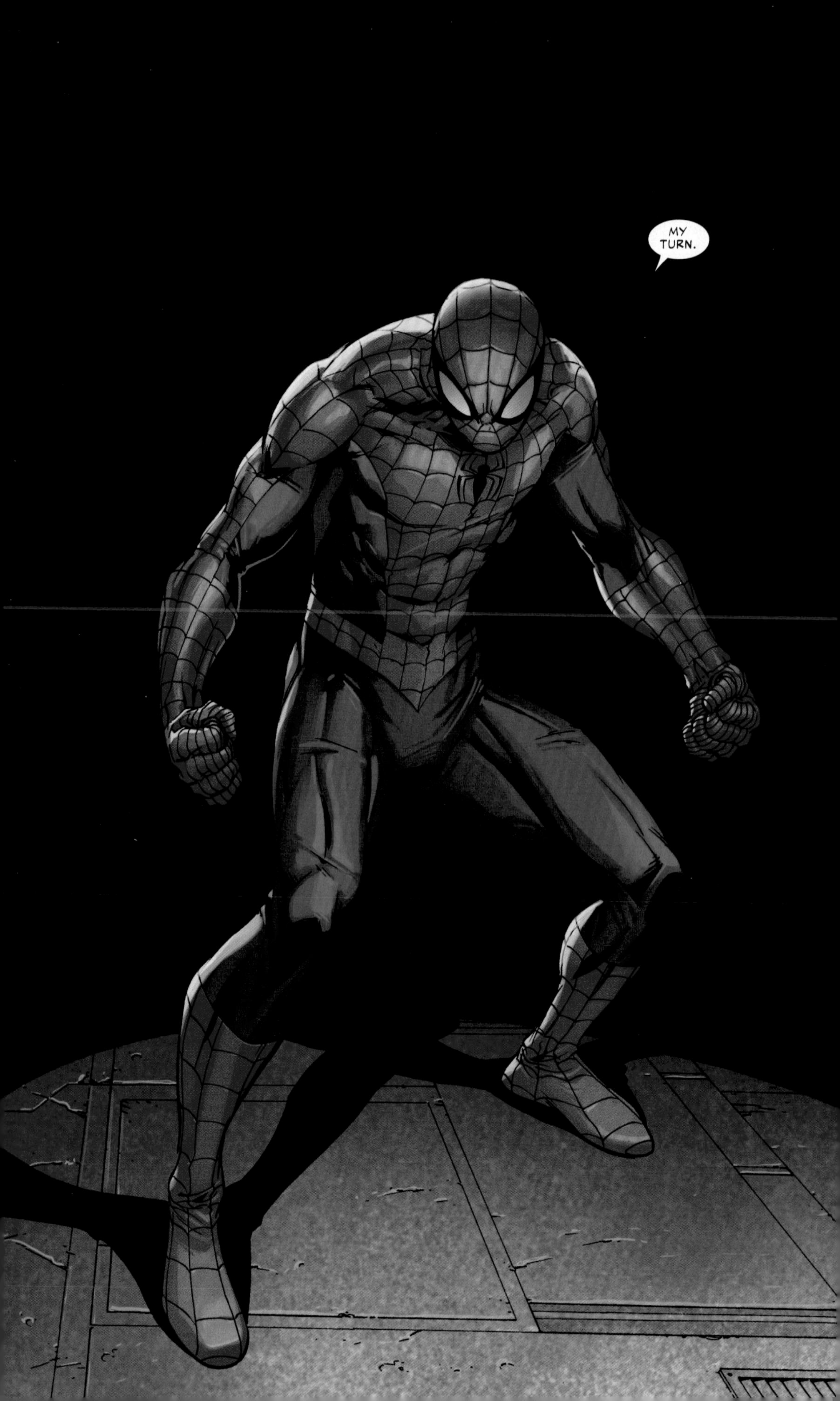
MY TURN.

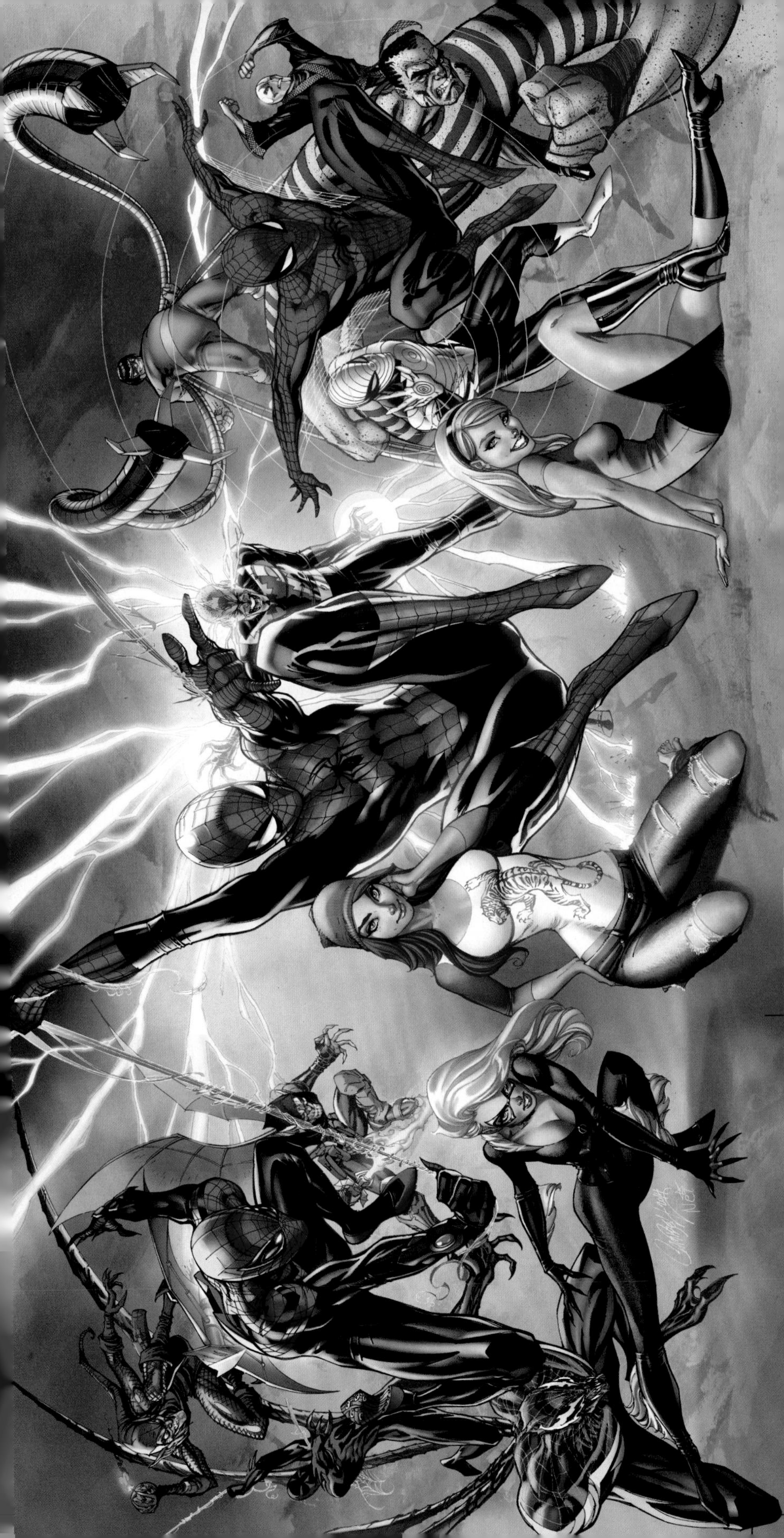

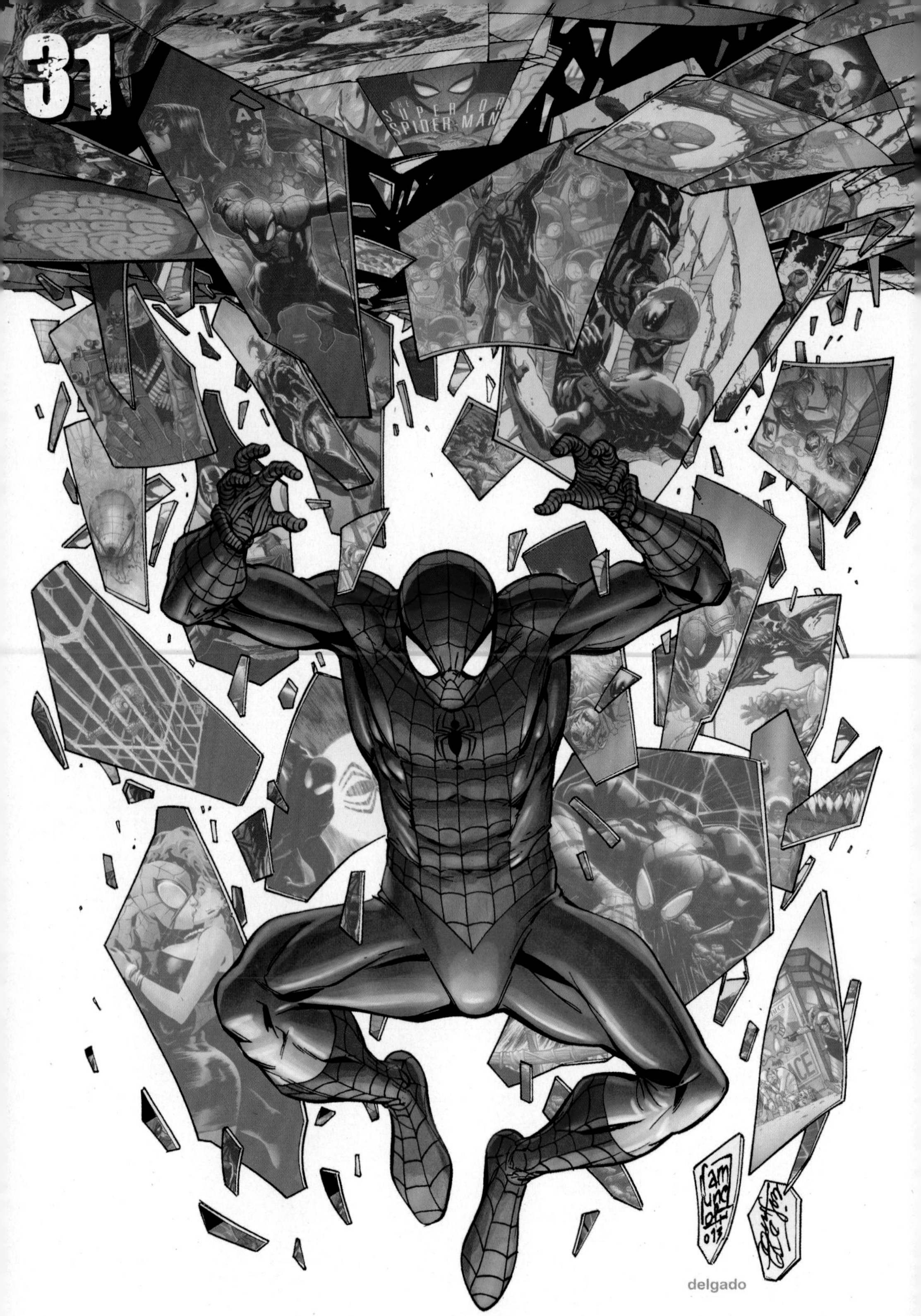
31
THE SUPERIOR SPIDER-MAN
delgado

AMAZING

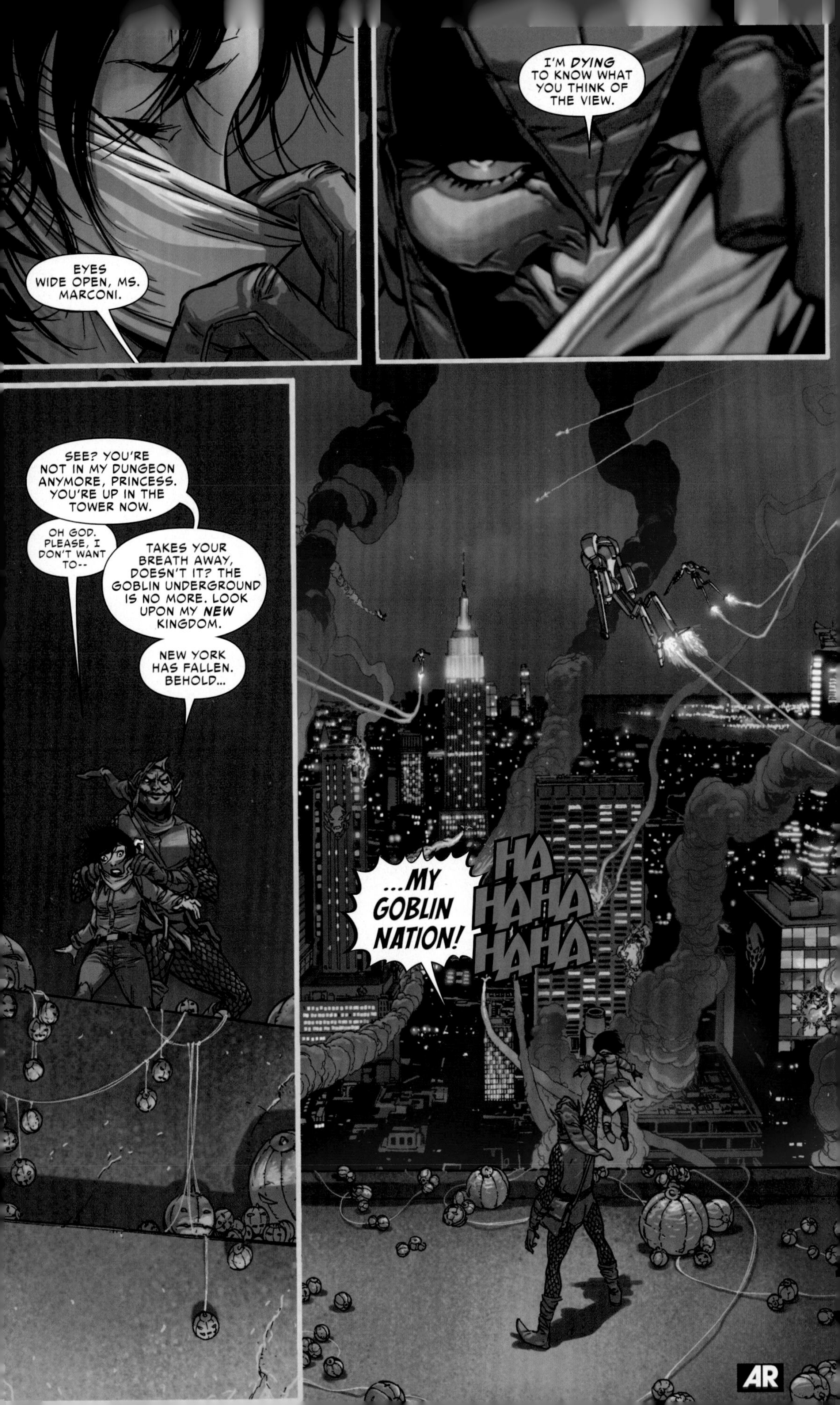
EYES WIDE OPEN, MS. MARCONI.
I'M DYING TO KNOW WHAT YOU THINK OF THE VIEW.
SEE? YOU'RE NOT IN MY DUNGEON ANYMORE, PRINCESS. YOU'RE UP IN THE TOWER NOW.
OH GOD. PLEASE, I DON'T WANT TO--
TAKES YOUR BREATH AWAY, DOESN'T IT? THE GOBLIN UNDERGROUND IS NO MORE. LOOK UPON MY NEW KINGDOM.
NEW YORK HAS FALLEN. BEHOLD...
...MY GOBLIN NATION!
HA HAHA HAHA
AR

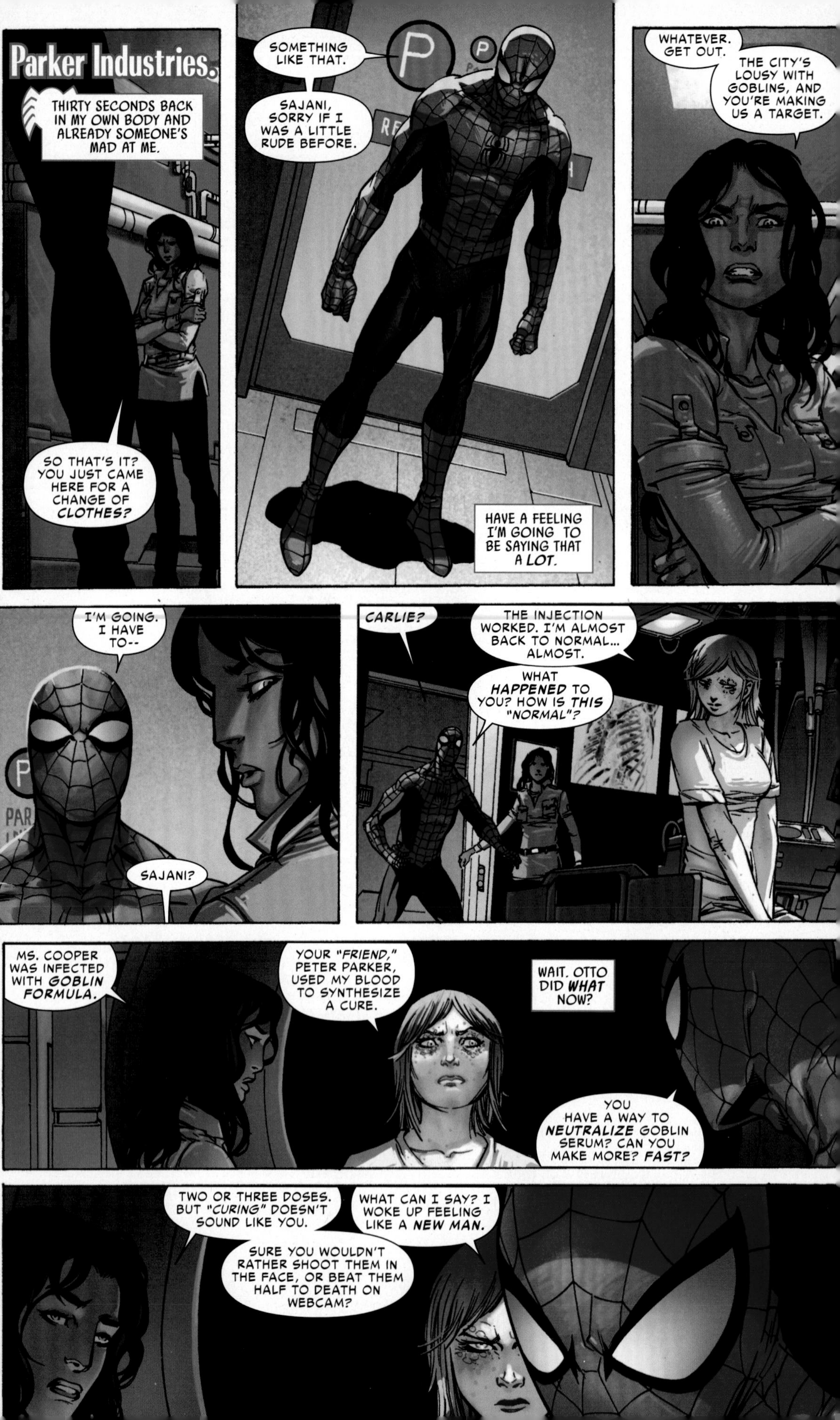

Parker Industries.
THIRTY SECONDS BACK IN MY OWN BODY AND ALREADY SOMEONE'S MAD AT ME.
SO THAT'S IT? YOU JUST CAME HERE FOR A CHANGE OF CLOTHES?
SOMETHING LIKE THAT.
SAJANI, SORRY IF I WAS A LITTLE RUDE BEFORE.
HAVE A FEELING I'M GOING TO BE SAYING THAT A LOT.
WHATEVER. GET OUT.
THE CITY'S LOUSY WITH GOBLINS, AND YOU'RE MAKING US A TARGET.
I'M GOING. I HAVE TO--
SAJANI?
CARLIE?
THE INJECTION WORKED. I'M ALMOST BACK TO NORMAL... ALMOST.
WHAT HAPPENED TO YOU? HOW IS THIS "NORMAL"?
MS. COOPER WAS INFECTED WITH GOBLIN FORMULA.
YOUR "FRIEND," PETER PARKER, USED MY BLOOD TO SYNTHESIZE A CURE.
WAIT. OTTO DID WHAT NOW?
YOU HAVE A WAY TO NEUTRALIZE GOBLIN SERUM? CAN YOU MAKE MORE? FAST?
TWO OR THREE DOSES. BUT "CURING" DOESN'T SOUND LIKE YOU.
SURE YOU WOULDN'T RATHER SHOOT THEM IN THE FACE, OR BEAT THEM HALF TO DEATH ON WEBCAM?
WHAT CAN I SAY? I WOKE UP FEELING LIKE A NEW MAN.

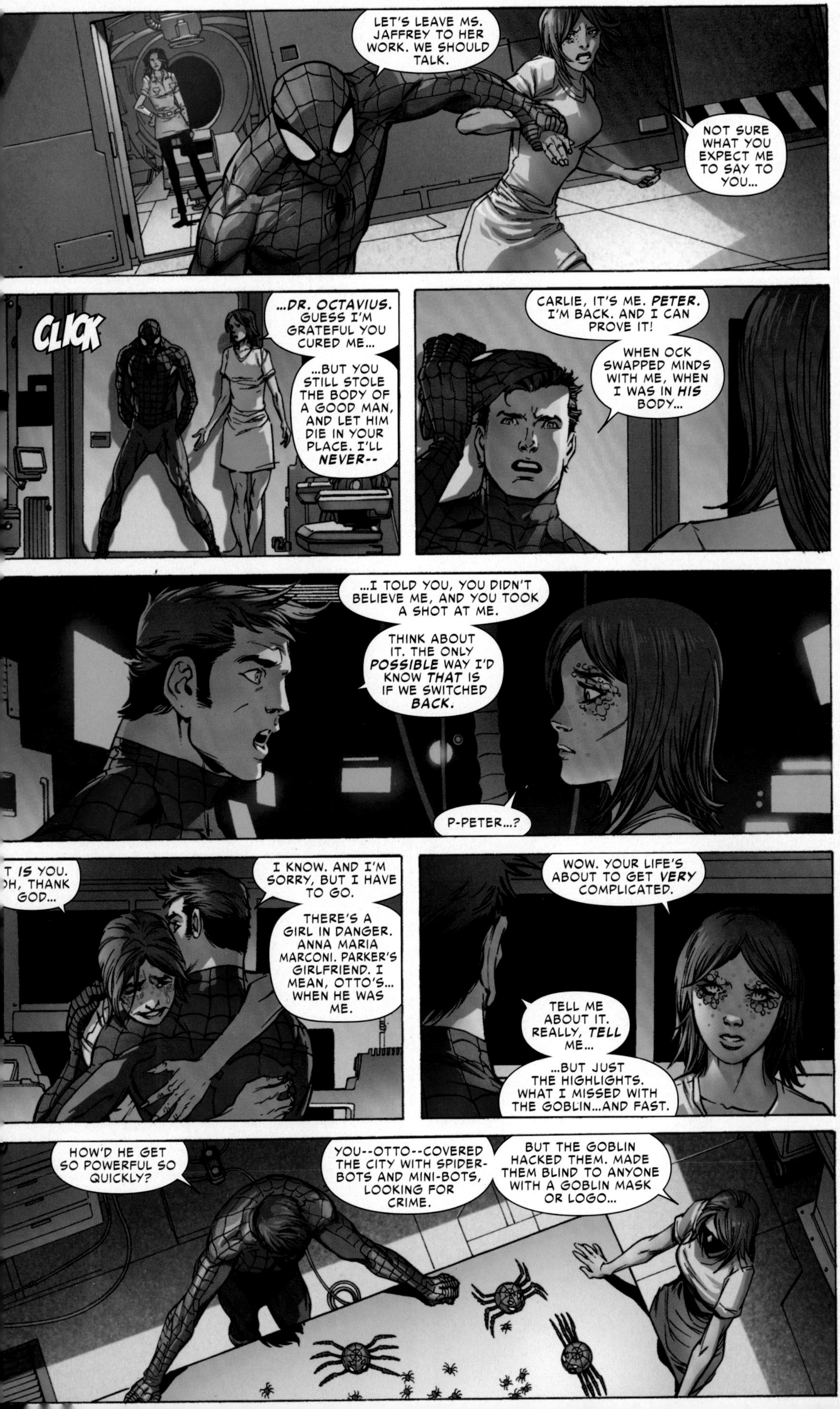
LET'S LEAVE MS. JAFFREY TO HER WORK. WE SHOULD TALK.
NOT SURE WHAT YOU EXPECT ME TO SAY TO YOU...
CLICK
...DR. OCTAVIUS. GUESS I'M GRATEFUL YOU CURED ME...
...BUT YOU STILL STOLE THE BODY OF A GOOD MAN, AND LET HIM DIE IN YOUR PLACE. I'LL NEVER--
CARLIE, IT'S ME. PETER. I'M BACK. AND I CAN PROVE IT!
WHEN OCK SWAPPED MINDS WITH ME, WHEN I WAS IN HIS BODY...
...I TOLD YOU, YOU DIDN'T BELIEVE ME, AND YOU TOOK A SHOT AT ME.
THINK ABOUT IT. THE ONLY POSSIBLE WAY I'D KNOW THAT IS IF WE SWITCHED BACK.
P-PETER...?
T IS YOU. OH, THANK GOD...
I KNOW. AND I'M SORRY, BUT I HAVE TO GO.
THERE'S A GIRL IN DANGER. ANNA MARIA MARCONI. PARKER'S GIRLFRIEND. I MEAN, OTTO'S... WHEN HE WAS ME.
WOW. YOUR LIFE'S ABOUT TO GET VERY COMPLICATED.
TELL ME ABOUT IT. REALLY, TELL ME...
...BUT JUST THE HIGHLIGHTS. WHAT I MISSED WITH THE GOBLIN...AND FAST.
HOW'D HE GET SO POWERFUL SO QUICKLY?
YOU--OTTO--COVERED THE CITY WITH SPIDER-BOTS AND MINI-BOTS, LOOKING FOR CRIME.
BUT THE GOBLIN HACKED THEM. MADE THEM BLIND TO ANYONE WITH A GOBLIN MASK OR LOGO...

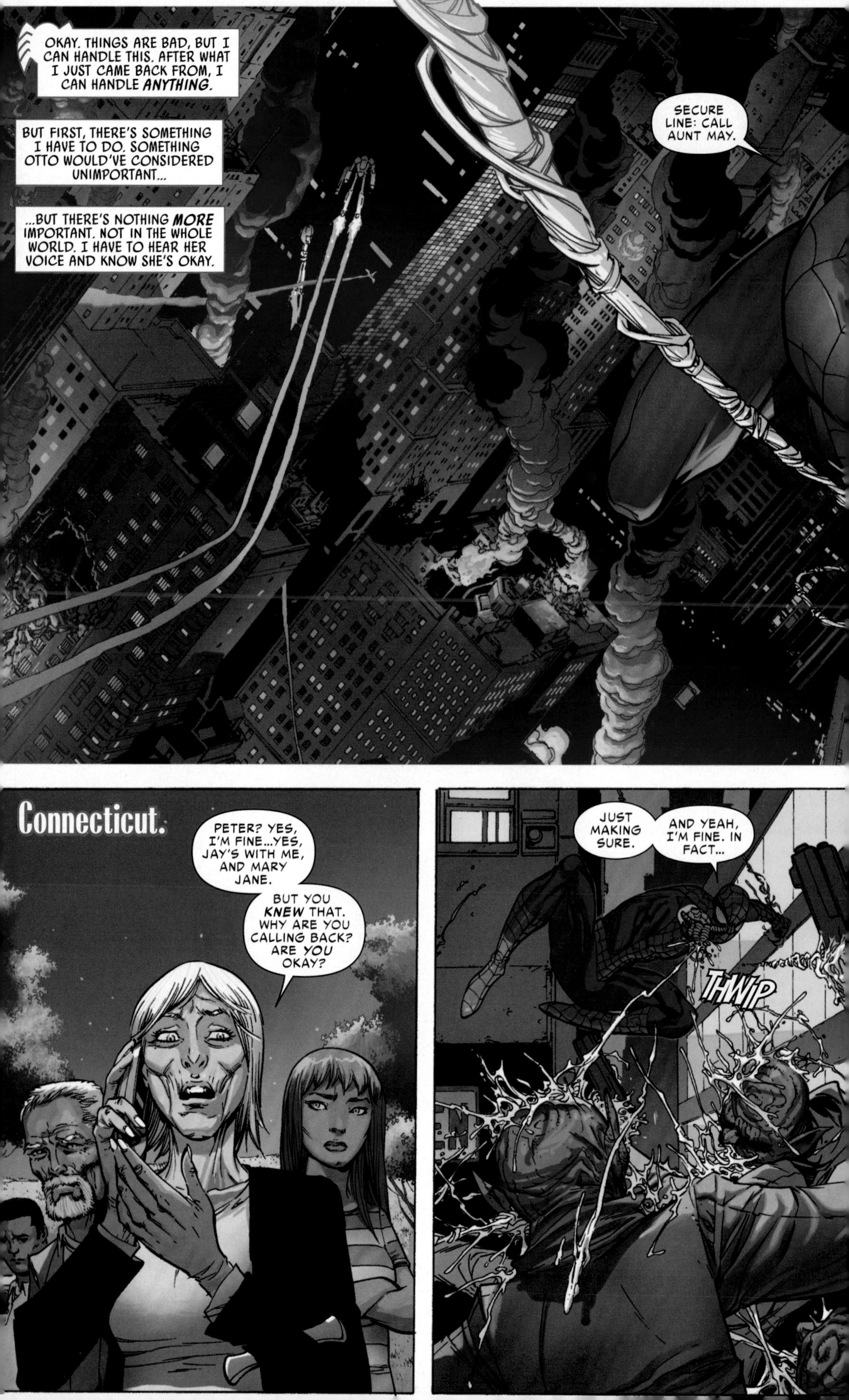
OKAY. THINGS ARE BAD, BUT I CAN HANDLE THIS. AFTER WHAT I JUST CAME BACK FROM, I CAN HANDLE ANYTHING.
BUT FIRST, THERE'S SOMETHING I HAVE TO DO. SOMETHING OTTO WOULD'VE CONSIDERED UNIMPORTANT...
...BUT THERE'S NOTHING MORE IMPORTANT. NOT IN THE WHOLE WORLD. I HAVE TO HEAR HER VOICE AND KNOW SHE'S OKAY.
SECURE LINE: CALL AUNT MAY.
Connecticut.
PETER? YES, I'M FINE...YES, JAY'S WITH ME, AND MARY JANE.
BUT YOU KNEW THAT. WHY ARE YOU CALLING BACK? ARE YOU OKAY?
JUST MAKING SURE.
AND YEAH, I'M FINE. IN FACT...
THWIP

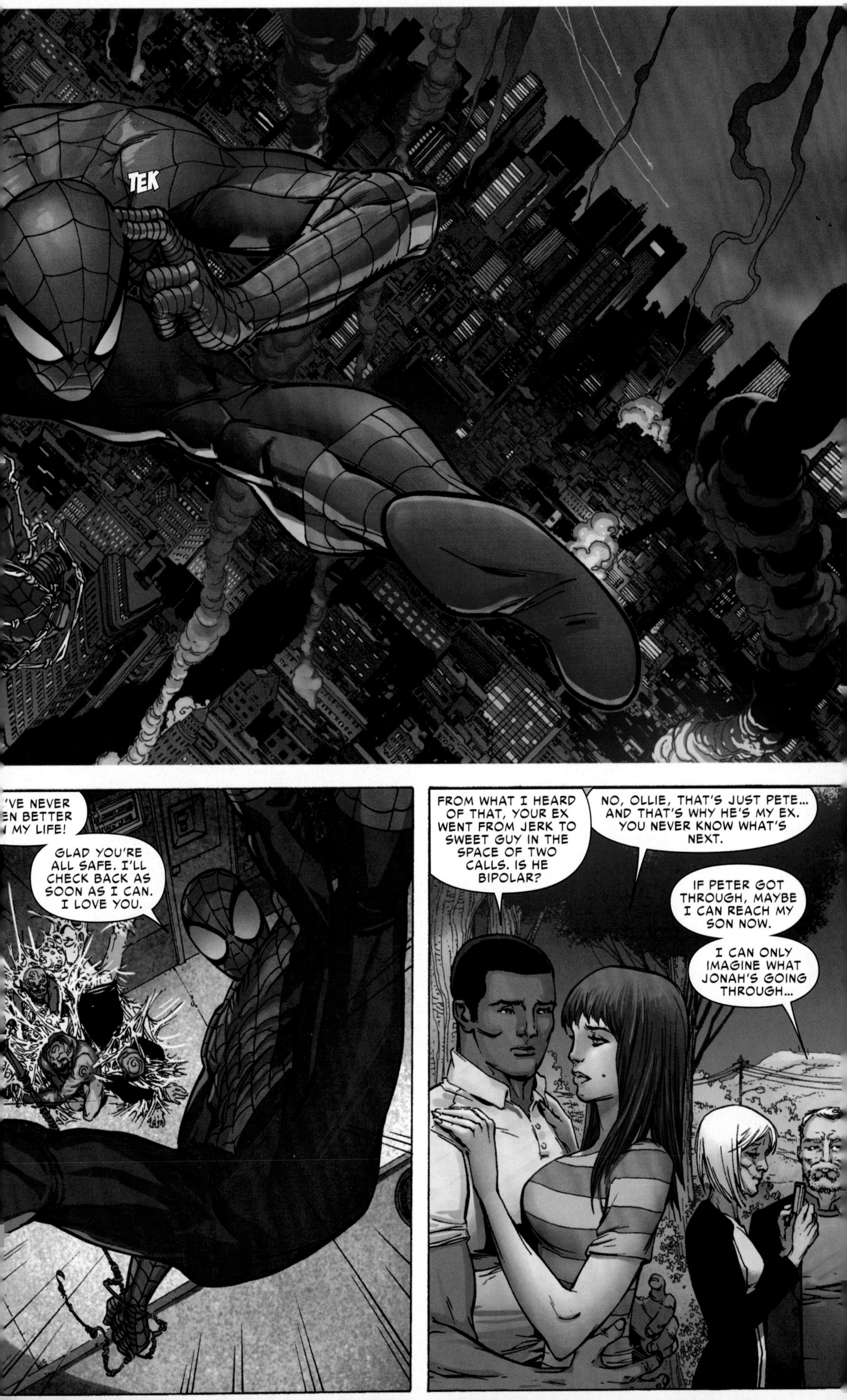
TEK
'VE NEVER EN BETTER N MY LIFE!
GLAD YOU'RE ALL SAFE. I'LL CHECK BACK AS SOON AS I CAN. I LOVE YOU.
FROM WHAT I HEARD OF THAT, YOUR EX WENT FROM JERK TO SWEET GUY IN THE SPACE OF TWO CALLS. IS HE BIPOLAR?
NO, OLLIE, THAT'S JUST PETE... AND THAT'S WHY HE'S MY EX. YOU NEVER KNOW WHAT'S NEXT.
IF PETER GOT THROUGH, MAYBE I CAN REACH MY SON NOW.
I CAN ONLY IMAGINE WHAT JONAH'S GOING THROUGH...

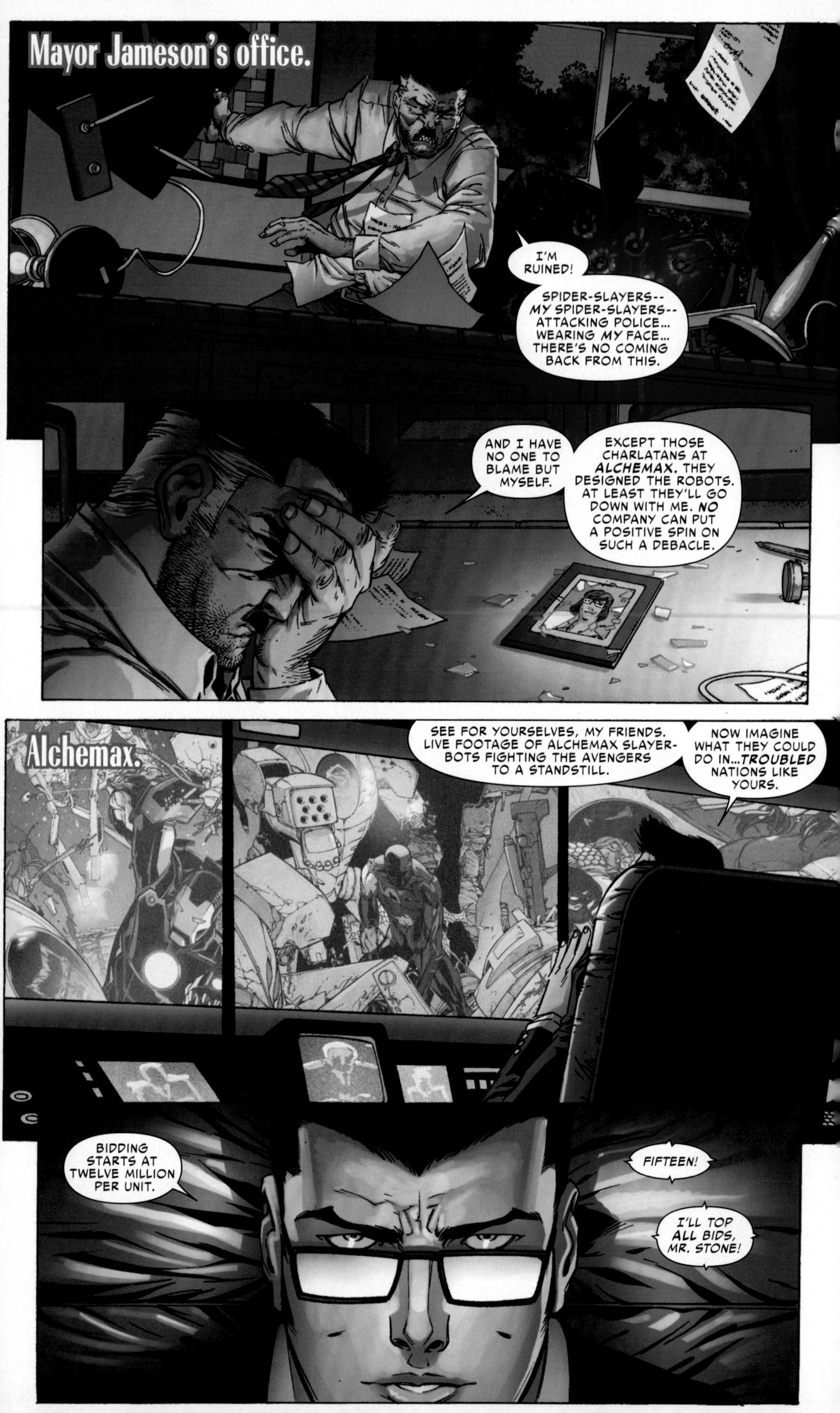
Mayor Jameson's office.
I'M RUINED!
SPIDER-SLAYERS-- MY SPIDER-SLAYERS-- ATTACKING POLICE... WEARING MY FACE... THERE'S NO COMING BACK FROM THIS.
AND I HAVE NO ONE TO BLAME BUT MYSELF.
EXCEPT THOSE CHARLATANS AT ALCHEMAX. THEY DESIGNED THE ROBOTS. AT LEAST THEY'LL GO DOWN WITH ME. NO COMPANY CAN PUT A POSITIVE SPIN ON SUCH A DEBACLE.
Alchemax.
SEE FOR YOURSELVES, MY FRIENDS. LIVE FOOTAGE OF ALCHEMAX SLAYER-BOTS FIGHTING THE AVENGERS TO A STANDSTILL.
NOW IMAGINE WHAT THEY COULD DO IN...TROUBLED NATIONS LIKE YOURS.
BIDDING STARTS AT TWELVE MILLION PER UNIT.
FIFTEEN!
I'LL TOP ALL BIDS, MR. STONE!

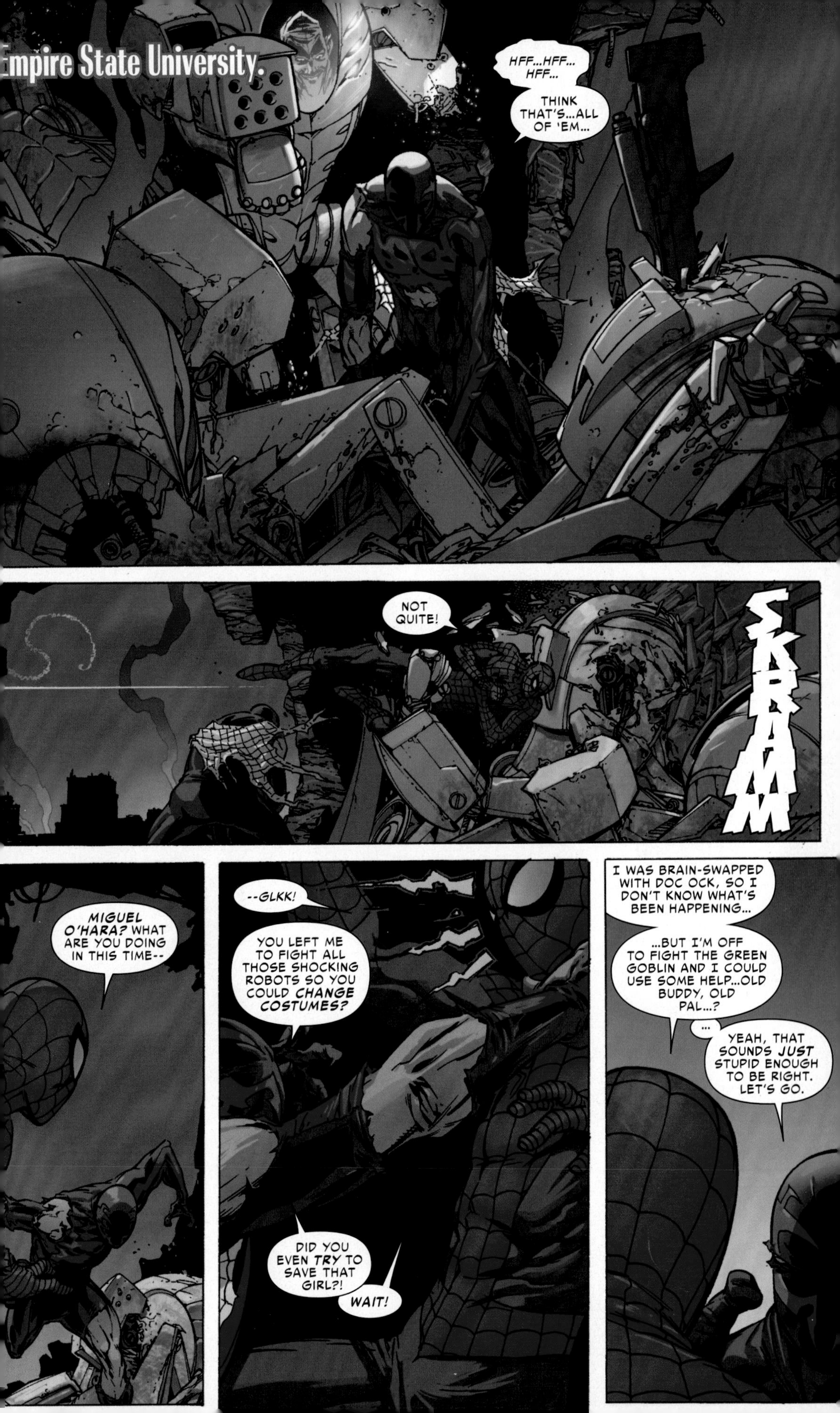
Empire State University.
HFF...HFF... HFF...
THINK THAT'S...ALL OF 'EM...
NOT QUITE!
SKRAM
MIGUEL O'HARA? WHAT ARE YOU DOING IN THIS TIME--
--GLKK!
YOU LEFT ME TO FIGHT ALL THOSE SHOCKING ROBOTS SO YOU COULD CHANGE COSTUMES?
DID YOU EVEN TRY TO SAVE THAT GIRL?!
WAIT!
I WAS BRAIN-SWAPPED WITH DOC OCK, SO I DON'T KNOW WHAT'S BEEN HAPPENING...
...BUT I'M OFF TO FIGHT THE GREEN GOBLIN AND I COULD USE SOME HELP...OLD BUDDY, OLD PAL...?
...
YEAH, THAT SOUNDS JUST STUPID ENOUGH TO BE RIGHT. LET'S GO.

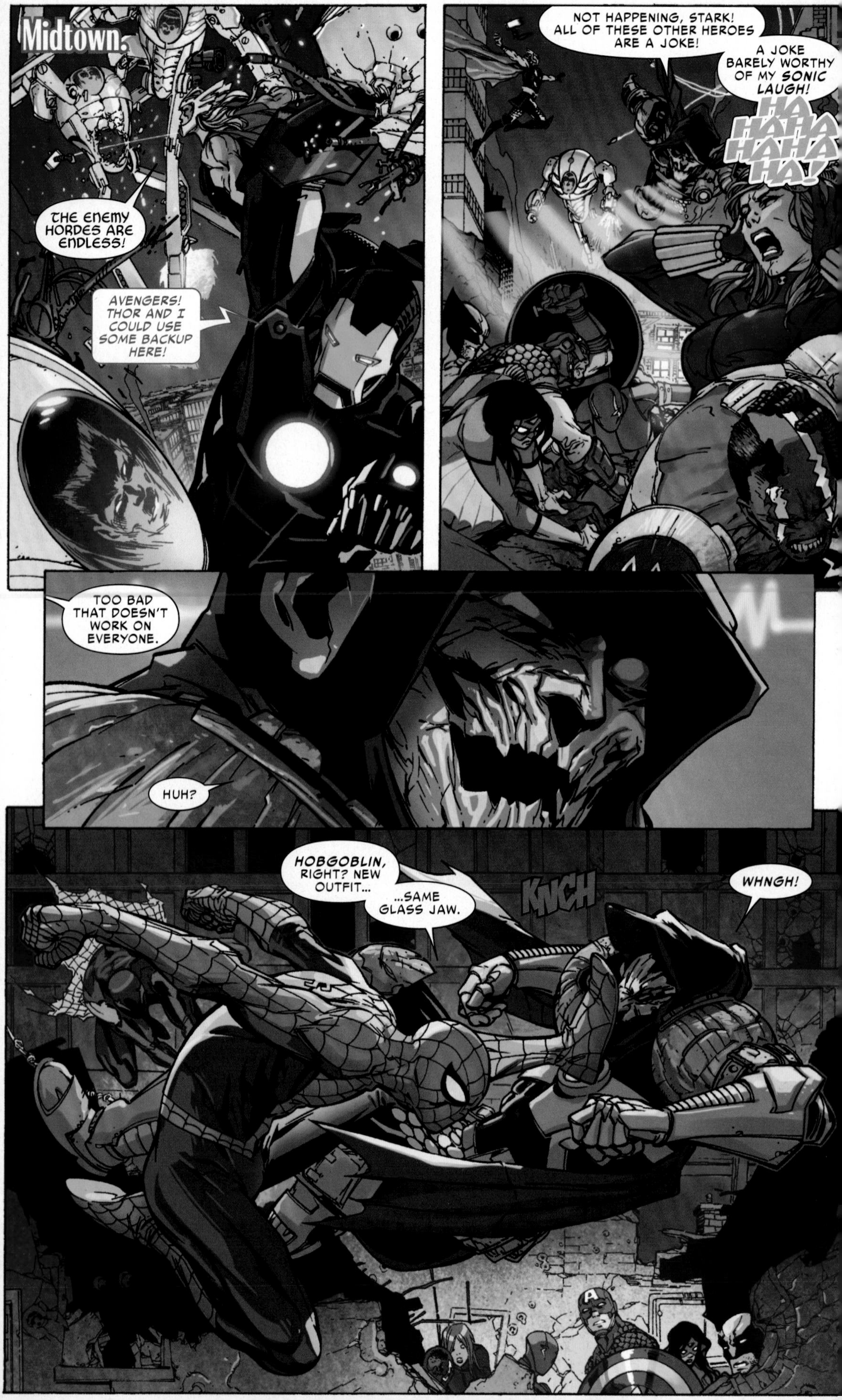
Midtown.
THE ENEMY HORDES ARE ENDLESS!
AVENGERS! THOR AND I COULD USE SOME BACKUP HERE!
NOT HAPPENING, STARK! ALL OF THESE OTHER HEROES ARE A JOKE!
A JOKE BARELY WORTHY OF MY SONIC LAUGH!
HA HAHA HAHA HA!
TOO BAD THAT DOESN'T WORK ON EVERYONE.
HUH?
HOBGOBLIN, RIGHT? NEW OUTFIT...
...SAME GLASS JAW.
KNCH
WHNGH!

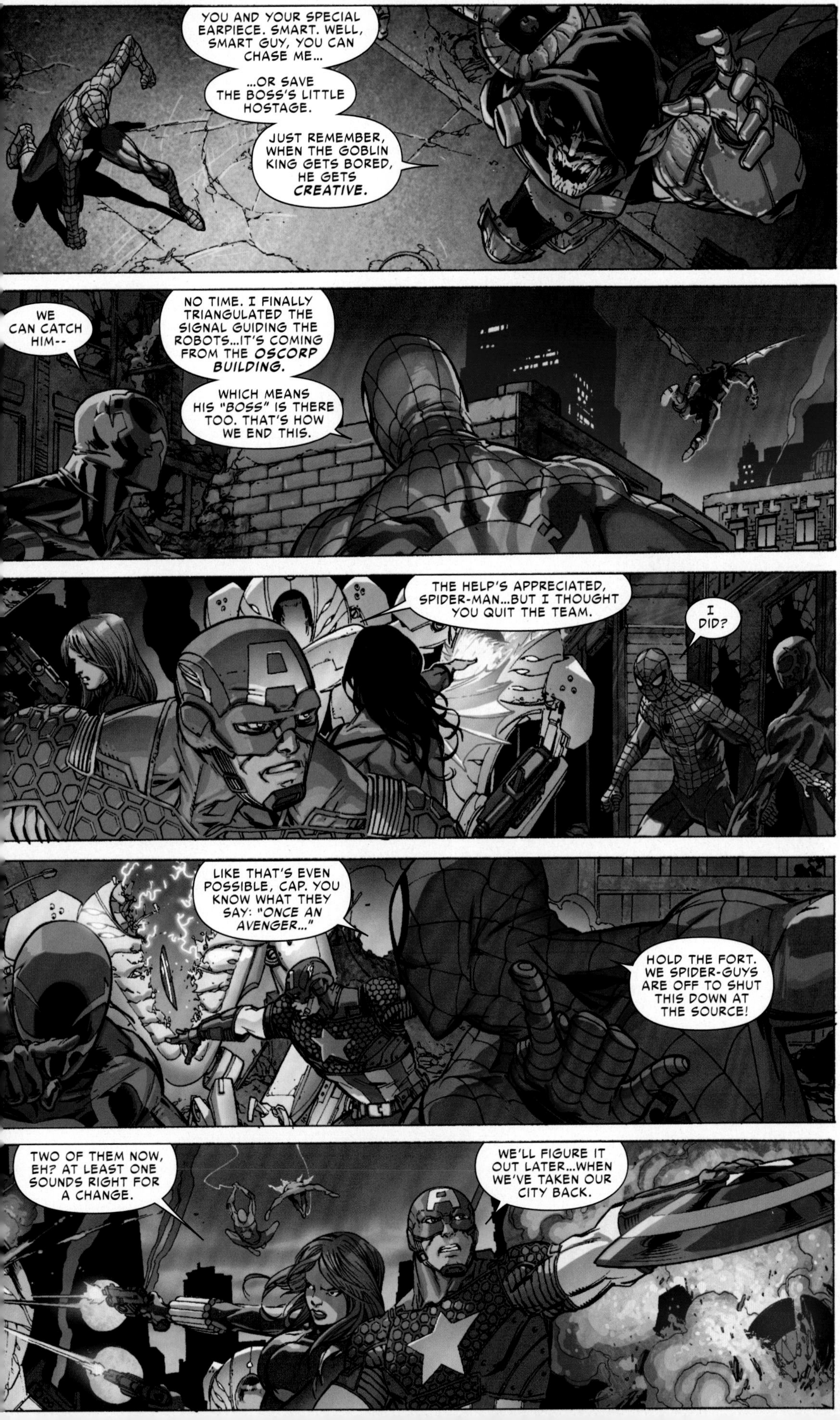

YOU AND YOUR SPECIAL EARPIECE. SMART. WELL, SMART GUY, YOU CAN CHASE ME...
...OR SAVE THE BOSS'S LITTLE HOSTAGE.
JUST REMEMBER, WHEN THE GOBLIN KING GETS BORED, HE GETS *CREATIVE*.
WE CAN CATCH HIM--
NO TIME. I FINALLY TRIANGULATED THE SIGNAL GUIDING THE ROBOTS...IT'S COMING FROM THE *OSCORP BUILDING*.
WHICH MEANS HIS "*BOSS*" IS THERE TOO. THAT'S HOW WE END THIS.
THE HELP'S APPRECIATED, SPIDER-MAN...BUT I THOUGHT YOU QUIT THE TEAM.
I DID?
LIKE THAT'S EVEN POSSIBLE, CAP. YOU KNOW WHAT THEY SAY: "*ONCE AN AVENGER...*"
HOLD THE FORT. WE SPIDER-GUYS ARE OFF TO SHUT THIS DOWN AT THE SOURCE!
TWO OF THEM NOW, EH? AT LEAST ONE SOUNDS RIGHT FOR A CHANGE.
WE'LL FIGURE IT OUT LATER...WHEN WE'VE TAKEN OUR CITY BACK.

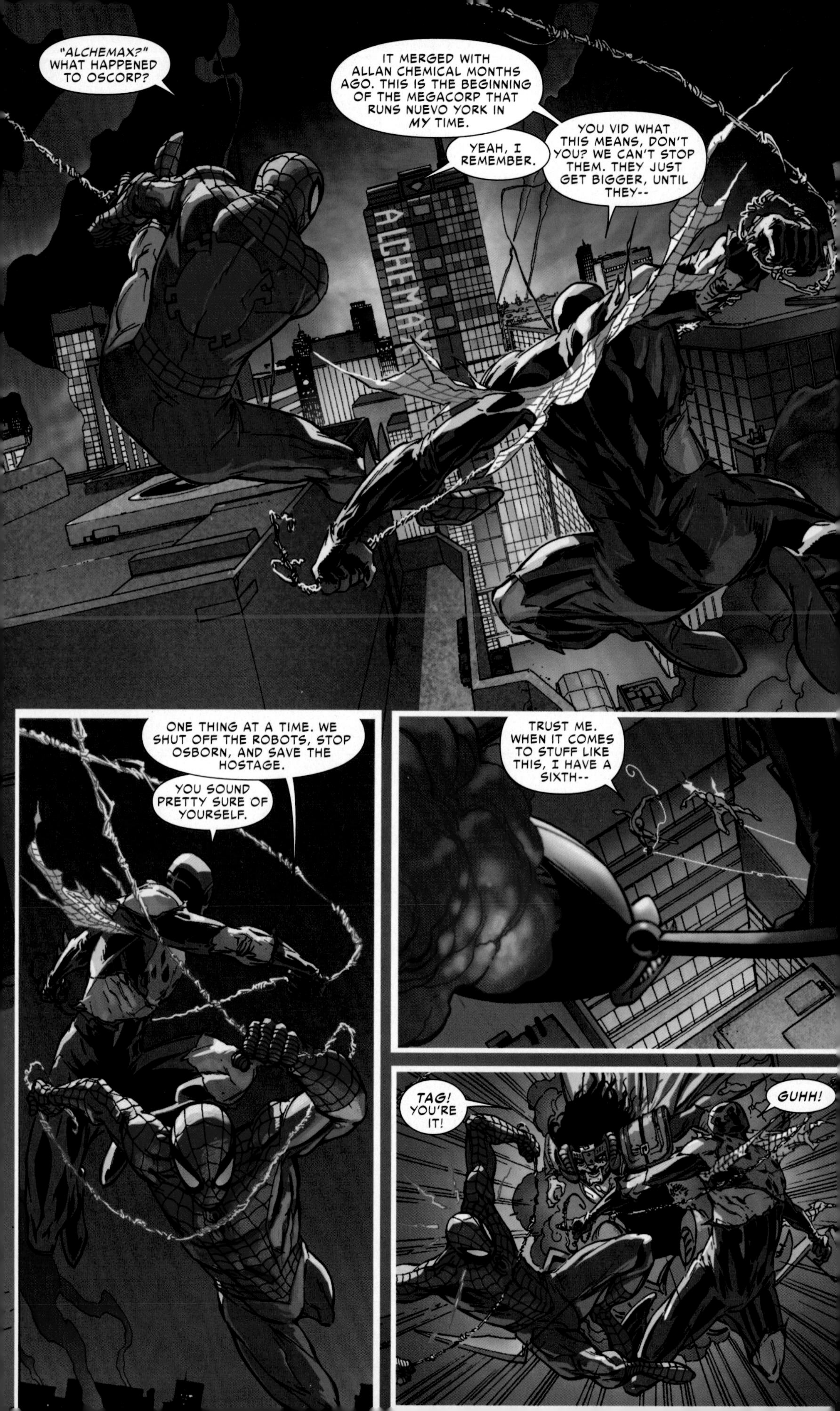
"ALCHEMAX?" WHAT HAPPENED TO OSCORP?
IT MERGED WITH ALLAN CHEMICAL MONTHS AGO. THIS IS THE BEGINNING OF THE MEGACORP THAT RUNS NUEVO YORK IN MY TIME.
YEAH, I REMEMBER.
YOU VID WHAT THIS MEANS, DON'T YOU? WE CAN'T STOP THEM. THEY JUST GET BIGGER, UNTIL THEY--
ALCHEMAX
ONE THING AT A TIME. WE SHUT OFF THE ROBOTS, STOP OSBORN, AND SAVE THE HOSTAGE.
YOU SOUND PRETTY SURE OF YOURSELF.
TRUST ME. WHEN IT COMES TO STUFF LIKE THIS, I HAVE A SIXTH--
TAG! YOU'RE IT!
GUHH!

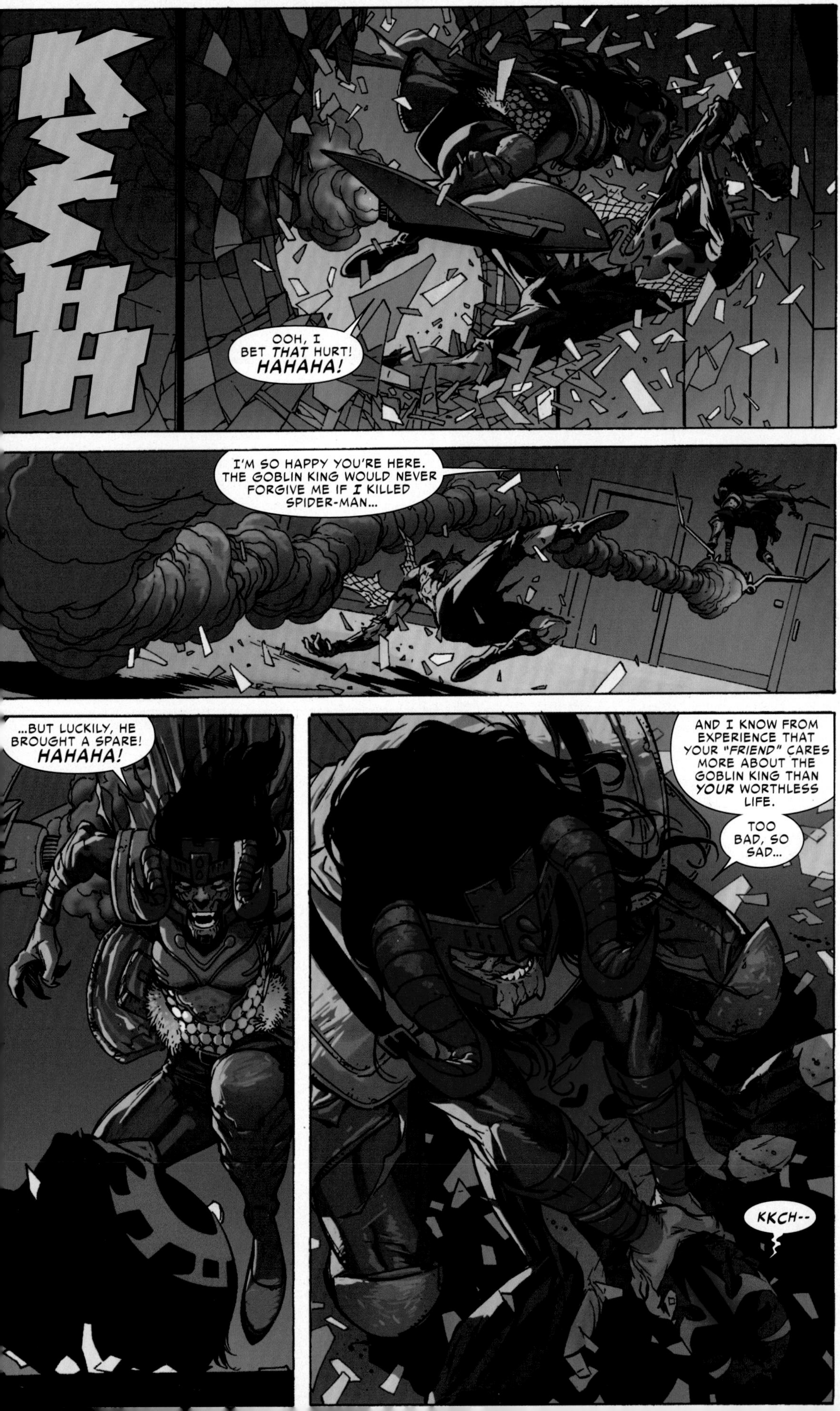
KSSHH
OOH, I BET THAT HURT! HAHAHA!
I'M SO HAPPY YOU'RE HERE. THE GOBLIN KING WOULD NEVER FORGIVE ME IF I KILLED SPIDER-MAN...
...BUT LUCKILY, HE BROUGHT A SPARE! HAHAHA!
AND I KNOW FROM EXPERIENCE THAT YOUR "FRIEND" CARES MORE ABOUT THE GOBLIN KING THAN YOUR WORTHLESS LIFE.
TOO BAD, SO SAD...
KKCH--

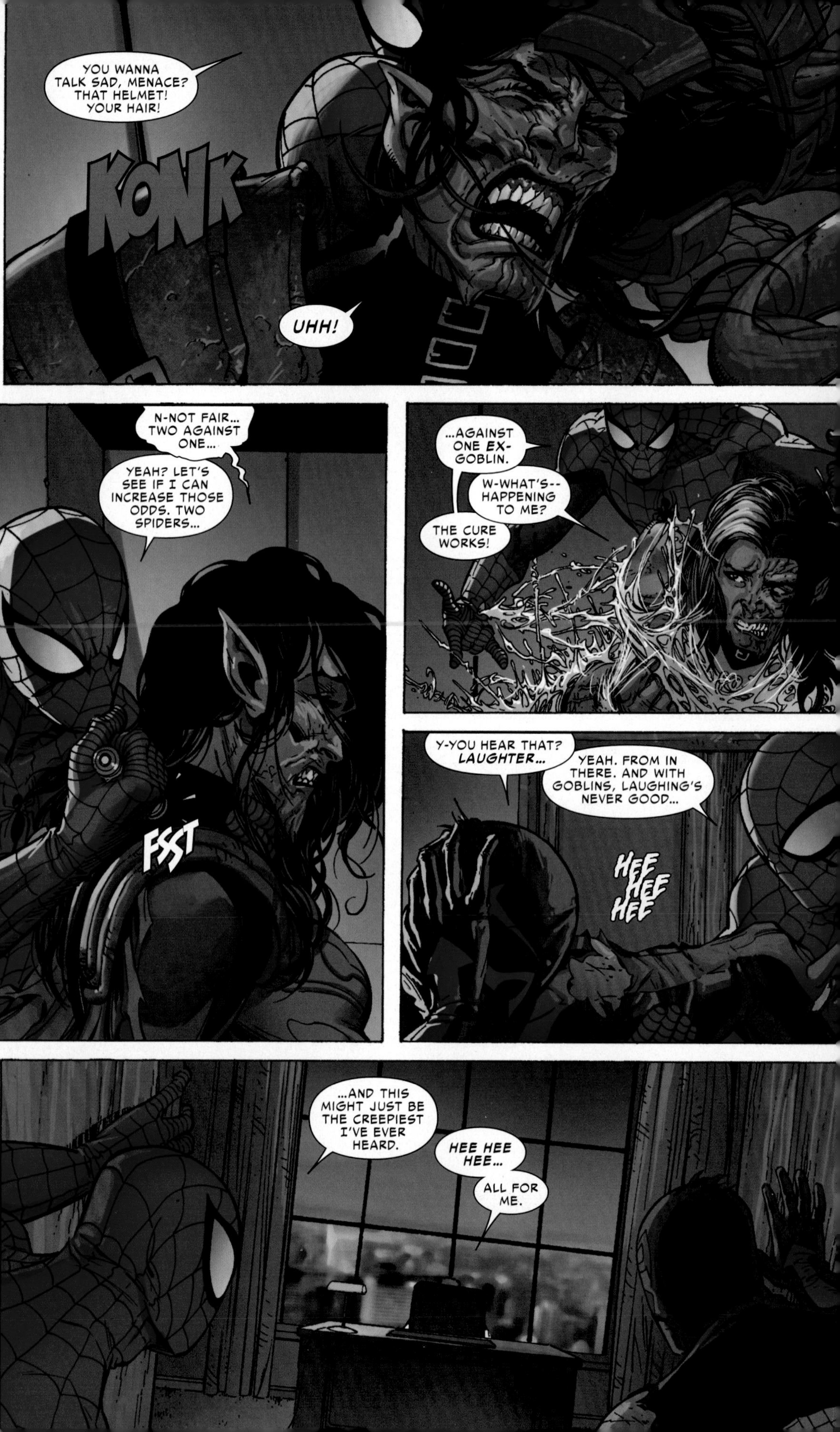
YOU WANNA TALK SAD, MENACE? THAT HELMET! YOUR HAIR!
KONK
UHH!
N-NOT FAIR... TWO AGAINST ONE...
YEAH? LET'S SEE IF I CAN INCREASE THOSE ODDS. TWO SPIDERS...
FSST
...AGAINST ONE EX-GOBLIN.
W-WHAT'S-- HAPPENING TO ME?
THE CURE WORKS!
Y-YOU HEAR THAT? LAUGHTER...
YEAH. FROM IN THERE. AND WITH GOBLINS, LAUGHING'S NEVER GOOD...
HEE HEE HEE
...AND THIS MIGHT JUST BE THE CREEPIEST I'VE EVER HEARD.
HEE HEE HEE...
ALL FOR ME.

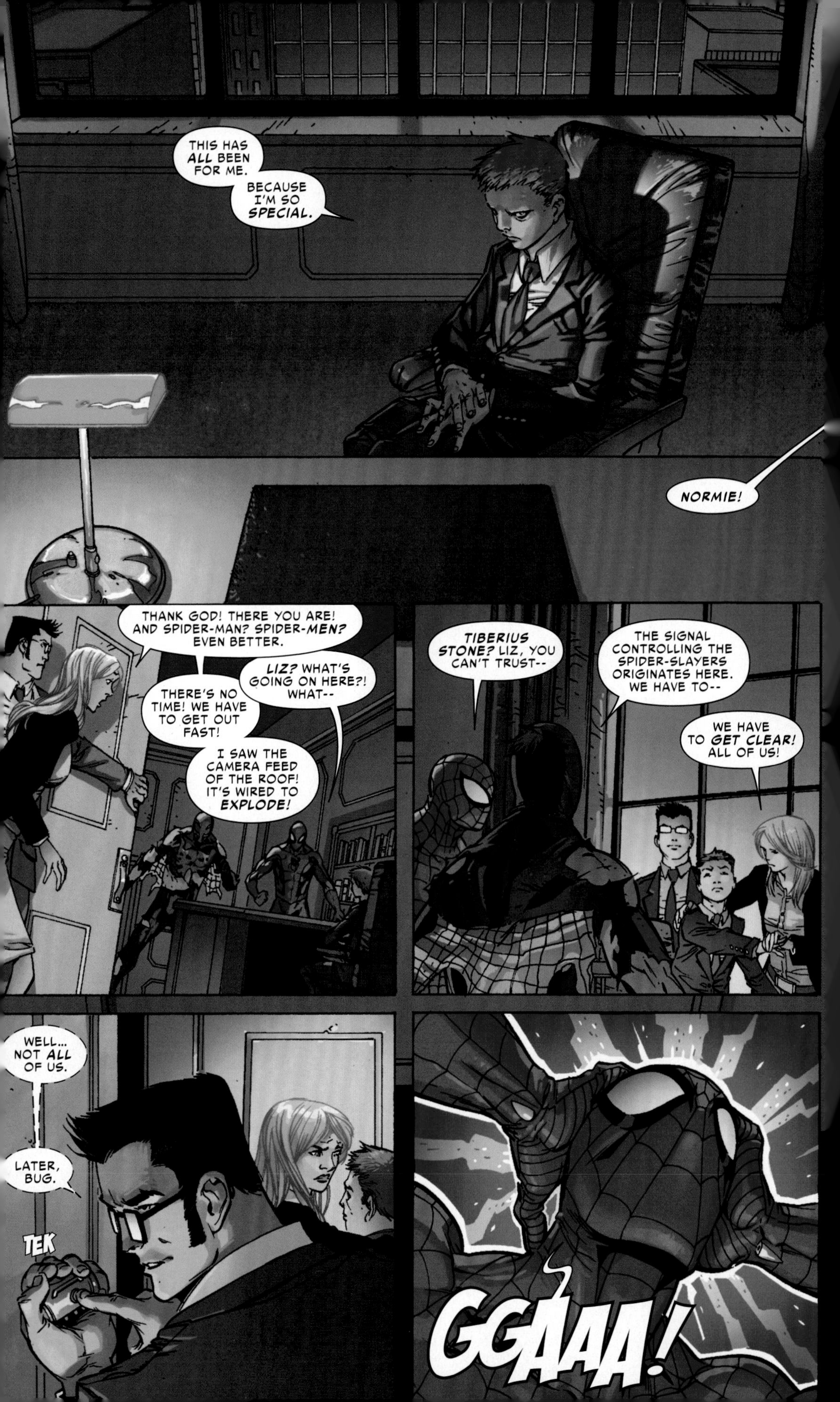
THIS HAS ALL BEEN FOR ME.
BECAUSE I'M SO SPECIAL.
NORMIE!
THANK GOD! THERE YOU ARE! AND SPIDER-MAN? SPIDER-MEN? EVEN BETTER.
LIZ? WHAT'S GOING ON HERE?! WHAT--
THERE'S NO TIME! WE HAVE TO GET OUT FAST!
I SAW THE CAMERA FEED OF THE ROOF! IT'S WIRED TO EXPLODE!
TIBERIUS STONE? LIZ, YOU CAN'T TRUST--
THE SIGNAL CONTROLLING THE SPIDER-SLAYERS ORIGINATES HERE. WE HAVE TO--
WE HAVE TO GET CLEAR! ALL OF US!
WELL... NOT ALL OF US.
LATER, BUG.
TEK
GGAAAA!

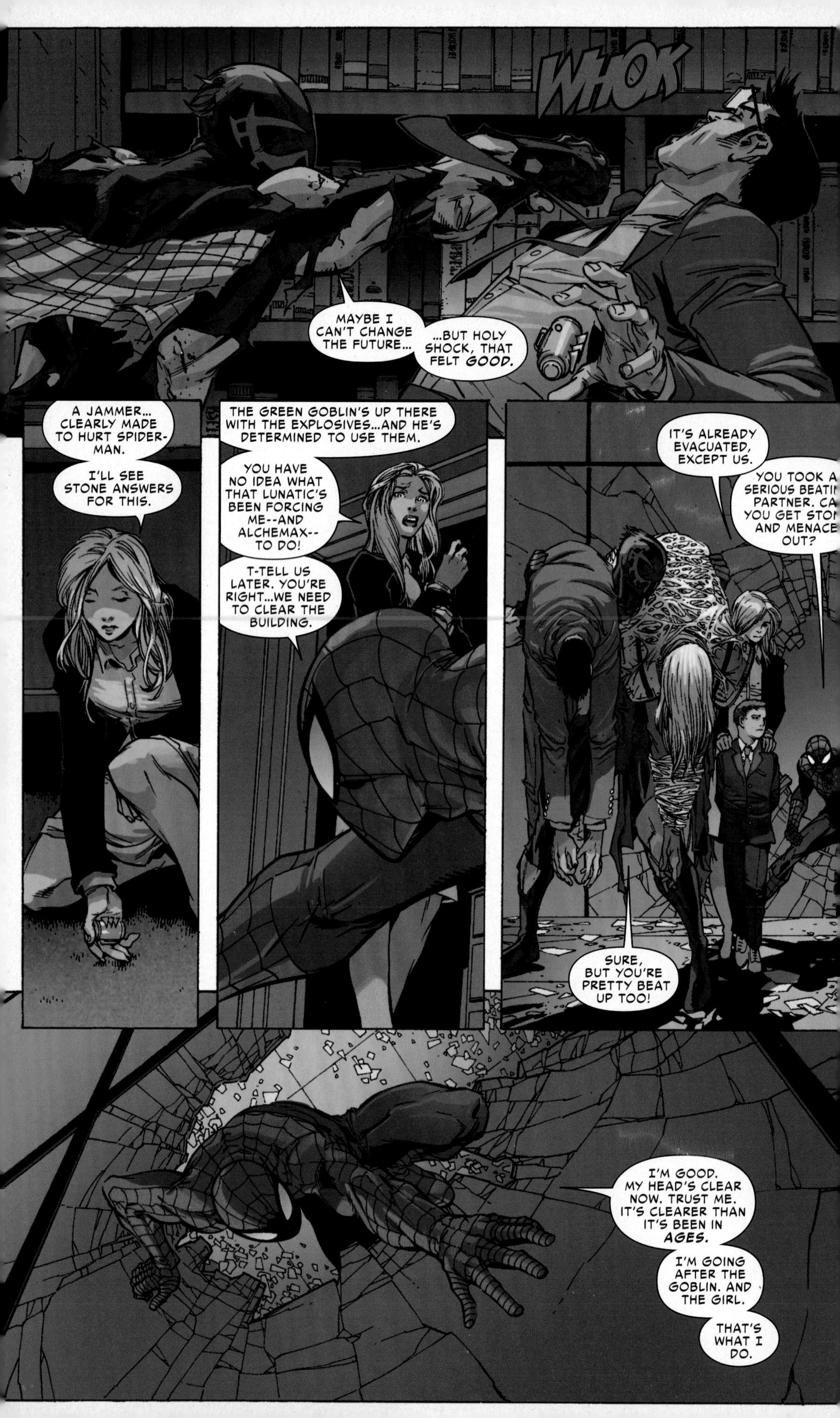
WHOK
MAYBE I CAN'T CHANGE THE FUTURE...
...BUT HOLY SHOCK, THAT FELT GOOD.
A JAMMER... CLEARLY MADE TO HURT SPIDER-MAN.
I'LL SEE STONE ANSWERS FOR THIS.
THE GREEN GOBLIN'S UP THERE WITH THE EXPLOSIVES...AND HE'S DETERMINED TO USE THEM.
YOU HAVE NO IDEA WHAT THAT LUNATIC'S BEEN FORCING ME--AND ALCHEMAX--TO DO!
T-TELL US LATER. YOU'RE RIGHT...WE NEED TO CLEAR THE BUILDING.
IT'S ALREADY EVACUATED, EXCEPT US.
SURE, BUT YOU'RE PRETTY BEAT UP TOO!
I'M GOOD. MY HEAD'S CLEAR NOW. TRUST ME. IT'S CLEARER THAN IT'S BEEN IN AGES.
I'M GOING AFTER THE GOBLIN. AND THE GIRL.
THAT'S WHAT I DO.

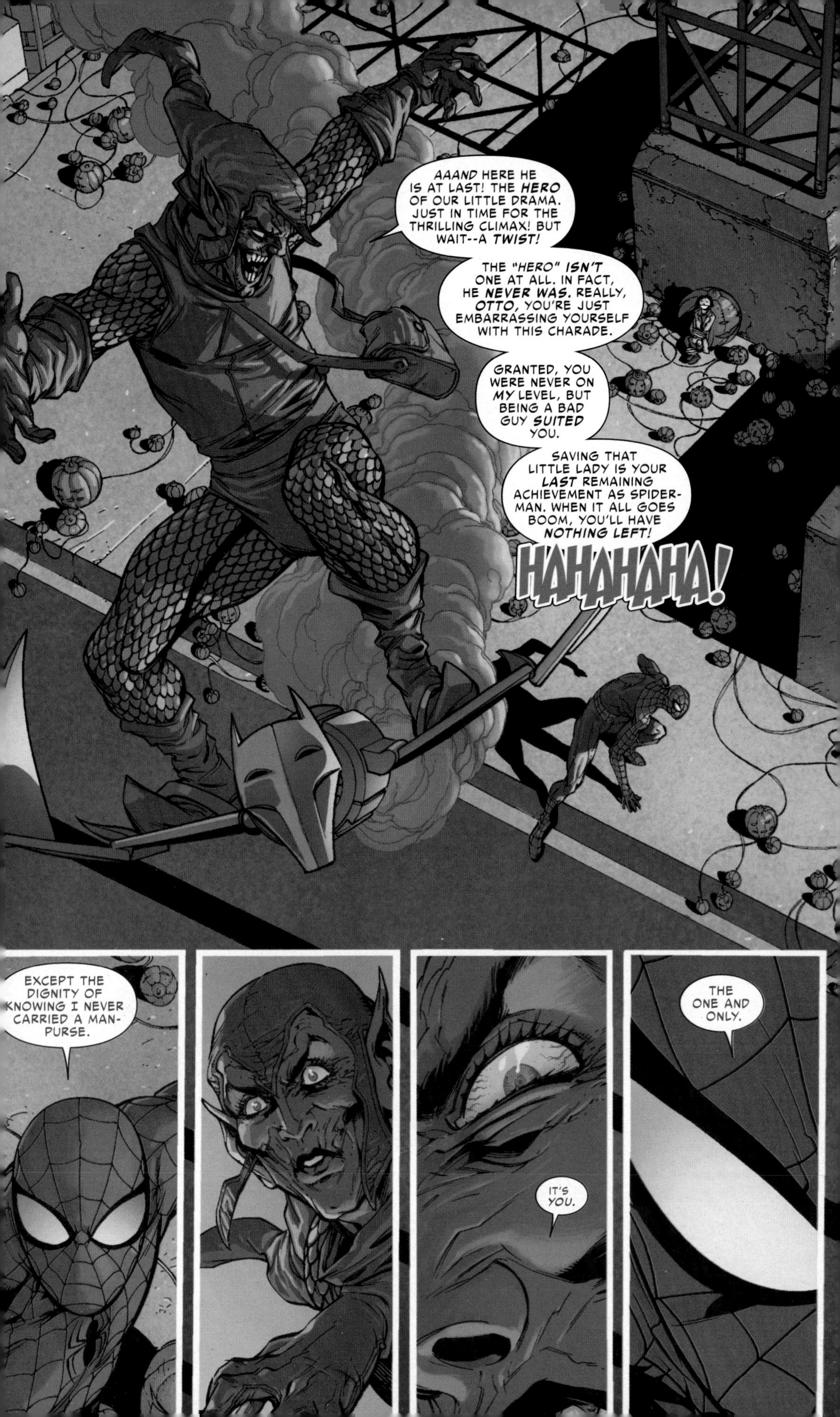
AAAND HERE HE IS AT LAST! THE HERO OF OUR LITTLE DRAMA. JUST IN TIME FOR THE THRILLING CLIMAX! BUT WAIT--A TWIST!
THE "HERO" ISN'T ONE AT ALL. IN FACT, HE NEVER WAS. REALLY, OTTO, YOU'RE JUST EMBARRASSING YOURSELF WITH THIS CHARADE.
GRANTED, YOU WERE NEVER ON MY LEVEL, BUT BEING A BAD GUY SUITED YOU.
SAVING THAT LITTLE LADY IS YOUR LAST REMAINING ACHIEVEMENT AS SPIDER-MAN. WHEN IT ALL GOES BOOM, YOU'LL HAVE NOTHING LEFT!
HAHAHAHA!
EXCEPT THE DIGNITY OF KNOWING I NEVER CARRIED A MAN-PURSE.
IT'S YOU.
THE ONE AND ONLY.

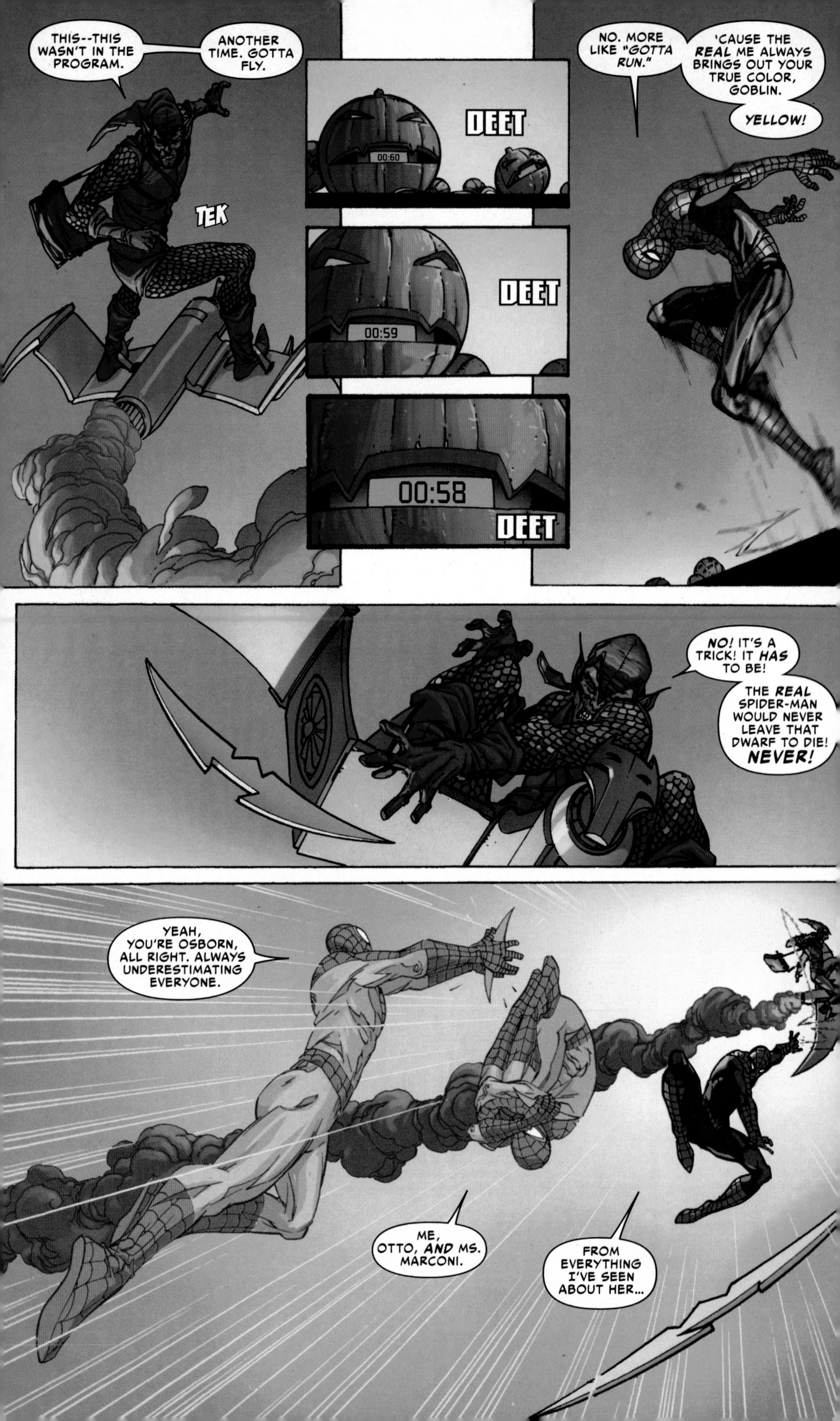
THIS--THIS WASN'T IN THE PROGRAM.
ANOTHER TIME. GOTTA FLY.
TEK
DEET
00:60
DEET
00:59
DEET
00:58
NO. MORE LIKE "GOTTA RUN."
'CAUSE THE REAL ME ALWAYS BRINGS OUT YOUR TRUE COLOR, GOBLIN.
YELLOW!
NO! IT'S A TRICK! IT HAS TO BE!
THE REAL SPIDER-MAN WOULD NEVER LEAVE THAT DWARF TO DIE! NEVER!
YEAH, YOU'RE OSBORN, ALL RIGHT. ALWAYS UNDERESTIMATING EVERYONE.
ME, OTTO, AND MS. MARCONI.
FROM EVERYTHING I'VE SEEN ABOUT HER...

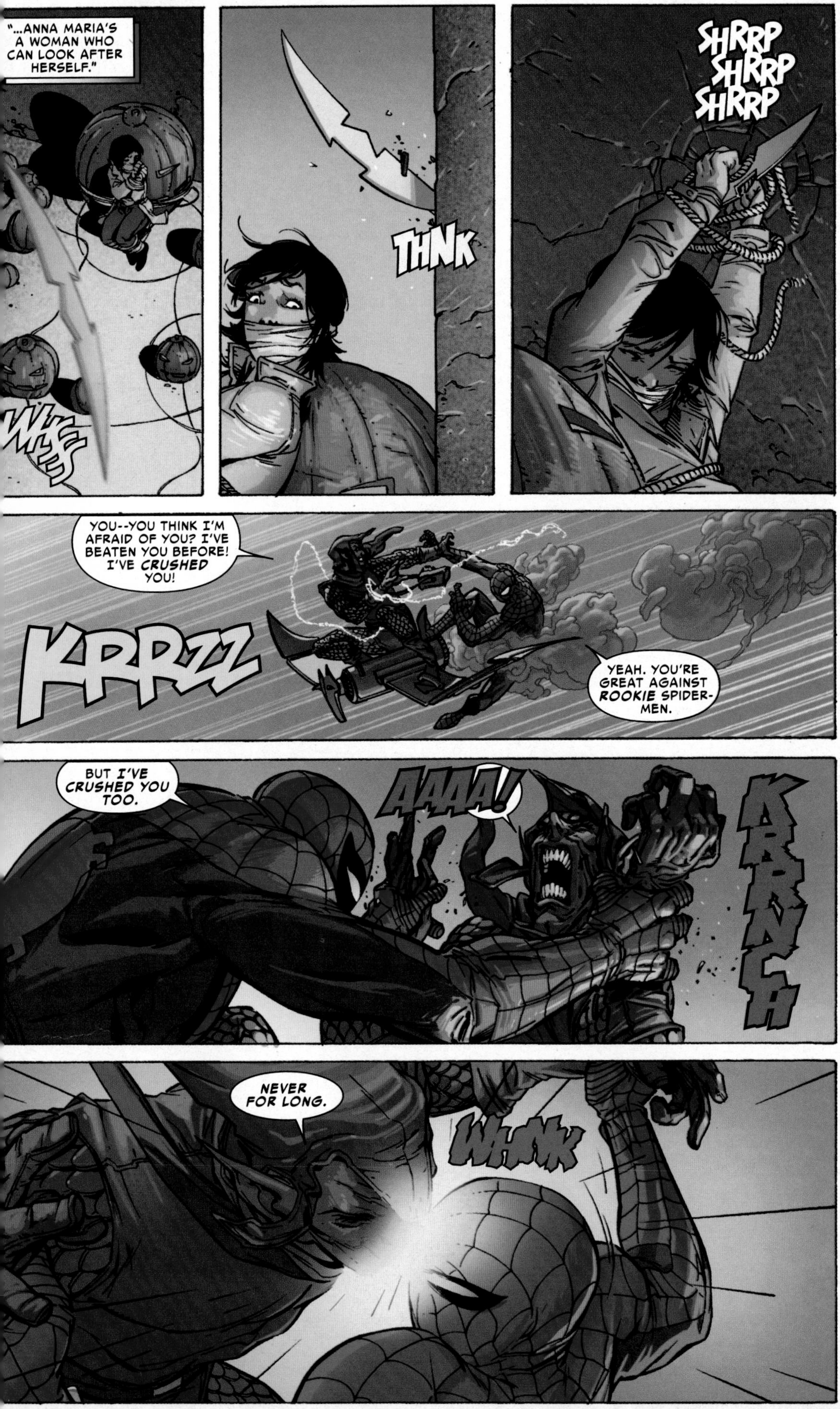
"...ANNA MARIA'S A WOMAN WHO CAN LOOK AFTER HERSELF."
THNK
SHRRP SHRRP SHRRP
YOU--YOU THINK I'M AFRAID OF YOU? I'VE BEATEN YOU BEFORE! I'VE CRUSHED YOU!
KRRZZ
YEAH. YOU'RE GREAT AGAINST ROOKIE SPIDER-MEN.
BUT I'VE CRUSHED YOU TOO.
AAAA!
KRRNCH
NEVER FOR LONG.
WHNK

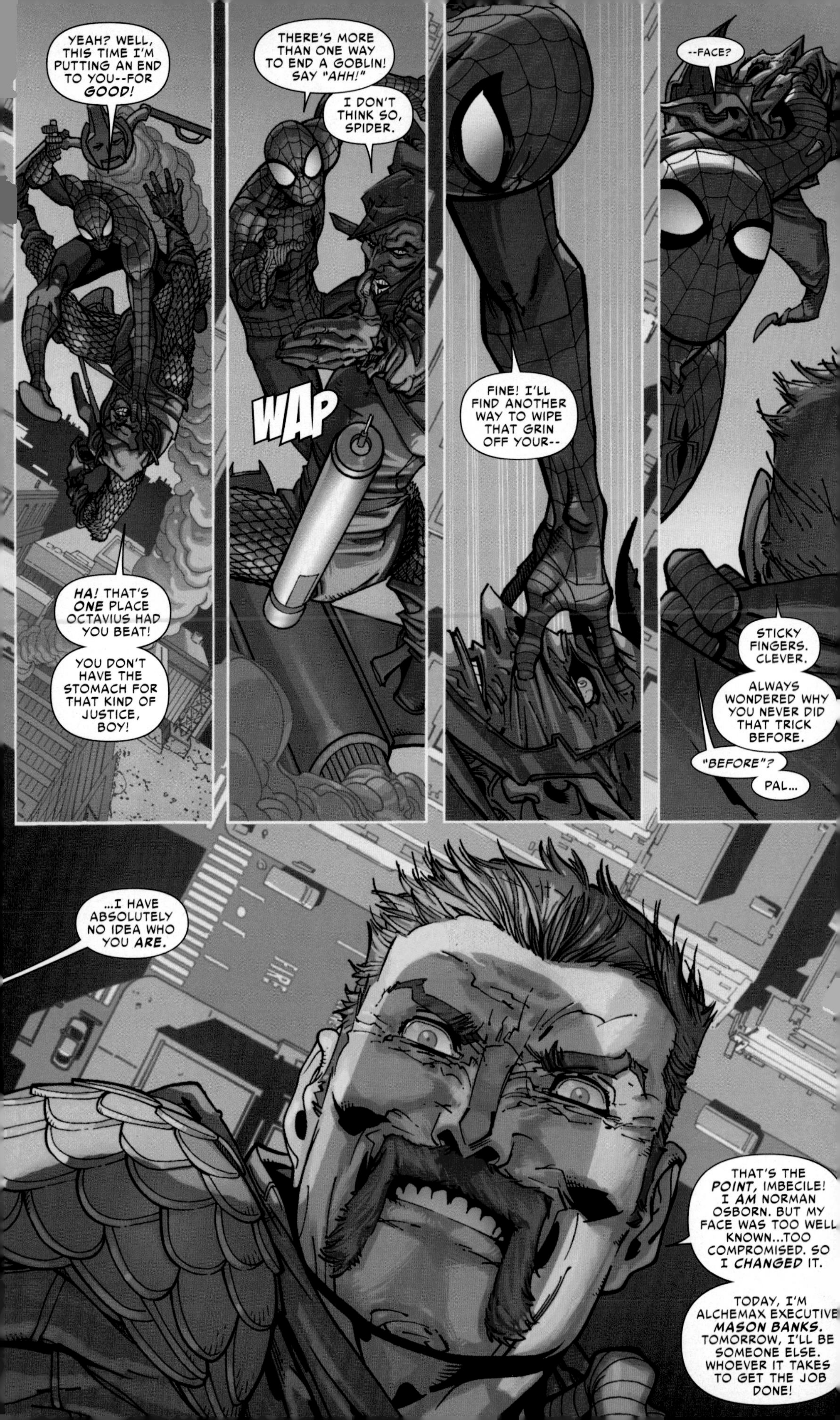
YEAH? WELL, THIS TIME I'M PUTTING AN END TO YOU--FOR GOOD!
HA! THAT'S ONE PLACE OCTAVIUS HAD YOU BEAT!
YOU DON'T HAVE THE STOMACH FOR THAT KIND OF JUSTICE, BOY!
THERE'S MORE THAN ONE WAY TO END A GOBLIN! SAY "AHH!"
I DON'T THINK SO, SPIDER.
WAP
FINE! I'LL FIND ANOTHER WAY TO WIPE THAT GRIN OFF YOUR--
--FACE?
STICKY FINGERS. CLEVER.
ALWAYS WONDERED WHY YOU NEVER DID THAT TRICK BEFORE.
"BEFORE"?
PAL...
...I HAVE ABSOLUTELY NO IDEA WHO YOU ARE.
THAT'S THE POINT, IMBECILE! I AM NORMAN OSBORN. BUT MY FACE WAS TOO WELL KNOWN...TOO COMPROMISED. SO I CHANGED IT.
TODAY, I'M ALCHEMAX EXECUTIVE MASON BANKS. TOMORROW, I'LL BE SOMEONE ELSE. WHOEVER IT TAKES TO GET THE JOB DONE!

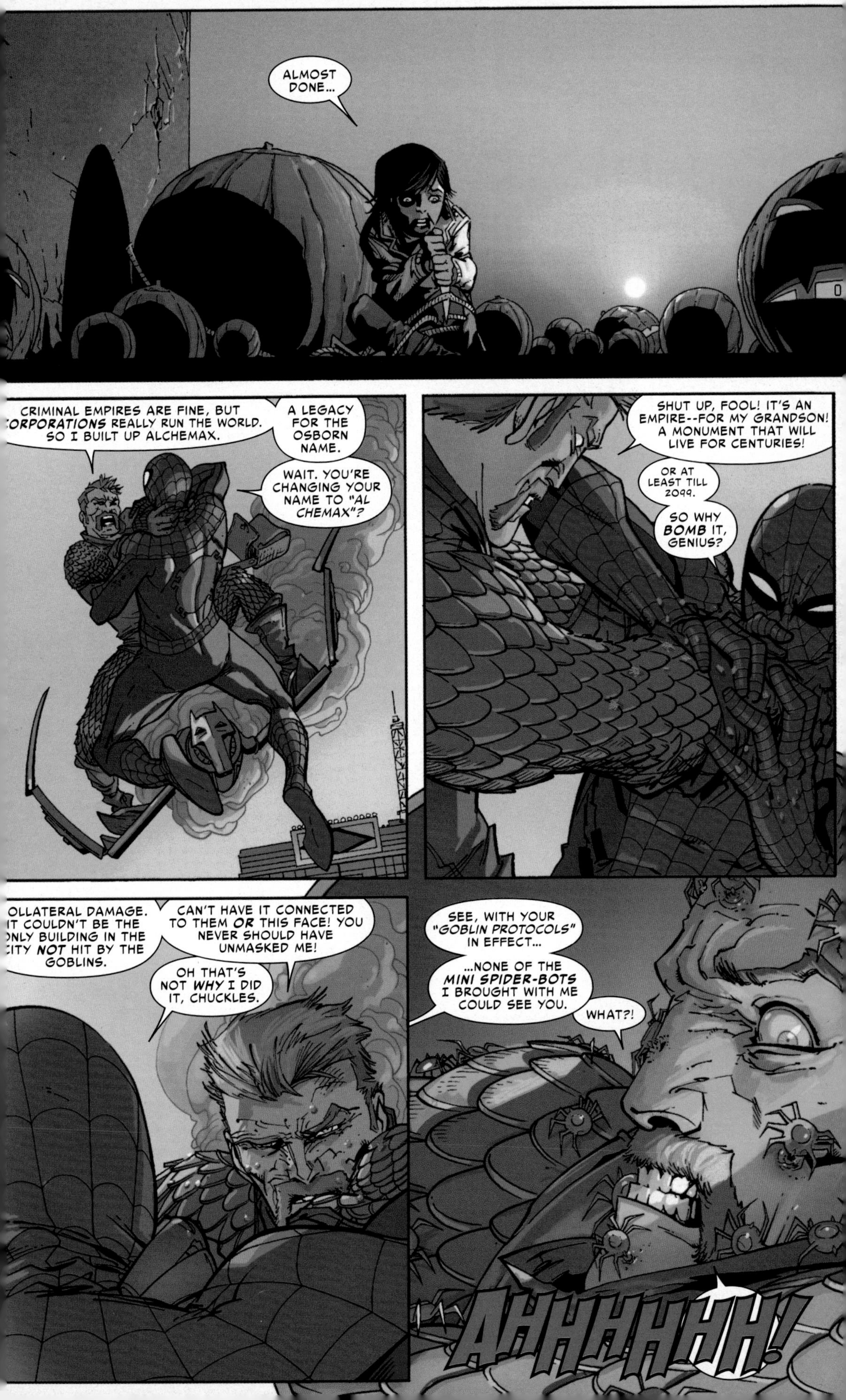
ALMOST DONE...
CRIMINAL EMPIRES ARE FINE, BUT CORPORATIONS REALLY RUN THE WORLD. SO I BUILT UP ALCHEMAX.
A LEGACY FOR THE OSBORN NAME.
WAIT. YOU'RE CHANGING YOUR NAME TO "AL CHEMAX"?
SHUT UP, FOOL! IT'S AN EMPIRE--FOR MY GRANDSON! A MONUMENT THAT WILL LIVE FOR CENTURIES!
OR AT LEAST TILL 2099.
SO WHY BOMB IT, GENIUS?
OLLATERAL DAMAGE. IT COULDN'T BE THE ONLY BUILDING IN THE CITY NOT HIT BY THE GOBLINS.
CAN'T HAVE IT CONNECTED TO THEM OR THIS FACE! YOU NEVER SHOULD HAVE UNMASKED ME!
OH THAT'S NOT WHY I DID IT, CHUCKLES.
SEE, WITH YOUR "GOBLIN PROTOCOLS" IN EFFECT...
...NONE OF THE MINI SPIDER-BOTS I BROUGHT WITH ME COULD SEE YOU.
WHAT?!
AHHHHHHH!

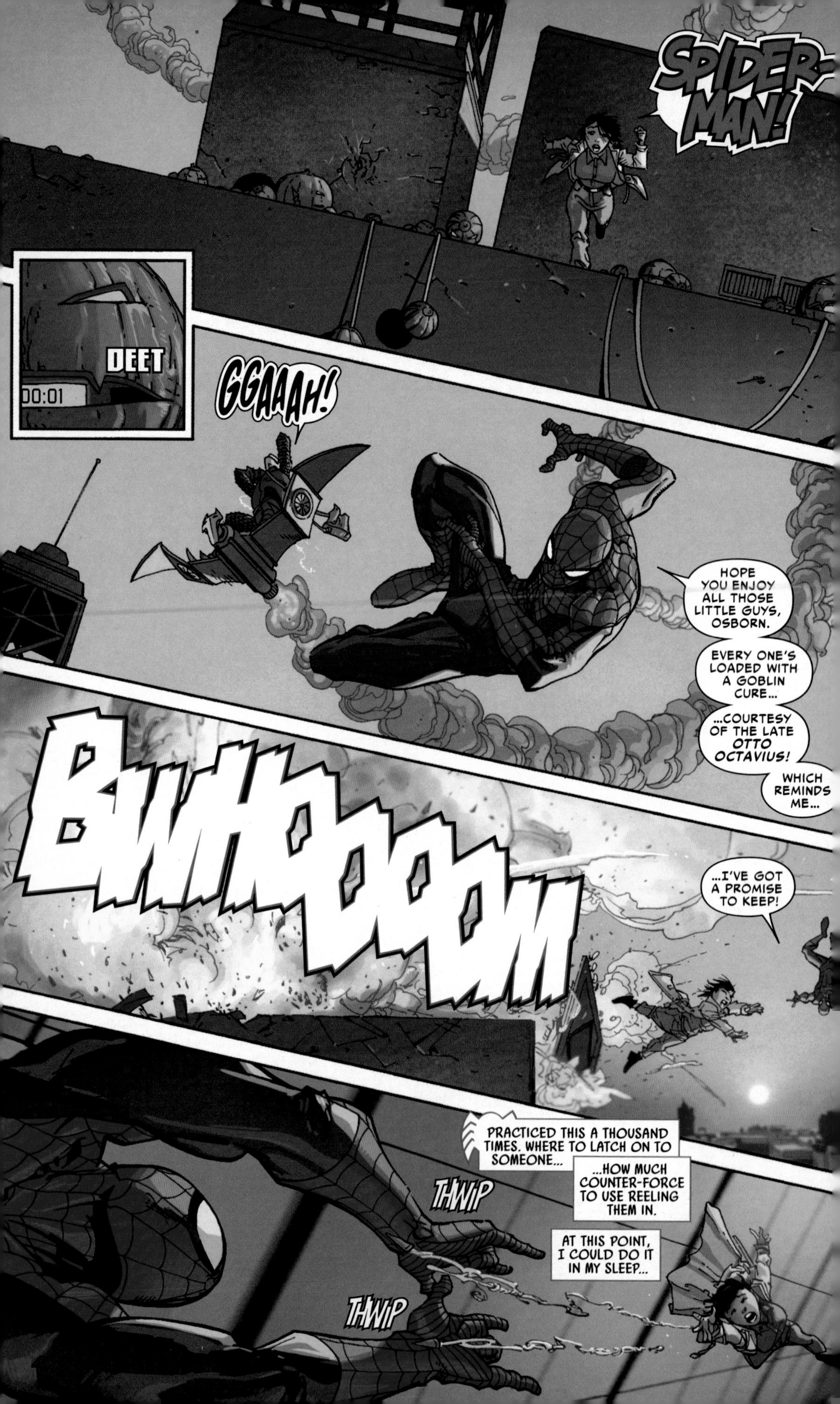
SPIDER-MAN!
DEET
00:01
GGAAAH!
HOPE YOU ENJOY ALL THOSE LITTLE GUYS, OSBORN.
EVERY ONE'S LOADED WITH A GOBLIN CURE...
...COURTESY OF THE LATE OTTO OCTAVIUS!
WHICH REMINDS ME...
BWHOOOOM
...I'VE GOT A PROMISE TO KEEP!
PRACTICED THIS A THOUSAND TIMES. WHERE TO LATCH ON TO SOMEONE...
...HOW MUCH COUNTER-FORCE TO USE REELING THEM IN.
AT THIS POINT, I COULD DO IT IN MY SLEEP...
THWIP
THWIP

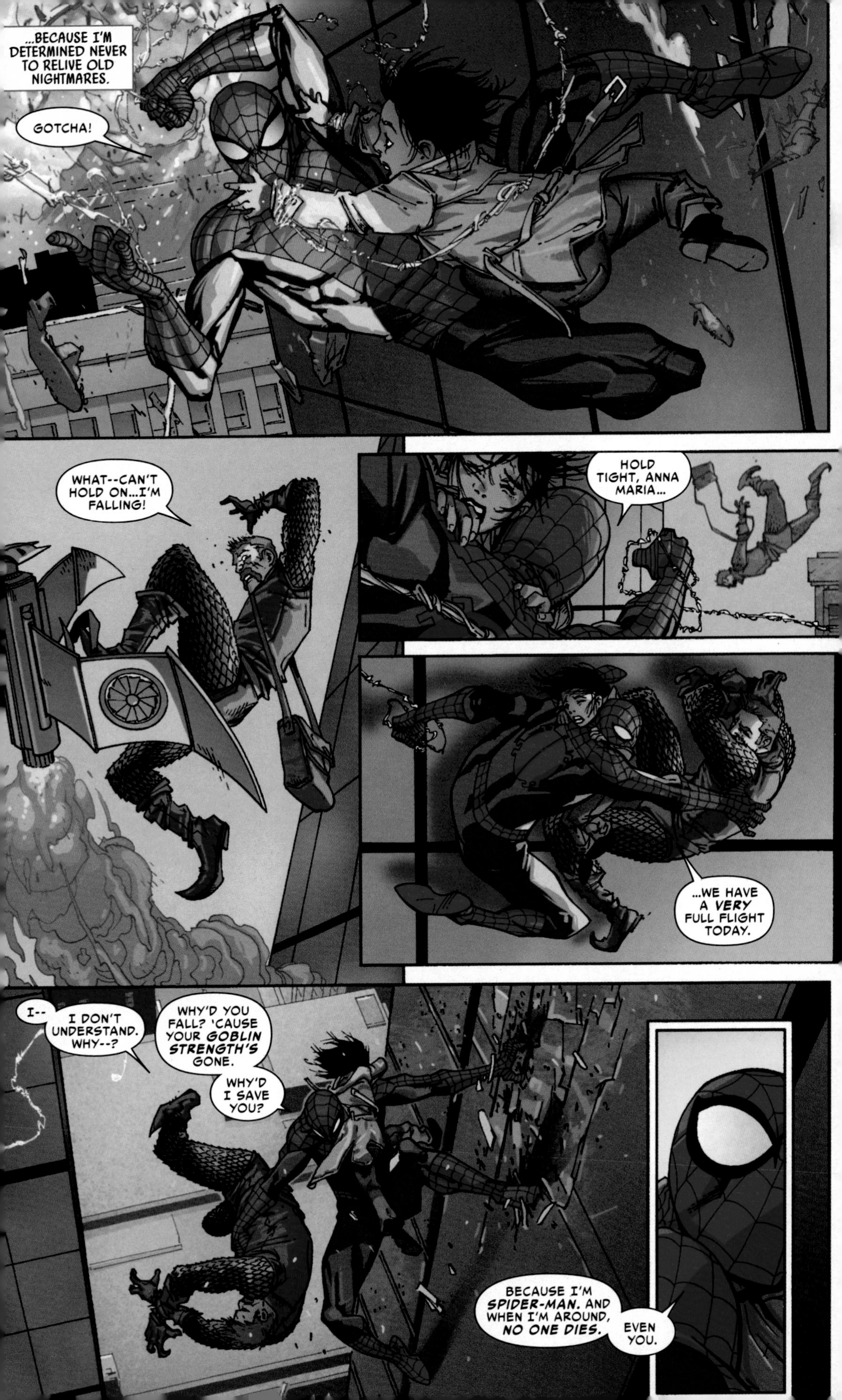

...BECAUSE I'M DETERMINED NEVER TO RELIVE OLD NIGHTMARES.
GOTCHA!
WHAT--CAN'T HOLD ON...I'M FALLING!
HOLD TIGHT, ANNA MARIA...
...WE HAVE A VERY FULL FLIGHT TODAY.
I--
I DON'T UNDERSTAND. WHY--?
WHY'D YOU FALL? 'CAUSE YOUR GOBLIN STRENGTH'S GONE.
WHY'D I SAVE YOU?
BECAUSE I'M SPIDER-MAN. AND WHEN I'M AROUND, NO ONE DIES.
EVEN YOU.

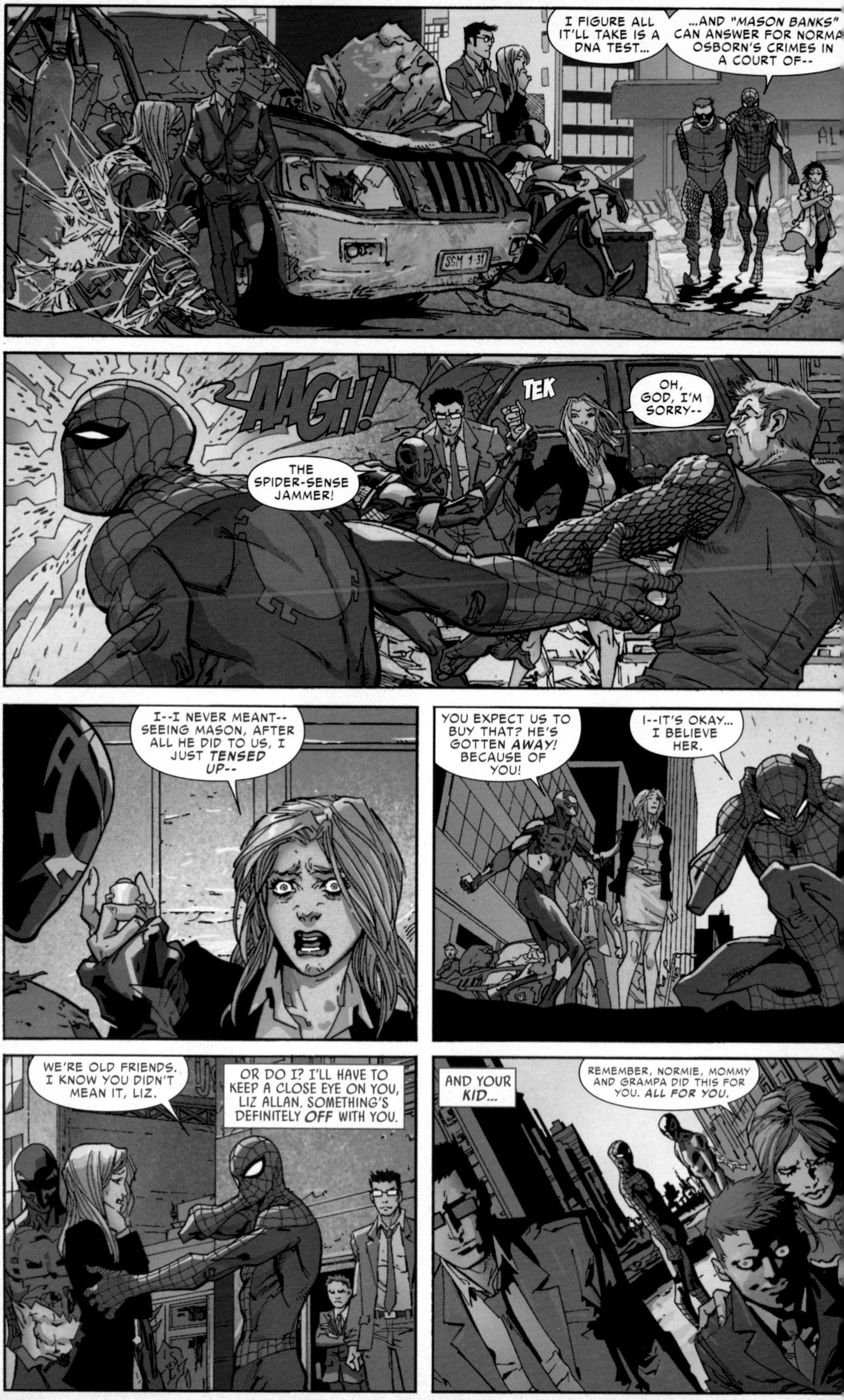
I FIGURE ALL IT'LL TAKE IS A DNA TEST...
...AND "MASON BANKS" CAN ANSWER FOR NORMA OSBORN'S CRIMES IN A COURT OF--
AAGH!
TEK
OH, GOD, I'M SORRY--
THE SPIDER-SENSE JAMMER!
I--I NEVER MEANT-- SEEING MASON, AFTER ALL HE DID TO US, I JUST TENSED UP--
YOU EXPECT US TO BUY THAT? HE'S GOTTEN AWAY! BECAUSE OF YOU!
I--IT'S OKAY... I BELIEVE HER.
WE'RE OLD FRIENDS. I KNOW YOU DIDN'T MEAN IT, LIZ.
OR DO I? I'LL HAVE TO KEEP A CLOSE EYE ON YOU, LIZ ALLAN. SOMETHING'S DEFINITELY OFF WITH YOU.
AND YOUR KID...
REMEMBER, NORMIE, MOMMY AND GRAMPA DID THIS FOR YOU. ALL FOR YOU.

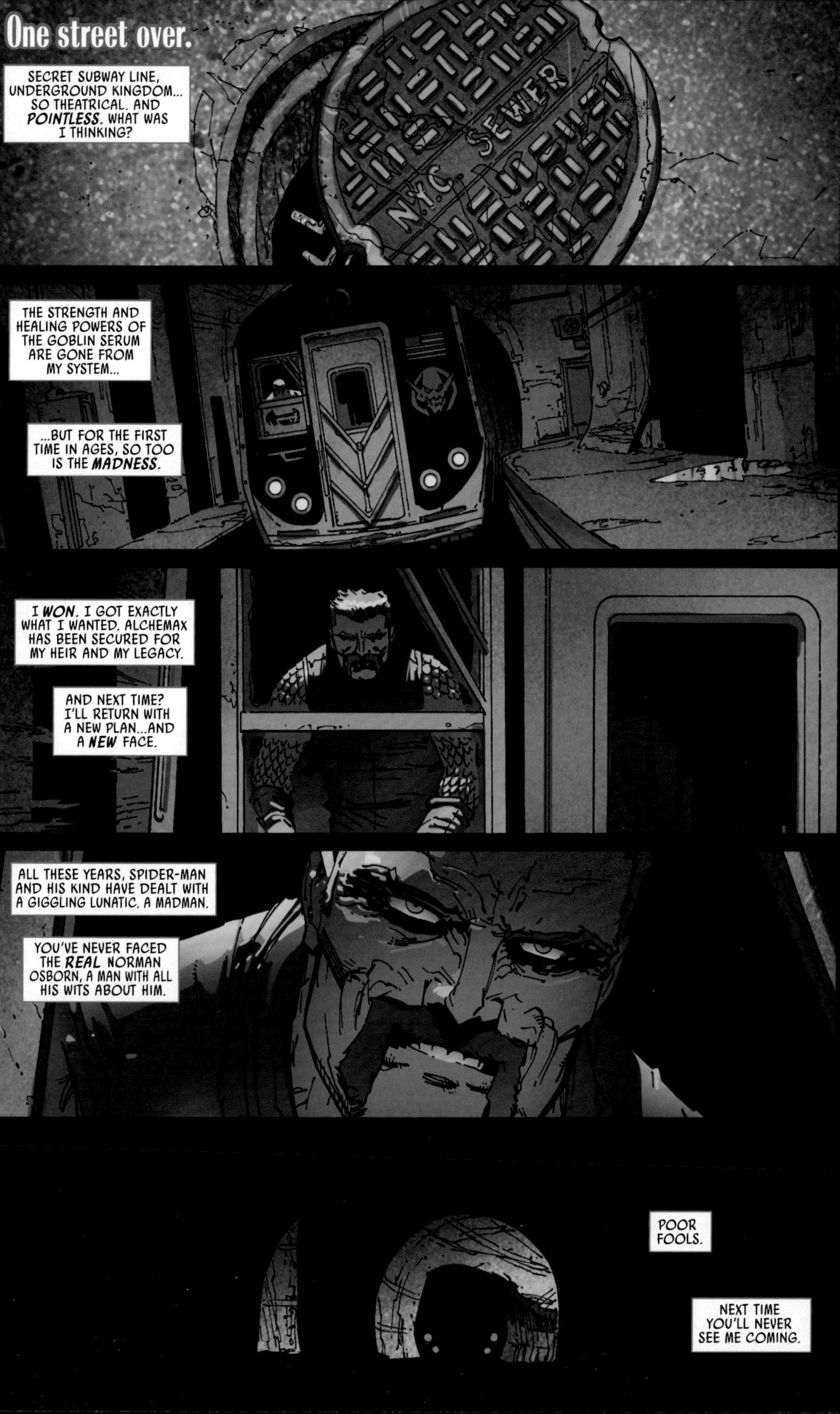
One street over.
SECRET SUBWAY LINE, UNDERGROUND KINGDOM... SO THEATRICAL. AND POINTLESS. WHAT WAS I THINKING?
N.Y.C. SEWER
THE STRENGTH AND HEALING POWERS OF THE GOBLIN SERUM ARE GONE FROM MY SYSTEM...
...BUT FOR THE FIRST TIME IN AGES, SO TOO IS THE MADNESS.
I WON. I GOT EXACTLY WHAT I WANTED. ALCHEMAX HAS BEEN SECURED FOR MY HEIR AND MY LEGACY.
AND NEXT TIME? I'LL RETURN WITH A NEW PLAN...AND A NEW FACE.
ALL THESE YEARS, SPIDER-MAN AND HIS KIND HAVE DEALT WITH A GIGGLING LUNATIC. A MADMAN.
YOU'VE NEVER FACED THE REAL NORMAN OSBORN, A MAN WITH ALL HIS WITS ABOUT HIM.
POOR FOOLS.
NEXT TIME YOU'LL NEVER SEE ME COMING.

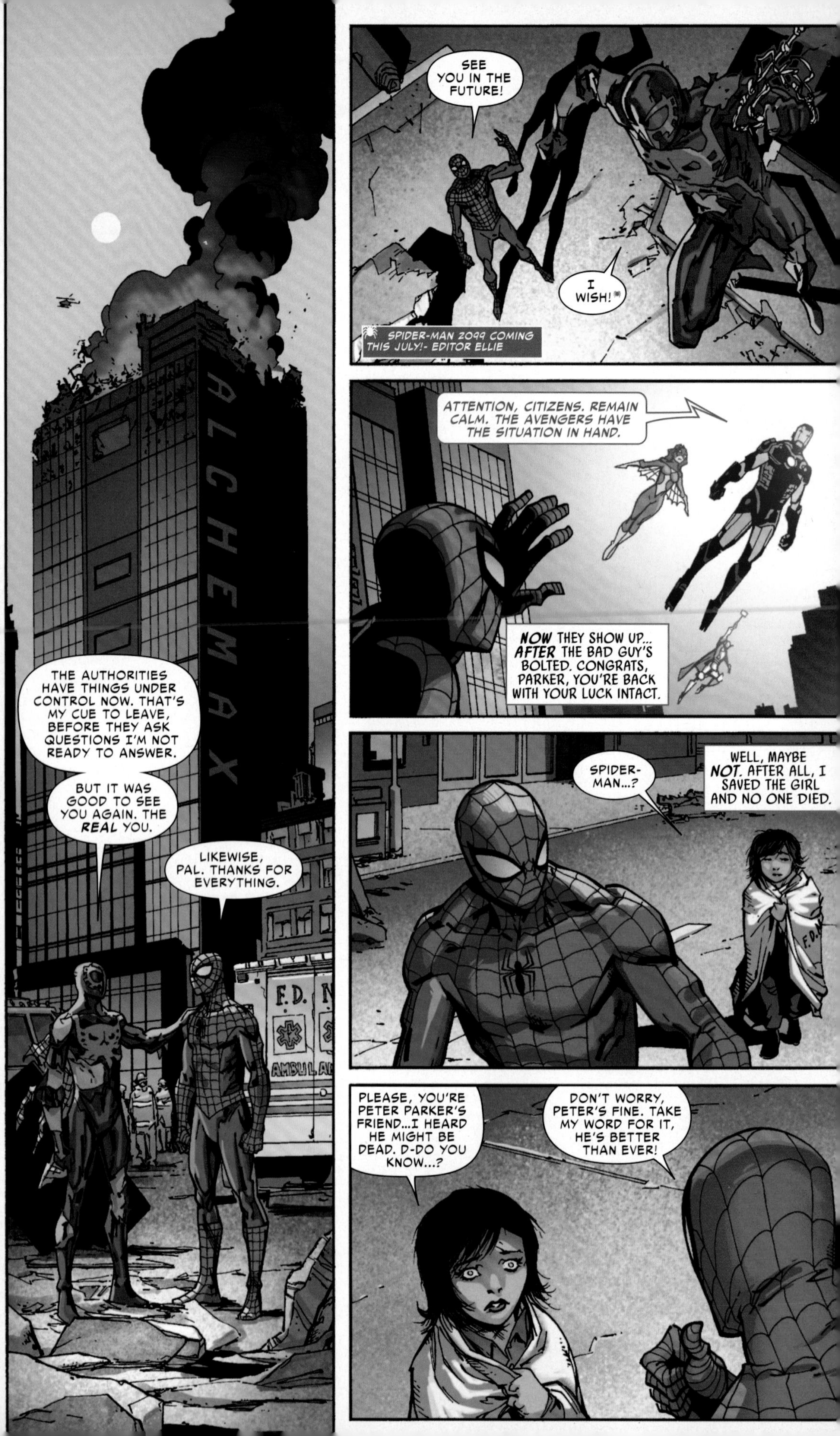
ALCHEMAX
THE AUTHORITIES HAVE THINGS UNDER CONTROL NOW. THAT'S MY CUE TO LEAVE, BEFORE THEY ASK QUESTIONS I'M NOT READY TO ANSWER.
BUT IT WAS GOOD TO SEE YOU AGAIN. THE *REAL* YOU.
LIKEWISE, PAL. THANKS FOR EVERYTHING.
F.D. N
AMBULAN
SEE YOU IN THE FUTURE!
I WISH!
SPIDER-MAN 2099 COMING THIS JULY!- EDITOR ELLIE
ATTENTION, CITIZENS. REMAIN CALM. THE AVENGERS HAVE THE SITUATION IN HAND.
NOW THEY SHOW UP... ***AFTER*** THE BAD GUY'S BOLTED. CONGRATS, PARKER, YOU'RE BACK WITH YOUR LUCK INTACT.
SPIDER-MAN...?
WELL, MAYBE ***NOT***. AFTER ALL, I SAVED THE GIRL AND NO ONE DIED.
PLEASE, YOU'RE PETER PARKER'S FRIEND...I HEARD HE MIGHT BE DEAD. D-DO YOU KNOW...?
DON'T WORRY, PETER'S FINE. TAKE MY WORD FOR IT, HE'S BETTER THAN EVER!

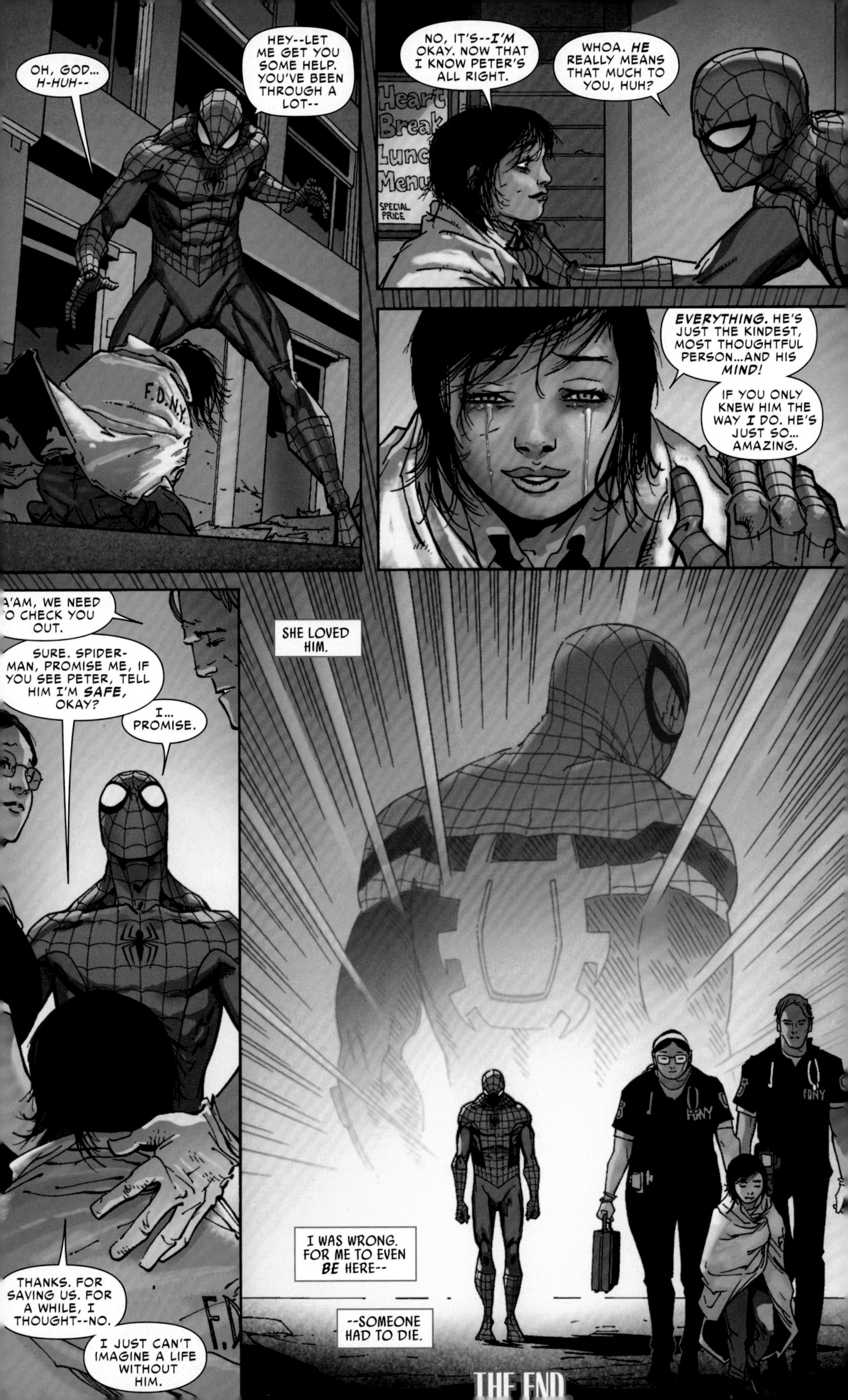
OH, GOD... H-HUH--
HEY--LET ME GET YOU SOME HELP. YOU'VE BEEN THROUGH A LOT--
F.D.N.Y.
NO, IT'S--I'M OKAY. NOW THAT I KNOW PETER'S ALL RIGHT.
Heart Break Lunc Menu SPECIAL PRICE
WHOA. HE REALLY MEANS THAT MUCH TO YOU, HUH?
EVERYTHING. HE'S JUST THE KINDEST, MOST THOUGHTFUL PERSON...AND HIS MIND!
IF YOU ONLY KNEW HIM THE WAY I DO. HE'S JUST SO... AMAZING.
A'AM, WE NEED O CHECK YOU OUT.
SURE. SPIDER-MAN, PROMISE ME, IF YOU SEE PETER, TELL HIM I'M SAFE, OKAY?
I... PROMISE.
THANKS. FOR SAVING US. FOR A WHILE, I THOUGHT--NO.
I JUST CAN'T IMAGINE A LIFE WITHOUT HIM.
SHE LOVED HIM.
I WAS WRONG. FOR ME TO EVEN BE HERE--
--SOMEONE HAD TO DIE.
THE END

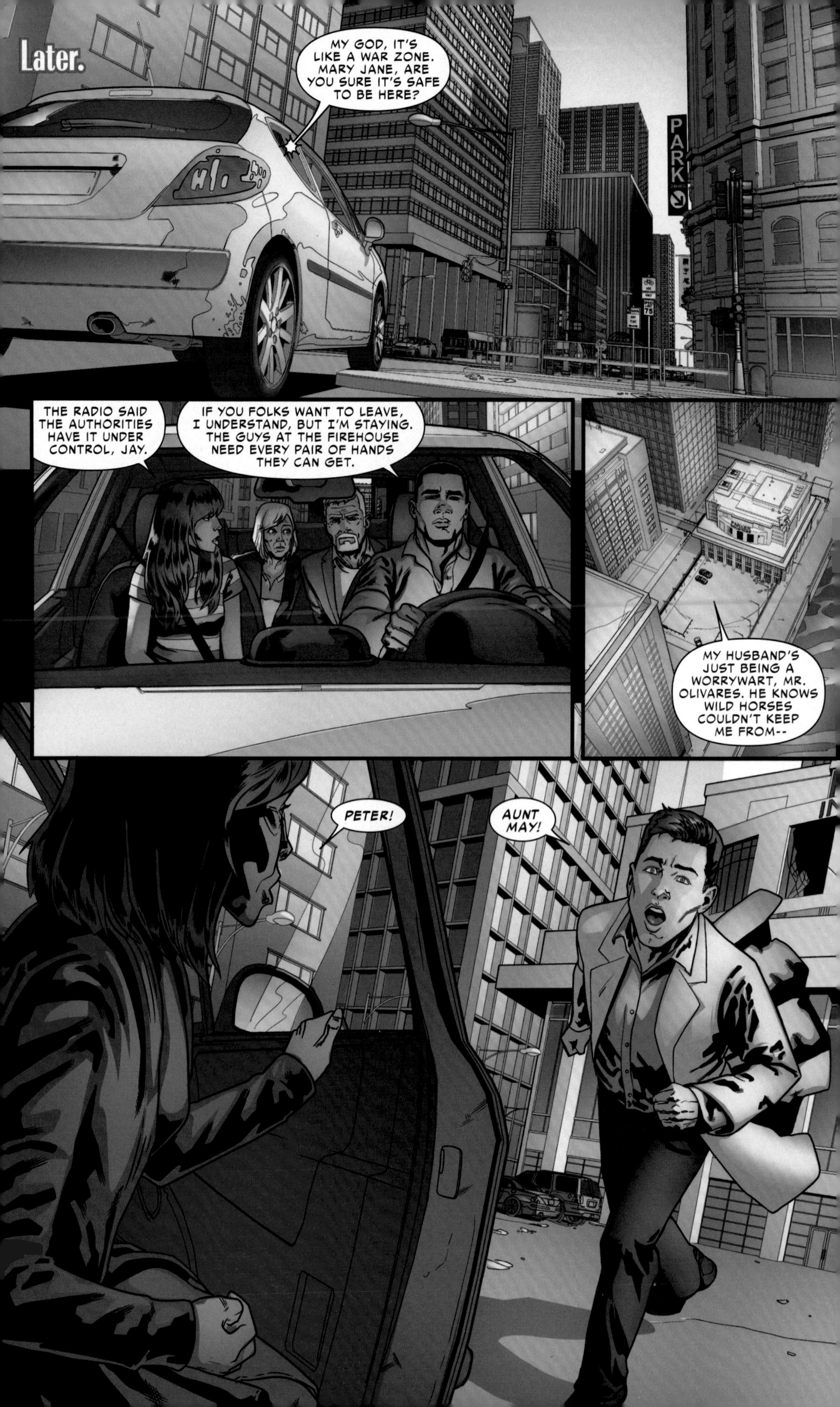
Later.
MY GOD, IT'S LIKE A WAR ZONE. MARY JANE, ARE YOU SURE IT'S SAFE TO BE HERE?
PARK
THE RADIO SAID THE AUTHORITIES HAVE IT UNDER CONTROL, JAY.
IF YOU FOLKS WANT TO LEAVE, I UNDERSTAND, BUT I'M STAYING. THE GUYS AT THE FIREHOUSE NEED EVERY PAIR OF HANDS THEY CAN GET.
MY HUSBAND'S JUST BEING A WORRYWART, MR. OLIVARES. HE KNOWS WILD HORSES COULDN'T KEEP ME FROM--
PETER!
AUNT MAY!

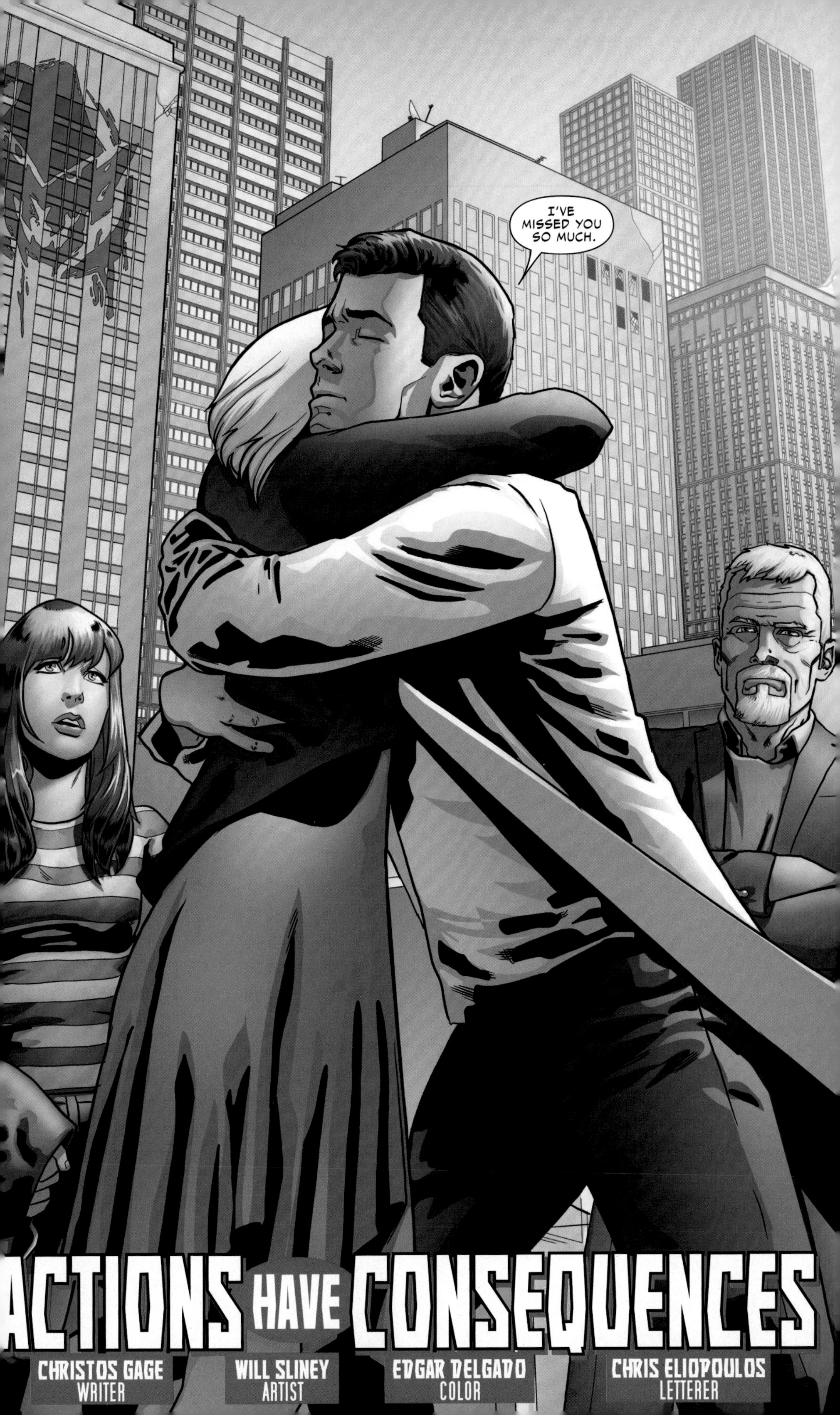
I'VE MISSED YOU SO MUCH.
ACTIONS HAVE CONSEQUENCES
CHRISTOS GAGE WRITER
WILL SLINEY ARTIST
EDGAR DELGADO COLOR
CHRIS ELIOPOULOS LETTERER

MJ, I HATE TO MISS MEETING YOUR INSANE EX, BUT MY BUDDIES NEED ME. YOU MIND IF I--

GO AHEAD. TAKE THE CAR. CALL ME LATER.

I'M SO SORRY. FOR EVERYTHING I'VE PUT YOU THROUGH...FOR EVERYTHING.

HUSH UP, PETER PARKER. I'M THE ONE WHO SHOULD BE SORRY.

I BEG TO DIFFER. PETER, THE LAST TIME WE SAW YOU, YOU BEHAVED UNCONSCIONABLY TOWARD YOUR AUNT.

THE LAST-- I--

YOU'VE BEEN CRUEL TO HER. COLD TO HER. AND YOU'VE LIED ABOUT YOUR CONTINUED WORK FOR SPIDER-MAN!

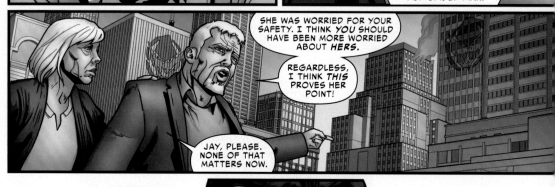

SHE WAS WORRIED FOR YOUR SAFETY. I THINK YOU SHOULD HAVE BEEN MORE WORRIED ABOUT HERS.

REGARDLESS, I THINK THIS PROVES HER POINT!

JAY, PLEASE. NONE OF THAT MATTERS NOW.

NO, HE'S RIGHT. I KNOW I HAVEN'T BEEN MYSELF LATELY. I HOPE YOU'LL GIVE ME A CHANCE TO EXPLAIN.

WE'RE LISTENING.

UH...

IT'S TRUE. I PUT YOU IN DANGER. AND NOTHING WILL EVER MAKE THAT OKAY.

ME WORKING FOR SPIDER-MAN--AND ANYONE KNOWING THAT--IS AN UNACCEPTABLE SITUATION. I *SHOULD* HAVE ENDED IT. BUT I...WASN'T IN A POSITION TO.

FINANCIALLY? I KNOW STARTUPS ARE A CHALLENGE, BUT IF YOU NEED MORE MONEY, WE MIGHT BE ABLE TO--

"MORE--"? NO. *PLEASE.* YOU'VE...ALREADY DONE MORE THAN I WOULD'VE EVER DREAMED OF ASKING YOU TO.

I'LL WORK IT OUT. ON MY *OWN.* THE WAY I ALWAYS SHOULD HAVE.

PARKER INDUSTRIES

I JUST TOLD SPIDER-MAN. I *QUIT.*

AND I KNOW THAT SOUNDS LIKE THE THING I SAY *ALL* THE TIME, BUT I'M CALLING A PRESS CONFERENCE TO MAKE IT OFFICIAL. I HOPE YOU'LL BE THERE.

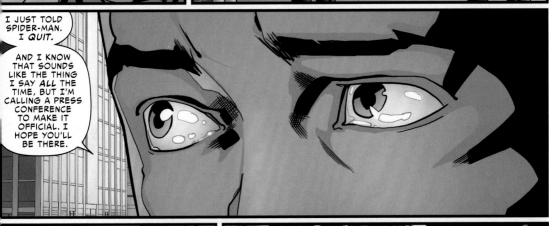

I DON'T DESERVE A SECOND CHANCE. BUT IF YOU'LL *GIVE* ME ONE...I PROMISE I'LL KNOW WHAT A GREAT GIFT THAT IS.

AND I'LL MAKE IT *COUNT.*

OH, PETER. OF COURSE WE WILL.

ALL RIGHT, SON.

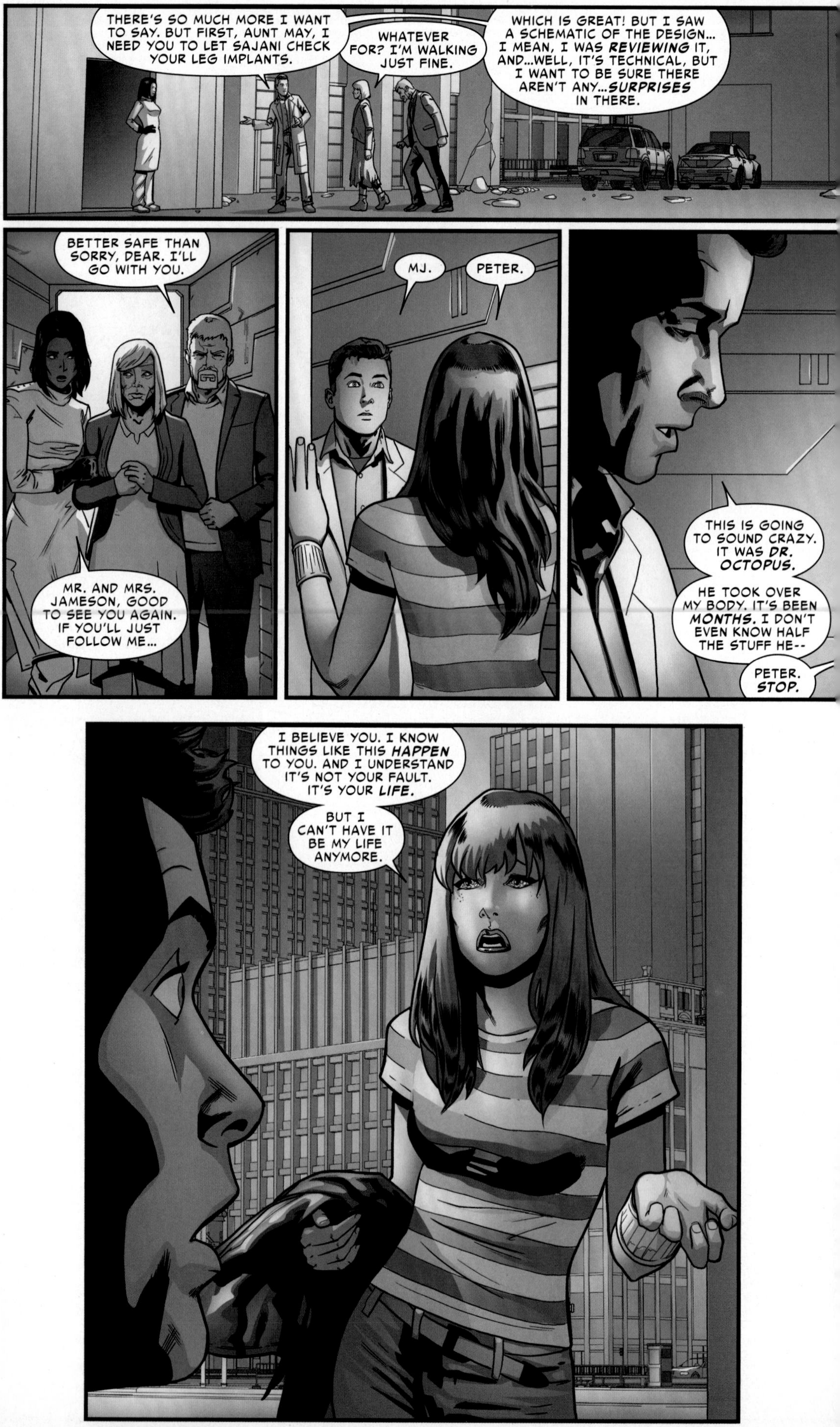
THERE'S SO MUCH MORE I WANT TO SAY. BUT FIRST, AUNT MAY, I NEED YOU TO LET SAJANI CHECK YOUR LEG IMPLANTS.
WHATEVER FOR? I'M WALKING JUST FINE.
WHICH IS GREAT! BUT I SAW A SCHEMATIC OF THE DESIGN... I MEAN, I WAS REVIEWING IT, AND...WELL, IT'S TECHNICAL, BUT I WANT TO BE SURE THERE AREN'T ANY...SURPRISES IN THERE.
BETTER SAFE THAN SORRY, DEAR. I'LL GO WITH YOU.
MR. AND MRS. JAMESON, GOOD TO SEE YOU AGAIN. IF YOU'LL JUST FOLLOW ME...
MJ.
PETER.
THIS IS GOING TO SOUND CRAZY. IT WAS DR. OCTOPUS.
HE TOOK OVER MY BODY. IT'S BEEN MONTHS. I DON'T EVEN KNOW HALF THE STUFF HE--
PETER. STOP.
I BELIEVE YOU. I KNOW THINGS LIKE THIS HAPPEN TO YOU. AND I UNDERSTAND IT'S NOT YOUR FAULT. IT'S YOUR LIFE.
BUT I CAN'T HAVE IT BE MY LIFE ANYMORE.

ONE MINUTE I'M BEING THREATENED BY THE *VENOM* SYMBIOTE. THE NEXT, THE GREEN GOBLIN'S MEN ARE TRYING TO KILL ME.

AT SOME POINT, THE "WHY" OF IT JUST DOESN'T MATTER.

YOU'VE MADE YOUR CHOICE ABOUT HOW TO LIVE. I UNDERSTAND IT...EVEN ADMIRE IT. FOR A LONG TIME, I LIVED IT TOO.

BUT LATELY, I'VE BEEN LIVING ON *MY* TERMS. A GREAT JOB. A GREAT GUY. IS IT *PERFECT?* OF COURSE NOT. BUT THE PROBLEMS ARE *NORMAL.* I CAN HANDLE THEM.

PETER...I'M GLAD YOU'RE BACK. I'M GLAD YOU'RE OKAY. *REALLY.*

BUT YOU AND I BOTH KNOW THERE'LL BE SOMETHING ELSE. AND SOMETHING ELSE AFTER THAT.

I'LL ALWAYS CARE FOR YOU.

BUT I CAN'T HAVE MY LIFE CONSUMED BY YOURS ANYMORE.

I...I WON'T.

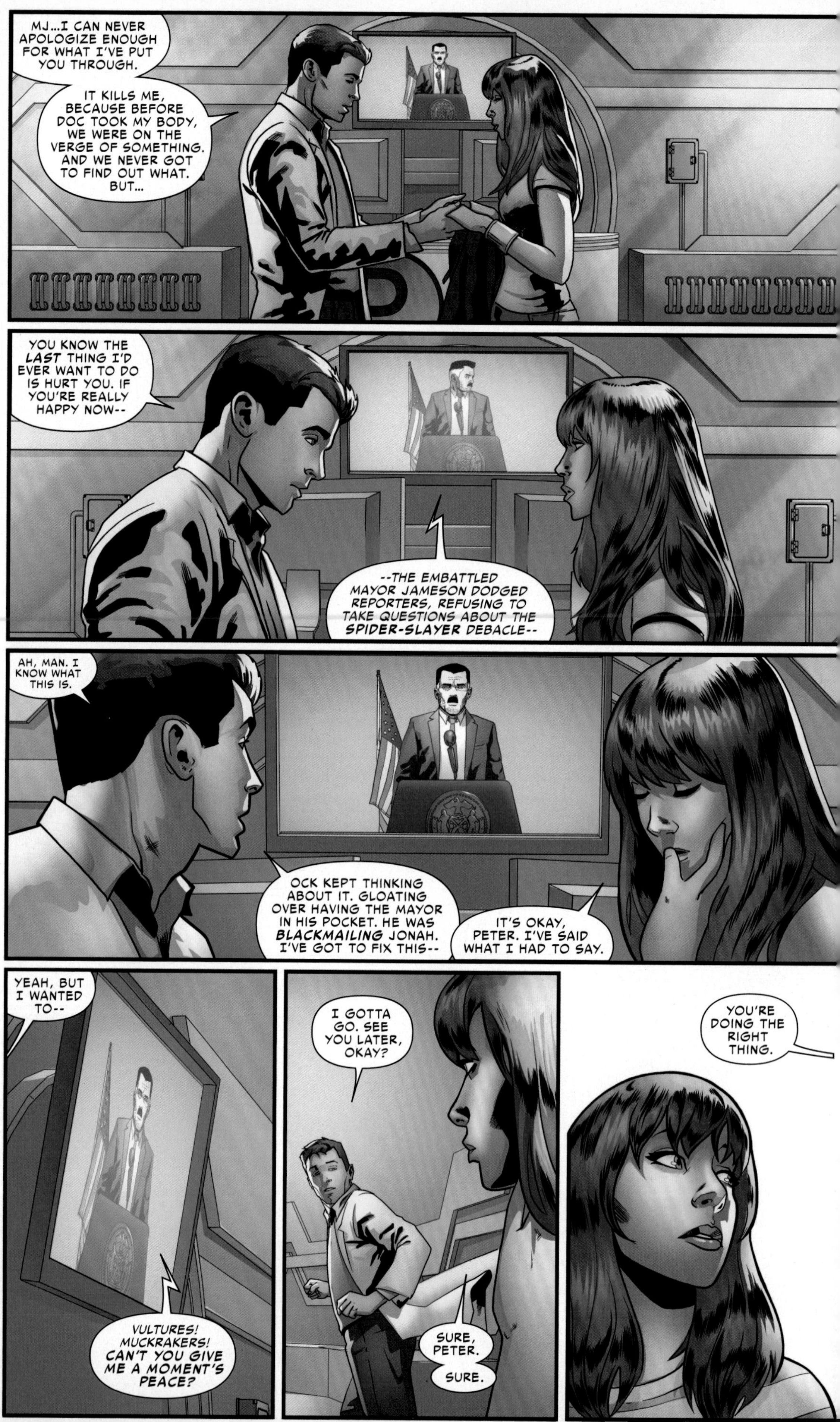
MJ...I CAN NEVER APOLOGIZE ENOUGH FOR WHAT I'VE PUT YOU THROUGH.
IT KILLS ME, BECAUSE BEFORE DOC TOOK MY BODY, WE WERE ON THE VERGE OF SOMETHING. AND WE NEVER GOT TO FIND OUT WHAT. BUT...
YOU KNOW THE LAST THING I'D EVER WANT TO DO IS HURT YOU. IF YOU'RE REALLY HAPPY NOW--
--THE EMBATTLED MAYOR JAMESON DODGED REPORTERS, REFUSING TO TAKE QUESTIONS ABOUT THE SPIDER-SLAYER DEBACLE--
AH, MAN. I KNOW WHAT THIS IS.
OCK KEPT THINKING ABOUT IT. GLOATING OVER HAVING THE MAYOR IN HIS POCKET. HE WAS BLACKMAILING JONAH. I'VE GOT TO FIX THIS--
IT'S OKAY, PETER. I'VE SAID WHAT I HAD TO SAY.
YEAH, BUT I WANTED TO--
VULTURES! MUCKRAKERS! CAN'T YOU GIVE ME A MOMENT'S PEACE?
I GOTTA GO. SEE YOU LATER, OKAY?
SURE, PETER.
SURE.
YOU'RE DOING THE RIGHT THING.

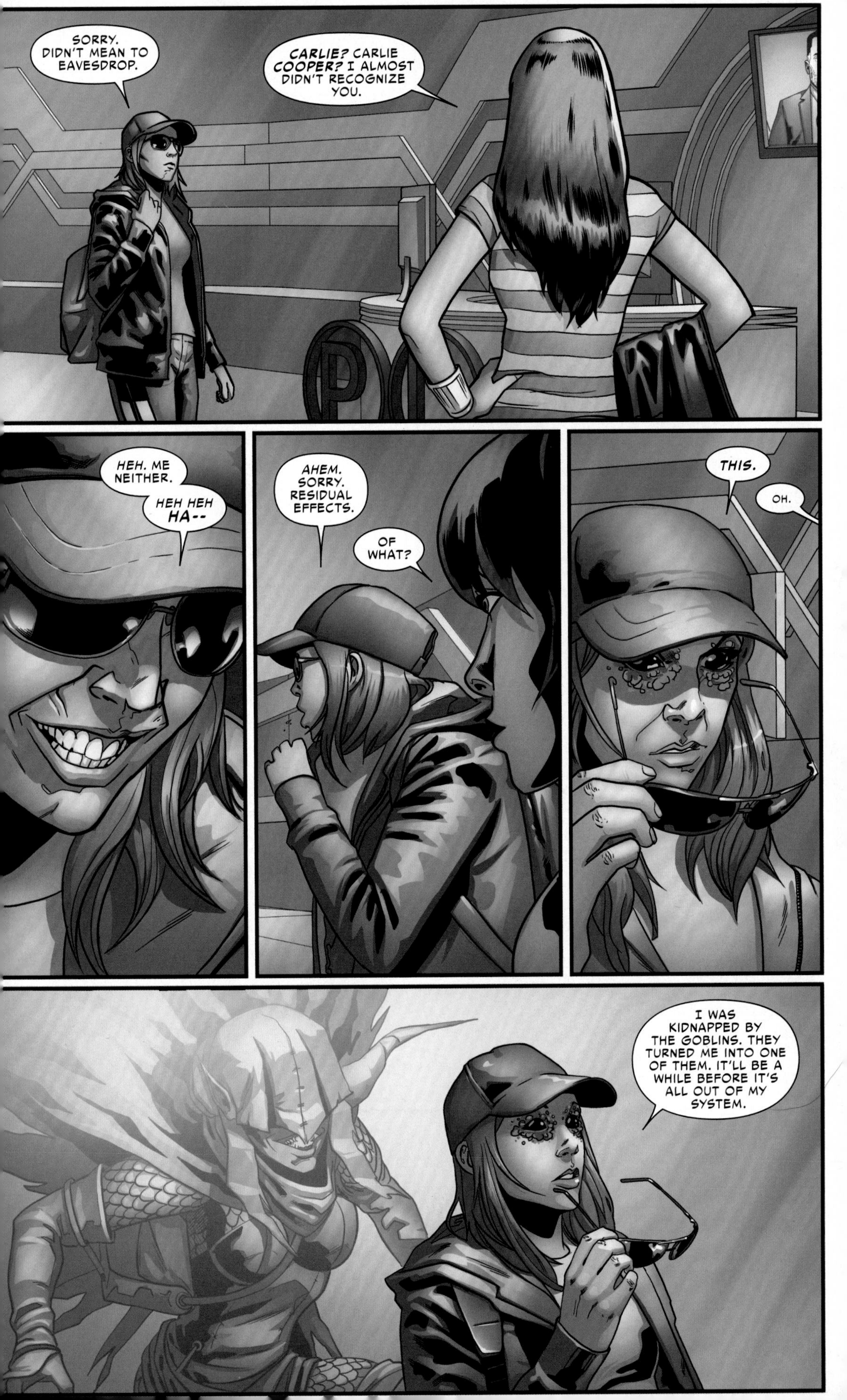
SORRY. DIDN'T MEAN TO EAVESDROP.
CARLIE? CARLIE COOPER? I ALMOST DIDN'T RECOGNIZE YOU.
HEH. ME NEITHER.
HEH HEH HA--
AHEM. SORRY. RESIDUAL EFFECTS.
OF WHAT?
THIS.
OH.
I WAS KIDNAPPED BY THE GOBLINS. THEY TURNED ME INTO ONE OF THEM. IT'LL BE A WHILE BEFORE IT'S ALL OUT OF MY SYSTEM.

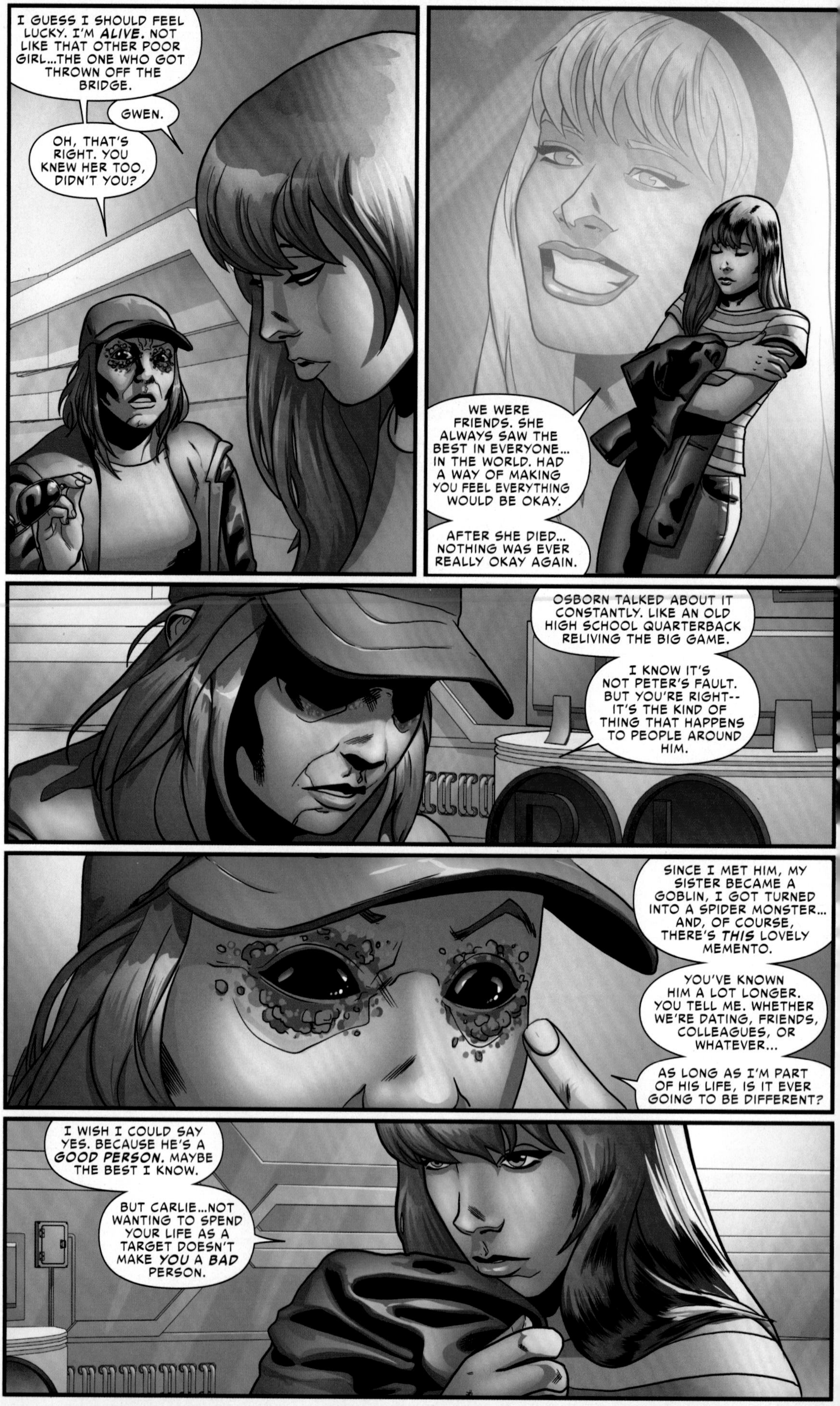
I GUESS I SHOULD FEEL LUCKY. I'M *ALIVE.* NOT LIKE THAT OTHER POOR GIRL...THE ONE WHO GOT THROWN OFF THE BRIDGE.
GWEN.
OH, THAT'S RIGHT. YOU KNEW HER TOO, DIDN'T YOU?
WE WERE FRIENDS. SHE ALWAYS SAW THE BEST IN EVERYONE... IN THE WORLD. HAD A WAY OF MAKING YOU FEEL EVERYTHING WOULD BE OKAY.
AFTER SHE DIED... NOTHING WAS EVER REALLY OKAY AGAIN.
OSBORN TALKED ABOUT IT CONSTANTLY. LIKE AN OLD HIGH SCHOOL QUARTERBACK RELIVING THE BIG GAME.
I KNOW IT'S NOT PETER'S FAULT. BUT YOU'RE RIGHT-- IT'S THE KIND OF THING THAT HAPPENS TO PEOPLE AROUND HIM.
SINCE I MET HIM, MY SISTER BECAME A GOBLIN, I GOT TURNED INTO A SPIDER MONSTER... AND, OF COURSE, THERE'S *THIS* LOVELY MEMENTO.
YOU'VE KNOWN HIM A LOT LONGER. YOU TELL ME. WHETHER WE'RE DATING, FRIENDS, COLLEAGUES, OR WHATEVER...
AS LONG AS I'M PART OF HIS LIFE, IS IT EVER GOING TO BE DIFFERENT?
I WISH I COULD SAY YES. BECAUSE HE'S A *GOOD PERSON.* MAYBE THE BEST I KNOW.
BUT CARLIE...NOT WANTING TO SPEND YOUR LIFE AS A TARGET DOESN'T MAKE *YOU* A *BAD* PERSON.

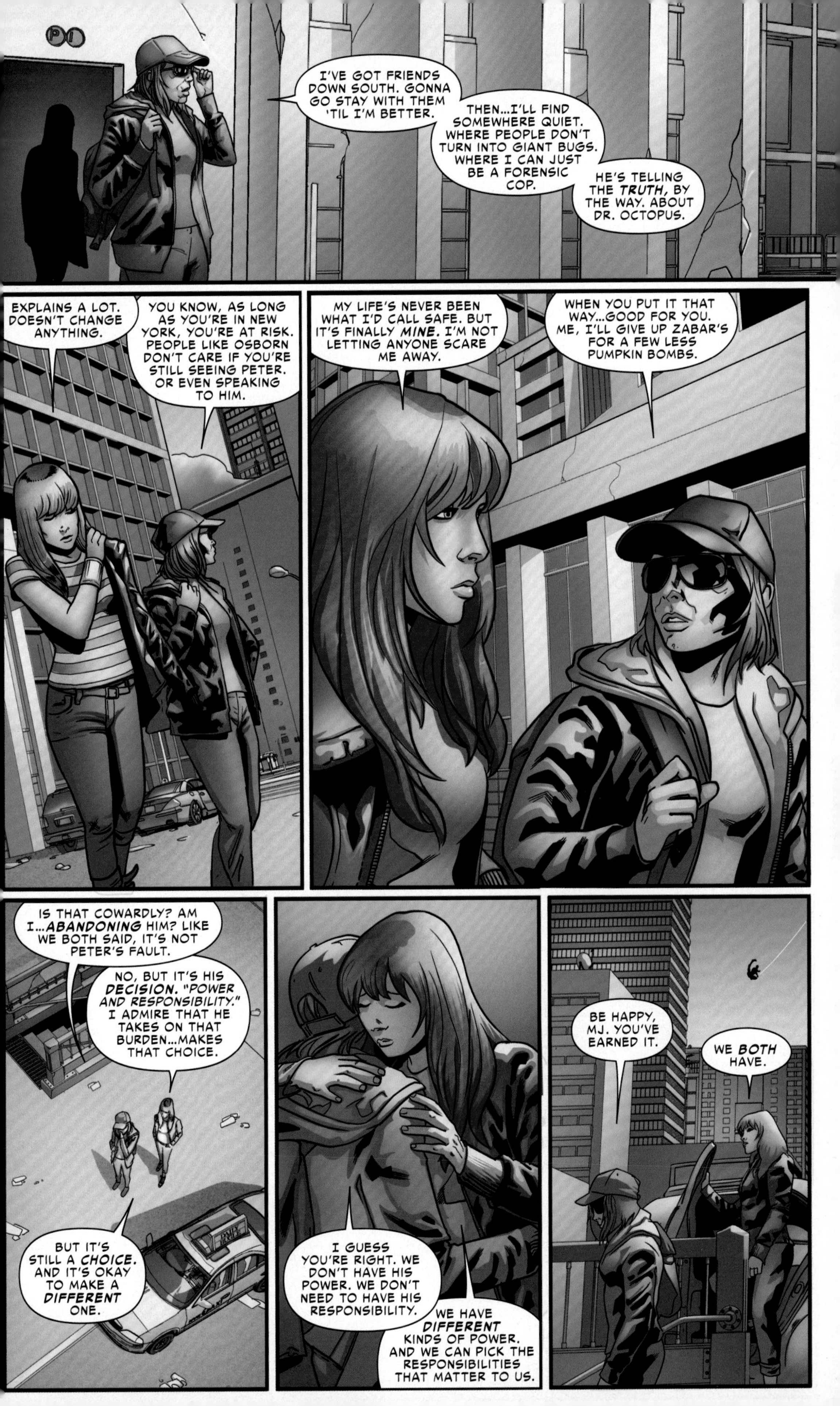

I'VE GOT FRIENDS DOWN SOUTH. GONNA GO STAY WITH THEM 'TIL I'M BETTER.
THEN...I'LL FIND SOMEWHERE QUIET. WHERE PEOPLE DON'T TURN INTO GIANT BUGS. WHERE I CAN JUST BE A FORENSIC COP.
HE'S TELLING THE *TRUTH*, BY THE WAY. ABOUT DR. OCTOPUS.
EXPLAINS A LOT. DOESN'T CHANGE ANYTHING.
YOU KNOW, AS LONG AS YOU'RE IN NEW YORK, YOU'RE AT RISK. PEOPLE LIKE OSBORN DON'T CARE IF YOU'RE STILL SEEING PETER. OR EVEN SPEAKING TO HIM.
MY LIFE'S NEVER BEEN WHAT I'D CALL SAFE. BUT IT'S FINALLY *MINE*. I'M NOT LETTING ANYONE SCARE ME AWAY.
WHEN YOU PUT IT THAT WAY...GOOD FOR YOU. ME, I'LL GIVE UP ZABAR'S FOR A FEW LESS PUMPKIN BOMBS.
IS THAT COWARDLY? AM I...*ABANDONING* HIM? LIKE WE BOTH SAID, IT'S NOT PETER'S FAULT.
NO, BUT IT'S HIS *DECISION*. *"POWER AND RESPONSIBILITY."* I ADMIRE THAT HE TAKES ON THAT BURDEN...MAKES THAT CHOICE.
BUT IT'S STILL A *CHOICE*. AND IT'S OKAY TO MAKE A *DIFFERENT* ONE.
I GUESS YOU'RE RIGHT. WE DON'T HAVE HIS POWER. WE DON'T NEED TO HAVE HIS RESPONSIBILITY.
WE HAVE *DIFFERENT* KINDS OF POWER. AND WE CAN PICK THE RESPONSIBILITIES THAT MATTER TO US.
BE HAPPY, MJ. YOU'VE EARNED IT.
WE *BOTH* HAVE.

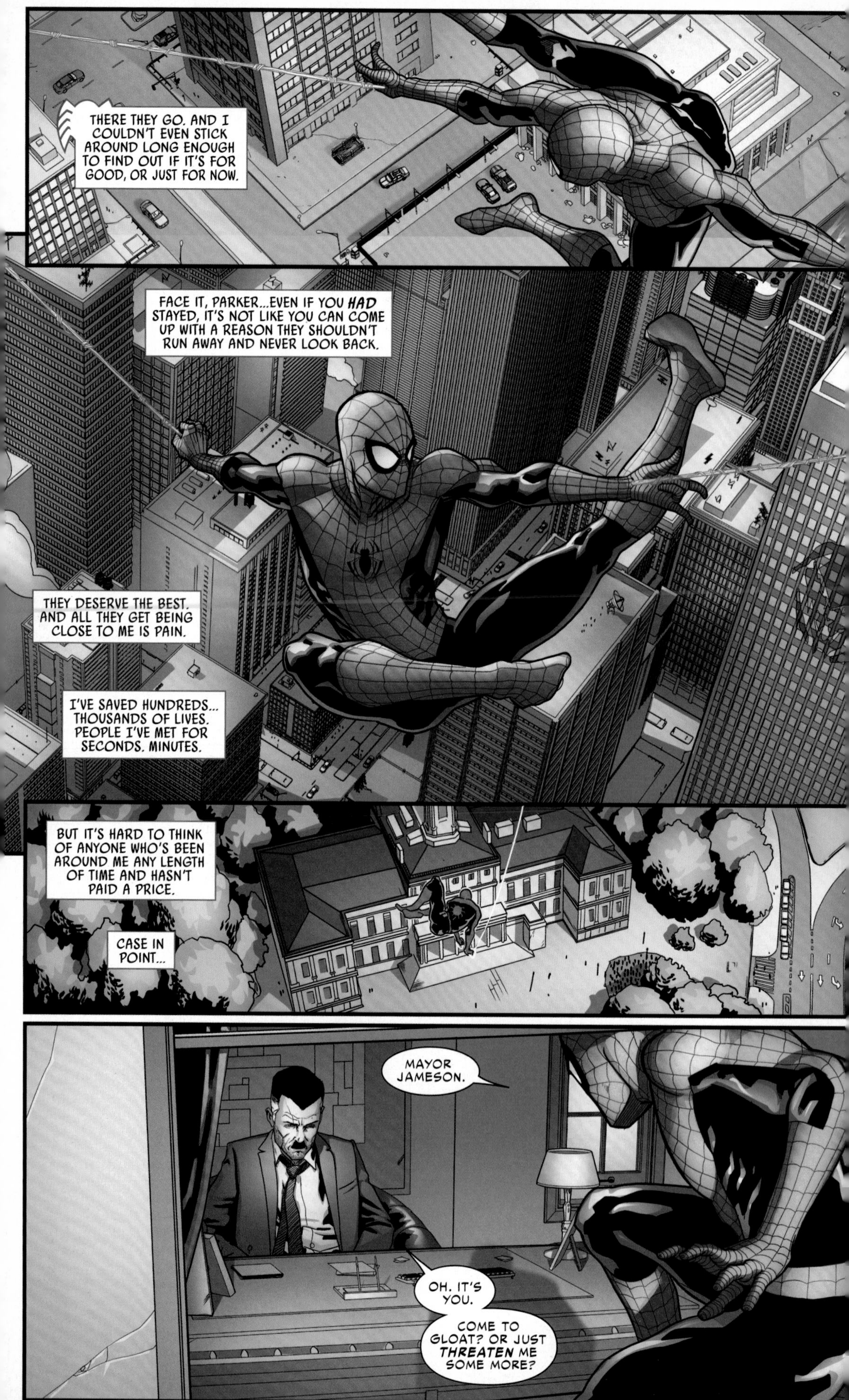

THERE THEY GO. AND I COULDN'T EVEN STICK AROUND LONG ENOUGH TO FIND OUT IF IT'S FOR GOOD, OR JUST FOR NOW.
FACE IT, PARKER...EVEN IF YOU *HAD* STAYED, IT'S NOT LIKE YOU CAN COME UP WITH A REASON THEY SHOULDN'T RUN AWAY AND NEVER LOOK BACK.
THEY DESERVE THE BEST. AND ALL THEY GET BEING CLOSE TO ME IS PAIN.
I'VE SAVED HUNDREDS... THOUSANDS OF LIVES. PEOPLE I'VE MET FOR SECONDS. MINUTES.
BUT IT'S HARD TO THINK OF ANYONE WHO'S BEEN AROUND ME ANY LENGTH OF TIME AND HASN'T PAID A PRICE.
CASE IN POINT...
MAYOR JAMESON.
OH. IT'S YOU.
COME TO GLOAT? OR JUST *THREATEN* ME SOME MORE?

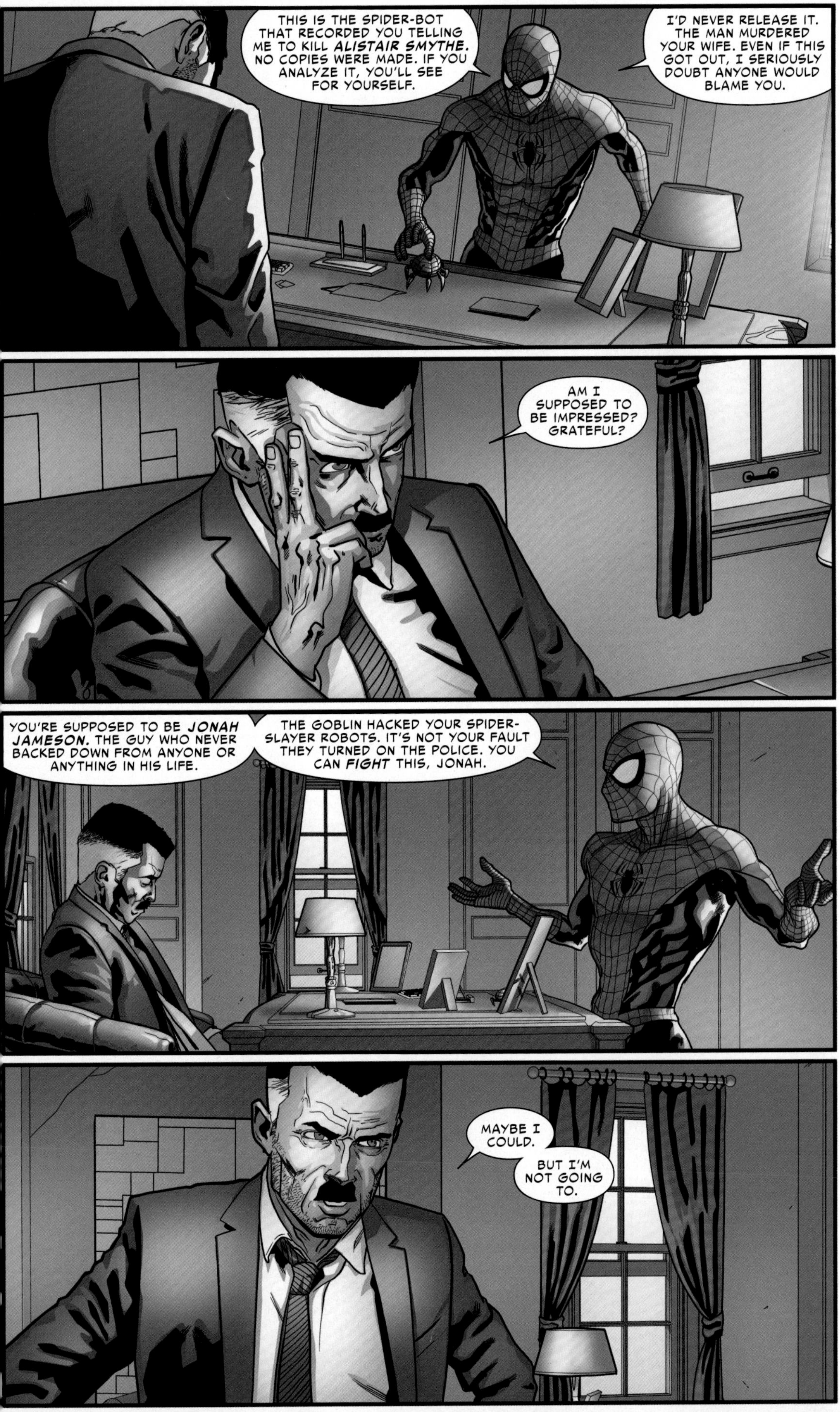
THIS IS THE SPIDER-BOT THAT RECORDED YOU TELLING ME TO KILL ALISTAIR SMYTHE. NO COPIES WERE MADE. IF YOU ANALYZE IT, YOU'LL SEE FOR YOURSELF.
I'D NEVER RELEASE IT. THE MAN MURDERED YOUR WIFE. EVEN IF THIS GOT OUT, I SERIOUSLY DOUBT ANYONE WOULD BLAME YOU.
AM I SUPPOSED TO BE IMPRESSED? GRATEFUL?
YOU'RE SUPPOSED TO BE JONAH JAMESON. THE GUY WHO NEVER BACKED DOWN FROM ANYONE OR ANYTHING IN HIS LIFE.
THE GOBLIN HACKED YOUR SPIDER-SLAYER ROBOTS. IT'S NOT YOUR FAULT THEY TURNED ON THE POLICE. YOU CAN FIGHT THIS, JONAH.
MAYBE I COULD.
BUT I'M NOT GOING TO.

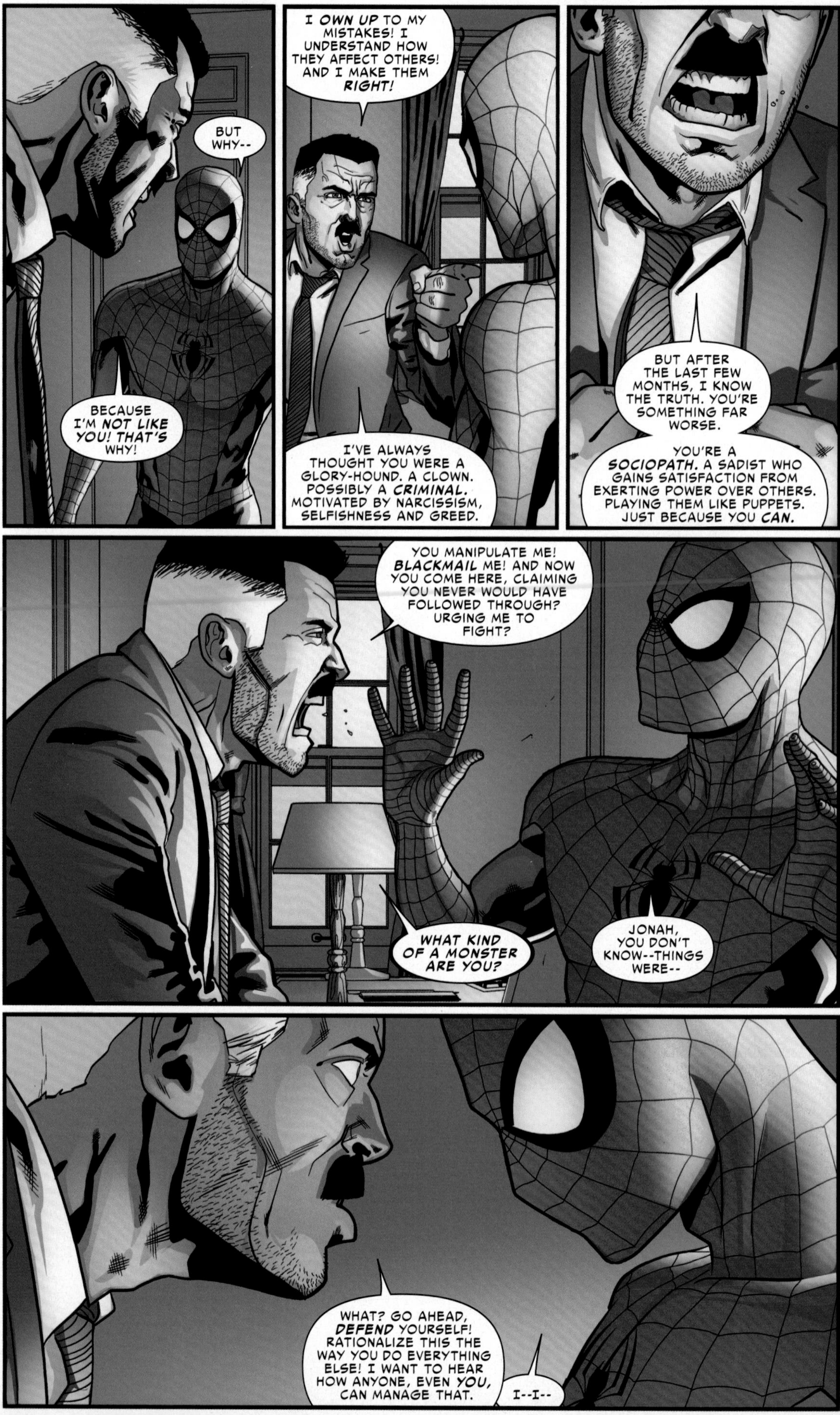

BUT WHY--
BECAUSE I'M NOT LIKE YOU! THAT'S WHY!
I OWN UP TO MY MISTAKES! I UNDERSTAND HOW THEY AFFECT OTHERS! AND I MAKE THEM RIGHT!
I'VE ALWAYS THOUGHT YOU WERE A GLORY-HOUND. A CLOWN. POSSIBLY A CRIMINAL. MOTIVATED BY NARCISSISM, SELFISHNESS AND GREED.
BUT AFTER THE LAST FEW MONTHS, I KNOW THE TRUTH. YOU'RE SOMETHING FAR WORSE.
YOU'RE A SOCIOPATH. A SADIST WHO GAINS SATISFACTION FROM EXERTING POWER OVER OTHERS. PLAYING THEM LIKE PUPPETS. JUST BECAUSE YOU CAN.
YOU MANIPULATE ME! BLACKMAIL ME! AND NOW YOU COME HERE, CLAIMING YOU NEVER WOULD HAVE FOLLOWED THROUGH? URGING ME TO FIGHT?
WHAT KIND OF A MONSTER ARE YOU?
JONAH, YOU DON'T KNOW--THINGS WERE--
WHAT? GO AHEAD, DEFEND YOURSELF! RATIONALIZE THIS THE WAY YOU DO EVERYTHING ELSE! I WANT TO HEAR HOW ANYONE, EVEN YOU, CAN MANAGE THAT.
I--I--

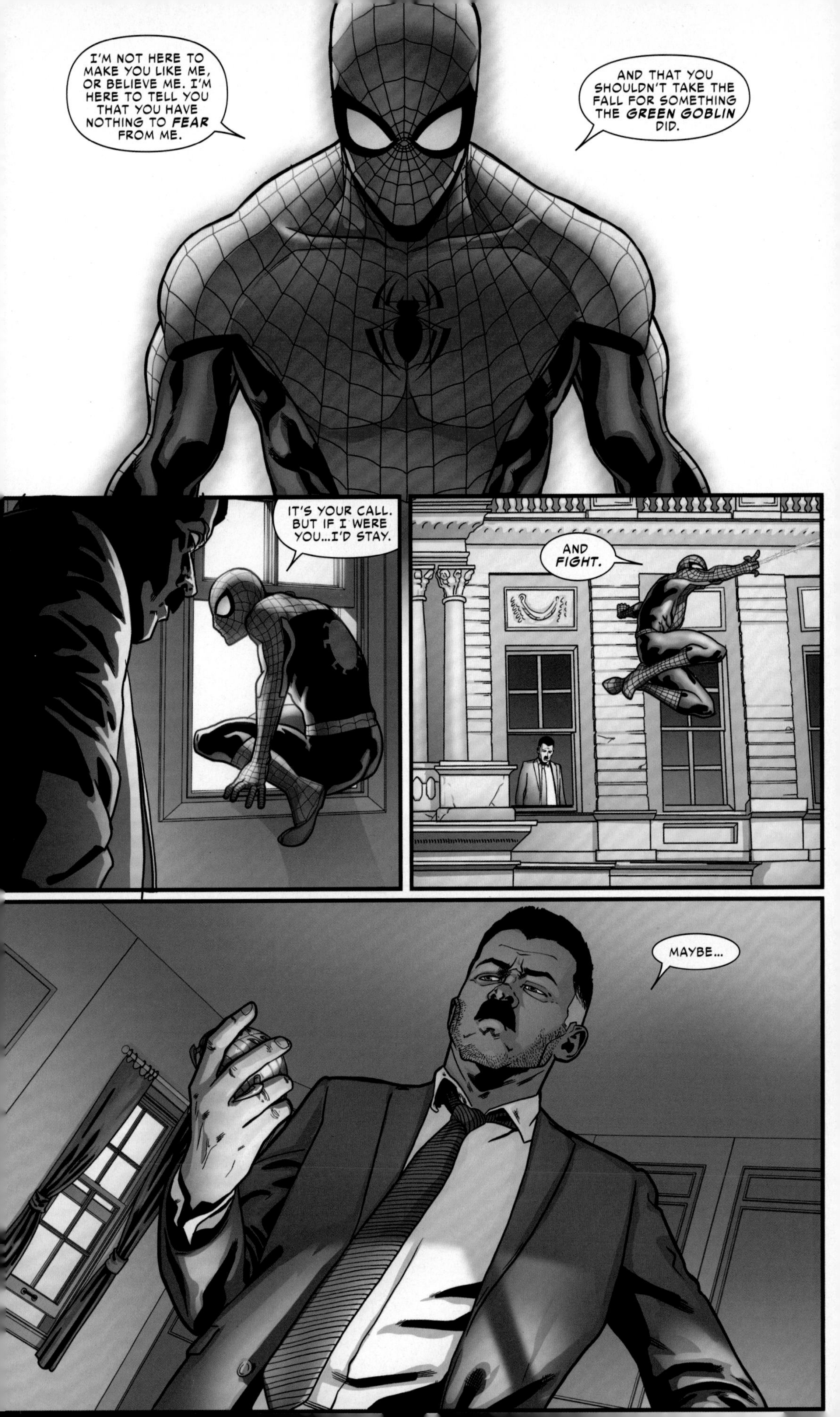
I'M NOT HERE TO MAKE YOU LIKE ME, OR BELIEVE ME. I'M HERE TO TELL YOU THAT YOU HAVE NOTHING TO *FEAR* FROM ME.
AND THAT YOU SHOULDN'T TAKE THE FALL FOR SOMETHING THE *GREEN GOBLIN* DID.
IT'S YOUR CALL. BUT IF I WERE YOU...I'D STAY.
AND *FIGHT*.
MAYBE...

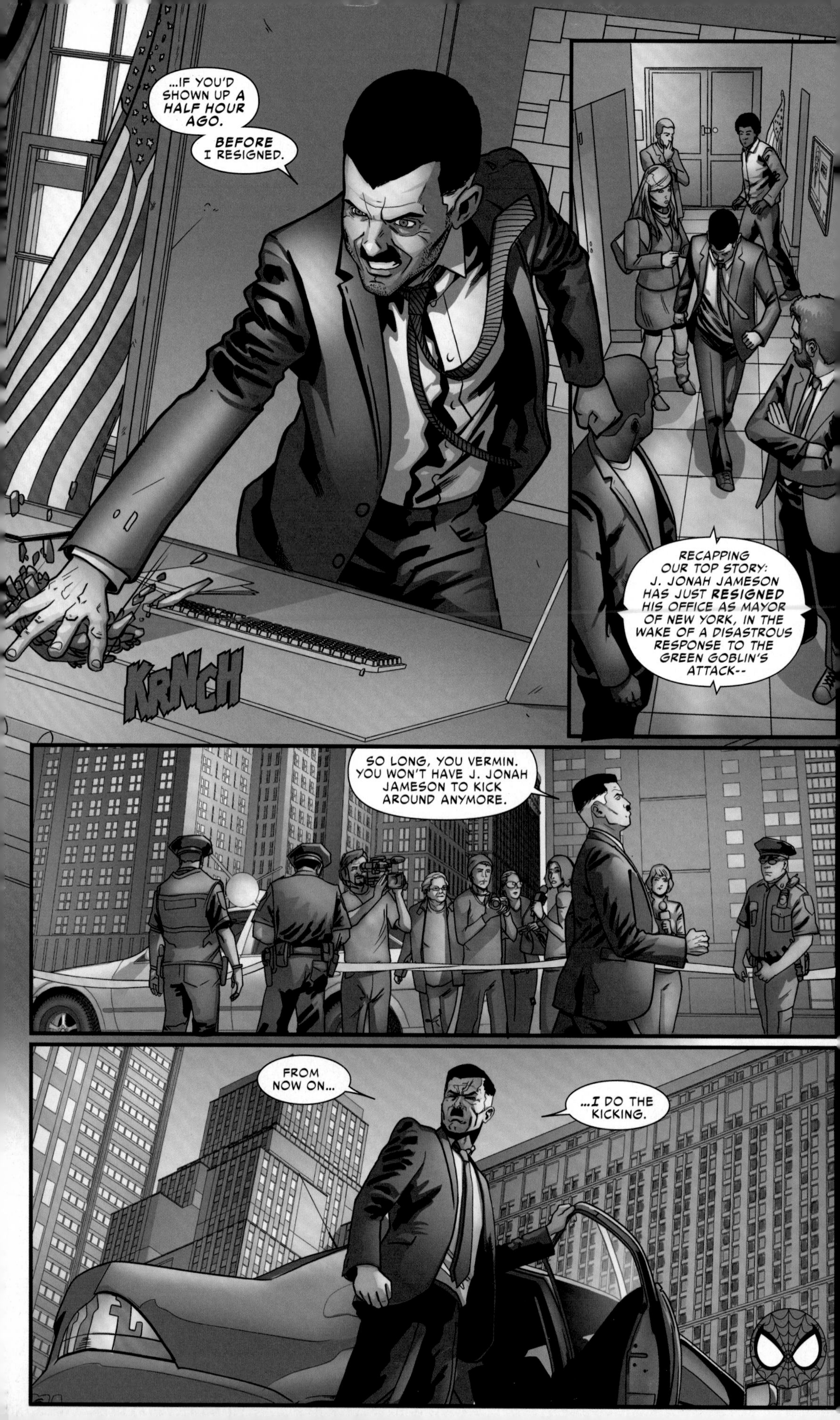
...IF YOU'D SHOWN UP A HALF HOUR AGO.
BEFORE I RESIGNED.
KRNCH
RECAPPING OUR TOP STORY: J. JONAH JAMESON HAS JUST RESIGNED HIS OFFICE AS MAYOR OF NEW YORK, IN THE WAKE OF A DISASTROUS RESPONSE TO THE GREEN GOBLIN'S ATTACK--
SO LONG, YOU VERMIN. YOU WON'T HAVE J. JONAH JAMESON TO KICK AROUND ANYMORE.
FROM NOW ON...
...I DO THE KICKING.

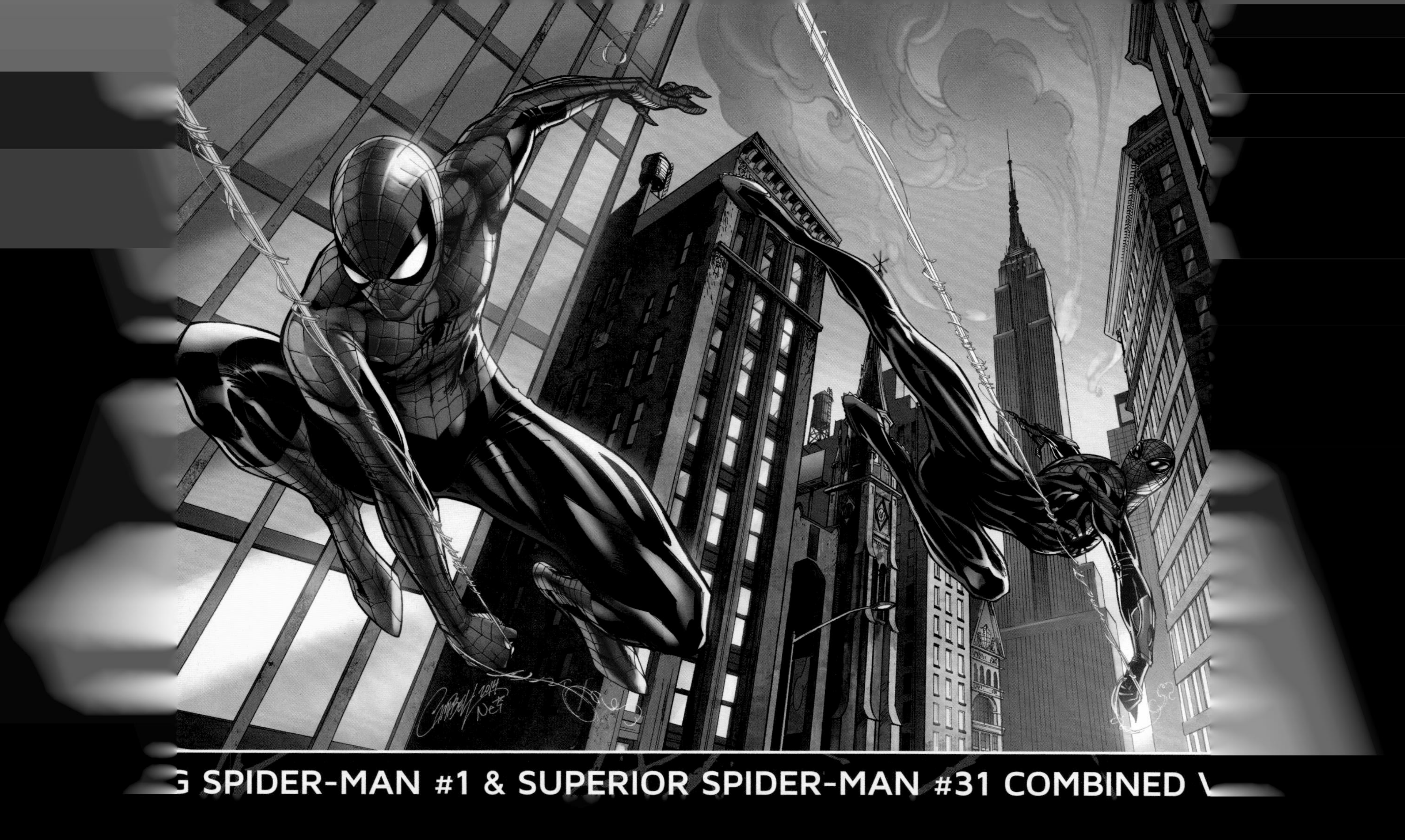

G SPIDER-MAN #1 & SUPERIOR SPIDER-MAN #31 COMBINED V

MARVEL AR AUGMENTED REALITY

MARVEL AUGMENTED REALITY (AR) ENHANCES AND CHANGES THE WAY YOU EXPERIENCE COMICS!

TO ACCESS THE FREE MARVEL AR CONTENT IN THIS BOOK*:

1. **Locate the AR logo within the comic.**
2. **Go to Marvel.com/AR in your web browser.**
3. **Search by series title to find the corresponding AR.**
4. **Enjoy Marvel AR!**

*All AR content that appears in this book has been archived and will be available only at Marvel.com/AR – no longer in the Marvel AR App. Content subject to change and availability.

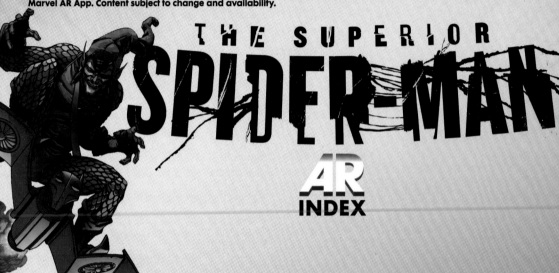

THE SUPERIOR SPIDER-MAN

AR INDEX